The Myth of Universal Human Rights

The Myth of Universal Human Rights

Its Origin, History, and Explanation,
Along with a More Humane Way

David N. Stamos

Paradigm Publishers
Boulder • London

Copyright © 2014 by Paradigm Publishers

Published in the United States by Paradigm Publishers, 5589 Arapahoe Avenue, Boulder, Colorado 80303 USA.

Paradigm Publishers is the trade name of Birkenkamp & Company, LLC, Dean Birkenkamp, President and Publisher.

Library of Congress Cataloging-in-Publication Data

Stamos, David N., 1957–
  The myth of universal human rights : its origin, history, and explanation, along with a more humane way / David N. Stamos.
      p. cm.
  Includes bibliographical references and index.
  ISBN 978-1-61205-241-0 (hc : alk. paper) — ISBN 978-1-61205-242-7 (pbk : alk. paper) — ISBN 978-1-61205-286-1 (Q-ISBN)

  1. Human rights. 2. Human rights—History. I. Title.
JC571.S7775 2012
323—dc23
                                                                                    2012024529

Printed and bound in the United States of America on acid-free paper that meets the standards of the American National Standard for Permanence of Paper for Printed Library Materials.

Designed and Typeset in Adobe Garamond by Straight Creek Bookmakers.

18 17 16 15 14   1 2 3 4 5

for my students

Contents

Acknowledgments

Frst and foremost I want to thank Jason Barry, my editor at Paradigm Publishers, for his wisdom and guidance, which was quite extraordinary here. The book was further improved by the perspicacity of Paradigm's project editor, Meredith Smith, and copyeditor, Antoinette Smith. Thanks are also due to the anonymous referees (especially the one who suggested a change in the order of the chapters) and to Ryan Chynces, who provided the spark that led away from a paper in progress to the writing of this book in the first place. In addition, I want to thank the individuals, organizations, and departments that provided me the opportunity to lecture on this topic and receive feedback on some of its ideas, specifically John Xu and Katie Kish of the Centre for Inquiry in Toronto, Mauro Buccheri of Founders College at York University, Brian Garrett of the philosophy department at McMaster University, and Andrew Sneddon of the philosophy department at the University of Ottawa. There are others I want to thank who contributed to this book in one way or another, many of them in terms of useful feedback on one or more parts of the manuscript at various stages of its growth in addition to my editor and the anonymous referees, namely, Robert Aunger, Joshua Bachynski, Jason Buccheri, Michelle Devlin, Megi Duraku, Amir Ghorashi, Sepideh (Sandra) Javadi, Matthew Kramer, Bernie Lightman, Tyler Lin, Adam Riggio, Samira Sahihi, Tamara Schwarz, Gloria Segovia, Neven Sesardic, John Shafer, Andrew Sharp, Marc Soscia, Julia Tourianski, Minwan (Mindy) Xu, and Carol Yuen. Finally, I want to unconventionally acknowledge the many nonhuman animals, both past and present, with whom I have had the pleasure to share life—in their own way, due to the wonder of their being, they helped to write the final chapter.

Preface

WHY A BOOK AGAINST HUMAN RIGHTS? It sounds downright devilish. What kind of person would want to write such a book? Does the author hate people? He must. Maybe he's a neo-Nazi and this is his own *Mein Kampf.* Surely this should not be allowed in this day and age!

These sentiments, and others like them, are bound to be the response of many to the very title of this book. And the answer to them all is simple and straightforward: a person who puts truth and evidence above ideology, a person who doesn't hate people but doesn't hate animals either, a person who believes that truth and compassion are not mutually exclusive but are often perfectly compatible, a person who greatly values life and believes that matters of ethics and justice are too important to depend on myths.

Imagine ancient Greece at its peak, during the fifth century B.C., with the public believing in Zeus and the rest of the ancient gods, and the few philosophers who dared to question or challenge the existence of those gods being persecuted for impiety and blasphemy. Today we look back at the situation with puzzlement, including condescension. It's so obvious to us that their gods were a myth. But this is because we have the vantage point of history. To *them* their gods were fully real. And not only were they fully real, but for all their faults the gods were the foundation of ethics and justice, as enshrined in their sacred stories, such as Homer's *Iliad.* All in all it was as if they could feel the truth pumping in their hearts, sometimes even as if the gods were speaking to them directly.

Today we look back at these people as wrongheaded and even naive. But do we *really* see that? Scroll ahead to the present day, to our modern world, and suppose, just suppose for the moment, that the belief that humans have human rights—moral claims and entitlements by virtue of being human, held equally, innately, and inalienably by all—could be proven false, beyond a reasonable doubt, that it could be proven that the dominant moral language of our world, both nationally and internationally, is a modern myth. How would you feel? What would you say? What would you do? Would you want a better way of dealing with matters of ethics and justice? Or would you want to be like the ancient Greeks with their myths?

This book is for those who want to know, in particular those who are truly interested in the topic of universal human rights: professional scholars, students, and educated laypeople alike. Written in a clear and informative style that meets the needs of each of these audiences, this book focuses on what I call the *consensus concept,* the concept of universal human rights touched on above, the concept enshrined in key documents such as the Declaration of Independence, ratified by the American Congress in 1776, and the Universal Declaration of Human Rights, ratified by the United Nations in 1948, the concept believed in by the vast majority of people who believe in universal human rights and who claim that their own or other people's human rights have been violated. There are other concepts of human rights, to be sure, formal or functional concepts that are parasitic on the consensus concept, but they are not to be confused with the consensus concept, even though I give them their fair share of attention in this book, too.

After the introductory chapter, which deals with a lot of preliminary matters, Chapter 2 provides the proof beyond a reasonable doubt that universal human rights do not exist. The argument relies on what scientists routinely call the *fact* of biological evolution, and whether the reader believes that evolution is a fact, one must be willing to follow the argument wherever it leads. Chapter 3 deals with human rights theory. By looking at a generous sample of scholarly defenses of human rights, both of the consensus and of non-consensus concepts, detailed concept and argument analyses are provided to show how and why they fail. Chapters 4 and 5 deal with history, Chapter 4 with extravagant claims that this or that ancient or medieval source was the first to have the modern concept of universal human rights, such as the Bible, Cyrus the Great, or the Koran, while Chapter 5 shows that the concept almost certainly began in 1640s London, in the heat of the English Civil Wars, from which it spread eventually to America and France and then to the rest of the world. Chapter 6 is devoted to explanation, to explaining why the consensus concept of universal human rights began and spread the way it did, and to explaining why the belief in the content of the concept is so strong in so many, to the point that universal human rights are "self-evident" and anyone who argues that they do not exist must be evil. The connection with genuinely democratic beliefs and values, using a theory known as *memetics,* is the key to explaining the former phenomenon, while the evolutionary psychology of fairness is the key to explaining the latter phenomenon. Chapter 7, the final chapter, is devoted to a better way of dealing with matters of ethics and justice, better not only because it makes no appeal to the use of fictions, but also because it is a fully humane way that gets its strength from our evolved moral nature taken as a whole. This method of "naturalized normative ethics" is developed in the chapter and then applied to six cases that are typically argued in terms of human rights: abortion, affirmative action, same-sex marriage, the treatment of animals, waterboarding, and political regime change.

All in all, the book is highly interdisciplinary, as it indisputably must be, for the question of universal human rights is not the domain of any one academic discipline but of many. Nor is it the domain of the scholarly few, who fancy themselves as thinking and speaking for the rest. The question of human rights, instead, is a question that concerns us all, every single one of us, and it's anyone's guess what future generations, thousands of years from now, will think when they look back at our time with all our talk about human rights. What they will actually think, of course, is one thing, a matter of future history, and none of us can know what that will be, but what they *should* think is quite another matter, and we can in fact actually know that, we in the here and now, which is what this book before you is all about.

Chapter 1

Introduction

Truly, I say to you, a prophet is never accepted in his own country.
—*Jesus (Luke 4: 24)*

Problem, Audience, and Myth

OUR WORLD ABOUNDS IN HUMAN RIGHTS TALK. We routinely hear of individual human rights, such as the right to life, to property ownership, to freedom from torture, to freedom of religion, and more controversially to social welfare, to health care, to holidays with pay, to gay marriage, to having lots of children, to suicide, and even to being fat. We also routinely hear of group rights, such as women's rights, gay rights, and aboriginal rights. The United Nations has the Universal Declaration of Human Rights, which was expanded into international human rights law, while state governments similarly declare human rights in their Constitutions, Bills, and Charters, as do Humanist Associations in their Manifestos. We have Human Rights Museums and routinely hear of recent human rights violations not only in places such as China and Zimbabwe but in our own backyard as well. We have human rights lawyers, Human Rights Commissions, Councils, and Tribunals, and organizations such as the American Civil Liberties Union. We have international watchdog organizations such as Amnesty International, Human Rights Watch, and Freedom House, which investigate human rights abuses and publish thick annual reports on human rights violations around the world. We even hear of captured terrorists who complain about the violation of their human

1

rights (though their sincerity is doubtful). The overall impression is that human rights are written into our very DNA itself, as birthrights constituting part of human nature.

But do they actually exist? Are they real? Despite all the good intentions behind the universal human rights phenomenon (and they are formidable), these questions need to be asked and they need to be taken seriously. If universal human rights really do exist, then we should want to know the nature of their reality, if only to determine their scope. And if they do not exist, but people talk as if they do, then we should not want people appealing to fictions in matters so important as ethics and justice but should want to find a better way.

Talking about human rights as if they actually exist, as objective properties of human beings, is the majority view among believers in human rights. As the political scientist Tony Evans puts it in his book, *The Politics of Human Rights* (2005), "natural rights foundationalism continues to inform most mainstream 'human rights talk'" (7). Accordingly, the consensus concept of universal human rights is the main focus of the book before you. But there is another approach, also examined in this book, that is the minority view among believers in human rights. Here the view is that universal human rights talk is simply an expression of normative values, a kind of shorthand for what people should think and do. In this case we should want to examine the values underlying the language to see if those values have a legitimate basis, and also to see if universal human rights talk is the proper vehicle for their expression, for it might after all be a kind of systematically misleading expression.

Either way, the majority or the minority, it is said that people "have" human rights. It is therefore legitimate to ask of both, "Where does the having come from and is it really having?" And given that the language of universal human rights constitutes the dominant moral discourse of our world today, the more general question of what people are talking about when they talk about universal human rights is one of the most important questions of our time and should not be ignored.

Immediately many will want to shift the focus to effects. They will want to focus on all the good that the universal human rights phenomenon has produced, such as reducing world hunger and improving the lot of minorities. One could just as easily argue that the widespread belief in universal human rights has produced a lot of harm, notably the creation of an international culture of entitlements and social justice the cost of which has run many countries to the brink of bankruptcy, such as Greece, Ireland, and Portugal, with the United States close behind. Whichever way one argues here, the debate does not seem to go anywhere. My focus is more basic, and actually more tractable. It is, primarily, the question of whether universal human rights are real in the first place. All else follows from that.

In this book it is argued that universal human rights are a myth, that they are not real. What is meant here by "myth" shall be clarified below. But first we need to specify the audience. Quite simply, this book should be of interest to *anyone interested in the topic of human rights,* and that is a great many people. On the one hand it includes many in the academic world, primarily in the fields of philosophy, law, politics, and history. Professional scholars should find the book attractive not only because it deals with human rights theory in an original, detailed, and interdisciplinary manner, but also because it provides detailed critical analyses of arguments on human rights by scholars that are well known in their respective fields, such as, to name a few, James Griffin's (2008) defense of human rights (ethics), Charles Beitz's (2009) defense of human rights (politics), Brian Tierney's (1997) argument that the medieval Decretists were the first to have the concept (medieval studies), Tony Honoré's (2002) argument that the Roman lawyer Ulpian was the first human rights lawyer (law), and Nicholas Wolterstorff's (2008) argument that not only is the concept of human rights to be found in the Bible but the Bible gave the modern concept to the world (philosophy of religion).

Students should also find the book interesting, and useful. This is partly because the style maintained throughout the book is that of teaching while arguing, but also because the book provides students with the analytical and conceptual tools required for doing their own analyses of arguments on human rights that are not specifically analyzed in this book, whether they are dealing with claims that this or that premodern source has the modern consensus concept of universal human rights or are dealing with arguments defending the modern consensus concept, or some aspect of it, or a related concept of human rights. As the literature is enormous in terms of both theory and history, course directors should have no problem providing their students (both undergraduate and graduate) with essay topics and research projects. The final chapter of the book is also very useful for students, as it provides a unique method (that of a naturalized normative consensus) for dealing with matters of ethics and justice and provides six examples of applications that are routinely dealt with in terms of human rights.

Finally, the general educated public should find this book of great interest, not only because it is clear and informative and written in a relatively nontechnical style, but because the belief in human rights has pretty much gone global ever since World War II, such that the language of universal human rights dominates our moral discourse both domestically and internationally. The topic of human rights, then, is not a dry scholarly exercise, confined to specialists, such as the species problem in biology (the question of what a species is), but is a question that vitally concerns most people today. A distinction made by William James (1897, 3–4) in a very different context helps to emphasize this point. We may say that the belief in universal human rights is "live" for most people in that it animates them in a number of ways, it is "forced" in the sense that the pervasiveness of the belief means that we cannot avoid the question but have to make a decision one way or another, and it is "momentous" in the sense that the stakes are not insignificant but very high—we are talking about life, after all, and how it should be lived.

In other words, professional scholars do not have a monopoly here, students should not think that the scholarly world revolves around them on this topic (or any other), and the general public needs to realize just how complicated and nuanced the problem of universal human rights has become. Accordingly, the book is written in a style that is meant to be accessible to all three of these main audiences: not long-winded, highly abstract, and dripping with scholarly footnotes, and not simplified to the point of being boring and unchallenging to the knowledgeable and erudite. The book is written, instead, in a style that reaches out to all three audiences, a style that teaches and argues in a clear and forceful manner, a style that should appeal to all three audiences as long as each remains mindful of the needs of the other two. The content, moreover, is an original argument and is in fact much like a long case presented to an intelligent jury and a seasoned judge: a clear, meticulous, detailed, step-by-step case that in the end is intended to command the assent of every reasonable and rational person who believes in the principle of proof beyond a reasonable doubt. Though the thesis is hardly a politically correct one (a point of which I am abundantly aware), it has to be recognized that *politics does not determine good scholarship* and *it is not wisdom to ignore evidence*. In the very least, if one has a genuine desire for truth, knowledge, and justice, then one should be willing to follow the argument wherever it leads, to paraphrase Plato's Socrates (*Phaedo* 107b, *Republic* 394d).

The term "myth" is used throughout the book in basically the normal way, but some elaboration is warranted right up front. For a start, there is a *consensus concept* of universal human rights and it is the main focus of the book. This concept is enshrined in key documents such as the American Declaration of Independence and the Universal Declaration of Human Rights and is held by the vast majority of people who believe in human rights. It is the concept of *moral claims and entitlements that all humans have by virtue of being human*. The belief based on this concept is an *ontological* belief, a belief about something that exists in the world, in this case something that humans *have*.

There are also non-ontological concepts of human rights, mentioned above as the minority view, which collectively may be called *formal* or *functional* concepts of human rights. Lacking the ontological content of the consensus concept, they retain its form and function. These concepts are usually found only among professional scholars and will be examined in the appropriate chapters. As non-ontological concepts lacking common currency, they might be said to be immune to the charge of myth. This is not necessarily true, as they are parasitic in various ways on the consensus concept. Indeed, the scholars who subscribe to them may be likened to the ancient Epicureans, who did not believe in the gods of their society (they had a radically different conception) but nevertheless piously practiced the sacrifices and ceremonies of the state religion (Summers 1995). At any rate, these finessed concepts of human rights raise separate problems and will be rejected for a number of reasons, partly because they are not explanations of, let alone defenses of, the consensus concept and belief, and partly because they fail to stand on their own.

The title of this book is a deliberate and unashamed imitation of *The Myth of Mental Illness* by the psychiatrist Thomas Szasz (1974). Szasz states his problem in terms of a conventional norm, namely, the majority of psychiatrists who "define their discipline in terms of nonexistent entities or substantives" (1). He argues that not only psychiatrists but also the general public have accepted the myth of mental illness in the sense of a "dogma" (xiii), one that has received the "imprimatur" (x) of the state.

To count as a *myth,* it should be noted, an alleged fact or story does not necessarily require state sanction, but it does require some degree of common currency in a community, if only for a short time. A myth must also have a beginning in time and place, such that myths may rightly be viewed as cultural artifacts. And myths, of course, have to be false. There is also something simple-minded about myths, which often seem to require a childish naïveté for belief in them, such as the Adam and Eve story. In the very least, mythological beliefs involve a serious lack of critical reasoning often combined with a dogmatic certainty that one is right, all of which should become obvious once the knowledge necessary to see through the myth becomes acquired. Myths, moreover, need not be about nonexistent objects or persons, such as the gods of ancient Greece or the demons of medieval Europe. They can also be about nonexistent properties and relations, such as the myth of King Tut's curse (property) and the myth that masturbation causes blindness (relation). A myth can also simply be in the story itself, such as the myth that Christopher Columbus discovered America. Finally, we do not call a belief a myth if the belief is part of human nature, such as the belief that color is part of the world or that moral qualities are similarly out there, apart from minds.

In the case of human rights, the norm or common currency we are dealing with does not concern a specific discipline or profession. It does not even concern a specific group or society. Instead, it concerns a number of disciplines (philosophy, law, politics, history), a number of institutions (domestic and international), and the general public considered globally. It is the widespread belief that in addition to the well-known basic facts about human beings—their overall intelligence, their many kinds of consciousness, their language ability, their moral abilities, and so on—there is a set of further facts, *moral* facts that all and only human beings have, namely, human rights. (Again, there are other modern concepts of human rights, and a representative sample of them shall be dealt with in the book where appropriate, but none of them should be confused with the consensus concept.)

Returning to Szasz, his meaning of "myth" is problematic given his phrase "entities or substantives." Clearly no psychiatrist ever thought of mental illness as an independent entity, but instead as a *property*, as something someone *has*. Likewise, we are not dealing with universal human rights as "entities or substantives," but instead as properties that, it is argued, humans do not in fact possess. Since the supposed properties are clearly moral ones, the argument is similar in a sense to John Mackie's argument against moral objectivism in *Ethics: Inventing Right and Wrong* (1977). *Moral objectivism* is the common belief that when we make a moral statement, such as that rape is wrong, we are not simply expressing how we feel or what we think someone ought not to do, but instead we are making a judgment about the act itself, that in addition to all the natural facts of the matter there is a further fact, the fact that rape is morally wrong. As Mackie puts it, "ordinary moral judgments include a claim to objectivity" (35), such that philosophical analyses of moral claims tend to overlook "the apparent authority of ethics" (33). It is therefore legitimate, says Mackie, to ask whether there really are such facts. His denial in turn is an "ontological thesis" (18), the thesis that in reality the world does not contain such facts. Thus his skepticism against moral objectivism is what he calls an "error theory" (35). The situation is similar, he says, to asking whether colors are really out there in the world. When we say, for example, "That shirt is red," we typically think we are referring to a color fact out there in the world in addition to all the other facts involved. Today it is standard in science to say that color is not really out there in the world, that instead we automatically and unconsciously project color onto the world, that color exists only in our visual images.

Without necessarily subscribing to Mackie's thesis in general, the skepticism against universal human rights defended in this book is similarly an "error theory"—or more accurately an "error proof"—the conclusion of which is that there are in fact no such objective properties, no such moral facts, and that those who think otherwise are guilty of projecting their belief onto the world, the human world. But it is also argued that the projection is not part of human nature (although human nature contributes to it), that instead it began roughly only a little more than 360 years ago, that it is a modern myth. In this sense the thesis of this book is not like Mackie's but more like Szasz's. At any rate, the case for it takes us right up to the final chapter.

The thesis is essentially negative, then, and many will view this book as pernicious or even as outright evil, in the very least as iconoclastic. I view the book, however, as ultimately positive, for in the final chapter, summarized below, it is argued that there is a much better way of dealing with matters of ethics and justice, a way that does not at all require an appeal to fictions.

It should be added that this book was not intended to be an exhaustive treatment of the subject. The quantity of literature on human rights is quite staggering, whether we are talking about concepts, theories, defenses, or histories. Emphatically, the point and purpose of this book is not to deal with it all. Instead, although a number of competing concepts, theories, defenses, and histories are explicitly dealt with, the primary purpose is to deal with the consensus concept and its history, the concept of human rights enshrined in numerous domestic and international documents, institutions, and agreements, which is also the concept that individuals around the world typically use when they talk about human rights and when they claim that their human rights have been violated.

To maintain that something is a myth and to provide a full explanation of that myth, whether as an error theory or as an error proof, one must accomplish three tasks. First, one has to prove, inasmuch as that is possible, that the myth is indeed false (given the difficulty of proving a universal existential negative, in the very least one has to show that there are no good reasons to believe the myth and plenty of good reasons not to). Second, one has to account for the origin and spread of the myth. Third and finally, in the case of *living* myths especially, one has to account for the persistence of the belief in the myth. These three tasks are reflected in the order of the chapters of this book, each of which shall now be summarized.

Chapter Summaries

Chapter 2, which immediately follows this introductory chapter, is devoted to proving the myth false. It might seem an astonishing claim, that one can actually prove that the modern belief in universal human rights is false, but that is indeed what Chapter 2 is all about. What is required first is to take evolution seriously, as seriously as the science of biology does, which is to say, as a fact proven beyond a reasonable doubt. The implications of this fact are enormous, as scholars inside and outside of biology are becoming increasingly aware. And one of the implications is that there cannot be such properties as universal human rights.

The proof that the widespread belief in universal human rights is a modern myth begins with the fact that the language of universal human rights includes the word "human." Whether one likes it or not, this word, whatever else it is used for, is fundamentally a biological term, a reference to the species *Homo sapiens*. In the literature on human rights one can often find it said that human rights are fundamentally a political or moral matter and so have nothing really to do with biology. But this is to put blinders on, to naively and willfully ignore much that is relevant to the matter. In short, it is to take the *human* out of "human rights."

Beginning with morality, if human rights are the rights that humans have by virtue of being human, we should want to know why only humans have these rights and not members of other species. Biology cannot be ignored here. Moreover, the moral theory or theories employed to justify the belief in human rights, including the appeal to moral intuitions, themselves require justification, such that again one cannot afford to ignore the nature of humans, given that biology is statistical and that humans have an evolutionary history.

Nor can hiding behind political theory help either, for every political theory boils down to a theory of human nature. At the one extreme you have the view of human nature as basically essentialistic, such as the views of Plato and Aristotle, each of which is the foundation of their political theories. At the other extreme you have the view of human nature as basically plastic, the so-called Standard Social Science Model, which holds that what we call "human nature" is really only the product of social and cultural forces. In either case one cannot afford to ignore biology, not only because modern evolutionary biology completely undermines species essentialism, but also because it undermines the Standard Social Science Model, given evolutionary theory (every species has a nature or norm) and the evidence gathered especially in recent decades by evolutionary psychology. In the very least, the claim that human nature is basically plastic is not at bottom a political or sociological claim but a hard-core scientific claim, a matter of biological fact, which if true ultimately requires an evolutionary explanation in order to account for it.

"Human," again, is fundamentally a biological term, in the sense that humans are members or parts of a biological species. This species, moreover, did not fall from the sky but was evolved ever so slowly by processes including natural selection. The importance of this for human rights is enormous. Evolution is a fact, not a theory, the well-established core or framework of the science of modern biology. As such, it requires us to think of humans not only statistically but both *synchronically* (horizontally as the tip of a branch in the evolutionary Tree of Life) and *diachronically* (as a vertical branch or long segment of a branch in the Tree, the human part). Humans, then, have not only social and cultural histories but collectively an evolutionary history, and it is the general failure to think of humans as having a diachronic history in evolution that gives a surface plausibility to the belief in universal human rights. As long as humans are thought of only synchronically, there seems to be little or no problem in thinking of human rights as moral rights that are held universally and equally. But therein lies the rub, for once the time dimension is added it becomes logically impossible to maintain the belief in universal and equal human rights in the context of the Tree of Life. I call this part of the argument the *diachronic thrust,* as it is a killer.

Chapter 3 is devoted to a critical examination of a number of modern scholarly defenses of the belief in universal human rights, defenses that might be thought to rise to the challenge, or to bypass it altogether. This chapter is for hard-core human rights theorists, although the style of writing in it is no different than the rest of the book. General readers can skip the chapter if they wish, but the price will be a considerable loss of learning. Scholarly readers, on the other hand, will probably find this chapter essential, not only because the scholarly literature on human rights theory is quite large and has been increasing in pace over recent years (which says something in itself), but also because many scholars will not be satisfied solely by an analysis based on evolutionary biology and (to be dealt with in subsequent chapters) history, memetics, and evolutionary psychology. They will want to see what is specifically wrong with various scholarly attempts at justifying the belief in universal human rights. For many human rights scholars, nothing else will do. But the reader should not think that what goes on in this chapter is the core of the book. It is not. One cannot possibly argue for the rejection of universal human rights talk by refuting one scholarly defense after another, for there are far too many of them and every year seems to bring more. But it certainly does help, in the context of the rest of the argument, to see how and why representative examples do fail.

Disputation or *polemic,* however, is not really the main purpose of Chapter 3. Analyzing the arguments of others is important, to be sure, but here the exercise is used to serve a deeper purpose, which is that of helping to bring to light much that needs to be observed about the topic of human rights. One thing we shall observe is a phenomenon I've noticed repeatedly not only when reading scholarly defenses of human rights but also when giving talks on the subject. Time and again I've noticed that scholars tend to lose sight of the ball, namely, the consensus concept of universal human rights enshrined in key documents such as the American Declaration of Independence and the Universal Declaration of Human Rights. In other words, they might begin but end up defending not the consensus concept but some other concept. It is important to notice this, for the human rights phenomenon is a *world* phenomenon, not the possession of the scholarly few. Their arguments also force us to look more closely at the language of human rights, the way people actually use the words that represent the concept. That is another purpose pursued in Chapter 3, along with taking a closer look at the concept of human rights as it is found in the Universal Declaration of

Human Rights. What we shall see is that both the words of the Declaration and the archival material behind it leave no doubt that the framers and signers of the Declaration thought of human rights not as a social construction but as part of human nature, as something that all humans are born with and possess equally regardless of whether they are part of a political state. Chapter 3 also examines the supposed relation between human dignity and human rights and the related issue of extending human rights to nonhuman animals. The problem of a *reductio ad absurdum* is one that affects not a few of the defenders of universal human rights, and in more ways than one.

The examples of scholarly defenses of human rights chosen for Chapter 3 are not only representative but also relatively famous within the field. Many will be surprised, of course, at whose arguments were not included, but that cannot be helped. The first argument examined is by Alan White (1984), a philosopher of language whose sole approach consists of conceptual analysis in the ordinary language tradition. The next argument is by Jack Donnelly (2003), a political scientist who defends the belief in human rights by an appeal to what he calls an "international normative consensus." The third argument is by Charles Beitz (2009), also a political scientist, who likewise defends human rights by an appeal to what he calls an "emergent political practice," such that he refers to human rights as "international human rights." His argument, however, is sufficiently novel and nuanced to warrant a separate analysis. The fourth argument is by Jack Mahoney (2007), a theologian who defends human rights in terms of what he calls the "wonder of our being." The next two arguments are by moral philosophers who defend the belief in human rights by focusing on human agency: Alan Gewirth (1978, 1996) by appealing to the requirements for rational purposive agency, and James Griffin (2008) by appealing to the requirements for what he calls "normative agency." The seventh and last argument is by the multidisciplinary scholar Martha Nussbaum (1997, 2006), who applies what she calls the "capabilities approach" to human rights, which identifies human rights with what she calls "central human capabilities."

The arguments of the last four of these scholars deal with human rights as moral *possessions,* as something that humans *have,* while the arguments of the first three of these scholars conceive of human rights solely in terms of what they *do,* and so are properly characterized as *formal* or *functional* approaches. Two famous examples of this latter approach, by Ronald Dworkin (1978) and John Rawls (1993), are dealt with in Chapter 6 instead of Chapter 3, as it is more important to discuss them in the context of memetics. The distinction between possessive approaches on the one hand and formal or functional approaches on the other is not always clear in the writings of human rights scholars, since those who explicitly disavow human rights as possessions can sometimes be found to use the language of possessives, as when Beitz (2009) repeatedly refers to human rights as something that people "have," while those who explicitly characterize human rights as moral possessions can sometimes be found to focus more on what they do than on what they are, as when Griffin (2008) characterizes human rights as "protections."

At any rate, what all of the scholarly defenses of human rights have in common, whether those dealt with in Chapter 3 or in Chapter 6—and I daresay all other defenses past, present, and future—is a serious failure to take evolutionary biology seriously. This failure, shared even more so by the general public, is devastating in its consequences, for what mostly undermines the belief in universal human rights is the fact and nature of evolution itself. While the diachronic thrust is given in Chapter 2 as the ultimate argument against the consensus concept of universal human rights, not all non-consensus concepts are necessarily defeated by that argument. A further argument is therefore given in Chapter 3, in addition to the specific critiques, an argument I call the *hypocrisy thrust*.

Chapter 4 takes us in a different direction. If universal human rights talk is illegitimate, either because universal human rights do not in fact exist or because the values underlying the talk do not have a legitimate basis, we should then want to look at how the belief began in the first place, how and why it spread the way it has spread, and why it persists and persists so strongly, including its mutation into a multiplicity of related forms (the modern non-consensus concepts of human rights).

Part of the reason for the persistence of the belief is the failure to take history seriously, human cultural history, and to do history responsibly. The latter, doing history irresponsibly, is the topic of Chapter 4. In the very least, one should think that anyone who believes in universal human rights, or at least in the language and values of universal human rights, or who rejects both, should truly want to know where the belief came from, its genealogy. This means they should want to get the history right, objectively as much as possible. What we shall find in many who attempt to accomplish this task, however, is a pattern quite striking, and it is a pattern that actually might be explained as an unconscious strategy for helping to spread and strengthen the belief in universal human rights itself.

The consensus concept of universal human rights, of course, did not pop into existence out of nothing, nor did it fall from the sky like manna from heaven. Instead, it evolved from earlier concepts, and in a twisted, historical way. That means that it has *predecessors*, but these should never be confused with the same concept (any more than an ancestor should be confused with a descendant). What we need is to ask, "When and where did the modern concept of universal human rights actually begin?" This, it turns out, is an extremely important question, and what we shall see in Chapters 4 through 6 is that there is a complex but profound answer to it, in terms of both concept and belief, an answer that helps to explain not only the origin of the belief in universal human rights, but also its spread and widespread persistence.

In dealing with the history of the concept, the question of predecessors—or "forerunners" or "contributors"—is especially troubling. In each case one has to ask whether they really deserve to be called such. Democritus and Epicurus, for example, did not have the modern concept of the atom, but they definitely contributed to it. Moreover, they deserve to be called "forerunners" of the concept because, given what we know of them, it is safe to say that if they could be plucked out of history and brought up to date on the evidence, then they would fully accept the modern concept.

The same is generally not true, however, of so-called contributors to or forerunners of the modern concept of universal human rights. It is important to see this, and this brings us back to our chapter summaries. Many have claimed that this person in history or that document in history was the first, or one of the first, to have the modern concept of universal human rights, or if not the actual concept then they contributed to it in some positive and important way. There are so many extravagant claims here, including those of professional scholars themselves, that the question of history needs to be cleared up.

Chapters 4 and 5 accordingly are devoted exclusively to history of ideas. As already mentioned, an important and central question for our topic concerns when and where the concept of universal human rights actually began. The concern here is indeed with *history of ideas,* not contextualist history, the modern vogue in professional history writing that attempts to explain the origin and spread of ideas purely in terms of the nitty-gritty facts of social and cultural influences. Instead, a genuine history of ideas approach is needed not only because a great many scholars have claimed to have found the origin of the concept of universal human rights in this source or that, but because getting it right is absolutely essential for seeing clearly that the international apparatus of universal human rights is, or is based on, a modern myth.

What we shall see in Chapter 4 is that, contrary to numerous people who think otherwise, including a great many academics, the concept of universal human rights is not to be found in ancient or medieval sources. It is not to be found in the Bible, whether the Old Testament or the New Testament, in Confucius, in Cyrus the Great, in the Koran, in ancient Greeks such as Plato and Aristotle, in ancient Romans such as Cicero and Ulpian, in medieval philosophers such as William of Ockham and Jean Gerson, in medieval canonists such as Huguccio, or in the Magna Carta. What we shall see, instead, is that the concept of universal human rights began in Europe during the dawn of the European Enlightenment. It did not begin, however, in political thinkers such as Grotius, Hobbes, or Pufendorf. Sufficiently detailed but relatively brief analyses shall be provided to show this, against professional scholars who claim otherwise. It shall also be made clear that none of the above sources, if they are taken instead to have contributed to the modern concept, would probably have accepted it had they become aware of it. They are not, then, it will be shown, like Democritus and Epicurus on the atom.

Chapter 4 will require some patience on the part of the reader. This is not only because the chapter is long and fairly detailed, but also because individual interests vary. A Christian, for example, might be interested only in the section on the Bible, a Muslim only in the section on the Koran, while a classicist might be interested only in the section on the Romans. Although the chapter and indeed the whole book can be read in a modular fashion, the book should be read from start to finish (not necessarily in one sitting, of course), as a page-by-page and chapter-by-chapter whole. One can jump around and pick and choose parts, but one has to realize that the historical/philosophical analyses provided in Chapters 4 and 5 provide an essential part of the book. Without a good understanding of the history of the modern concept of universal human rights, the rest of the argument of the book cannot possibly be fully appreciated.

Chapter 5 is devoted to getting the history right, inasmuch as that is possible. What we shall see, quite astonishingly, is that the modern concept of universal human rights—both the concept and the belief—originated in the crucible of the English Civil Wars of the 1640s, specifically in the thinking of a group of Independents known as the Levellers. It is here that one finds the first clear and unequivocal expression of the concept of universal human rights in history, especially in the writings of Richard Overton, one of their leaders. Though as a political movement the English Levellers were quashed only a few years after they began, their ideas survived and spread beyond the confines of England a few decades later, principally in the writings of the English philosopher John Locke, in his *Two Treatises of Government*. During the convulsions of the 1640s, England was also the very same place and time of the first beginning in history of genuinely democratic beliefs and values, for the Levellers were the first true democrats in history. The basics of their democratic ideas were also furthered in Locke's *Two Treatises*, which unlike the pamphlets of the Levellers was read very widely. From Locke's *Two Treatises* the concept of universal human rights spread in connection with genuinely democratic thinking to the American and French Revolutions, to the United Nations, and then to much of the rest of the world, in the form of various Declarations, Constitutions, Bills, Charters, Drafts, and Covenants, along with a staggering number of books, chapters, articles, and, more recently, websites.

The whole has the appearance of the spread of a virus, and Chapter 6 is devoted to explaining its origin and spread. A large part of the explanation involves *memetics,* the approach to ideas that looks at ideas as having people (rather than people as having ideas) and as spreading for their own and not their hosts' sake. Developed by the biologist Richard Dawkins in his book devoted primarily to biological explanation in terms of *selfish genes* (Dawkins 1976), memetics is the truly revolutionary idea of applying the same principles of biological explanation to the units of cultural evolution, *memes.* As far as I am aware, the present book is the first and only attempt at applying memetic analysis to the origin and spread of the belief in universal human rights. In this sense alone it is original, and also quite daring.

After a preliminary section explaining the basics of memetics and providing a rather detailed defense against the two main criticisms of it, it is argued in Chapter 6 that the belief in universal human rights originated and spread in *symbiosis* with the origin and spread of modern democratic beliefs and values, from the Levellers through Locke to Jefferson and eventually to most of the rest of the world. Just as symbiosis in biology occurs because it increases the chance of survival and reproduction of at least one of the symbionts, *mutualism* in the case of both symbionts, it is likewise argued that the symbiotic origin and spread of the belief in universal human rights with the belief in democracy was not a coincidence but occurred primarily for the sake of the ideas themselves, as a kind of mutualism.

This kind of explanation will certainly seem counterintuitive at first sight, but the power of explanation in the present case is strengthened (and certainly made more interesting) when it is put into the context of *inference to the best explanation.* This is because memetics, it is argued, not only gives us a *powerful* explanation of the origin and spread of the belief in universal human rights, but also gives us the *best* explanation in contrast to competing explanations, such as the rise of capitalism, a shift in the discourse of power away from kings, or the rise of a new genre of literature known as the epistolary novel.

Following this, evolutionary psychology is then employed to help explain the psychological force and vivacity of the belief in universal human rights, since memetic analysis alone cannot do this. In particular, the theories on fairness by the sociobiologist Robert Trivers (reciprocal altruism) and the primatologist Frans de Waal (egocentric fairness) are applied to the topic. An evolved sense of fairness, it is argued, pre-adapted us for a deep acceptance of the meme complex of universal human rights that was to come.

The overall argument of the book, then, is highly interdisciplinary (as it must be), combining evolutionary history with history of ideas, political history, philosophical analysis, memetics, and evolutionary psychology. Consequently, it takes a truly interdisciplinary mind to fully appreciate the argument as a whole. That being said, the argument is not all over the place but is essentially two-pronged: taking biological history seriously reveals the false nature of the belief in universal human rights as well as the psychological predisposition to believe in them, while taking cultural history seriously reveals the mythological nature of the origin and spread of the belief.

It should be added that the argument taken collectively is not given as an *absolute proof* that the belief in universal human rights is false. No one could possibly prove beyond any and all doubt that all humans right now at this moment do not in fact have these mysterious properties called "universal human rights." The conclusion that human rights are a myth, instead, is given as an *inference to the best explanation* of the evidence, both evolutionary and cultural. This is the best that one can hope to do with such a topic. Given the evidence, the most reasonable conclusion is not that universal human rights are real but we just haven't fully understood them yet, or that some strong evidence will be forthcoming to justify the belief in them, but that they just don't exist, and ultimately that the beliefs and values used to justify them are illegitimate. The nature of the "proof," then, is *proof beyond a reasonable doubt*.

In the final chapter, Chapter 7, a very different way of dealing with moral and legal issues commonly identified with human rights is developed and applied. If it is true that universal human rights really do not exist, that they are a myth, and that the beliefs and values used to justify them are illegitimate, then appeals to human rights in moral and legal cases, such as matters of oppression and international law, rest on a false and hence precarious foundation. Sooner or later it is to be expected that the educated public as a whole, and with them possibly much of the rest of the world, is going to see that the Emperor has no clothes. The reference here, of course, is to "The Emperor's New Clothes," the delightful fairy tale written by Hans Christian Andersen and first published in 1837. With his new clothes, made of a "magical cloth" that was a sham, cloth the weavers claimed to be "invisible to people who are stupid or bad at their job," the Emperor walked through the streets to show off. "But suddenly a small child looked at the Emperor and cried, 'He's got nothing on at all!' Everyone heard. They looked at the Emperor. Then they looked at each other and looked at the Emperor again. At last all the people shouted, 'He's got nothing on at all!' And the Emperor knew that they were right" (Biro 2005, 76–77). The story is not a perfect parallel, of course, but it does have much to recommend it. In the end, Andersen has the Emperor blush and continue on his merry way, with his head held "higher than before."

I suspect that many will respond in much the same way to the main argument of this book. Even if they accept it, they will continue with the pomp and circumstance of human rights talk, believing that the ends justify the means, in this case fictional and illegitimate means. But a blatant disregard for truth is highly unlikely to produce a regard for truth, which is exactly what is needed for matters of ethics and justice. What is surely wanted, then, is a more secure foundation on which to place our moral and legal concerns, or to vary the metaphor, a new and better Emperor.

Accordingly, in the final chapter it is recommended that ethics and justice be *demythologized,* meaning not only that they be freed of theological concepts and programs such as divine-command ethics (which they pretty much have in the Western world, at least institutionally), but that they be freed of the modern myth of universal human rights, along with the anthropocentrism that goes along with it and the related concept of person. What should remain is a concern for matters of ethics and justice grounded in realities that are unequivocal and that everyone (or just about everyone) can relate to—specifically the realities of pain and pleasure, sympathy and empathy, kin and reciprocal altruism, fairness, and reason—a grounding that must include not only humans but also nonhuman animals within the boundaries of the moral universe. After providing a sketch of a hypothetical country I call Naturalia, the chapter closes by looking at a sample of six issues that are routinely dealt with today in terms of universal human rights—abortion, affirmative action, same-sex marriage, the treatment of animals, waterboarding, and political regime change—and by indicating how they might be dealt with by a fully and completely naturalized approach to ethics and justice, one that appeals to our full moral being. A naturalized approach to ethics and justice is, of course, by no means new, but the particular method developed and applied in this chapter is a novel one with surprisingly powerful results. In all of this there is no delusion of changing the moral world order of our modern time, only the hope of changing the individual reader in some way for the better.

Conceptual Errors and Fallacies

Before we turn to the following chapters, it is necessary to discuss a number of errors that commonly occur whenever the topic of human rights comes up. Some of these errors are conceptual, some of them inferential.

Beginning with the conceptual, one problem is the failure to distinguish *human rights* from *conventional rights.* The latter are man-made: they are given and taken away by individuals, governments, companies, and institutions. For example, citizens in a democracy have the right to vote, noncitizens do not; executives in a corporation each have the right to a particular parking space, which is taken away when they are no longer employed by the company; students who pay their tuition for a course have the right to submit work and receive a grade, others do not. Conventional rights are real, as real as the conventional agreements upon which they are based. But they are not *human* rights. Nor does it make any sense to say that there are *conventional* universal human rights. The United Nations is not the world government (far from it)—nobody has a birth certificate or citizenship paper declaring that they are a citizen of the world—nor is there a world corporation of which every human is an employee, or a world institution of which every human has membership. Perhaps the day will come when the opposite of one of these situations will become a reality, but we are not there and have never been, and the day, if ever it should come, is surely a long way off.

Human rights, on the other hand, are said to be *universal,* in the sense that *all* humans have them. Any conception of human rights that denies that all humans have them or, what is the same, affirms that only some humans have them, is not the modern consensus concept, the concept enshrined in the American Declaration of Independence, the Universal Declaration of Human Rights, and so much more. This simple point should follow from the label. If one is a human, and human rights exist, then one has human rights.

This creates a problem for those who conceive of group rights as human rights. For example, some feminists want to include women's rights among human rights (e.g., Bunch 1990). Certainly "sexism kills," on an alarmingly large scale, and it ought to be fought, but if women and only women have certain rights, such as the right to an abortion, if that is what they really mean, then the rights they are claiming cannot be *human* rights, since humans are not composed of just women. To count as human rights, women's rights would have to be phrased in such a way that they are not really women's rights after all but the rights of all humans, in a realistic and clear sense. (It will do no good to say that men have a right to an abortion, too, if ever they should happen to get pregnant.) In all of this the keyword in human rights is "human." Human rights, to be worthy of the name, must be had by all humans, not just by some.

What it is about humans that gives them these rights, of course, is another matter. As we shall see especially in Chapter 2, it is often said that universal human rights are the rights that one has simply because one is human. The word "simply" is remarkable, for it smacks of the arbitrary. What is wanted is something more than mere anthropocentrism, the analog of sexism and racism that Peter Singer (1975) calls *speciesism.* That problem is addressed mainly in Chapter 2 and no more will be made of it here.

Another key feature of the modern consensus concept of human rights is that human rights are *plural.* Immanuel Kant, therefore, as a prime example, in his

The Metaphysics of Morals (1797), is not at all dealing with the same concept as the modern consensus concept when he states that "*Freedom* (independence from being constrained by another's choice) ... is the only original right belonging to every man by virtue of his humanity" (393). What makes matters worse is that Kant claims that this "*natural right* ... rests only on a priori principles," meaning that it is a necessary postulate for humans to be moral agents. This means that *human natural right* is immune to criticism from an empirical, a posteriori point of view. As we shall see in the following chapters, this position cannot be maintained.

The consensus definition, as we shall see time after time, is that there are a number of universal human rights, not one, although complete lists are routinely avoided. In this sense, the belief in universal human rights suffers from the same problem that plagued Plato and other believers in the abstract paradigms he called Forms, the problem of scope. If Forms exist, then how many are there? There is a Form for justice, a Form for beauty, and a Form for triangle, fine, but is there also a Form for hair, a Form for mud, a Form for dirt (*Parmenides* 130b–d)? When we look at the history of growth of human rights talk, and the proliferation of types of human rights claims, the same problem arises: the proliferation has the appearance of a *reductio ad absurdum* and threatens the very foundation of the concept's legitimacy.

Aside from this problem, the essential plurality of the modern concept of universal human rights kills the equation with any singular concept whatsoever, not only freedom but others such as human dignity or moral equality. One either has dignity or does not, or has it to some degree, but no one talks of someone having human *dignities*. With regard to moral equality, of course, there are various senses in which some people are morally equal and unequal with one another. Two people can be morally equal in terms of heroism, for example, but morally unequal in other ways. But that is not at all what is usually meant when it is said that all humans are morally equal. What is meant, instead, is that all humans are morally equal by virtue of being human. This is the idea of *equal moral worth*. As Gregory Vlastos (1962) points out, this is not to be confused with *merit* (which does in fact vary between humans), such that "there can be strictly and literally no superior or inferior persons, individuals, men" (74).

Given these important distinctions, then, when one finds in a written work the concept of the moral equality of all human beings, one cannot automatically assume that the author also had the concept of universal human rights. The two are not the same concepts; the former is singular, the latter is plural. Nor are they logically related. This should be evident from the fact that there is no contradiction in claiming that all humans are morally equal but do not have natural rights. Singer, for example, claims that all sentient animals have interests, and therefore are morally equal, worthy of equal moral consideration, but his argument is explicitly not based on natural rights, the existence of which he doubts very much (see Chapter 7). Similarly, as odd as it sounds, there is no contradiction in claiming that all humans have dignity but do not have a natural right to be treated with dignity, or that all humans have freedom but do not have a natural right to be free. In all of this, throughout the whole book, one must never lose sight of the ball, which is the consensus concept of human rights, a concept that consists in large part of a plurality of putative rights that all humans have by virtue of being human.

Another essential feature of the modern consensus concept of universal human rights is that they are *equal* rights. This is to say that all human rights, whatever they are, are had by all humans *equally*. As Donnelly (2003) puts it in terms of justification, "one either is or is not a human being" (10). Again, as we shall see throughout this book but especially in Chapter 2, this is unquestionably part of the consensus concept, the concept found in the Universal Declaration of Human Rights and so much more. Any other concept of human rights, according to which some humans have them more than others (unequal), or some humans have them and some not (non-universal), is not at all the same concept, and anyone who defends either of the latter should not claim that he or she is defending the modern consensus concept of human rights. Donnelly's way of stating the equality of human rights, by the way, clearly makes sense only given a synchronic conception of humans, as there are no living or recent intermediates between humans and our closest cousins, the chimpanzees and bonobos. That, as pointed out above, is a problem that will be exploited in Chapter 2. But leaving aside that problem for the moment and thinking only synchronically, it is surely odd, if not nonsensical, for human rights to be *human* rights, to say that some humans have human rights more than others and some not at all.

A further key feature of the consensus concept of universal human rights is that human rights are *innate* or *inborn,* meaning that humans are literally born with them, whether they acquired them at conception or during gestation. Any concept of human rights as state-given, then, is not the same concept as the consensus concept, although this is sometimes contested and often overlooked. What we shall see in Chapter 3 is that the concept of human rights enshrined in the American Declaration of Independence and the UN's Universal Declaration of Human Rights and the many documents they spawned is that of innate rights, rights that all humans are born with, irrespective of whether their birth is in a political or pre-political context.

Finally, logically independent from the previous feature is that human rights are *inalienable,* meaning that they are not the sort of thing that can be given or taken away (either by oneself or by someone else). Along with the previous four features, this means that human rights are part of the human condition. As Donnelly (2003) puts it in defense of the modern consensus concept, "one cannot stop being human" (10). What this means is that I cannot give to a dog, for example, my human right to own property or any other putative human right, any more than I could give it my membership in the human species.

It needs to be added here that this idea that human rights are inalienable, which as we shall see later is definitely part of the modern consensus concept, should not be confused with the idea that human rights are *absolute,* that they cannot be overruled in particular circumstances. In the very least, human rights claims, as with all rights claims, often come into conflict with one another. The equality of human rights means only that all humans have them equally, not that all human rights are equal. This is a common point in both principle and practice and it helps to clarify the inalienable sense of the concept of human rights. Moreover, human rights are not the only fundamental claims in matters of ethics and justice, whether in principle or in practice, such that they can and often do come into conflict with other kinds of claims. As Vlastos (1962) puts it, to say that human rights are inalienable is to say only that they constitute a "*prima-facie* justification." This justification can sometimes be overpowered in particular circumstances by a counterclaim with a different justification, but as Vlastos puts it, a prima facie justification is one that is justified "unless there are stronger counter-claims in the particular situation in which it is made, the burden of proof resting always on the counter-claims" (47n23). When a person or state, then, which believes in universal human rights, overpowers an individual's claim to a human right, it is not necessarily the case that they are violating that individual's human right. They might have a stronger justification than the strength of the justification for that individual's human right, the latter being the fact that the individual is a human. Logically speaking, *inalienable* does not mean *absolute.*

Apart from the issue of justification, what must be reemphasized at this point is that the belief in universal human rights, as commonly understood in the world, is an existence claim, that in addition to the various observable facts about humans there is a set of further facts, a set of moral claims and entitlements that all and only humans have. These facts are generally understood as possessions, as something humans *have,* as facts about humans regardless of whether they are aware of them.

Some, however, have attempted to introduce confusion at this point. The philosopher Brian Orend (2002), for example, argues that for imprisonment to be justified from a human rights point of view, "The most plausible conclusion to draw here is that we should reject the assumption that human rights are properties of persons, woven into the very fabric of our being" (19). Orend would have us believe that human rights as possessions, as the innate and inalienable endowment of all human beings, is not part of the "bedrock beliefs," not part of the "most cherished beliefs," of what he calls the "contemporary human rights movement" (39), the "human rights community" (15), of which he considers himself a member. But the very "assumption" that he is talking about is a vital belief of the majority of that community, evidenced alone by its central documents, not only the American Declaration of Independence but also the UN's Universal Declaration of Human Rights and the numerous national and international documents that followed it. Again, as Tony Evans (2005) puts it, "natural rights foundationalism continues to inform most mainstream 'human rights talk'" (7). The view that Orend expresses, it turns out, is that of a minority within the human rights community, an intellectualist elite that (like many elites in other fields) likes to speak for the beliefs of the rest. Rather than look closely at the central documents and institutions of the modern human rights movement and at expressions by prominent individuals within that community (both of which we shall do in Chapters 2 and 3), Orend uses a philosophical argument in an effort to elucidate the consensus concept of that community, an argument that fails not only because it ignores the evidence to the contrary, but also because it ignores the important distinction between inalienable and absolute.

Another philosopher, Alan White (1984), argues more abstractly that rights claims are factual claims but they do not denote, since "facts are not themselves items that exist in space and time" (10). We cannot point to facts, he says, since facts are neither created nor destroyed, neither here nor there. But this is loading the dice in one's favor. Facts are merely features of reality, of which we can have true and false propositions (Frankfurt 2006, 54–55). And granted, human rights claims are not claims about physical facts but about moral facts. Yet they still are claims to something that humans either do or do not in fact have, claims moreover that are supposed to be based on observable or indirectly observable facts, such as being human or more specifically having human intelligence or reason. The philosophical use of wordplay to avoid this fundamental feature of the vast majority of universal human rights talk is a case where, to borrow the words of Bishop George Berkeley in the early eighteenth century, "we have first raised a dust and then complain we cannot see."

Clever wordplay on this topic (and others) also comes from adherents of the ideology common in the humanities and social sciences known as *postmodernism,* which rejects as illusions any distinction between objectivity and subjectivity, fact and fiction, truth and falsity. Triumphantly we are told that we live in the "age of postmodernism," which means that, in line with political correctness, different perspectives and interpretations must be allowed to fully vent (this turns out usually to mean that women and minorities count more than others) and no one perspective or interpretation can be deemed as epistemologically privileged (see Stamos 2008, 31–33). What this means for human rights, in the words of Richard Rorty (1993), a prominent postmodernist, is first that "one important intellectual advance made in our century is . . . a growing willingness to neglect the question 'What is our nature?' and to substitute the question 'What can we make of ourselves?'" (115), and second, that "the question whether human beings really have the rights enumerated in the Helsinki Declaration is not worth raising" (116).

This book (despite its title) does not subscribe to the ideology of postmodernism. I am a realist. In line with natural science, law, business, and everyday life, I take it that there are objective facts in the world, like money in the bank, and that many of them are not only knowable but also important to know, such as whether there are facts (including probabilities) about human nature. That Rorty could not be more wrong about human nature and about human rights is a theme that runs throughout the pages of this book. For the moment, I will leave the reader with an analogy: imagine a man going to the bank to take out money he doesn't have in his account and arguing with the teller that there is no objective truth about the matter, that it is a matter of perspective, even that it is a matter of "What I can make of myself." The appropriate response of the teller is to either laugh or to call the manager (and then the police if the customer persists). The laughter part evokes a famous saying by H. L. Mencken: "One horse-laugh is worth ten thousand syllogisms" (Mencken 1949, 17). One does not refute postmodernism by showing how silly it is (or pernicious), nor can postmodernists be converted to realism by argument, something Harry Frankfurt (2006, 19) appears to try to do. But in the very least it is important to make clear where one stands on the matter.[1]

---

1. There is a strong analogy here with *psychopaths* (see Stamos 2011), who lack moral virtues and values, such as sympathy, empathy, and conscience, and look down upon those who have them. Similarly postmodernists lack *epistemic* virtues and values, such as testing theories against evidence, Ockham's Razor, and the importance of truth, and look down upon those who have them. The former lack the stuff of morality, the latter the stuff of knowledge. So just as there is no point arguing with a psychopath for why he or she should be moral (a point I shall return to in Chapter 7), there is no point arguing with a postmodernist for why he or she should pursue knowledge. The analogy breaks down when it comes to numbers. Psychopaths number roughly 1 percent in the human population, a number that is higher in corporations, where the attributes of psychopaths are often valued (Hare 1995; Babiak and Hare 2006). Postmodernists, on the other hand, probably number far fewer than 1 percent in the human population, but considerably higher than 1 percent in universities and colleges among faculty, depending on the division (virtually zero in the natural sciences, upwards of 50 percent in the humanities, the social sciences, and philosophy, depending on the department). The irony of it all is that colleges and universities are supposed to be devoted to the pursuit of knowledge, not to the pursuit of anti-knowledge.

Taking the issue of universal human rights as a matter of objective possessions, a further feature of the modern consensus concept, and the last one we shall focus on, is that, in line with rights talk in general, expressions containing the phrase "a right" are logically distinct from phrases such as "the right thing to do" or "acting right." (Sometimes in the literature on human rights the term *subjective right* is used for the former and *objective right* for the latter, which is misleading since human rights realists believe that human rights exist objectively, irrespective of our subjective awareness.) That "a right" is not logically the same as "the right thing to do" or "acting right" should be obvious not only from the fact that "right" in the first case is a noun and that "right" in each of the other two cases is an adverb combined with a verb, but because the phrases "the right thing to do" and "acting right" can exist and get along in the world completely without the concept of "a right." Nor does the latter logically follow from the former. For example, suppose that my giving money to a homeless person I happen to be passing by on the street is the right thing to do or a right action. It might be right because charity is a virtue (virtue ethics), or because it produces more happiness than unhappiness (utilitarianism), or because I'm treating the poor human as a person and not merely as a thing (Kant), or because it is a prima facie duty (Ross), or because it is important to care (feminist ethics), or because it will impress my girlfriend (ethical egoism). For each of these theories, what makes my action right is not a supposed right of the homeless person to receive money from me or anyone else; in fact, none of the theories is based on rights at all. In short, then, an action being *right* and someone having *a right* must never be confused.

A further number of errors need to be highlighted on the topic of universal human rights, errors that are not so much conceptual as they are inferential. These are errors in reasoning routinely committed by those who claim to see the modern belief in universal human rights existing either explicitly or implicitly in premodern sources.

One common error is *presentism,* reading the present into the past. Professional historians often warn against this, as one of the cardinal sins to be avoided when dealing with history.[2] Given that universal human rights is a large part of the consciousness of most people today, at least in the West, the urge to read the modern belief into premodern sources needs to be resisted in the interest of objectivity and good scholarship. Laypeople all too easily fall into this trap, but as we shall see

---

2. A striking example of presentism is the increasingly popular reading of modern scientific ideas into the Koran, such as cell biology, evolutionary biology, and the Big Bang, exemplified in the footnotes of Ali (2001).

throughout Chapter 4, professional scholars, too, those who should know better, including even professional historians, are prone to the same weakness. Clearly there is something about the topic of human rights that brings out this common error in people, pretty much regardless of their education.

What typically goes hand in hand with presentism is *wishful thinking*, what may be called the *ought-is fallacy*. This fallacy permeates the general public but is also common in the academic world. There *ought* to be a God, because the meaning of life demands it, so every reason is found to conclude that there *is* a God. Gender *ought* to be a social construction, including the male-female dichotomy, because social justice demands it, so every reason is found to conclude that gender *is* a social construction. Human races *ought not* to exist, because that would undermine racism and satisfy political correctness, so every reason is found to conclude that human races *do not* exist. In each case the pattern is the same, and the belief in universal human rights is no exception. There *ought* to be universal human rights, because we need them to fight social injustice worldwide, so earlier cultures/philosophies/religions *must* have independently "discovered" them. Maybe they did, but fallacious reasoning is not going to demonstrate it.

One often finds the above combined with a healthy dose of *ethnocentrism*, putting one's ethnic group above others, considering it superior in some way. Determining whether universal human rights exist, and which culture first began proclaiming them, is not to be settled in the manner of flag waving at a soccer match. This human, all-too-human proclivity must likewise with the others be resisted in the interest of good scholarship, and not only whether it is a matter of one's own ethnic group, but likewise whether it is a matter of one's own religion, country, or scholarly field.

Yet another common and related error is known as *gerrymandering* (also *cherry picking* and *quote mining*), picking and choosing passages that seem to fit one's preconceived view and either ignoring the ones that do not or reinterpreting them (*exegesis*). Walter Kaufmann (1958, 219) claims that gerrymandering is not accidental but essential to theological exegesis, and he might be right. What is unquestionable is that the game of gerrymandering, often played unconsciously and with full sincerity, of which we shall see some prime examples in Chapter 4, is antithetical to objectivity and has no place in the pursuit of truth.

Finally, there is the *genetic fallacy* widely conceived. Narrowly conceived, the fallacy consists of rejecting an argument, idea, practice, or institution because of its genesis, such as rejecting an argument because it came to the arguer in a dream, or rejecting an institution because of its racist origins. More widely conceived, the fallacy involves accepting as much as rejecting because of origin (Damer 2005, 83). But the fallacy may be conceived even more widely still, as including a specific version, the reasoning that because B evolved or originated from A, therefore there must be some of the content of B in A. We shall see this in Chapter 3 with regard to natural law theory. Even if it is true that the modern belief in universal human rights evolved from natural law theory prevalent in the Middle Ages, it does not automatically follow that the concept of universal human rights existed in the Middle Ages. Modern chemistry evolved from medieval alchemy, but it would be a gross mistake to say that medieval alchemists had chemistry, or that alchemy contains the basics of chemistry, or that alchemy entails chemistry. Similarly, if it is thought that the belief in universal human rights evolved from the belief in biological equality, or from the belief in moral equality, or from the belief in human dignity, or from a system of duties and obligations, or from a system of man-made rights, it does not follow that any of these beliefs contain or entail the concept of universal human rights. In each case, it is the *assumption* that makes the reasoning fallacious, the assumption that because B evolved from A, the latter necessarily includes or entails B. It is not true for the evolution of biological species B from A, or the evolution of natural language B from A, or the evolution of business B from A, so why would it be any different when it comes to concepts?

For whatever the causes or reasons, conceptual sloppiness and fallacious reasoning dominate most thinking on universal human rights, as we shall see in detail in later chapters.

Chapter 2

Evolution and Universal Human Rights

His reason ought to conquer his imagination.

—*Charles Darwin (1859, 188)*

The Theological Foundation of Universal Human Rights

THE THEORETICAL FOUNDATION OF UNIVERSAL HUMAN RIGHTS TALK was originally theological, more specifically creationism, with universal human rights having been made part of human nature at the time of God's creation of man. Locke in his *Two Treatises* repeatedly refers to God, Creation, and Adam and Eve, as did the Levellers before him. Jefferson, Paine, and others were likewise explicit in their creationism.[1] In our modern time, with the eclipse of creationism, the theological foundation still often finds expression, though within the context of a debate over that very foundation. John F. Kennedy, for example, in his Inaugural Address

---

1. Paine was a deist, in the modern sense of the term, albeit still a creationist (as we shall see below), believing in a creator God with no subsequent supervision or intervention, while those who think that Jefferson was also a deist in the same sense of the term, or even an agnostic or atheist, need to go beyond his often-cited letter to his nephew Peter Carr and examine his correspondence more fully (e.g., Peterson 1984, 1080–1082, 1120–1126, 1466–1470). In a letter to John Adams, for example, he writes of "the God whom you and I acknolege [*sic*] and adore, the Creator and benevolent governor of the world" (1466).

delivered in January 1961, stated that "the same revolutionary beliefs for which our forebears fought are still at issue around the globe—the belief that the rights of man come not from the generosity of the state, but from the hand of God." Kennedy, echoed today in the current presidential race, openly sided with the hand of God, as did Malcolm X a few years later. In his speech "The Ballot or the Bullet," delivered in 1964, Malcolm X stated that "Civil rights means you're asking Uncle Sam to treat you right. Human rights are something you were born with. Human rights are your God-given rights.... any time anyone violates your human rights, you can take them to the world court." One can also find human rights theorists, professional scholars such as Leo Strauss (1953, 3–8) and Richard Tuck (1979, 1–2, 176–177), who find fault with secular conceptions of human rights (or their rejection) and hanker after the past, if not to creationism then to theological conceptions of a wider sort.

There are a number of problems that should be obvious here. One is that theology is a highly insecure foundation on which to rest the reality of human rights. Anyone who does not see this, who fails to see this, suffers either from a lack of education or from a lack of objectivity. This is because not a single argument for God's existence is a done deal, not the Argument from Design, or the Argument from Contingency, or the Argument from Religious Experience, or any of the others. In the field devoted to studying these arguments, known as philosophy of religion (which includes more than just philosophers), one can find professional scholars who side with one or the other of each argument and its variants, with no consensus whatsoever, or if there is a consensus it is on the negative side. Any good course or anthology on philosophy of religion will readily show this (e.g., Pojman 2003). Long gone, then, are the days when one could rest satisfied with the belief that the existence of God is self-evident or could be proven to all rational and reasonable beings.

A related problem is that belief in God has been shown to vary inversely with IQ and education, such that the higher the IQ or education, the less religious belief statistically, especially when the education is in the natural sciences (Bell 2002; Larson and Witham 1999). Moreover, there is an inverse relationship between belief in God and countries with social programs, such that countries with the highest levels of social programs also have the highest levels of atheism and agnosticism (Zuckerman 2007). All of this should be troublesome to those who want to base the reality of universal human rights on a theological foundation.

The final problem, and arguably the biggest, is that evolutionary biology cannot be ignored but needs to be taken seriously. This is because the evidence in favor of its basic framework, beginning with the work of Charles Darwin and leading to the present, has become so massive that the modern scientific world calls evolution a *fact*, not a theory, in the sense of *beyond a reasonable doubt* (Stamos 2008, 232–234). But don't take my word for it, read top-notch professional biologists (e.g., Miller 2008; Coyne 2009; Dawkins 2009). In the very least, what this means is that a creationist foundation for universal human rights lacks intellectual respectability.

But that was the original foundation. Moreover, it was combined with a kind of essentialism, the view that all members of a species are essentially the same, in this case humans. This is true even of Locke. While it is true that in his *Essay Concerning Human Understanding*, published in 1689, he did indeed argue against species (including the human species) as having an underlying essence (see Stamos 2003, 40–45), he nevertheless claimed in *Two Treatises* not only that all humans are "of the same species and rank," but that they are all born "to the same advantages of Nature, and the use of the same faculties," such that they "should be equal one amongst another without Subordination or Subjection" (II.2.§4). Even more apparently, the pamphleteer Thomas Paine, the spirit of the American and French Revolutions, made essentialism the explicit foundation of universal human rights. As he put it in his *Rights of Man* (1791), referring explicitly to the Mosaic account of creation, not only did God make male and female with no other distinction between them "even implied," but God made man (male and female) "all of *one degree*," such that "all men are born equal, and with equal natural rights, in the same manner as if posterity had been continued by *creation* instead of *generation*" (463). Generation (reproduction) as repeated creation is just about as clear a statement as one can get on the notion of species fixity and essentialism.

The Foundation in Human Nature

Ever since Darwin, species essentialism has been dead, not only because species fixity is incompatible with the evolution of one species from another but because the process of natural selection cannot possibly work without underlying variation. And today it is known as a fact that variation for species and populations is the norm, not an underlying essence. In fact, biology is statistical in just about every way, such that no two organisms have identical DNA except for clones and monozygotic (identical) twins, and even then only if they underwent no mutation in their life histories. The statistical nature of the genotype, moreover, affects the statistical nature of the phenotype (the outward expression of the genes). If humans have human rights, then, one would expect them to be statistical, not essentialistic.

The problem only becomes worse once we turn from individual variation to group variation. Mutation and recombination ensure that each and every population or species has genetic variability. But sexually reproducing species and geographically wide-ranging species are going to have even more genetic variability, which brings us to the politically hot-button topics of gender and race. Given evolutionary history, it is only to be expected that the human sexes, reaching far back before the evolution of our own species, *Homo sapiens,* would have evolved an innate division of labor between the sexes, based on the reproductive asymmetries of the sexes—following the title of the book by Joe Quirk (2006), the fundamental fact of human gender is that *sperm are from men and eggs are from women.* Given, then, a vast evolutionary history of small hunting-gathering groups fighting for survival in hostile environments, which included competition with related groups as well as a variety of dangerous predators, it is only to be expected that statistical differences would have evolved between the sexes in physical traits, such as size and strength, and in hormones, such as testosterone and estrogen, as well as in behavioral traits, such as reproductive strategies, talkativeness, and single-tasking versus multitasking.

In the case of the human races, we are all of one species, as with the sexes, but statistical differences would likewise be expected to have evolved. The fundamental difference is that while the two sexes have always existed together, the human races are the result of branching evolution from a common origin. Every biological species has its evolutionary origin in a particular time and locale, and if it spreads outward from that area into novel habitats and niches, then it is expected to evolve statistical differences (providing that it does not first go extinct). The human species, having its origin in a part of Africa, spread outward via the Middle East to virtually all terrestrial areas of the globe. What is to be expected are not only innate statistical differences in physical traits, such as skin color and immunity to various diseases, but also statistical differences in behavioral traits, such as IQ, cooperativeness, competitiveness, and aggression (each with their different categories or kinds). Take just about any trait one may choose: if a species gradually spreads geographically, then geographical variation is going to be its norm. And in the case of humans, that is exactly what biology has found, including evolutionary psychology.

But for the political sensitivity of it all, absolutely none of the above is controversial in the slightest within the science of biology. It is only controversial outside of biology, and only then because it is shocking to our modern moral and political sensibilities, including political correctness.

The common response is to say that universal human rights is not a claim about biological equality (for clearly we are not all biologically equal) but instead is a claim about *moral* equality. This, however, does not remove the basic problem.

First, *equality,* as with the term *similarity,* suffers from a lack of meaning unless a particular respect is specified. With respect to moral capacity, clearly we are not all morally equal, whether the capacity is sympathy, empathy, conscience, altruism, fairness, or whatever else we should choose to add to the list. Full-fledged psychopaths are one end of the spectrum here.

With respect to merit, clearly again we are not all morally equal, given the extremes of our individual and group behavior from humanitarianism to genocide. Whether the behavior that is counted is outward behavior or inner behavior including motives does not matter. It should be abundantly obvious that we all cannot possibly be morally equal if the equality is based on meritorious behavior.

Another possibility is that our moral equality is based on the mere fact that we are human. One often finds this in discussions on human rights, not only that all humans have human rights and have them equally, but that human rights are the rights that one has "simply" because one is human—"rights that are had by every human being simply insofar as he or she is human" (Gewirth 1996, 6), "the rights that one has simply by virtue of being human" (Hayden 2001, xv), "the rights one has simply because one is a human being" (Donnelly 2003, 1), "rights held by individuals simply because they are part of the human species" (Ishay 2008, 3). If one really means this, then the claim is fundamentally arbitrary.

One reason is that *human* is a species term and there is no consensus in biology on what a species is.[2] One might try to get around this problem by conceptualizing species synchronically (at a given slice of time), since all modern species concepts contain this dimension for species (they just don't all define species synchronically). In this way one might then be able to make the case that we are all equally human. The problem now is that, depending on how one defines "species," there are currently in existence upwards of 30 million species on Earth. Why would humans and only humans have those special rights called "human rights"? Any answer that simply affirms that humans have natural moral rights and the members of the rest of the species on Earth do not (or have them to a lesser degree) smacks of anthropocentrism and is guilty of *speciesism,* the arbitrary privileging of members of one's own species over members of other species. What is needed is some further reason than mere species membership, something rooted in human nature and lacking in other species.

One answer often given, even back in human rights talk before evolutionary biology made things more interesting, is the human possession of *reason*. Locke, our most important example, makes it sufficiently clear in his *Two Treatises* that he thinks that reason is what primarily separates humans from the brutes. "Reason,"

---

2. In biology a species is a basic kind of living organism, one not reducible to or composed of other basic kinds of living organism. The problem is that different species concepts use different criteria to divide organisms into species, with different results. See Stamos (2003, 2007).

he says, "which God hath given to be the Rule betwixt Man and Man, ... [is] the common bond whereby humane kind is united into one fellowship and societie" (II.15.§172). Man's reason, he adds, "places him almost equal to the Angels" (I.6.§58). And as "*the Voice of God in him*," reason makes it evident to man that he has "a right to make use of those Creatures ... that were necessary or useful to his Being" (9.§86). Thus, "being furnished with like Faculties, sharing all in one Community of Nature, there cannot be supposed any such *Subordination* among us, ... as the inferior ranks of Creatures are for ours" (II.2.§6). And indeed Locke equates liberty with reason, stating that "we are *born Free,* as we are born Rational" (6.§61) and that "The *Freedom* ... of Man and Liberty of acting according to his own Will, is *grounded on* his having *Reason*" (§63).

In a similar vein, Mary Wollstonecraft, in her *A Vindication of the Rights of Woman* (1792), argues that the French Constitution is flawed and needs to be rewritten, because it does not explicitly include women in the "rights of man." Her fundamental argument is that reason constitutes "man's pre-eminence over the brute creation," that women have been excluded from the "natural rights of man" because of the perception that "they want reason" (69), and that in fact women have an equal potential in this regard but it has gone unnoticed because "the female world [is] oppressed" (275).

Human reason, however, is today no longer the premier human trait given as justification for the belief in human rights. The Universal Declaration of Human Rights, for example, refers in its Preamble to "the human family" and claims that "all members of the human family" have "inherent dignity" and "equal and inalienable rights," while in Article 1 it states that "All human beings are born free and equal in dignity and rights. They are endowed with reason and conscience...." Nowhere does it *base* human rights on human reason or human dignity or any other particular trait or set of traits. Instead it asserts in its Preamble a consensus among the member nations of the United Nations and a reaffirmation of a "faith in fundamental human rights." The implication, of course, is that there is something distinct about "the human family" that warrants this faith. The African Charter on Human and Peoples' Rights (1981) is a little more explicit, since it claims that "fundamental human rights stem from the attributes of human beings" (359), but it does not specify what those attributes are. Whether specified or not, what must be recognized is that if we are not going to go the theological route on human rights (and that includes natural law theory), then human rights have to be based on specifically human traits, whatever those are taken to be. In other words, we are going to have to deal with *human nature.*

And it will do no good to deny human nature. The denial of human nature defines what has come to be known as the Standard Social Science Model (SSSM), the idea, actually an ideology, that there is in fact no such thing as human nature, that what we call "human nature" is in fact the result of environmental forces (social, political, cultural), not biological ones. This ideology is common to sociology, political science, cultural anthropology, behaviorist psychology, Marxism, women's studies, and to a large extent gay studies and philosophy (e.g., existentialism and phenomenology). As Jack Donnelly (2003) puts it in his defense of human rights that we shall examine in the next chapter, "'Human nature' is a social project more than a presocial given, ... human beings create their 'essential' nature through social action on themselves" (15). This is a major example of the widespread failure to take biology seriously, or more accurately in many cases the widespread *desire* (mainly political, including political correctness) to *not* take biology seriously. No one has a problem with the idea of rabbit nature or wolf nature, but when the topic of human nature comes up it becomes controversial in the extreme. Critics slap on labels such as "essentialism" and "biological determinism," without a fair-minded desire to listen to a reply. The devil is in the details, however, as the saying goes, and there has accumulated throughout especially the past few decades a mountain of evidence in favor of the view that there is such a thing as human nature, that the human phenotype is not just physical but also includes behavioral and mental traits (as evolved capacities and instincts). As with phenotypic traits in general, the expression of these behavioral and mental traits will be the result of a combination of factors, genetic and environmental. But this plasticity does not negate the existence of the genotype or its influence, an underlying multifaceted norm or nature in a statistical, synchronic sense (see Barkow et al. 1992; Crawford and Krebs 1998; Pinker 2002; Buss 2005b; Dunbar and Barrett 2007; Stamos 2008).

In short, there is no getting around human nature when it comes to human rights. If human rights are the rights that one has by virtue of being human (and this is the consensus concept), then we cannot sidestep or ignore what "being human" means.

A serious problem now is that no matter what trait or traits one takes to be specifically human, the important fact is not only that not all humans have them equally, but that some humans are so deficient in any one of them that one can find nonhuman animals that have more of the specified trait. This is commonly known (albeit indelicately) as the *problem of marginal cases*. The problem arises whether one takes the trait to be reason, autonomy, language, self-awareness, conscience, moral behavior, the ability to imitate, or anything else (see, e.g., Singer 1975; Corbey 2005). Locke in his *Second Treatise* seems to be at least partly aware of this problem (in his case, that some humans can lack reason as much as animals), for although he thinks that reason, as we have seen above, is the "Rule" among humans and is lacking in animals, he recognizes the temporary exception of "*Children*" and "*Madmen*" and the permanent exception of "Lunaticks and Ideots," such that "if through defects that may happen out of the ordinary course of Nature, any one comes not to such a degree of Reason, wherein he might be supposed capable of knowing the Law, and so living within the Rules of it, he is *never capable of being a Free Man*" (6.§60). Locke's only solution is to say that "he is . . . continued under the Tuition and Government of others, all the time his own Understanding is uncapable of that Charge." Locke, however, does not seem to see the problem that defects in the course of nature creates for human rights, since if human rights are based primarily on human reason, then defective humans, humans who permanently lack the distinctive human ability to reason, will automatically lack "the *Equality*, which all men are in, in respect of Jurisdiction or Dominion one over another." Consequently, they will lack "that *equal Right* that every Man hath, *to his natural Freedom*" (§54). In other words, permanently defective humans have the potential to render "universal human rights" a contradiction in terms (if they are universal, then they are not human, and if they are human, then they are not universal). Locke might have thought he got around this problem, if he thought of it at all, by placing human rights on the foundation of God's fiat, but a secular conception of human rights must look elsewhere.

The problem of marginal cases does not reside simply in determining what the defining trait or traits of humans should be taken to be (clearly no simple matter). The problem instead is that *no matter what those traits are taken to be*, human nature is going to be statistical. This is a fact that follows from modern biology. As we shall see in the next chapter, one might then accept this fact and argue in one way or another, as White and Gewirth and Griffin and Nussbaum and so many others do, that human rights are based on the nature of the *typical* human being, the human who is not the unfortunate victim of accidents of history such as the human born, say, with half a brain, or the human who suffered a brain injury or disease that destroyed his or her language capacity, or the human born with genes that helped make him or her a psychopath (usually him). In this way, it is thought, human rights can be justified as universal (or almost universal), as rights that all (or almost all) humans have by virtue of being human.

A major problem here, elaborated in the next chapter, is that these approaches deviate from the consensus concept of human rights, the concept enshrined in the American Declaration of Independence and the Universal Declaration of Human Rights and so much more, which literally and strictly includes the concepts of universal and equal. Extending human rights to underdeveloped and defective humans acknowledged as lacking in personhood simply because of misfortune (White) fails because animals could likewise be considered misfortunate in not being evolved as persons, so that universal human rights would have to be extended to nonhumans. Extending human rights to underdeveloped and defective humans because of an underlying similarity to normal humans (Gewirth) fails not only because similarity is a matter of respects but also because similarity is a matter of degree, of more or less, and equal human rights require identity, not degree. Not extending human rights to underdeveloped and defective humans because they fall under the required threshold (Griffin) fails because it does not meet the universality requirement. And extending human rights to underdeveloped and defective humans based on the "species norm" (Nussbaum) fails because it appeals to an arbitrary criterion: mere membership in the human species, which is speciesism.

Finally, one might argue that all humans are morally equal not because of anything that humans *have*, whether in common among themselves or when compared with other animals, that humans are morally equal not because of any *is*, but because of an *ought*, that all humans are morally equal because they *ought* to receive equal moral consideration, that despite their innate differences they should be treated as moral equals, on the same level with one another, with no one human or group enjoying a higher moral status than any other.

But this sense of equality does no better than any of the others. The arguments of the ethicist Peter Singer are especially relevant here. As Singer (1975) points out, the *principle of equality* has been prominently used, particularly since the liberation movements of the 1960s, with respect to matters of gender and race (and since then to other matters, such as people with disabilities, but I will keep it simple). The principle does not require that the sexes be in fact equal, or the human races, nor does it require that they be treated equally. It does not require, for example, that white males get affirmative action, too. What it requires, instead, is that people of different sexes and races be given *equal moral consideration*. An implication of this principle is that differences such as genitalia or skin color should not be taken into account, that in themselves they are morally irrelevant. What this really means is that people's interests should be treated on the same level, with no sex or race having its interests privileged over another. The principle of equal moral consideration, then, prominent in the contexts of combating sexism and racism, is really underneath it all the *principle of equal consideration of interests*. But what is the foundation of having interests? The answer is simple: *sentience*. As Singer puts it, "The capacity for suffering and enjoyment is *a prerequisite for having any interests at all*, a condition that must be satisfied before we can speak of interests in a meaningful way" (7). The problem that arises now for the principle of equality is that humans are not the only sentient beings on Earth, such that if we really do believe in the principle of moral equality, so as to avoid sexism and racism, then we cannot, without being inconsistent, confine it to the human species alone. To do so would be speciesism, the equivalent of sexism and racism with respect to species other than one's own: it is to privilege membership in one's own species over membership in other species, just as sexists and racists have done with their respective sexes and races. *Speciesism* was coined by the psychologist Richard Ryder, but it was Singer who gave the term its currency, and it is interesting here to look at his exact definition: "a prejudice or attitude of bias in favor of the interests of members of one's own species and against those members of other species" (6).

At this point lofty slogans are often touted in response, such as "human dignity," "the dignity of man," or "the sanctity of (human) life," in order to privilege human interests over nonhuman interests, but as Singer quite rightly points out, "fine phrases are the last resource of those who have run out of arguments" (239). The bottom line is that if one truly believes in the moral equality of the human sexes and races, then one cannot confine that equality to humans alone. And by the same line of reasoning, one cannot confine universal, equal, innate, and inalienable moral rights to humans either, "simply" because they are human.

All of this is devastating for the modern belief in universal human rights. But the worst is yet to come.

Taking Evolution Seriously

Increasingly in the academic world it is said that we need to take Darwin seriously, or more accurately that we need to take evolution seriously. But rarely is it appreciated what "taking evolution seriously" fully means. For a start, it means recognizing the populational nature of species. It means recognizing that every individual organism, and consequently every generation, contains new mutations and that mutations are generally random, both with respect to the environment and with respect to their foundation in quantum indeterminism. It means taking seriously the statistical processes of genetic drift and natural selection, and seeing that only the latter produces adaptations. It means recognizing that evolutionary processes have in themselves no goal or purpose. It means taking seriously the enormous timescale of evolution, which is measured minutely in thousands of years and ultimately in hundreds of millions of years. It means recognizing that evolutionary history moves generally from the simple to the more complex and that it is fundamentally a branching process, if only at the higher levels of complexity. And finally, it means recognizing that evolution has far-reaching implications and consequences for topics and fields outside of biology as normally circumscribed, such as epistemology, ethics, religion, and human nature.

In the specific case of universal human rights, it should be seen that taking evolution seriously sounds the death knell of what Mahoney (2007) on human rights calls "a single moral family" (ix). The argument is a particularly striking example of what the philosopher Daniel Dennett calls the "universal acid" of Darwinism. As he puts it in his book *Darwin's Dangerous Idea* (1995), Darwin's theory of evolution by natural selection "eats through just about every traditional concept, and leaves in its wake a revolutionized world-view, with most of the old land-marks still recognizable, but transformed in fundamental ways" (63). Dennett himself, however, has underestimated Darwin's acid in one of the topics where it matters most, namely, the moral distinction between man and all other animals. In commenting on Jeremy Bentham's rejection of the doctrine of universal human rights as "nonsense upon stilts" (we shall return to Bentham in the final chapter), Dennett defends the doctrine pragmatically as "*good* nonsense—and good only because it is on stilts, only because it happens to have the 'political' power to keep rising above the meta-reflections—not indefinitely, but usually 'high enough'—to reassert itself as a compelling—that is, conversation-stopping—'first principle'" (507).

This is like dropping the ball on the one-yard line (and not because of the long, run-on sentence). A first principle is a foundational claim not thought to be in need of defense, like an axiom in mathematics. One might expect universal human rights to be treated as a first principle in legal theory and political science, but one hardly expects it from a Darwinian. There are even some who do not count themselves as Darwinians, even though they pay lip service to evolution (and that includes a great many academics), who believe that universal human rights are in need of defense. In the next chapter we shall encounter the arguments of a number of scholars who felt the need and attempted to rise to the challenge. We shall also see that their attempts fall far short of their mark. At any rate, the time has surely come to take Darwin's universal acid and pour it where Dennett himself, for whatever his reasons, has refrained.

What shall be argued here is that the moral distinction that is universal human rights is fatally undermined by taking Darwin and evolution seriously, and not so much because of the basic principles of population biology examined in the previous section, but mainly because of the nature of evolutionary history itself. More specifically, the conclusion that shall be defended is that evolutionary biology entails that the dominant moral discourse of our modern world is fundamentally false, that humans do not and cannot possibly have universal, equal, innate, and inalienable moral rights if evolution is a reality. In short, the ultimate point is that *if evolution is true, then human rights must be false.* Let us now see how this is so.

From an evolutionary point of view, *Homo sapiens,* as with other biological species, did not pop into existence out of nothing, nor did it jump into existence from a previously existing species, analogous to the birth of Athena in Greek mythology from the head of Zeus. Instead, the human species evolved *gradually* from earlier species in a branch-like fashion, as part of what Darwin (1859) called "the great Tree of Life" (130). This is standard in evolutionary biology and there is nothing controversial here if one takes evolution seriously.[3]

What we get, moreover, is not simply the gradual emergence of humans from nonhumans, from an earlier species something like modern chimpanzees, an evolutionary relay. This is a popular (outside of science) and seriously misconceived picture of human evolution. What we get, instead, is a branch-like or more properly bush-like picture of human evolution, with the species we call *Homo sapiens* being the last remaining branch in a pattern that contained many similar branches, many of which existed contemporaneously. For a long time we were contemporaneous with *Homo neanderthalensis,* which went extinct roughly 27,000 years ago, or the recently discovered *Homo floresiensis,* which is thought to have gone extinct on the island of Flores in Indonesia as recently as 12,000 years ago. Anatomically modern humans, our species, *Homo sapiens,* goes back roughly 200,000 years. Before that the fossils give us more and more differences the farther back we go, and often with more and more overlap. Roughly 1.8 million years ago, for instance, *Homo ergaster* (also known as African *Homo erectus*) inhabited what is now northern Kenya along with *Homo rudolfensis, Homo habilis,* and *Paranthropus boisei* (formerly *Australopithecus boisei*), and possibly even more hominid species. In the words of the paleoanthropologist Ian Tattersall (2000), "we were not alone." He prefaces this with the word "once," but the modern picture is that no matter how we define "we," *for the most time* "we" were not alone. This is true whether we define "we" as *Homo sapiens,* or all members of the *Homo* family, or more extensively to include Australopithecines such as Lucy, whose complete skeleton is thought to be between 3.2 million and 3.8 million years old.

The question for human rights realists then becomes: "How far back do human rights go?" Two hundred thousand years? But evolution is gradual, not saltational, so what of the generations before anatomically modern humans? And what of Neanderthals? Did they have human rights, too, or not? And what of Lucy? And so on.

A thought experiment is important here: What if living representatives of every human or human-like species in the history of life on Earth were suddenly discovered in a remote valley in Africa, or instead were cloned from fossil DNA? Even if we confine ourselves to the branch, of which we are a part, that goes back 5 million to 7 million years, the time of the ancestral species that led to modern chimpanzees and bonobos on the one hand and modern humans on the other, the

---

3. This picture of evolution is modified somewhat by processes such as endosymbiosis and hybridization and if one takes seriously the theory of punctuated equilibria. For more on the role of these concepts in evolutionary theory, see Stamos (2003).

result would be morally devastating. Human rights realists get up in arms over the abortion of human fetuses but not over the killing and torture of chimpanzees, because the former have human rights and the latter do not. But what if living representatives of all the historical intermediates between us and the human-chimp ancestral species were either found or grown? What would then become of the human rights defense? It would become arbitrary. As Richard Dawkins (1986) puts it, explicitly in reference to human rights and abortion and the torture and killing of chimpanzees, "The only reason we can be comfortable with such a double standard is that the intermediates between humans and chimps are all dead" (263). Again as he puts it (1993), "We need only discover a single survivor, say a relict *Australopithecus* in the Budongo Forest, and our precious system of norms and ethics would come crashing about our ears. The boundaries with which we segregate our world would be all shot to pieces" (85).

In reply, one might argue that the facts are what they are and only the facts matter, not thought experiments. But the fact remains (leaving aside the importance of thought experiments) that it is chance, not necessity, that any of the intermediate forms between modern humans and the human-chimp ancestral species are extinct. This fact has moral significance. As Dawkins (1993) puts it, "If the contingencies of survival and extinction had been different, the gap [between humans and non-human apes] would be in a different place. Ethical principles that are based upon accidental caprice should not be respected as if cast in stone" (87).

Further difficulties remain, however, the most important of which I prefer to call the *diachronic thrust*. The thrust of the difficulty trades on a distinction common in the literature on what is known as *the species problem,* the problem in biology and philosophy of biology of determining what a species is. (The massive size of the literature on this problem is another problem in itself.) I alluded to this problem in the previous section. *Species* is a key concept in biology, and part of the species problem is determining whether species are objectively real or man-made (certainly the organisms themselves are real, but not necessarily the groupings of them into species). Since most biologists are species realists, by far the greatest part of the species problem concerns the species category, the problem of determining the correct concept and definition (or plural) of what a species is. A common distinction that partly defines the debate is the synchronic/diachronic distinction, the question of whether the reality of species consists primarily at a cross section of time or through time as a branch (or a distinguished segment of a branch) in the Tree of Life. The language in the debate varies: "horizontal"/"contemporaneous"/"synchronic"/"non-temporal" versus "vertical"/"cladistic"/"temporal." (The same debate occurred in linguistics over the nature of languages and was settled a little less than a hundred years ago in favor of a synchronic conception following the work of Ferdinand de Saussure.) The figure below, an oldie but goodie taken from a book by the great paleontologist George Gaylord Simpson (1961, 164), illustrates perfectly the distinction:

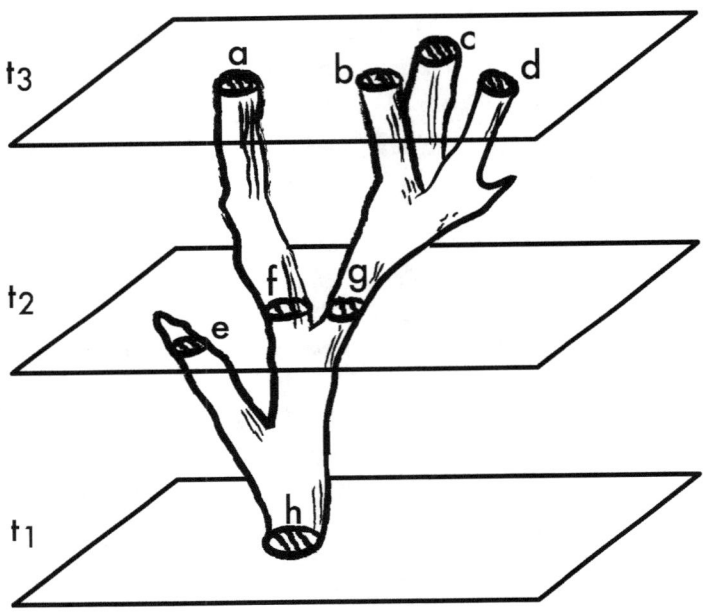

In a series of publications (Stamos 2002, 2003, 2007) I have argued not only that species are real but that their reality should be conceptualized as primarily horizontal, for a combination of pragmatic, logical, ontological, biological, and analogical reasons (reasons I need not get into here). By *horizontal* or *synchronic* I did not mean a time-instant but rather a period of time too short for speciation (the evolution of a new species) to occur, which to be safe I placed at roughly 3,000 years (a minimum number of generations would have been a better idea). Within this time frame most species are, in the words of Darwin (1859), "tolerably well-defined" (177). Defenders of the belief in universal human rights could possibly appeal not only to this distinction but to this conception and defense, so that *Homo sapiens* is a species only meaningfully and distinctly in relation to other contemporaneous species (such as *b* at t_3 in the figure above).

But with that move they will have retreated into a dead end from which there is no escape. The problem now has nothing to do with a trait-based approach to species, with viewing species in terms of their characteristic traits. The problem of marginal cases is bad enough. Neither does it have to do with the branch-like or bush-like evolution of the *Homo* genus, and the thought experiment that went with it.

The problem now, instead, has to do with an evolutionary approach to individual species, with viewing an individual species alone as an evolving entity. The problem is that if one takes evolution seriously (as one must), then one cannot possibly avoid the diachronic thrust. This is because even if one conceives of species as primarily synchronic entities, they also have a diachronic history. This is devastating to the belief in human rights, because human rights are believed to be not only universal but also *equal* rights, rights that all humans have equally. There is no escaping this. It is the modern conception. It is part of the American Declaration of Independence penned by Jefferson in 1776, that "all men are created equal ... with inherent and inalienable rights" (Peterson 1984, 19). It is part of the 1789 French Declaration of the Rights of Man and of the Citizen, that "men are born and remain free and equal in rights" (Hayden 2001, 350). It is part of Paine's *Rights of Man* (1791), that "every generation is equal in rights to the generations which preceded it, by the same rule that every individual is born equal in rights with his cotemporary" (463). It is part of the Universal Declaration of Human Rights passed by the United Nations in 1948, that "the equal and inalienable rights of all members of the human family is the foundation of freedom, justice and peace in the world." And on and on, either explicitly or implicitly, in every Convention, Charter, and Draft on human rights proclaimed since then. What all of it means, clearly enough, is that according to the consensus concept of human rights, all humans, right now, right across the board, have equal human rights, whether male or female, infant or senior, healthy or sick, black or white, genius or idiot, loquacious or dumb, saint or psychopath.

It is important at this point to look at some prominent individual expressions of this claim in recent human rights literature, both explicit and strongly implicit claims, if only to better appreciate the diachronic thrust. According to Maurice Cranston (1967), for instance, "Human rights are a form of moral right, and they differ from other moral rights in being the rights of all people at all times and in all situations" (169), and clearly he thinks of them as being about "equality among men" (164). Ronald Dworkin (1978) tells us that "many rights are universal, because arguments are available in favour of these rights against any collective justification in any circumstances reasonably likely to be found in political society. It is these that might plausibly be called human rights" (365), to which he adds "the fundamental ideal of a political community as a community of equals" (368). Louis Henkin (1990) states that "human rights are those moral-political claims that, by contemporary consensus, every human being has—or is deemed to have, or should have—upon his or her society and government" (143), and he laments the fact that the American Constitution, with all its Amendments, still to this day does not explicitly recognize that "all men were created equal" (94) and that both government and the people should "respect each other's rights, including their equality" (95). According to Patrick Hayden (2001), "Because all persons everywhere share that which makes us human, the rights that belong to us naturally are also universal," and he adds that "the concept of natural rights implies that all humans are in some way equal because they possess the same basic rights" (5). Jack Donnelly (2003) claims that human rights are equal rights because "one either is or is not a human being, and therefore has the same rights as everyone else (or none at all)" (10). Michael Ignatieff (2007) writes that "The idea of rights implies that my rights are equal to yours. If rights aren't equal, they wouldn't be rights, just a set of privileges for separate groups of individuals" (55). Jack Mahoney (2007) writes that "what human rights reveal is that humanity forms a single moral family, all of whose members are united in human solidarity and thus owe to each other a mutual moral respect based on their shared dignity as awe-inspiring human beings" (ix). Micheline Ishay (2007) states that "Today ... one may think of human rights as universal, inalienable, and indivisible, as rights shared equally by everyone regardless of sex, race, nationality, and economic background" (xxi). Lynn Hunt (2007) points out that "For rights to be *human* rights, all humans everywhere in the world must possess them equally and only because of their status as human beings" (20).

There is no need to multiply examples any further. If our species, *Homo sapiens,* is thought of only synchronically rather than diachronically, then the claim that human rights are equal rights has some plausibility. And this in fact, usually unthinkingly, is how most who believe in equal human rights think of humans, in *human* time, a slice of time encompassing recorded human history. They are not creationists, or at least most of them are not, but they might as well be. They are thinking of humans in much the same way that Overton, Locke, Jefferson, and Paine thought of them. But that is no longer acceptable. This is not because we live in the *postmodern* age (we do not), but because we live in the *post-Darwin* age. Ever since Darwin, who placed biology on a new foundation (this is his main legacy, combined with his discovery of the process of natural selection), it has no longer been intellectually respectable to doubt that species are not fixed but evolve. The evidence accumulated ever since Darwin is overwhelmingly massive, beyond any reasonable doubt whatsoever. Hence, in modern science evolution is treated as a *fact*, not as a theory. The intellectual world, including moral philosophers and political scientists and others who write on human rights, typically pays lip service to this, but it has failed to take seriously the deep implications of biological evolution for human rights.

Thinking of *Homo sapiens* as basically synchronic, then, cannot be used to obscure the fact that our species, like all other species, evolved gradually, one day after another, with a new mutation here, a new mutation there, a gradual accumulation of new genes and gradual changes in the frequencies of genes in the gene pool sifted generation after generation by the process of natural selection. The utterly devastating consequence of this—and we need to keep our eyes on the ball to see this—is that if the rights that humans have by virtue of being human are held equally by each and every human living today, then they would have to have been held equally by each and every human living yesterday as well, with absolutely no difference between yesterday and today (since humans come in a variety of ages and most humans living today lived yesterday as well), and absolutely no difference between yesterday and the day before that, and so on for day after day, year after year, century after century, throughout thousands of millennia. In short, if human rights are synchronically equal, not varying statistically (and that is the modern, consensus conception), then they would have to be diachronically equal as well, without any increments. But that makes absolutely no sense given the fact of evolution and that the human species is part of the evolutionary Tree of Life. In other words, there is a logical incompatibility here, between the modern concept of evolution and the modern concept of universal human rights. One cannot logically have both. One must make a choice. And given the mountains of evidence in favor of evolution, the choice should be obvious.

This is the *diachronic thrust*, the deathblow to the myth of universal human rights, and more than anything else what it leaves us with is, in the memorable phrase of Bentham, "nonsense upon stilts." In some mysterious, mystical way, of course, it is still possible to believe that every human living right now has these imperceptible properties called "human rights." But there is not a single reason to believe this and there are enormous reasons not to. What of the many humans who died yesterday, for example, or a thousand years ago, and so on? Why would they not be included? Obviously they must be included, but then the diachronic thrust kicks in and does its job.

Nor will it help to take a nominalistic position on biological species, saying only individual organisms are real, not the species to which it is claimed they belong. This is because as long as the word "human" is taken to denote not only individuals existing right now but also individuals existing in the past (and that is obviously the standard in human rights talk), then the diachronic thrust kicks in once again and does its job, relegating any dividing line for "human" in the past to the dustbins of the arbitrary and ad hoc.

It will also not help to deviate from the consensus concept of universal human rights, the concept of human rights as moral claims and entitlements that all humans possess innately, equally, and inalienably, to non-consensus parasitic concepts, concepts that reject human rights as possessions but retain the elements of universality and equality. Brian Orend (2002), for example, claims that "A human right, like any other right, is *not* a property of persons; rather, it is *a reason to treat persons in certain ways*," which he calls "a more compelling and contemporary theory of human rights" (18). Orend adds that what he calls "elemental equality" (64), in other words "*a baseline level of equality for all*," is "present in the idea of human rights" (16), that "universal entitlement" and "a baseline level of moral equality genuinely shared by all" are two of the "bedrock beliefs" of "the contemporary human rights movement," two of its "most cherished beliefs" (39), and that "Everyone is treated as an equal to begin with" is in line with "the human rights tradition" (60). As we saw in the Introduction, Orend claims that human rights in the modern human rights community are logically and actually qualified by forfeiture, such that "a human can, by performing horrible deeds, give up or lose his entitlement to the objects of his human rights claims" (59). And after examining different kinds of reasons that may constitute human rights as reasons, Orend concludes that the best one is "the 'positive' value of protecting people's vital need to both have and lead a minimally good life, coupled with the 'negative' value of not violating a foremost duty we all have, namely, to not inflict grievous harm on our fellow human beings" (98).

The problem is that if universal human rights are conceptualized now as *reasons* to treat humans in certain ways, rather than as properties of humans, and these reasons are deemed to "genuinely" *apply equally* to all humans (granting the exception of forfeiture), then this equality in reasons for the ascription of human rights must apply equally not only to all humans living today but to all humans living yesterday as well, with absolutely no difference between yesterday and today (since humans come in a variety of ages and most humans living today lived yesterday as well, with an equality in needs for a minimally good life). But then that is to say that the reasons that apply equally synchronically must also apply equally diachronically. At this point the diachronic thrust returns, for humans are not the sort of species that remains the same over time (like chemical species), but instead are the sort of species that changes incrementally over time (albeit slowly and unnoticeably), such that there is a logical incompatibility between this dynamic concept of humans and the static concept of equality found not only in the consensus concept of human rights but also in variations of the concept, such as Orend's. Logically one cannot have it both ways, any more than one can logically have the belief in a static, accurate map of the world *and* the belief in plate tectonics.

In short, given the diachronic thrust that demonstrates the falsity of the consensus concept of universal human rights, including the illogicality of the egalitarian variations that are parasitic on it, and given the nature of the origin and spread of the belief in universal human rights that we shall examine later in this book, the inescapable conclusion is that the dominant moral discourse of the modern civilized world is a relatively recent myth, plain and simple. And coming to this realization is a kind of awakening.

In the next chapter we shall examine a number of scholarly defenses of universal human rights, prominent defenses that take human rights to be either moral properties of humans or moral reasons for treating humans in certain ways. In addition to seeing what is particularly wrong with each theory, we shall also see that, in one way or another, they each fall to the diachronic thrust.

Chapter 3

Scholarly Defenses of Universal Human Rights

> God of Abraham, God of Isaac, God of Jacob. Not of the philosophers and the scholars.
>
> *—Blaise Pascal (note written in 1654)*

PROFESSIONAL SCHOLARS ARE A CONTENTIOUS LOT. Typically territorial, highly critical, and often impatient with the arguments of others, they are known to resort to names and nastiness over cool and calm reflection. But they are also the prime repositories of knowledge and insights into whatever big question one may wish to choose. The general public typically looks upon professional scholars with a great deal of suspicion (as my brother-in-law likes to put it, Ph.D. means "piled high and deep"). But they should not. There typically is more to be learned from professional scholars than from anyone else, while on the other hand professional scholars on the whole need to make at least some of their arguments more accessible to those whom they view as beneath them, especially when it comes to topics that are of great importance to us all. In the very least, clarity of exposition is an epistemic virtue, and sometimes a moral virtue as well.

That being said, what we shall see when we examine the arguments of the scholars below are two recurring problems. First, in thinking they are defending or at least clarifying the concept of universal human rights, they each and every one of them have taken their eyes off the ball and ended up defending a different concept. In baseball, it is often the background of the sun that causes an outfielder to miss a fly ball. But scholars cannot blame light of any sort when they fail to keep their eyes on the concept they purport to be analyzing and defending, for they more than anyone else are supposed to be highly sensitive to the meanings of concepts. Perhaps there is something about the topic of human rights that causes them to do this; I don't know, but I've noticed it time and again, both in paying attention to their writings and when having discussions on this topic. For whatever reasons, scholars on the topic of human rights have a difficult time maintaining focus on the concept at hand, the consensus concept of universal human rights, the core concept enshrined in the American Declaration of Independence and the Universal Declaration of Human Rights and so much more. In a way, then, my complaint is akin to Pascal's remark penned during his conversion experience, that the God of the philosophers (e.g., Augustine, Boethius, Anselm, and Aquinas) is not at all the personal God of the Bible, the concept of the vast majority of Christian believers.[1]

There are human rights theorists, of course, who know full well and make it quite clear that the concept of human rights they are defending is not the concept of human rights as universal, equal, innate, and inalienable. But even there, what is remarkable is that these scholars tend to either ignore or downplay the fact that there is an enormous disconnect between their concepts of human rights and the consensus concept. It is for this reason that I have called these non-consensus concepts *parasitic,* for they seem to want to feed off the power of the consensus concept rather than exist on their own, and it is also because it is highly doubtful that they would exist in the first place or be taken seriously were it not for the existence of the consensus concept.

In either case, coming to the realization that with many human rights scholars one is not dealing with the consensus concept of human rights but with some other concept is to experience a kind of awakening. In either case, one has to be clear about what one is dealing with.

---

1. It does not matter what was actually going through Pascal's mind when he wrote his note to himself during his peak religious experience on November 23, 1654 (Eliot 1958, ix), the mystical epiphany that changed his life. (Since he begins the line at the head of this chapter with the word "Fire," his insight might have been preceded by a brain hemorrhage.) The important point is that anyone who studies philosophy of religion cannot help but notice that there is in fact an enormous difference between the God of the Bible, the God worshipped by billions of people around the world, and the God of religious philosophers and theologians, a God that is simple (no parts, no attributes), eternal (outside of time), unchanging (not even in will), and beyond human comprehension, a God that is best captured by what is called *negative theology* (saying what God is not). That enormous difference is mainly the point of the analogy that I want to make.

There is another kind of awakening that should occur, which is to realize that both kinds of scholarly defenses of human rights display an abysmal failure to take evolution seriously. It is not just confined to the scholars chosen for this chapter (they are leading scholars, by the way, and a representative sample). The failure is epidemic. Moreover, one sometimes even gets the impression that the failure is an arrogant denial that evolution has anything to do with their topic. In philosophy you routinely get, "That's science, not philosophy, we only do philosophy here." It is no doubt the same in political science and in jurisprudence. This arrogance in excluding the importance of science—especially the science of evolutionary biology—and its relevance to fundamental concepts and theories outside of science is seriously misplaced. (A prime example outside of our topic is Derek Parfit's work on personal identity, which is based not just on thought experiments but on split-brain research.) In the case of human rights, we are all talking about *human* rights, after all. And since *human,* whatever else it is, is fundamentally a biological concept, evolution cannot help but be relevant. But more to the point, evolution, the theory so massively corroborated that it has gained the status in science of a fact, completely and totally undermines the modern concept of universal human rights. This was the theme of the previous chapter, and it needs to be kept in mind as we now turn to some famous (meaning highly cited, highly discussed) scholarly defenses of universal human rights.

The order of their treatment is not chronological but topical, the first three—White, Donnelly, Beitz—defending human rights not as objective properties of human beings but nevertheless as fundamental reasons for treating human beings in certain ways (Dworkin and Rawls shall be reserved for Chapter 6), the remaining four—Mahoney, Gewirth, Griffin, Nussbaum—defending human rights as objective properties that human beings actually have.

Alan White

Prior to his death in 1992, Alan White was Ferens Professor of Philosophy at the University of Hull in England. In his book on rights, White (1984) rejects the approach to rights that focuses on the necessary and sufficient conditions for being a bearer of rights. As he recognizes, that approach creates the problem of extremes (the problem of marginal cases), in that whatever trait or traits are chosen, the choice will either exclude those we want to say have rights (e.g., children, the senile) or include those we don't want to say have rights (e.g., animals, trees, inanimate objects). For White, focusing on traits does not get to the essence of the matter, which like focusing on symptoms only provides a superficial analysis.

For White, instead, the proper approach is linguistic, following the school of philosophy known as *conceptual analysis* (or more accurately, but less commonly, *conceptual elucidation*), which is to chart the ways in which we use a term in ordinary language to understand its meaning. White applies this theory of meaning to rights. Looking at how we actually talk, he notices that the concept of "a right" does not operate individually but instead as part of a "set," that it has "normal companions" (91). For a start, "A right is something which can be said to be exercised, earned, enjoyed, or given, which can be claimed, demanded, asserted, insisted on, secured, waived, or surrendered." He notices, also, that a right is "related to and contrasted with a duty, an obligation, a privilege, a power, a liability." He notices finally that "In the full language of 'a right' only a *person* can logically have a right because only a person can be the subject of predications" (90).

By "logically" White is using the term in the sense of Gilbert Ryle's *logical geography*, which Ryle (1949) defines as "the logic of the propositions in which they [concepts] are wielded, that is to say ... with what other propositions they are consistent and inconsistent, what propositions follow from them and from what propositions they follow" (10). In this sense of the term, then, "logical" does not connote timeless, so what Ryle means would better be termed *conventional geography*. This is because languages themselves are not timeless.

What White is doing, then, is basing his answer to who or what has rights on ordinary language. He makes this even more explicit when he turns to law. He states that "the law has always linked together the notions of a person and of the bearer of rights, duties, privileges, powers, liberties, liabilities, immunities, etc." (90). The link, he says, was never strictly with human beings, as at times it has included gods and corporations. But even so, he adds, it is not stretching the concept of rights too far when we today link them with "infants, children, the feeble-minded, the comatose, the dead, or generations yet unborn," for it is simply "a misfortune, not a tautology, that these persons cannot enjoy, claim, or waive, their rights or do their duty or fulfil their obligations" (90). Something similar might be said of nonhuman animals, of course, that it is a misfortune of evolutionary history rather than a tautology that they did not evolve the qualities of personhood (whatever those are). But aside from that, it is odd that White uses the term "person" here at all, for in the case of an infant, for example, although there is a human being (a biological term) there is no actual person (a moral and legal term) but only a potential person, and a potential person is not an actual person any more than an acorn is an oak tree. At any rate, White's main point is that in applying the concept of rights to those such as infants and the comatose we are not thereby violating the logical geography of the concept of rights because we are still fundamentally linking that concept with its correlative concepts such as demanding, exercising, waiving, and so on.[2]

In connecting rights with persons rather than with sentient beings or living beings, White then claims that his approach is not guilty of "speciesism" because, he says, "it is not being argued that it is right to treat one species less considerately than another, but only that one species, that is, a person, can sensibly be said to exercise or waive a right, be under an obligation, have a duty, etc., whereas another cannot, however unable particular members of the former species may be to do so" (92). White equivocates here on the word "species," for the "species" in "speciesism" as used by Singer (1975)—and White does refer to Singer in his book—refers to *biological species,* whereas "person" is being used by White not as a biological species but as a *moral/legal kind,* the kind of being that can assert rights and so on.

Right away, then, if by "person" White does not mean "human being" (and he cannot, for as he must recognize, the logical geographies of both terms are not entirely the same, not in philosophy or in law), then the question naturally becomes, "What is a person?" Remarkably, White provides no answer. He is content simply to analyze the concept of a right with his Wittgensteinian blinders on. And that is where the problems fundamentally begin.

Conceptual analysis, as a movement in Anglo-American philosophy, began with the Austrian philosopher Ludwig Wittgenstein, whose collection of cryptic and unsystematic thoughts published between the covers of his *Philosophical Investigations* (1953), originally written in 1945, quickly became the model for many philosophers of how to do philosophy. Wittgenstein's central claim might seem innocuous enough: "For a *large* class of cases—though not for all—in which we employ the word 'meaning' it can be defined thus: the meaning of a word is its use in the language" (§43). The problem begins when he apparently defines the role of philosophy: "Philosophy may in no way interfere with the actual use of language; it can in the end only describe it" (§124). Again: "Philosophy simply puts everything before us, and neither explains nor deduces anything.—Since everything lies open to view there is nothing to explain. For what is hidden, for example, is of no interest to us" (§126). Once more: "we may not advance any

---

2. White's claim here must be counterbalanced against what he says later in his book, specifically that "To say something, for example a foetus, an animal, or nature, of whom it makes no sense to say it can exercise, waive, claim, secure, or surrender, a right or have a duty, privilege, obligation, power, etc., can nevertheless have a right is to stretch the ordinary notion of a right so as to blur the distinction between 'having a right' and such notions as 'being right,' 'deserving' etc." (171). Apparently White cannot make up his mind on whether the unborn (and by extension human infants and the brain dead) are persons and therefore bearers of rights.

kind of theory. . . . We must do away with all *explanation,* and description alone must take its place. . . . Philosophy is a battle against the bewitchment of our intelligence by our language" (§109).

And there is the first fundamental problem. Philosophy, traditionally the "love of wisdom," the systematic answering of the big "What is *x?*" questions, has for Wittgensteinians absolutely nothing to do with explanations or investigations into the nature of reality. Its job instead is only to chart and make explicit what Wittgenstein's follower Ryle (1949), as we have already seen, calls the *logical geography* of terms in ordinary language, the ways that members of a language community do and do not use their words. Wittgenstein rejected much of what he had written in his earlier (similarly cryptic and unsystematic) work, the *Tractatus* (1922), which gained him a reputation for genius and a large cult following. But he clearly retained the idea that "Darwin's theory has no more to do with philosophy than any other hypothesis in natural science" (§4.1122). This prejudice, this dogma, is unfortunately still widespread in philosophy today, and for a variety of reasons, not just because of Wittgenstein (you get the same thing in Continental philosophy), especially given that the heyday of conceptual analysis has come and gone.

All of this helps to put White's argument into perspective. Conceptual analysis is important as a *preliminary* to philosophical investigations (traditionally conceived) into the nature of reality, but it runs aground as the be-all and end-all of philosophy. To see this it helps to look specifically at what is wrong with White's argument.

First, the concept of person that is at the center of his analysis has troubled philosophers and theologians for many centuries and is by no means a settled concept, even if we accept the Wittgensteinian approach to meaning (see the collection of classic and contemporary writings on the concept of person in Stephens 2006).

Second, even if we confine ourselves to linguistic usage, what we find, in addition to what White claims, is that the concept of person is linked with the concept of personality (in fact the former is the root of the latter). In other words, if we look at how we talk, a person is the sort of entity that has a personality. Language use, then, would not be expected to exclude nonhumans from personhood, such as cats and dogs, for the logic of cat and dog talk (i.e., when we talk about cats and dogs) includes personality talk. And we are not stretching the term when we say, for example, that old Duke is lazy, or that Prince is pugnacious. When we speak thusly we are speaking literally, not metaphorically, not as when we attribute a personality to a car, for example. So maybe then we should distinguish between different kinds of persons, for our present topic between the kind whose "normal companions" include rights and the kind whose "normal companions" do not.

Language use creates a further problem for White's analysis in a very different way. As pointed out in the Introduction, it is common to distinguish between conventional rights and human rights. In his analysis of the logical geography of rights talk, however, White fails to notice this distinction. This is important because the logical geographies of the two concepts are not entirely the same. Conventional rights are rights that we indeed can acquire, demand, exercise, waive, and so on, but human rights, rights that we are supposed to have by virtue of being human, do not share the exact same logical geography (providing we keep our eyes, of course, on the consensus concept). For example, a human right is not a right that one can acquire. One can acquire a right to a particular parking space or the right to drive a car, for example, but one cannot acquire a human right, such as the right to freedom of religion. This is because one is either human or one is not. One does not acquire the state of being human. One was either born human or one was not. Similarly, one cannot give away a human right. I cannot give to a dog, for example, my right to freedom of religion. Thinking otherwise does not make any sense, because the logic of human rights talk and the logic of conventional rights talk are not entirely the same.

A fourth problem for White's analysis involves the plurality of language communities and language change. It has been known for centuries, of course, that natural languages are not static but change both regionally and over time and that there is a significant degree of relativity between language communities. White might reply to this in the case of rights talk by claiming a cross-cultural consensus or link between rights talk and person talk (someone else might even claim that the link is a Chomskyan universal built into the human brain). What his reply would fail to address, however, is the fact that language use tends to lag behind the current state of knowledge, whatever that is. For example, we still use the terms "sunrise" and "sunset," and routinely so, even though as a knowledge community we gave up the geocentric view of the universe many centuries ago, with the Sun orbiting around the Earth. In other words, there is a disconnect between the logical geography of the terms "sunrise" and "sunset" and our state of knowledge about the world.

The lesson here should not be lost on rights talk, for even if what White says is true about person talk and rights talk, it might actually be another example of a time-lag disconnect between language use and knowledge of reality. In this particular case, I suggest that our growing knowledge about both human and nonhuman animals, from Darwin to the present, provides us with a case analogous to the one about sunrise and sunset. The more we know about ourselves and about nonhuman animals, the more we realize that our legal and moral talk must change. For a rights theorist, that might have to mean not that the concept of animal should gain conventional rights talk as "normal companions," but that it should gain natural rights talk as new companions. Or it might mean that the concept of person must change. The time-lag mentioned above between knowledge and language use involves a time dimension that is very small compared with the one used routinely by evolutionary biologists and geologists. It is the difference between language evolution and species evolution, the former which is measured from decades to centuries, the latter upwards in millions of years. Since person is a concept linked with human and human is a concept linked with evolutionary time, the implications of these links cannot be ignored, as we have seen in the previous chapter.

The fundamental lesson here is that the meaning of a term should not as a rule be confined to its use, but should instead reflect what we know about the world. In many cases of meaning, we need to go beyond words and sentences and their relations to each other and delve into *ontology*, into what there is and what there isn't and the nature of what there is. The problem with linguistic philosophy is that it tends to treat language as a barrier between us and the rest of the world, as if language as lovers of wisdom is all we can or really need to know. This view is both stifling and mistaken. The information going into our brains is not just linguistic. If we really want to try to answer the "What is *x*?" questions, where *x* is a fundamental concept, we need to go beyond language and examine any evidence and argument or theory that might be relevant. To confine ourselves to anything less, such as the empirics of language, is to take the *sophia* out of philosophy. In the very least, *it is not wisdom to ignore evidence.*

John Mackie (1977), discussed briefly in the Introduction, makes a similar criticism of the meaning of moral language in general in his argument against moral objectivism. As Mackie points out, and quite rightly, "ordinary moral judgments include a claim to objectivity," both "the categorical imperative aspect" and "the claim to objective validity or truth" (33). The "claim to objectivity," of course, is usually not explicit but implied, but either way it constitutes a kind of *naive realism.* And as Mackie further points out, "it is precisely for this reason that linguistic and conceptual analysis is not enough. The claim to objectivity, however ingrained in our language and thought, is not self-validating. It can and should be questioned" (35). For Mackie it is a factual matter, not to be settled by paying careful attention to how we talk, whether for example the moral quality we call "good" really exists out there objectively in the world. As he puts it, "the problem of what goodness is cannot be settled conclusively or exhaustively by finding out what the word 'good' means, or what it is conventionally used to say or to do" (19).

The same is true of "human rights." It is very important to look at how we use this term, especially as the concept is enshrined in documents such as the American Declaration of Independence and the Universal Declaration of Human Rights. From all of this we can derive a consensus meaning, and that is something every human rights theorist has got to know. But whether human rights actually exist, whether it is factually true that all and only humans have equally an innate and inalienable set of moral claims and entitlements, cannot possibly be settled by looking at how we use words.

In sum, if we really want to know—and that is an important part of what it means to be a lover of wisdom—then it is a mistake to follow Wittgenstein, as White does, and confine ourselves to ordinary language. And it is especially a mistake to exclude Darwin and modern evolutionary biology if we want to know the real meaning of "human rights," or for that matter anything else in morality and justice. I was recently asked, "So what is a moral philosopher to do?" My answer was, quite simply, "Take evolution seriously." What that means for morality and justice is something we shall turn to in the final chapter.

Jack Donnelly

The second argument examined here, by Jack Donnelly (2003), involves some Wittgensteinianism but in a very different way. The Andrew Mellon Professor in the Graduate School of International Studies at the University of Denver in Colorado, Donnelly rejects defending human rights on the foundation of human nature, for he rejects the concept of human nature and reinterprets it as a social construction. He is quite explicit in this. In a section titled "Human Rights and the Social Construction of Human Nature," he rejects what he calls the scientific concept of human nature in favor of what he calls "human potential," which he says is "widely variable" (14). His "social constructivism," he tells us, is not based on "postmodern or poststructural social theory," but rather on the ordinary language philosophy tradition headed by Wittgenstein and followed by the Anglo-American tradition, which he studied as a graduate student. The attraction should be obvious: language philosophy loosens one from the shackles imposed by the science of human nature.

Free of those shackles, Donnelly is then able to connect universal human rights with something other than human nature. For Donnelly, the quest for a solid foundation for human rights is an illusion, something beyond our grasp. A foundation implies something beyond question, like an axiom in a mathematical proof. There is no such foundation for human rights, something beyond question, something intuitively true even just to all those within the circle of human rights talk. Not God, not human nature, not human needs—all of these are rejected by Donnelly. But in favor of what? Not something arbitrary, and not something merely conventional. For Donnelly, the only brute fact that human rights can comfortably rest upon is the fact that "there is a remarkable international normative consensus on the list of rights" (17), to which he adds the word "fortunately."

This is Wittgensteinianism with a new face: human rights talk now exists internationally, as an emergent language community, and there is no reason to look beyond communal use for the justification of human rights talk. The justification is in the use.

But there is more. Human rights talk is intricately connected with the concept of human dignity, Donnelly points out, but not in the sense that human dignity grounds human rights, but rather in the sense that "Human rights are 'needed' not for life but for a life of dignity," a life "worthy of a human being" (14). Hence, what grounds human rights is "man's moral nature," a *prescriptive* moral account of human possibility" (14), not actual human reality but "beyond actual conditions of existence" (15), a "deeper human moral reality," what people "might become." Hence, he says on the same page, "Human rights are at once a utopian ideal and a realistic practice for implementing that ideal," and they "ultimately rest on a social decision to act as though such 'things' existed" (21). Indeed, Donnelly appears to believe that the international human rights social project is the only way to achieve the potential dignity inherent in human life.

This is ultimately a pragmatic justification of universal human rights. It is reminiscent of William James's attempt in his essay "The Will to Believe" (1897) at justifying the pragmatic theory of truth, that in believing something to be true we can often make it true. James was ultimately concerned with "the question of religious faith" (25), but he applies his pragmatic theory of truth to other topics, including moral questions and personal relations such as getting people to like us or winning a woman's heart, such that those who mainly "stand aloof" and wait for sufficient evidence will probably lose out. "The desire for a certain kind of truth," he says, "here brings about that special truth's existence" (24). Again he says, "There are . . . cases where a fact cannot come at all unless a preliminary faith exists in its coming" (25).

Walter Kaufmann's (1958) critique of James on truth also applies to Donnelly's approach to human rights, not only in that the pragmatic approach to truth "makes a virtue of wishful thinking" (116), but in that faith is not necessary for success. To use Kaufmann's example, I might not have the faith to believe that I can jump across the ditch in front of me, but I still might do it if I try hard enough. "What matters," says Kaufmann, "is not faith but effort" (117). And it will do no good to claim that the needed effort cannot come about without the faith. That in itself is a matter of faith, and one of which there is a good deal of evidence to the contrary.

Kaufmann's claim about wishful thinking applies perhaps more to James than to Donnelly, but the fundamental problem is still the same. Donnelly wants us to join him and others and various international communities to move from *ought* to *is*, what is sometimes called "wishful thinking" but what might be called the *ought-is fallacy* (this is because the move from *ought* to *is* need not be *merely* wishful thinking). Consider a fictitious example. I am an American and have a famous politician for a parent and think I ought to be the president of the United States; therefore, I am going to pretend that I am, and maybe if I (and others) pretend hard enough, I will actually realize my potential. Thinking that I ought to be the president, however, hardly means that I now am, even if I should become later. Similarly, that humans ought to be born with human rights does not automatically mean that they are, even if believing that they are will make their lives fuller. The logical problem needs to be separated from the pragmatic one. Logically, that something ought to be does not automatically entail that it is, even if believing that it is might actually bring it to be. In the case of universal human rights, if we don't really have them, if we're not really born with them, but enough of us come to believe in them and act on that belief, then that might result in most if not all of us living a life of human dignity to the maximum, but it would do nothing to change the fact that we were not born with them in the first place and hence do not really have them. In other words, it would not change the fact that those rights are not natural but man-made, a man-made illusion at that. Moreover, one has to wonder whether a charade on such a massive scale can prevent enough people from seeing that the Emperor has no clothes. Illusions given seriously and not as entertainment tend to be self-defeating after all; they tend to backfire in the faces of those who create and perpetuate them.

But there is an even deeper problem with Donnelly's position. In stating that "Human rights thus can be seen as a self-fulfilling moral prophecy," that "they demand, as rights, the social changes required to realize the underlying moral vision of human nature" (15), Donnelly fails to appreciate that there are *many* logically possible moral visions of human nature and that the particular decision to choose any one of them is itself a moral decision, a moral choice—or an *immoral* one, depending on one's moral theory. A Nietzschean, for example, would view Donnelly's moral vision as a slave morality, attempting to reduce all humans to a single level, and thereby being anti-nature, because it rejects hierarchy. But more important, someone like Singer would view it as immoral because of the gap it attempts to maintain between humans and nonhuman animals. Universal human rights are *human* rights after all, not animal rights or sentient animal rights. The vision that Donnelly shares with many others views only the human potential for dignity as worthy of rights talk, of an international social convention and schedule of implementation, and *that* is a moral decision, or rather an immoral one, for animals arguably also have a need for dignity, in the very least a need to not suffer the gross indignity of being raised as a resource on a factory farm or being experimented upon in a science lab.

The problem could be extended even further. If we base the belief in human rights on a moral vision of what humans could become rather than on what they currently are, why stop with humans? One notices that purported human rights are always good and positive for their bearers, never, for example, something bad like the right to be eaten alive. So why not dehumanize these human rights and conceptually extend them to nonhuman animals? And to be fair, because fairness is a moral quality intricately connected with the concept of human rights, we can make animal rights only good or positive ones so that they, too, can maximize their potential. The idea is not as crazy as it sounds; it sounds crazy only because it is foreign. To one who has raised pets, for example, from a feral state to a domestic state, who has seen an enormous change in the animal from one of fear and viciousness and self-protection to one of play and deep affection, the idea of attributing natural rights to animals (rights beneficial to them) might seem important if not necessary for fulfilling their moral vision.

Some might want to extend the recognition of human rights only a little, to the great apes, which in fact is the common denominator among the signees of A Declaration on Great Apes (Cavalieri and Singer 1993). The Declaration demands "the extension of the community of equals to include all great apes" (4), which involves attributing to great apes "basic rights," not only the right to life but "the right to appeal" if only through an advocate, the fundamental criterion being that we are all "intelligent beings with a rich and varied social life" (ix).

Or one might go further, extending basic human rights to all higher animals, as Tom Regan (1983) does. He argues that not just humans but all higher animals have natural rights, animals not merely with consciousness but also with what he calls "the subject-of-a-life" (243), that is, animals with beliefs and desires, a capacity for pleasure and pain, a sense of self not only in the present but over time, and a sense of personal welfare. The argument, in short, is that being a subject-of-a-life entails "inherent value" (243), inherent value admits of no degrees but is "categorical" because "One either *is* a subject of a life, in the sense explained, or one is *not*" (245), and inherent value entails moral, natural rights, rights to respectful treatment such as the right to life, rights that are "valid claims" in the sense that "certain treatment is owed or is due, either to oneself or to another (or others)" (327).[3]

---

3. The main problem here, of course, is not only the rejection of degrees of consciousness and accordingly of inherent value, but that there is no necessary connection between having inherent value and automatically being owed something by others, such as not being treated merely as a thing.

Or one could go further still, extending basic human rights not just to higher animals but to all living things, as part of a program that has come to be called *biocentric ethics*. This is strongly implied in Albert Schweitzer's teaching of *reverence for life* (Schweitzer 1949, ch. 26), where he not only distinguishes between the rights "political rulers exalt at banquets and tread underfoot in their actions" and what he calls "true rights" (328), but he also claims that reverence for life "establishes no dividing line between higher and lower, between more valuable and less valuable life," the main reason being that any contrary judgment must be based on "a purely subjective criterion" (Schweitzer 1933, 235). For Schweitzer, the fundamental moral fact of my existence is that "I am life which wills to live, in the midst of life which wills to live" (1949, 309), and a fully developed ethics, the ethics of reverence for life, is the natural extension of reverence for my own life to all other living things, "in analogy to the will-to-live which is within myself" (308).

More recently, in a paper that has become famous in environmental ethics, a biocentric ethics has been defended by the philosopher Paul Taylor (1981), who likewise argues that the concept of higher and lower life and inherent worth is anthropocentric and is "nothing more than the expression of an irrational bias in our own favor" (527). For Taylor, what makes all living things have inherent worth, and therefore equally worthy of respect, is that they "all are equally teleological centers of life in the sense that each is a unified system of goal-oriented activities directed toward their preservation and well-being," such that "*Conceiving of it as a center of life, one is able to look at the world from its perspective*" (525). For reasons he does not explain, Taylor explicitly rejects the idea of extending the concept of moral rights to nonhuman living things (527), but one can easily imagine combining Regan's view with Taylor's, such that inherent value based on teleology is taken to entail equal inherent value, which is taken to entail equal moral rights.[4]

---

4. The essential problem with Taylor's view is that he confuses *teleology*, which is genuine (mental) goal-directed behavior, with what biologists call *teleonomy*, which is mechanical goal-directed behavior. All living things have teleonomy (and some nonliving things, too, such as heat-seeking missiles) by virtue of their genotype and associated functions, but not all living things have teleology. Hence it is mistaken to say that we, who are truly teleological, can meaningfully look at merely teleonomic living things *from their perspective*, since the latter literally do not have a perspective. Schweitzer (whom I enormously admire and do not like to criticize) makes a similar mistake with his use of the word *will* in "will-to-live." Nonmental living things cannot possibly have a will in the literal sense, so that it makes no sense to say that I can (let alone should) extend my reverence for my own life based on my own will-to-live "in analogy" to living things that literally lack a mind. In both cases, equivocation (the latter based on mysticism, the former on I know not what) obscures important moral facts.

Or one might go even further still, extending basic human rights not just to all living things but to certain nonliving things as well, as the conservationist Aldo Leopold does in his *A Sand Country Almanac* (1949), published a year after his death and one of the early classics of the environmental movement. In his chapter "The Land Ethic," Leopold claims not only that "birds should continue as a matter of biotic right" (211), but also that the land ethic—where "land" includes "soils, waters, plants, and animals"—"does affirm their right to continued existence, and, at least in spots, to their continued existence in a natural state" (204). Leopold considers this not only a natural but also a necessary extension (ecologically necessary) of the gradual evolution of moral concern, from an ethics that involves only human tribes to an ethics that involves all humans and eventually the land, an ethics of "love, respect, and admiration for land, and a high regard for its value," by which he means "value in the philosophical sense" (222), not the economic sense. Similarly, in an exposition and defense of *deep ecology* (the term was coined by the Norwegian ecophilosopher Arne Naess in 1972), Bill Devall and George Sessions (1985, 65–73), both university professors (of sociology and philosophy, respectively), claim from a "basic intuition" that "all things in the biosphere have an equal right to live and blossom and to reach their own individual forms of unfolding and self-realization within the larger Self-realization," that they are all "equal in intrinsic worth"—"life," they point out, "is used here in a more comprehensive nontechnical way to refer also to what biologists classify as 'nonliving'; rivers (watersheds), landscapes, ecosystems"—that with regard to dominance and hierarchy "Deep ecological consciousness allows us to see through these erroneous and dangerous illusions," and that only with this consciousness can we truly achieve "self-realization," defined as "the realization of 'self-in-Self' where 'Self' stands for organic wholeness."

What we have here, far from being a higher form of consciousness, is simply a *reductio ad absurdum* of rights talk and the problem of scope briefly discussed in the Introduction. Why not extend the equal right to exist (and possibly other rights), simply by virtue of its being in existence, to anything that exists at all, such as a rock or a piece of shit? Certainly one can have a "basic intuition" about that, too. But that just shows how ridiculous the whole matter has become, a symptomology of what one wants to believe and nothing more. What should be clear is that once we start to extend human rights beyond humans as something that nonhumans should have as well, there is then none but an arbitrary stopping point, and the idea easily reduces to absurdity (not to mention poetic nonsense, such as the "self-in-Self"). As with every successful *reductio ad absurdum*, there was something at the starting point that was mistaken. The mistake, the central theme of this book, is the belief that humans are born with rights at all, rights that all humans have by virtue of being human. Human history combined with memetic analysis makes that belief highly suspicious, while evolutionary biology seals its fate.

Charles Beitz

Charles Beitz is the Edwards S. Sanford Professor of Politics at Princeton University, and it is perhaps not surprising that as a political scientist he makes an argument (2009) that in many respects is similar to Donnelly's. But it also has some features that merit a separate analysis.

For a start, Beitz rejects theoretical approaches to human rights based on one or more aspects of human nature. He devotes an entire chapter to this topic, which includes analyses of the arguments by James Griffin and Martha Nussbaum. As I provide my own analyses of their arguments below, I'll say nothing of Beitz's analyses, except to highlight some of his main points against what he calls "naturalistic theories." One is that Beitz is skeptical of human rights as an "ontological property," the idea "that human rights are 'out there,' existing in some separate normative order." What matters to him, instead, is that this idea "is not part of international doctrine" (54). One might wonder why international doctrine is given preference over philosophy, but Beitz turns this upside down. "It is," he says, "this additional critical force—the use of a philosophical conception of human rights to argue for limitations of content and reform of international doctrine—that requires a justification" (68). Beitz also wants human rights to be more flexible than naturalistic accounts would allow. "International human rights are not even *prospectively* timeless," he says. "As the social, economic, and technological environment evolves, the array of threats may change. So, perhaps, may the list of human rights" (58). But perhaps his biggest complaint is that "It was explicitly agreed by the framers [of the Universal Declaration of Human Rights], as a general matter, that international doctrine should not embrace its own justification, and in particular that it should not presuppose that human rights are 'natural'" (72).

Even if this last part is true (it is not, and we shall see why below), it does not follow that a naturalistic defense of human rights is not desirable. Surely the international practice is in need of some sort of justification. But aside from that (a problem we shall also return to below), one has to wonder whether the fundamental differences between Beitz and other theorists on human rights are in large part territorial rather than philosophical. Fortunately, the topic of human rights is inherently an interdisciplinary one, such that any territorial disputes make the topic only more interesting.

In addition to his chapter against naturalistic theories of human rights, Beitz has a chapter devoted to examining and rejecting what he calls "agreement theories." The idea here is either that there is a common intercultural core of moral values connected with human rights, or an overlapping consensus of such values, or a "progressive convergence" in the evolving moral systems of cultures around the world. The overall idea here is akin to the methodology of Grotius, the "father of international law" whose views we shall examine more closely in the following chapter. Much of Grotius's argumentation on natural law was based on what he perceived to be an international consensus, which Grotius called "the law of nations." In *De Iure Belli ac Pacis* (Campbell 1901), he says the law of nations derives "its authority from the consent of all, or at least of many nations" (I.1.§14). The problem here, of course, returning to agreement theories of human rights, as Beitz makes very clear, is that the supposed agreement is more in the eye of the beholder, evident alone in the way different cultures treat women, children, and the infirm. For Beitz, the bottom line is that "Human rights doctrine as formulated in the leading international instruments does not set forth a culturally or politically ecumenical or syncretistic position" (74). Nor does a progressive convergence approach yield more hope, since not only is progress also in the eye of the beholder, but the entire approach, in line with agreement theories in general, "simply assumes the truth of the conclusion" (92). It is at best, then, a theory that "We cannot know whether it will turn out true" (94).

For Beitz, the most important fact about human rights is what he calls "an emergent political practice" (xii). This practice, he says, "dates from the settlement of World War II and the adoption in 1948 of the Universal Declaration of Human Rights" (14). The emerging practice involves "the major treaties intended to give legal effect to its provisions" (8). Much like Donnelly, Beitz focuses on the existence of an international "discursive community" in which human rights constitute "a distinctive class of norms as sources of reasons" (9). Hence repeatedly throughout his book Beitz refers to human rights as "international human rights," as if to use the phrase synonymously with "human rights."

Beitz recognizes that international human rights, as a practice, "is not a mature social practice," since there is much disagreement in the international community about issues such as the scope of human rights and about the means of enforcement. Nevertheless, the practice has emerged to the point that it is legitimate to find the answer to the question "What are human rights?" simply by looking to "the meaning of the term within the practice" (106).

By now this should be all too familiar: it is the Wittgensteinian idea of meaning all but in name. According to Beitz, the practice of international human rights is basically a "two-level model" (108), where the "first level" is that of individual states, the duty of an individual state to protect the human rights of its own citizens, and the "second level" is that of international concern, where the international community has the duty of making sure that individual states fulfill their first-level duties and of admonishing them if they do not, which may include international sanctions and even military action. This second level, he says, is "a distinctive feature, perhaps the most distinctive feature, of contemporary human rights practice" (115).

This distinctive feature also helps to determine, according to Beitz, what should be the content or scope of international human rights, in other words, what should count as a human right and what should not. The principle, quite basically, is that "Human rights are standards for domestic institutions whose satisfaction is a matter of international concern" (128). Although rather vague, the principle is not without important implications. For one, it means that human rights "should not depend exclusively on beliefs and norms that are specific to a single culture or way of life" (137). Hence there can be no human right to be a Christian, for example, but there can be and is a human right to "being able to follow one's religion" (138). Although Beitz has a chapter devoted to three controversial cases of human rights (antipoverty rights, women's rights, and democratic rights), his book tends not to discuss more specific controversial cases, such as abortion or the right to being fat. Presumably with regard to the latter (though not clearly the former) he would say that the supposed human right is not really a human right because it is not a proper matter of international concern. The same would seem to follow for the supposed human right to paid vacations, and so much more that one reads or hears about in the news.

Beitz's approach is very much like, and is very much an elaboration of, the approach of John Rawls on human rights (which we shall examine in Chapter 6 in the context of memetics), and Beitz is quite explicit about this, pointing out the many similarities. For Beitz, much like Rawls, there is not a human right for just any human interest, nor are human rights determined "in terms of a single moral value" (138). Human rights, instead, "delineate the boundaries of acceptable pluralism in international affairs" (100). What Beitz calls the "second level" of international human rights probably marks the greatest point of difference in Beitz's view compared with Rawls's, the role of the international community in individual states' affairs. As Beitz puts it, "Rawls's understanding of the functions of human rights is narrower than what is found in present international practice" (101).

In all of this, Beitz takes "the functions of human rights in international practice as basic." He adds that "international human rights is the name of a collective political enterprise—a practice—with distinctive purposes and modes of action"

(103). Put in other words, he says "we treat international human rights as a normative practice to be grasped *sui generis* and consider how the idea of human rights functions within it" (12). Beitz takes the main virtue of this approach to be that "Such a view allows that people might agree about the nature of international human rights but disagree about their content or the kinds of considerations that ground them" (104).

This claim that international human rights are "basic" is fundamental to Beitz's defense of human rights, and it invites comparison with a similar debate in a very different field. In philosophy of religion, most notably, it is debated whether belief in God is "properly basic," which is to say whether the belief is rational, beyond criticism, and not in need of any justification. On the one hand you have those such as Alvin Plantinga, who embrace the Calvinist idea that belief in God is a "natural instinct" triggered by being raised in a Christian community or by reading the Bible or by viewing the starry heavens, so that the existence of God is "self-evident," while on the other hand you have those such as Michael Martin, who reject the natural instinct claim and point out that any community whatsoever could claim that its basic beliefs are properly basic, so that the claim is a version of relativism that loses credibility when all communities are taken together, each with their basic beliefs (see Pojman 2003, 414–435).

Beitz, of course, does not appeal to a natural instinct nor could he be bothered by the problem of competing communities, since the belief and practice he takes to be properly basic has no competing communities but is the international community as a whole. This, however, does not exactly remove the difficulty, for there are uncountable numbers of people and numerous subcommunities that do not share the belief in human rights as well as ideologies that are antithetical to it, and no one can say what the future holds in terms of an international consensus. So does a belief and practice become properly basic just because it has emerged as the majority belief? That would not make any sense, any more than the idea that truth is democratic.

This raises a related question, the problem of moral authority. As an emergent international practice, which Beitz says has "a certain authority in guiding our thinking about the nature of human rights" (10)—elsewhere he says "the human rights system has accumulated a measure of moral authority" (208)—one has to wonder, says Beitz, "why the practice considered as an empirical phenomenon should be allowed any such authority" (10). To this objection Beitz replies by stating first that "the practice exists," and second that "we have a *prima facie* reason to regard the practice of human rights as valuable" (11). A prima facie reason, however, is not much of a reason: as a principle of moral authority it could be used for just about anything. In terms of moral authority, one therefore requires more. Beitz does state that "the human rights of international doctrine, taken as a package, are in their own terms an effort to identify the social conditions necessary for the living of dignified human lives" (57). But one has to notice, then, that human rights according to such a view constitute a means only, not an end, which raises the question of whether there are better means available for the desired ends. I shall argue in the final chapter that there is a better way, one that does not involve fictitious entities or, in Beitz's view, a massive international social construction.

This brings us to a further and deeper problem. As we have seen above, Beitz rejects the view of human rights as an "ontological property," as something "out there," in favor of a formal or functional view. This is a very different kind of "properly basic" belief, then, not like the belief in God or what Hume scholars call *natural beliefs*, natural propensities to believe in an external world, other minds, and causation (to which we can add color as a useful example). This approach saves Beitz from an awful lot of problems, but it also comes at an enormous cost, which is the basic intentions he attributes to the framers of the Universal Declaration of Human Rights. He says they

> disowned the thought that human rights are the expression of any single conception of human nature or human good or of any but the most general understanding of the purposes of human social organization. They took it as an ineliminable fact that people would differ about these matters. They therefore aspired to a doctrine that could be endorsed from many contemporary moral, religious, and cultural points of view and that was suited to be implemented by means distinctive to characteristically modern forms of social organization. [8]

Quite simply, as we have seen above in this section, he states that the framers believed that international doctrine "should not presuppose that human rights are 'natural'" (72).

This is where Beitz loses sight of the ball: he reads the international human rights doctrine as a social constructionist thesis. This is not only implicit in the above but also explicit in a number of places. For example, in summarizing Rawls's view he approvingly says, "Human rights constitute a 'political doctrine' *constructed* for certain political purposes" (99, italics mine). And again, in a very different context, in answer to the question "What are human rights?" he says they are "a political doctrine *constructed* to play a certain role in global political life" (49, italics mine).

The problem is that none of this is true. Human rights were never thought of as merely a social construction by the framers of the Universal Declaration of Human Rights or arguably by the framers of later Declarations, Charters, and Covenants. (And they certainly are not thought of as man-made by most people who believe in human rights.)

It is important to see the magnitude of the error here. Beitz distances his concept of international human rights from earlier natural rights theorists, such as John Locke and Thomas Jefferson. "It is not difficult," he says, "to conceive of the Lockean rights in this way," as "pre-institutional," but, he adds, "The same cannot be said of some of the rights found in the contemporary human rights documents" (55), such as the right to "political asylum" or to "free elementary education."

To see the error here, one has only to notice that postinstitutional rights can still be thought of as natural rights just so long as humans are supposed to be political animals by nature, which of course was Locke's view, as we shall see in Chapter 5. This points to a very serious error in Beitz's account, which is that he has completely overlooked or purposely disregarded the enormous conceptual continuity between Locke's *Two Treatises,* Jefferson's American Declaration of Independence, and the United Nations' Universal Declaration of Human Rights. The continuity is both historical and conceptual, and it is important to see this if we are going to gain a proper understanding of human rights.

Let us start in the middle. The American Constitution, of course, is not one of the documents in question, since it does not explicitly mention human rights. But it did have a forerunner, specifically the Declaration of Independence and the Articles of Confederation, which were mandated by Congress in close tandem (the former was formally adopted on July 4, 1776, the second was first drafted on July 12). As Donald Lutz (1998) puts it, they together constituted the two main parts of "the first national compact" and thereby created "a people," such that "the 1789 Constitution implicitly retained the Declaration of Independence as the first half of our second national compact, a fact that has been ratified by more than two hundred years of our celebrating the Fourth of July as our national founding" (376).

This is important, given the connection that we shall see in Chapter 5 between the thinking of Locke and the Levellers before him and the Founding Fathers of the United States of America, such as Jefferson and Adams. It is also important given, as we shall see in Chapter 6, that the United States was the main driving force behind the framing of the Universal Declaration of Human Rights, such that the Declaration has been described as America's "Sermon on the Mount" (Secretary of State John Foster Dulles quoted in Norman and Zaidi 2008, 195). The enormously important fact, ignored by Beitz, is that the core concept of universal human rights found in Locke and Jefferson is not absent in the Universal Declaration of Human Rights but is its central concept.

Beitz states that "Those interested in the theory of human rights are not at liberty to interpret this idea in whatever way best suits their philosophical commitments" (xii). But this is exactly the liberty he himself has taken in his book. For all of his rhetoric, he has misrepresented the beliefs and intentions of the minds directly behind the drafting of the Universal Declaration of Human Rights, as well as the minds behind the international Declarations, Covenants, Charters, and Drafts that followed it. And this is easy to prove.

For a start, Beitz states quite categorically, as we have seen above, that although human rights are "usually framed as an ontological property," "it cannot be said—and in any case, it is not part of international doctrine—that human rights are 'out there,' existing in some separate normative order" (54). But this is simply not true. When we turn to the Universal Declaration of Human Rights itself, we find in the Preamble that "the recognition of the inherent dignity and of the equal and inalienable rights of all members of the human family is the foundation of freedom, justice and peace in the world." As Mary Ann Glendon (2001) points out with regard to legal positivism (the view that rights exist only as laws of the state), "The Declaration implicitly rejected the positivist position by stating that fundamental rights are recognized, rather than conferred" (176). If this is true, as it apparently is, then the framers could not have thought of human rights simply as an emergent practice.[5]

The Universal Declaration of Human Rights further states that "All human beings are born free and equal in dignity and rights" (Art. 1). This again implies that human rights exist prior to the existence of international agreement, and indeed prior to the existence even of a state. This is also implied by the statement that "every individual and every organ of society, keeping this Declaration constantly in mind, shall strive by teaching and education to promote respect for these rights and freedoms" (Preamble). The inclusion of "every individual" again implies the belief that human rights exist prior to the state, certainly not that they are the result of international agreement.

The same is implied when the Universal Declaration of Human Rights mentions the role of individual states and of the United Nations: "Member states have pledged themselves to achieve, in co-operation with the United Nations, the promotion of universal respect for and observance of human rights and fundamental freedoms" (Preamble). Nothing here implies that human rights emerged solely as a practice from this international pledge; instead, the words "respect for and observance of" imply that human rights were believed to preexist as part of human nature and are the reason for the pledge.

---

5. This is not to imply that Beitz is a legal positivist when it comes to international human rights. He explicitly rejects this position, whether of "legal (or proto-legal) rules," in favor of human rights as "background norms" (210). His overall position is that legal rules, especially international ones (given the great disparities in power between states), cannot possibly capture the "normative force" of human rights or the "critical discourse" involved among agents.

One can also see this by examining the archival material involving the delegates who voted on the Universal Declaration. As Johannes Morsink (1999) puts the entire matter, the "denial of the connection between human nature and human rights goes against what is in the text and all through the supporting archival material" (294). With regard to the archival material, a good example is the haggling over what exactly "born" is to mean in "All human beings are born free and equal in dignity and rights" (Art. 1). Some, such as the South American delegates, wanted the word to refer to conception, while some others, such as the Russian delegates, wanted the word to have only a legal sense. Morsink quotes the French delegate Salomon Grumbach, who took the first sentence of Article 1 to mean that "the right to freedom and equality was inherent from the moment of birth," to which Morsink adds, "This sentiment prevailed in the vote" (293).

But without even knowing the background, it ought to be abundantly clear that the Universal Declaration of Human Rights, even though it adds economic and social rights and is silent on whether God is the ultimate source of human rights, is in the ontological tradition of the American and French Declarations before it. As Morsink (1999) puts it in his chapter on the topic, in reference to what he calls the "inherence view of human rights" (209), "Even a casual reader of the Universal Declaration will see that there is a similarity of language between this 1948 United Nations document and the classical declarations of the eighteenth century" (281). The words "born," "equal," "all," "inherent," and "inalienable" alone should make this apparent, while the phrase "human family" merely improves on the ambiguous word "man."

In support of his very different view, Beitz turns to Jacques Maritain, the French philosopher who was part of the UNESCO Committee on the Theoretical Bases of Human Rights. This Committee sent out questionnaires to the leading scholars and statesmen of the world to see whether a common theoretical basis could be found for human rights, all of this while the drafting process for the Universal Declaration of Human Rights had begun. In support of his own view, Beitz thrice quotes Maritain, who in conclusion wrote that human rights are "practical conclusions which, although justified in different ways by different persons, are principles of action with a common ground of similarity for everyone" (21, 54). According to Beitz, "This conception of international human rights as a public doctrine open to a variety of justifications is indispensable to a proper appreciation of its historical uniqueness" (21). He further quotes Maritain, who said to a visitor at one of the UNESCO meetings, "we agree about the rights *but on condition that no one asks us why*" (21). As Glendon (2001) points out, "Maritain and his colleagues did not regard this lack of consensus on foundations as fatal" (77).

But to point to all of this quite misses the point, and not because Maritain was not part of the Drafting Committee of the Declaration, or because the UNESCO findings were rejected by the Human Rights Commission because they were not consulted and so did not distribute the findings to the members of the United Nations (Normand and Zaidi 2008, 185). The point is that even though the drafters of the Declaration were satisfied not to settle on a theoretical foundation for human rights (otherwise a *Universal* Declaration of Human Rights would not have been possible), but instead were satisfied with merely an expression of "faith in fundamental human rights," as they put it in the Preamble, they nevertheless were agreed that human rights are an *ontological property* of all human beings; they did not at all think of them simply as an emergent practice of international agreement. In other words, what they agreed upon was an ontological thesis in league with moral language in general, the thesis (discussed earlier in this chapter and in the Introduction) known as *moral realism*: in this case, *universal, equal, innate, inalienable, human* rights—*not* international human rights. The latter is a different concept altogether.

This rather obvious reading of the intentions behind the Universal Declaration of Human Rights finds even more support, and explicitly so, in many of the Covenants, Conventions, Drafts, and Constitutions that followed its lead. For example, the United Nations International Covenant on Civil and Political Rights (1966), with regard to "the equal and unalienable rights of all members of the human family," states that "these rights derive from the inherent dignity of the human person" (Ishay 2007, 507). "Derive from" are the key words here. The United Nations International Covenant on Economic, Social, and Cultural Rights (1966) uses the exact same words (513). The American Convention on Human Rights (1969) is even more explicit: "the essential rights of man are not derived from one's being a national of a certain state, but are based upon attributes of the human personality ... they therefore justify international protection" (519). Similarly, according to the African Charter on Human and Peoples' Rights (1981), "fundamental human rights stem from the attributes of human beings, which justifies their national and international protection" (533).

What needs to be added to all of this are the state constitutions and court cases that have appealed and continue to appeal to the Universal Declaration of Human Rights for their authority. According to Morsink (1999), more than sixty domestic constitutions "grant some measure of authority to an outside standard of judgment" (xi) while at least twenty-six explicitly acknowledge the authority of the Universal Declaration of Human Rights. For example, the Preamble of the Constitution of Haiti (1987) states that "The Haitian people proclaim this constitution in order to: Ensure their inalienable and imprescriptible rights to life, liberty and the pursuit of happiness; in conformity with the Act of Independence of 1884 and the Universal Declaration of Human Rights of 1948" (xii).

In all of this, from the Universal Declaration of Human Rights to the present, it should be clear that we are dealing with an ontological thesis, even though, unlike earlier Declarations, the theoretical foundation was left open. Again, as the political scientist Tony Evans (2005) puts it, quoted in the Introduction, "natural rights foundationalism continues to inform most mainstream 'human rights talk'" (7). The foundation is debated, to be sure, over foundations such as "the existence of a deity, self-evidence and human need," to further quote Evans. But no matter. Beitz clearly has lost sight of the ball.

The important point is that the consensus concept of human rights was and still remains basically the same from the English Levellers to the present (the latter with all of its international agreements), which is that human rights are *human* rights, not *international* human rights, that they predate modern and ancient states and belong to all humans equally whether in a state of nature or in a political or international setting. In all of this, contrary to Beitz, there is a core and it has remained fundamentally the same.

It is extremely odd, then, that Beitz would state right at the beginning of his first chapter that "Everyone has human rights" (1)—keyword, the possessive "has"—and that he would repeatedly refer to human rights or international human rights as "objects" (e.g., xi, 2, 44, 45, 102). These would seem to be systematically misleading expressions given that Beitz thinks of human rights (and wants us to think of them) not as objects at all but as an international social construction. Beitz might reply that he indeed wants us to think of human rights as objects but as man-made objects, not as natural objects. That is still an odd use of the word "object." A deeper problem, however, is that human (unlike the dollar or soccer) is not at all a social construction. Instead, it is a biological category, a natural kind, a species, such that one cannot help but take human nature seriously if one is going to defend the reality of human rights. If all there is to human rights is that they are an international social construction, then one has to answer, "Why put the word *human* in there at all?" If one simply appeals to the international practice, then one is guilty of speciesism (Singer 1975), the kind of chauvinism that puts humans morally above other species simply because they are human. The fact that the chauvinism is international does not make it any better. To avoid the charge of a fundamentally arbitrary practice, then, one would have to say something about humans per se, something about their *nature*, that warrants them *having* these "objects" called "human rights," perhaps something about their moral worth.

That is the focus of our next four scholars. But the argument thus far brings us to one further and final consideration, what is arguably the culminating point against non-consensus concepts of universal human rights. It is an argument that applies equally to the consensus concept of universal human rights, but since non-consensus concepts, the formal or functional concepts of universal human rights, lack the ontological content of the consensus concept, they might appear to be untouched by taking evolution seriously, including ultimately the *diachronic thrust* presented in the previous chapter. This is not necessarily true, but it so happens that a further argument is at hand, against collectively all non-consensus concepts of universal human rights, analogous in power to the diachronic thrust leveled against the consensus concept.

Quite simply, the argument concerns the *values* of which human rights talk are merely an expression according to the defenders of the non-consensus concepts of universal human rights. The problem is not only that anthropocentrism but that speciesism is being used to fight the injustices of sexism, racism, the hierarchical oppression and exploitation of the poor and disabled, and so on. In other words, a doctrine filled with prejudice, inequality, and hierarchical oppression and exploitation in a wide domain (humans vis-à-vis animals) is being used to fight prejudice, inequality, and hierarchical oppression and exploitation in a more restricted domain (humans vis-à-vis humans). It all falls to pieces once one really thinks about it, about the sheer hypocrisy of it all, especially in light of the discussion on moral equality presented in the previous chapter.

And as a practical matter there is no point pretending that the values underlying the belief in universal human rights are values of justice or are legitimate in the fight for justice. For as many have pointed out, you cannot reap justice when you sow injustice, any more than you can grow a rose from a weed. Gandhi put it best in, for example, his pamphlet *Hind Swaraj,* or *Indian Home Rule,* published in 1909:

> Your belief that there is no connection between the means and the end is a great mistake. Through that mistake even men who have been considered religious have committed grievous crimes. Your reasoning is the same as saying that we can get a rose through planting a noxious weed. [quoted, ironically, in Ishay 2007, 318]

In other words, returning to our topic, you cannot rid the world of prejudice by being prejudiced, or of inequality by being inequitable, or of hierarchical oppression and exploitation by being hierarchically oppressive and exploitative. But that is what universal human rights are ultimately all about.

In sum, the values underlying the expression of universal human rights are incompatible, incoherent, painfully dissonant—I hesitate to add the words "inconsistent" or "contradictory" because of the problems involved with calling values true or false—and in the end incapable. I call this argument the *hypocrisy thrust.* Non-consensus concepts of universal human rights, such as Beitz's, since they lack the ontological content of the consensus concept, might not appear to be fully undermined by taking evolution seriously, even if it is admitted that they are seriously harmed. Where the diachronic thrust might fail, then, the hypocrisy thrust finishes the job.

Jack Mahoney

We now turn to defenses of universal human rights based on human nature. The first is by Jack Mahoney (2007), which shares an important feature emphasized in Donnelly's argument and to a lesser extent in Beitz's argument, namely, a focus on human dignity. Now while Mahoney is a Catholic theologian, Emeritus Professor of Moral and Social Theology at the University of London no less, he recognizes the problem of trying to justify the belief in universal human rights by an appeal to God or to scriptures. The problem, quite simply, as he well recognizes, is that many people, especially among intellectuals, do not believe in God, and even if they did, another problem is that scriptures, including Christian scriptures, do not contain the concept of universal human rights.

Mahoney, therefore, in his chapter "Establishing Human Rights," proceeds to provide what he considers to be an original defense of the concept. But first in that chapter, before he gets to his answer, he examines and then critically rejects a number of recent attempts at justification, and it is important to summarize his discussion here. The appeal to "natural law and a shared human nature" (J. Maritain, M. Cranston, R. Trigg, J. J. Thomson) is rejected by Mahoney because natural law is an outdated concept, a theological piece of nostalgia for the time when morality was thought to be divinely instituted into nature (or at least human nature) and every law was thought to require a lawgiver, all of which is rejected by our modern, secular/scientific society. Moreover, the move from human nature to moral duties commits "Hume's law, or the 'naturalistic' fallacy, which moves effortlessly from a description of how things regularly are to a moral claim that this is how things ought to be."[6] Turning next to modern humanism, which is typically antireligion, Mahoney notices (correctly, I might add) that human rights are simply declared rather than argued for (J. Fowler), an approach he rejects for failing to see human rights as problematic and in need of justification. The attempt to justify human rights talk as linguistic utterances necessary for a good society and for convincing others of accepting our moral ideals (M. MacDonald, G. B. Herbert, J. L. Mackie)

---

6. Hume's (1740) *is-ought fallacy* is here confused with Moore's (1903) *naturalistic fallacy*, which is not the same. For discussion and references, see Chapter 7 n9.

is rejected by Mahoney as postmodernist, as rejecting objective moral values and appealing to human rights as "word play" rather than as real entities. The approach that sees human rights as internationally agreed standards (J. Charvet, P. Sieghart) is rejected as reducing human rights to arbitrary convention. The approach that views human rights claims against others as necessary for one's freedom and well-being (A. Gewirth, J. W. Nickel) is rejected because subjective need does not entail the objective existence of rights against others. The appeal to intuition, which views human rights as intuitively obvious truths and so as not requiring argument (J. Finnis), is rejected as being useless against someone who does not share the same intuitions and hence for abandoning argument at a point where it is definitely needed. The approach that views human rights as a modern collective conviction, an intersubjective worldwide consensus and wonder (R. F. Drinan, R. Gillon, N. Bobbio) is rejected not only because a consensus can change, but also because *appeal to consensus* is a fallacy for the simple fact that truth is not democratic. The related view that human rights are a socially constructed worldwide normative consensus and that this is their only justification or grounds (J. Donnelly, R. Rorty) is rejected for dismissing the possibility of moral objectivity and for providing no good answer to one who asks the fundamental question, "Why should I be moral?"

The right direction, says Mahoney, is when we turn to the topic of human dignity. He notes from a variety of authors (F. Klug, R. Dworkin, P. Alston, J. Mann) not only that human dignity is the basis of morality but also that human dignity is repeatedly stressed in the Universal Declaration of Human Rights and is given as the only foundation of human rights. (I question that it is given as the foundation.) For Mahoney, then, the problem now becomes one of justifying the belief in human dignity. If he can do that, he believes he then has found the needed justification for the belief in human rights.

In a nutshell, Mahoney claims that "'the wonder of our being' seems well suited to explain why human beings possess an intrinsic dignity, and are therefore worthy, or deserving, of the deepest moral respect, as bearers of moral human rights" (150). Following thinkers as diverse as Shakespeare, Pascal, Teilhard de Chardin, and Julian Huxley, Mahoney connects "the wonder of our being" primarily with our ability to think, what he calls "the intrinsic wonder of the thinking human person" (146). Contemplating questions such as "Why is there anything?" and "Why is there something rather than nothing?" he looks at the processes of evolution, both cosmic and biological, and is filled with "awe, or natural reverence" (147) that beings such as us ever emerged from such processes. By "human thought" Mahoney includes "intelligence, reasoning, reflection, imagination, consciousness, and self-consciousness, as well as the human power of rational choice" (148). With this concept of human thought, and following the biologists Pierre Teilhard de Chardin and Julian Huxley (the former a Catholic priest, the latter an atheist),

Mahoney sees humans in their evolution passing through a "threshold" into a new mode of being, into genuine personhood. It is this personhood that gives humans their "inherent dignity," and since the Latin adjective *dignus* means "'worthy' or 'deserving'" (150), human dignity is the ground of universal human rights.

This argument for universal human rights, of course, is terribly flawed and in a number of ways. For a start, the concept of inherent dignity, as pointed out in the Introduction, is not the same as the concept of universal human rights. The former concept is singular, the latter plural. They are therefore not the same concept. Nor can one logically infer one from the other. This should be evident from the fact that without contradiction one can affirm one of the concepts and reject the other. In other words, there is no contradiction in affirming that humans have inherent dignity while rejecting that they have human rights. (i) I can affirm, for example, that not only humans but also higher animals such as dogs and cats have inherent dignity by virtue of certain mental capacities that they share in common, but no one would infer from this that dogs and cats have human rights (that would be ridiculous). This alone proves that the concept of inherent dignity does not entail the concept of human rights. (One could always claim that inherent dignity and human rights are synonyms or are coterminous, but that would be cheating, an example of the fallacy known as *question-begging definition*.) What is needed is an argument connecting human dignity (whatever that means) with the existence in humans of moral claims and entitlements, which is no small task. (ii) Similarly, I can affirm that all humans are born with certain moral claims and entitlements, but at the same time reject that they have inherent dignity. I might think that humans are inherently disgusting creatures but think that they nevertheless were born with certain rights. I can do this in the case of man-made rights. I can think that Mr. Smith is a disgusting human being with no dignity in any sense of the term but yet affirm that he has a right, say, to that parking space over there. If I can do this in the case of man-made rights, there is no logical reason why I cannot also do it in the case of natural rights. The former are conventional rights, the latter are birthrights, and whether real or supposed, neither presuppose nor entail inherent dignity.

In short, the perceived connection between human dignity and human rights is nothing but a psychological connection, an ingrained habit of mind born from repeatedly finding the two concepts together, both in the current discourse on human rights and in historical documents such as the Universal Declaration of Human Rights.[7]

---

7. The connection might also have a memetic connection, but I won't pursue that here. It would certainly be an interesting exercise to trace the connection of the universal human rights meme with the inherent human dignity meme, especially since the latter appears to be a later addition to the former.

A further problem with Mahoney's argument is that it is theological in disguise. Many years ago, in an article titled "Do We Survive Death?," Bertrand Russell (1957) replied to an argument similar to Mahoney's (differing only in its conclusion) made by the English mathematician Dr. E. W. Barnes, when the latter was the Bishop of Birmingham. Barnes was amazed at the intelligence of humans and their ability to know right from wrong. For Barnes it followed that God exists and it would have been unintelligent of God not to have made humans immortal. Russell turned the argument upside down. He wrote, "it is only when we think abstractly that we have such a high opinion of man. Of men in the concrete, most of us think the vast majority very bad" (93). Russell's point, if we wish to deal with the topic of humans in a secular manner (and that is Mahoney's expressed purpose on human rights), can be taken in Sartre's sense of human nature, which is that there is no such thing and we are what we do, or in the sense of an evolved statistical human nature that we find in evolutionary psychology and human sociobiology, the latter of which includes instincts not only for foods high in sugar, salt, and fat but also a rape instinct in males in addition to an instinct for war (see Ghiglieri 2000; Smith 2007). But either way in the modern debate over human nature (the Standard Social Science Model versus evolutionary models), Russell's point stands: the supposed wonder of our being is greatly diminished once we take humans in the concrete into account, either their behavior or their inner nature, so much so that humans hardly seem deserving of special rights.

Mahoney's argument suffers from this and further difficulties. We can look at the human brain, in particular human intelligence, and wonder at it in the abstract. But it is only self-aggrandizing anthropocentrism that makes us focus on the human brain and no other species-specific adaptation, such as the trunk of the elephant (Pinker 1994, ch. 11). Our overly large, metabolically greedy brain evolved for functions such as abstract reasoning and language, but we seem to elevate those features over others simply because we are the ones who have them.

But worse, intelligence is not a moral concept, nor does it bear any necessary or intimate connection with moral worth. We do not consider people with the intelligence of Einstein, for example, as having more moral worth than the village idiot. (If in doubt, simply imagine Hitler with the intelligence of Einstein.) This is because intelligence is not connected with moral worth. We judge people morally based on their motives and character, not on their intelligence. And when we turn to their actions, we judge those either by the motives behind them or by their consequences. Very little of this has anything to do with intelligence. Mahoney (2007) claims that "the wonder of human rational existence" makes humans worthy of "the deepest moral respect" (157). But that is not what we base moral respect on in practice. It is, instead, motives and character, and we can go much further than Russell in finding humans mainly bad. Man's inhumanity to man, man's even greater inhumanity to animals, and man's destruction of the environment, resulting in what biologists call mass extinction #6 (the previous one, #5, was caused mainly by a large meteor 65 million years ago), should dampen any enthusiasm about the wonder of man, the world's top predator and "most dangerous animal" (Smith 2007). Russell (1957) thought that if humans were created by a higher being rather than by "muddle and accident," then the Creator "must have been that of a fiend" (93)—I would use the term "psychopath" (Stamos 2011)—so that he chose muddle and accident (evolution by natural selection) as the more likely candidate. Mahoney's argument for the existence of universal human rights no more gives him the conclusion he wants than did the similar argument by Barnes.

But there is something even more basically wrong with Mahoney's argument. Grant for the sake of argument "the wonder of our being," grant that this wonder vastly exceeds objectively the wonder of any other species that has ever existed on this planet, and grant that "human beings possess an intrinsic dignity," from any or all of this it by no means follows that human beings "are therefore worthy, or deserving, of the deepest moral respect, as bearers of moral human rights." The fundamental, the central problem is not with connecting the wonder of man with intrinsic dignity (the latter does not logically follow from the former), or with connecting intrinsic dignity with deserving moral human rights (nonhumans might have intrinsic dignity, too), but with connecting the wonder of man or man's intrinsic dignity with *having* moral human rights. This is because, quite simply, *deserving does not entail having.* One might well be deserving of being a multimillionaire, for example, but one would be totally deluded because of it to think that one actually has those millions. Everyone knows this. (Of course, the matter would be different if one added that there is a God who provides whatever is deserved, but then one has a theological argument after all, and an acutely fanciful one at that.) In the final chapter it shall be argued that the belief in universal human rights functions—not primarily, of course, but largely—to put a barrier between humans and animals and that there is a better way to deal with matters of ethics and justice.

Alan Gewirth

Prior to his death in 2004, Alan Gewirth was the Edward Carson Waller Distinguished Service Professor Emeritus of Philosophy at the University of Chicago. Gewirth's argument, in short (1996, 17–19), is that a purposive agent "logically must accept" that his goals as an agent are valuable or good, at least for himself, the agent also must accept that his freedom and well-being are "necessary goods," from which he also must accept that "I must have freedom and well-being," from which he "logically must also accept" that "I have rights to freedom and well-being." The rights to freedom and well-being Gewirth calls "generic rights," also "fundamental rights," because they are the most basic for rational purposive agency, and also because from them more specific rights logically flow. From the conclusion established thus far the agent must then logically accept "that all other actual or prospective agents have these rights equally with his own." At this point, says Gewirth, "the rights in question become moral rights, because the agent is now committed to taking favourable account of the interests of other persons as well as of himself," and "since all humans are actual, prospective, or potential agents, the generic rights are now seen to be human rights."

This argument has a number of serious flaws. For a start, Alasdair MacIntyre (1981) remarks on the sudden introduction of the concept of right in Gewirth's argument. It is clear, he says, that "the concept of right needs justification both because it is at this point a concept quite new to Gewirth's argument *and* because of the special character of the concept of a right" (67). The special character, of course, as MacIntyre correctly notices, is that of a "possession," and a moral one at that. As MacIntyre further points out, "the claim that I have a right to do or have something is a quite different type of claim from the claim that I need or want or will be benefited by something." Since the two concepts are different concepts, that is, they have different content, an argument is needed to link them together, and that is missing in Gewirth's argument.

But we can go further, and in a direction that departs from MacIntyre's own view. According to MacIntyre, the concept of the possession of a right presupposes "the existence of a socially established set of rules," so that a claim to a right without such a society "would be like presenting a check for payment in a social order that lacked the institution of money" (67). This, however, is true only of *conventional* rights; it is not in fact part of the modern concept of universal *human* rights, the consensus concept emphasized over and over again in this book. In focusing on the social, however, MacIntyre's criticism does point to a serious flaw in Gewirth's argument. Up to a point Gewirth is dealing only with the individual, who logically accepts that he has "generic" or "fundamental rights." Gewirth says these rights then "become" human rights once the individual takes into account the existence of actual or potential rational purposive agents in addition to himself. The choice of the word "become" is extremely odd, since human rights as commonly understood are not the sort of things that come into existence upon any sort of cognition; we either have them or we don't, regardless of what we think. This leads to a further point, which is that Gewirth's argument is not really about *having* human rights.

To see this, let us grant for the sake of argument that Gewirth is indeed keeping to the modern consensus concept of human rights and that he has established what a rational purposive agent must think. The problem that Gewirth now faces is that he has not indeed established that a rational purposive agent in fact *has* those rights. The most that his argument can be allowed to prove, instead, is that a rational purposive agent logically must *think* that he has the generic and then human rights. Gewirth (1978, 21) seems to recognize this problem when dealing with objections, but then he makes it clear that he has failed to see it.

The problem is that what a person logically must *think* and what a person logically must *have* are entirely separate things. This is true for absolutely everything except for thoughts themselves. If I think a thought, then I logically must have that thought. But if I think a thought, it logically does not follow that I also must have what that thought refers to, unless of course it refers only to itself. The consensus concept of human rights, of course, is not that kind of thought. Instead, it refers to something that is extra-mentally real, moral claims and entitlements that all humans equally have by virtue of being human. This point was emphasized in the previous four sections of this chapter and needs to be emphasized again.

That Gewirth *wants* to defend this concept of human rights, but he in fact does not—in other words, that he has lost sight of the ball—becomes especially evident in his attempt to apply his defense of human rights to marginal cases. In his later work, Gewirth (1996) states that "human rights ... are had by every human being simply insofar as he or she is human" (6) and that his argument "eventuates in a principle of equal and universal human rights" (xi). In response to the problem that marginal cases create for his argument, however, the fact that severely mentally deficient humans lack the necessary purposive agency for human rights, Gewirth waffles. On the one hand he appeals to "the Principle of Proportionality: when humans or other entities are less than normal agents ... they have the generic rights to the degree to which they approach being normal agents" (65). But Gewirth does not stay there, not even apparently for cases of permanent disability. He does this by an appeal to "human dignity." Rational purposive agents, he says, "must [logically must in his view] ... attribute worth to themselves." Hence, "In the case of comatose and other subnormal humans, it is their underlying similarity to normal human agents that grounds the attribution of dignity and rights to them" (66). (See also Gewirth 1978, 120–125.)

All of this, again, should make one think that Gewirth's argument, despite his language and apparent intention, is not really about the *existence* of human rights, but only about what purposive agents *should think,* which is clearly not the same thing at all. The problem specifically with his argument above is that his initial argument for human rights *does not* logically extend to all humans; if it works at all it applies only to those who fit his concept of rational purposive agents. He therefore does not deal with the modern consensus concept of *human* rights at all.

But he *wants* to, so he appeals to the concept of "underlying similarity" between normal humans who do meet his criterion and all the rest who do not.

The problem now is the old chestnut of *similarity*, for many philosophers and others hold that similarity is purely subjective, such as Nelson Goodman, who considers similarity "insidious," "a pretender, an imposter, a quack," a "false friend." Goodman's argument is not entirely convincing (see the discussion on Goodman and others in Stamos 2003, 340–349), such that one can accept that there are objective similarity relations and that our judgments of similarity can be objective (more or less). Let us grant this position for the sake of argument. The problem remains that Gewirth has not made clear what in the case of humans he means by "underlying similarity." He cannot mean "overall similarity," of course, for "underlying" does not mean "overall." So he must be referring to similarity in one or more underlying respects. But it is not clear what that could mean. Does he mean similarity in the sense of belonging to the same species, *Homo sapiens*? If he does, then his claim would be trivial, a mere matter of membership, and a further example of speciesism. Does he then mean similarity in DNA? Indeed what else could he mean? But some humans are more similar genetically than others, with monozygotic twins being the most similar and members of different sexes and races being the least similar.

This is not a minor problem. Human rights, as Gewirth recognizes, are supposed to be "equal and universal," but similarity cannot possibly do the job, whether the focus is on DNA or anything else. This is because, quite simply, similarity is a matter of *degree,* which when it reaches 100 percent ceases to be similarity at all but *qualitative identity.* Human rights, however, are not a matter of degree. According to the consensus concept, human rights are an *equal* possession of all human beings, not varying more or less. Similarity cannot possibly give this. In trying to extend human rights to all humans, then, Gewirth has lost sight of the ball.

The problem only becomes worse when we change our focus from humans existing during a short slice of time, a synchronic conception of humans, to a diachronic conception, humans existing over a large stretch of time, the dimension that evolutionary biologists routinely deal with. The problem now is the *diachronic thrust,* and it is absolutely destructive of Gewirth's argument and so many more.

James Griffin

James Griffin is White's Professor of Moral Philosophy Emeritus at Oxford University. His argument (2008) has some similarities to Gewirth's, mainly in that they both base human rights on human agency, but the differences between the two approaches clearly far outweigh any similarities, such that they need to be analyzed entirely separately.

For a start, Griffin recognizes that the concept of human rights we have today is the Enlightenment notion, minus the theological grounding that the concept originally enjoyed. That loss of grounding has left the concept with a high degree of "indeterminateness," with few and unclear criteria for when to use it correctly. What we have been left with, he says, is the idea that a human right is "*a right that we have simply in virtue of being human*" (2, 13). His approach, then, is to make the sense of the term "more determinate" (2), in accordance with our modern secular world. But his approach is not at all like White's, that of simply charting out and specifying the term's logical geography. In the case of human rights especially, that approach cannot work, because there is enormous debate on whether, for example, the right to welfare is really a human right, similarly for the right to democratic participation, women's rights, and aboriginal rights. There is not a consensus of use, then, as there might be with the concept of human right in general.

But even if there were a consensus of use, Griffin points out, an international consensus or agreement on whether something is a human right, a settling of the *extension* of the term (settling examples of what the term points or refers to) does not settle the *intension* of the term (what the term means in terms of criteria of use). To give a simple example, even if we all agree when it comes to pointing to chairs that they each are chairs, that does not settle the meaning of "chair," in the sense of the cluster of criteria that determine correct or incorrect use. Determining the intension of the term remains to be done. In the case of human rights, Griffin recognizes that international agreements have come far in helping to settle the extension of the term, in helping to settle the *list* of human rights, but even if a canonical list were to be agreed upon (which is hardly the case), the problem remains that "we cannot establish the existence of a human right just by declaring it to be one" (5). Elsewhere he says, "We are after the existence conditions for a human right" (38).

So Griffin clearly is concerned not just with words and the way we use them, but with criteria of use and objective reality in their reference. Recognizing, again, that international agreements have made an important contribution, especially beginning with the Universal Declaration of Human Rights, Griffin also thinks that ethics needs to make an important contribution, for the concept of human rights is not merely a political or legal concept but also a moral one.

Griffin, then, in short, attempts to improve the intension of the term "human right" by grounding the concept in what he calls "normative agency." The approach is to look at what is needed for normative agency, not just what the term means, and from there to draw out a clear meaning of "human rights." The approach is not logical in the sense of logical geography, as already noted, but neither is it logical in the sense that he attempts to analytically derive the existence of human rights from examining the meaning of normative agency. That is the kind of approach Gewirth uses, as we have seen in the previous section, only he focused on rational purposive agency, not normative agency (not quite the same concept, as we shall see). Griffin is quite explicit in distinguishing his approach from Gewirth's. Griffin's approach, instead, is what he calls a "proposal," specifically "that we see human rights as *protections* of our normative agency" (italics mine). The proposal is based, he says, "on a hunch that this way of remedying the indeterminateness of the term ['human rights'] will best suit its role in ethics" (4).

By "normative agency" Griffin does not simply mean "agency," the mental ability to perform actions, since higher animals in general have that. Nor does he simply mean "rational agency," because it is not specific enough. Instead he means "agency involved in living a worthwhile life" (45). This involves having the capacity to have "a conception of a worthwhile life," not necessarily a life plan. It also involves the ability to be a "self-decider," what is normally called *autonomy*. Next, there also must be "liberty," in the sense of not being blocked from pursuing what one thinks is a worthwhile life. And finally, "By 'agency' we must mean not just having certain capacities (autonomous thought, executive action) but also exercising them" (47), in other words, "succeeding, within limits, in realizing the aim of the exercise" (48). Normative agency, then, if I have understood Griffin correctly, is *active autonomy combined with the concept of a meaningful life,* and it is the values involved in normative agency that provide the foundation for human rights. "If one of those parts [in normative agency] is missing," he says, "we do not have the values that, according to the account, are the ground of human rights" (48).

It is this conception that allows Griffin to call his theory of human rights a "personhood account" and also to connect it with human dignity, since for Griffin normative agency is the ground of the phrase "the dignity of the human person" (45, 47) found in the Universal Declaration of Human Rights. This allows Griffin to provide what he calls a "minimalist" approach to human rights. If human rights are conceptualized as the rights that humans have simply by virtue of being human, then there is nothing to stop them from being thought of as coextensive with human interests. In the very least, we will have human rights as claims and protections of a "fully flourishing life" (53). Griffin is surely sensible here, for a "fully flourishing life" can be understood in many different ways, with no end to nonsense claims about human rights, such as the right to being fat. If, on the other hand, the concept of human rights is made "more determinate," by limiting human rights to what is needed as protections of our normative agency, then "not any human interest will be a ground of a human right" and we will have a "less free-wheeling, more criteria-governed use of the discourse of 'human rights'" (53).

Problems begin for Griffin's approach, however, when we focus on the term "human" in "human rights." "We differ in social status; we are equal in human status. In that sense," he says, "it is undeniable that human rights are based on our equal human status." But then he adds, "if one wants to identify the existence conditions for human rights, one would not look to the equality of our human status but to the human status itself, and the personhood ground already captures that" (40). So it is not being human that grounds the belief in human rights, but something typical about being human. And that something, for Griffin, as we have seen, is normative agency. The problem, as Griffin readily acknowledges, is that not all humans are equal with respect to normative agency. Agency in humans, including normative agency, comes in degrees. There are "mental defectives" and young children, neither of whom meet the requirements of normative agency, and yet they are humans. Nevertheless, says Griffin, "the vast majority of adult mankind are capable of reaching (a factual claim) this valuable state (an evaluative claim)," and "normative agency is the typical human condition" (45).

As the typical human condition, Griffin makes it clear that he wants to keep his conception grounded in concrete reality, in human beings, rather than abstract out the concept of normative agency from them. If we go the latter route, he says, which is what Kant did when he combined the concept of person with the noumenal self, then "It turns the holder of rights into a highly spare, abstract entity." We are animals after all, not embodied spirits. "If one peels away everything about us that is shaped by nature or nurture," he says, "not enough is left" (34). So not only is human autonomy "deeply embedded in the causal network," but "human rights cannot therefore be entirely ahistorical" (35).

So human rights are not based simply on being human, but on being a flesh-and-blood human and a typical one at that. By avoiding an "ahistorical" conception of humans and of human rights, one might think that Griffin takes evolution seriously. But his discussion is not expanded to include evolutionary time. Instead, he confines his account to a synchronic conception of modern humans. What matters most for Griffin is what he calls a "borderline" or "threshold," such that "anyone who rises any degree above the threshold, is equally inside the class of agents, because everyone in the class thereby possesses the status to which we attach high value" (45). The borderline or threshold, then, is applied to *particular individuals,* not to the human species as a whole.

One might apply this idea to the species as a whole, however, and hence to human evolution. The question then becomes: "At what point did humans as a species pass through the threshold of normative agency and hence into acquiring human rights?" Clearly the question is unanswerable. But even if it were answerable, analogous to answering when the typical modern human child passes the threshold in its growth and development, the passing in the evolutionary answer would have to be gradual, involving in the very least a threshold period of roughly 5,000 to 50,000 years, assuming that one accepts the variant of Darwinian evolution known as *punctuated equilibria,* according to which speciation (the evolution of one species from another) is geologically rapid (Eldredge 1985, 121).

This is not in itself a serious problem for Griffin's theory of human rights. He is concerned mainly with humans in the here and now. Moreover, applying the concept of a borderline or threshold should not in itself be seen as problematic. After all, night and day are real despite dusk and dawn. In fact, thresholds and threshold effects are widespread parts of everyday life, including the world of biology as a whole (such as the threshold effect in ecology, where trees, for example, can handle a certain toxin to a point and look healthy, beyond which they start to die). The main problem, instead, is what this means for human rights in the here and now. And what it means is that Griffin has lost sight of the ball.

For a start, it is normally thought that human rights are rights that humans are born with. But this cannot be Griffin's view. This is because humans are not born beyond the borderline or threshold of normative agency. No human is. Instead, then, as Griffin puts it, "We should see children as acquiring [human] rights in stages—the stages in which they acquire [normative] agency" (95). It follows that what Griffin is giving us is not actually a fleshing out, not a making more determinate, of the modern consensus concept of human rights. The implications of this are enormous. For one, it means that human fetuses, babies, and young children do not have human rights, but that humans who are older typically do. It might be replied that the former *potentially* have human rights, and that that is good enough. But potential rights are not the same thing as actual rights. In fact they are not rights at all. To give a simple example, an official candidate for president of the United States is potentially the president, but that does not automatically give him or her the keys to the White House. In short, using whatever example one likes, potentiality does not give actuality. At most, then, what Griffin gives us is a view very different than the modern consensus concept of human rights. If human fetuses, babies, and young children have any natural rights at all from his perspective, they would not be *human* rights. (And that, of course, opens the door to animal rights.)

A second and related difficulty, focusing still on the potential/actual distinction, concerns adults. It is difficult to see how Griffin can think that he is fleshing out the existence conditions of the modern consensus concept of human rights when the existence conditions he provides do not give us *universal* human rights,

rights that all humans have, even if we confine ourselves to adult humans. This is because not all adult humans meet the minimum requirements for normative agency as he defines it, and some of them never will. There are, as he readily acknowledges, adults in an irreversible coma, adults with advanced dementia, and the "severely mentally defective" (95). Does this mean that they lack human rights? If they do, and they do in his view, then *universal* human rights become *typical human* rights, and that is not the same thing. Griffin says as much when he says, "human rights, on the personhood account, are not universal in the class of human beings: they are restricted to the sub-class of human normative agents" (50). The subclass, granted, is according to Griffin "the vast majority of adult mankind" (45). And he adds that there is more to morality and justice than rights, so that we can have not just obligations but "the weightiest obligations" (95) to those humans who lack normative agency. But even so, what has to be recognized is that this is not the modern consensus concept of human rights, which is that of *universal* human rights. What Griffin offers, then, is not a defense of that concept but instead a *reconceptualization*, a change in *both* the intension and extension of the term "human rights."

The reconceptualization might be found to be necessary after all, as it seems to avoid the *diachronic thrust* argument presented in the previous chapter—in fact it does not, as it is still generated by the focus on typical human adults—but it comes at an enormous cost, one that most human rights realists would not be willing to accept. For once one restricts human rights to a subclass of humans rather than to all humans alive today, the door then becomes open to further restrictions. One concept of "normal human" all of a sudden finds itself in competition with other concepts of "normal human," and it is difficult to see an end to it.

Finally, even if one accepts Griffin's "proposal" and accepts that a belief in basic human rights offers protection for the functioning of normative agency and therefore provides a good reason to believe in those rights, one nevertheless has to notice that it by no means follows that those rights actually exist. Griffin stipulates the "existence conditions" of human rights, and he clearly conceives of human rights as facts, as moral facts. Hume's classic distinction between facts and values is something he explicitly rejects, as involving a "narrow conception of fact." There are strong reasons, he says, for believing that "basic human interests are features of the world" (35). One can agree with this, but it nevertheless does not commit one to a belief in human rights (widely or narrowly conceived). This is because, to give an analogy, having bodyguards might be important for me to go about my daily business, they might be needed, but it doesn't automatically follow that I in fact have them. Similarly, human rights might be important protections for human normative agency, but it doesn't automatically follow that humans in fact have them. To return to Hume, human rights might be nothing more than projections onto the human scene. This is Hume's view with regard to so-called moral facts as a whole. As Hume (1740) puts it in a striking passage with regard to murder (I am here elaborating), you see the knife, you see the thrust, you see the blood and you hear the scream, and then you see the lifeless body, but you do not see that extra thing called "wrong" or "vice." What you find instead, he says, is "a sentiment of disapprobation, which arises in you, towards this action" (1.§1). So too, it may be maintained, with seeing a human right violated, in the case of murder the right to life. What happens, arguably, is not that a natural human right is violated, but that the violation is a projection onto the scene by a believer in a modern myth, the myth of universal human rights. Nothing more.

Martha Nussbaum

The final scholarly defense of human rights we shall examine is by Martha Nussbaum, the Ernst Freund Distinguished Service Professor of Law and Ethics at the University of Chicago (Law, Philosophy, Divinity, Classics). Nussbaum is famous for developing, independently and then partly in league with the Indian economist and philosopher Amartya Sen, a "capabilities approach" to human rights. This approach has been saved for last since it is more inclusive than the previous three approaches, in the sense that it takes into account more of human nature, and also because of all the approaches examined in this chapter it is arguably the most challenging (which is why it receives the longest discussion). Nussbaum's account, moreover, is preferable for examination here rather than Sen's not only because hers focuses more on constructing an actual list of central capabilities and the methodology underlying it (as Nussbaum herself points out), but also because her writings are featured more in anthologies on human rights (e.g., Hayden 2001; Ishay 2007) and in critical discussions on human rights (e.g., Beitz 2009). According to the latter, "Nussbaum's approach ... more clearly exemplifies an interpretation of the idea of rights that belong to human beings 'as such'" (62). It shall be argued below, nevertheless, that in addition to internal problems her approach no more captures the consensus concept than any of the others examined in this chapter. But to see this we need to begin by clarifying the capabilities approach itself.

It is trivially true, of course, that human beings are capable of a great many things, simple things like tying their shoes and helping a fallen robin back into its nest to massive enterprises like flying to the moon and committing genocide. But beneath all of this numerosity there are what Nussbaum (1997) calls "central human capabilities," the capabilities that "have value in themselves, in making a life fully human" (223). Hence Nussbaum's list of central human capabilities includes being able to live a normal length of life, having adequate nourishment and shelter, having opportunities for sexual enjoyment, having choice in matters of reproduction, being able to love and care for others, including animals, being able to exercise one's intellect and imagination, being able to express emotions such as grief and anger, being able to laugh and play and enjoy friendship, and being able to own property and to participate in one's government. This list is not the complete list that Nussbaum gives, nor does she mean for any list she gives to be complete. Instead, her lists are "empirical" and meant to be "open-ended and humble," something subject to "cross-cultural inquiry" and capable of being "remade" (223).[8]

Despite this last part, to which Nussbaum adds that "the items on the list are to some extent differently constructed by different societies" (223), we should not be confused by this apparent concession to cultural diversity. Nussbaum is no relativist or social constructionist. With regard to women's issues especially, she has much to say against cultural relativism and cultural justifications for harm. In her book *Sex and Social Justice* (1999), for example, she argues against the relativism and postmodernism that is rampant in anthropology and other social sciences, and against the charge that she is guilty of essentialism and other nonsense, in favor of what she calls "universalism." As she puts it with regard to the latter, "What activities characteristically performed by human beings are so central that they seem definitive of a life that is truly human? In other words, what are the functions without which (meaning, without the availability of which) we would regard a life as not, or not fully, human?" (39). By a "truly human life" she has in mind a standard, cross-cultural, gender-neutral optimum, a life that, if it is lacking in any one of the central human capabilities, "will fall short of being a good human life" (42). More recently, in her book *Frontiers of Justice* (2006), Nussbaum states her belief that the basic list of central human capabilities "can gather broad cross-cultural agreement, similar to the international agreements that have been reached concerning basic human rights" (78).

Unlike the Universal Declaration of Human Rights, however, the capabilities approach clearly takes biology much more seriously in the sense of "human nature," while recognizing that humans are both biological and cultural entities. In searching for the human universals that make for a good and full human life, her approach is clearly in the tradition of Aristotle's biology, and she is quite explicit in her Aristotelianism. Aristotle argued that every biological species has a nature

---

8. Nussbaum's lists of central capabilities are divided into ten groupings and are virtually unchanged throughout her writings examined here. In addition to Nussbaum (1997, 223–225), see also Nussbaum (1999, 41–42; 2003, 41–42; 2006, 76–77).

and humans are no different, that there is such a thing as human nature and that the fully happy and complete human is the fully functioning human. Since man is not only an animal but the rational animal, and a social animal as well, ethics and politics along with contemplation are necessary dimensions of human happiness and fulfillment.

There is clearly much about Aristotle's thinking that Nussbaum does not accept (such as his species fixism, his theory of natural slavery, and his male chauvinism), but she does accept the idea that human nature is a biological reality rather than a social construction and that as such it involves objectively existing central capabilities for fulfillment. In short, her approach is a modernized Aristotelianism.

Where Nussbaum most profoundly differs from Aristotle is in her shift from functions to capabilities, since the fully human life need not necessarily be the fully functioning one in her view. What matters, instead, is that the capability be there. This is where culture and individual choice combine with biology. To mix together two of her examples (1997), a deeply religious person might prefer to fast rather than to eat nourishing meals, or to abstain from sex, but would such a person then be leading less than a fully human or flourishing life? Aristotle would say yes, as much as if a bird would refrain from flight, but not so Nussbaum, since for her a fully human life involves the *capabilities* for these activities plus the *choice*. It is this element of choice that makes the difference between fasting and starving, between celibacy and forced virginity. Similarly, to use another of her examples, what is wrong with female genital mutilation (aka "female circumcision") is that it removes the basic human capability for sexual enjoyment and thus removes in females their choice in exercising that function. The same would have to be said for indoctrination and brainwashing, by the way, given the damage they do to human intellectual capabilities, and so on for many more examples. Nussbaum says that unlike the Catholic natural law tradition, which traces back to Aristotle, she does not believe in "pushing individuals into the function" (227). Rather, she believes in humans having the means to exercise the function but leaving it up to them to choose whether they will in fact exercise it. "Citizens," she says, "must be left free to determine their course after they have the capabilities" (226). *That* is the fully human life, the life of "dignified free beings who shape their own lives" (228).

This is where Aristotle meets Rawls, for Nussbaum combines a modernized functional approach of humans with Rawls's theory of justice as fairness, which entails via the "original position" in the *veil of ignorance* thought experiment a very high degree of liberalism, as Rawls (1971) puts it "the most extensive basic liberty compatible with a similar liberty for others" (60). This is a very odd mix, Aristotle and Rawls, since Aristotle's approach is rooted in the biology of human nature while Rawls's approach is most appropriate for "disembodied spirits," as

E. O. Wilson puts it (1975, 287). Interestingly, what both approaches do have in common, however, is that neither provides a natural or human rights theory. Nussbaum herself admits that "Aristotle's theory was grossly defective because it lacked a theory of basic human rights" (215). We shall see this in the next chapter. And what we shall see in Chapter 6 is that Rawls's theory of justice is not based on human rights either. Human rights are not part of the "original position" (only equality in reason and self-interest are), nor are they entailed by the veil of ignorance thought experiment. Instead, as we shall see, human rights for Rawls are a useful fiction, a social construction, the contractarian function of which is to set the "outer boundary" of what a just state or society can do.

Nussbaum's central capabilities approach turns out to be an ally of the naturalized approach to ethics and justice that I develop in Chapter 7, but given that the dual foundation of her approach in Aristotle and Rawls does not intrinsically include an appeal to universal human rights, one must seriously wonder whether Nussbaum's approach itself is really a human rights approach.

Nussbaum herself affirms that it is, and it is interesting to compare her 1997 paper with her 2006 book here. Beginning with the former, in the paper's ultimate discussion on human rights and the capabilities approach, she states that "there are some areas in which the best way of thinking about rights is to see them as, what I have called, *combined capabilities* to function in various ways" (228). Given that at the beginning of her paper she sketches a number of different ways of thinking about human rights, it would seem that she is providing what she thinks is the best way, especially given her claim that the language of human rights lacks "theoretical and conceptual clarity" (212). By a "combined capability" Nussbaum means an "internal capability" combined with "suitable external conditions" (227) for its exercise, where by an "internal capability" she means a capability not requiring an external condition for its functioning. Examples given of combined capabilities are the rights to political participation, to religious freedom, to freedom of speech, to seeking employment outside of the home, and to freedom from unwarranted search and seizure.

There are other capabilities that Nussbaum connects with human rights. According to Nussbaum, some capabilities deserve to be called "basic capabilities," in that they refer to "the innate equipment of individuals that is the necessary basis for developing the more advanced capabilities" (226–227), among which are the basic capabilities of reason and imagination. Human rights, in the sense of a "justified claim" that one has "by virtue of being human," reside, she says, "very close" to what she calls basic capabilities, "since typically human rights are thought to derive from some actual feature of human persons, some untrained power in them that demands or calls for support from the world" (229).

"Very close," of course, does not mean numerically the same or identical. Nevertheless, Nussbaum does claim that "capabilities and rights should be seen to be equivalent" in cases such as the supposed human right to religious freedom, where the state is called upon to defend an "urgent and justified claim" that a citizen has "just by virtue of being human" (229).

On the other hand, however, Nussbaum claims that in some cases a human right "is prior to capability, and a ground for the securing of a capability" (229), such as the right to seek employment outside the home. This, by the way, is the same example she gives when she defines a "combined capability," as we have just seen above. She also claims that a capabilities approach need not bring itself "nearly so close to rights" (233). A capabilities approach might take a less liberal approach, for example, focusing on function and authoritarian rule in promoting individual discipline rather than choice. In such a case, she says, "the relationship between capabilities and rights will shift accordingly" (233–234).

Nevertheless, with regard to "political and religious liberties" Nussbaum claims that "it seems evident that the best way to think of the secured right is as a capability." However, she also claims that "There is another set of rights, largely those in the area of property and economic advantage, which seem to me analytically different in their relationship to capabilities," such that "material rights may … plausibly be analyzed in terms of resources, or possibly in terms of utility" (230).

In *Frontiers of Justice* (2006), however, Nussbaum makes a full-fledged connection between her capabilities approach and human rights. Repeatedly she states that "I view the capabilities approach as one species of a human rights approach" (78, 284, 285–286, 291). She uses the word "species" because there are different theories of human rights, and she clearly thinks that her approach is the best: it clarifies, for example, the *basis* of human rights, in the central capabilities; it takes a clear position on a number of debates, affirming that human rights are pre-political, that they include not just first-generation rights (political and civil liberties from state interference) but also second-generation rights (social and economic entitlements); and it gives us what she calls a "benchmark" in terms of determining "what it really is to secure a right to someone" (287), in other words "goals for the international community as a whole, and for humanity as a whole" (291). In short, she states quite clearly that "the capabilities approach should not be seen as a rival of the human rights approach" (291).

If they are not rivals, then why not just replace the language of human rights with the language of human capabilities? After all, she says (1997), in an almost Wittgensteinian tone that threatens to bring us full circle to the beginning of this chapter, "a different language has begun to take hold in talk about people's basic entitlements. This is the language of capabilities and human functioning" (214). A major piece of evidence she cites is that ever since 1993 the *Human Development Reports* of the United Nations Development Programme, influenced largely by Amartya Sen, "have assessed the quality of life in the nations of the world using the concept of people's capabilities, or their abilities to do and to be certain things deemed valuable" (214). But Nussbaum's answer is not to follow or to promote that trend. This is because she recognizes that human rights talk, unlike human capabilities talk, has to it a "moral resonance" (212). Hence she specifies four reasons human rights talk should be retained: (i) "rights language reminds us that people have justified and urgent claims to certain types of urgent treatment" (231), such that "appealing to rights communicates more than appealing to basic capabilities" (232); (ii) an appeal to a list of human capabilities "has only a vague normative resonance," whereas an appeal to a list of human rights provides "a sense of the justified claim that all humans have to such things, by virtue of being human" (232); (iii) the language of human capabilities implies choice, whereas the language of human rights "helps us to lay extra emphasis on this very important fact" (232); and (iv) "the language of rights preserves a sense of the terrain of agreement, while we continue to deliberate about the proper type of analysis at the more specific level" (232–233).

This last point was elaborated by Charles Beitz, as we have seen above, who attempted to remove the naturalistic basis of the concept of human rights, and in so doing departed enormously from the consensus concept. But Nussbaum, too, has departed enormously from the consensus concept, only in a different way. This is because the language of human rights does not have the same *meaning* (whether intension or extension) as the language of central human capabilities, and also because the core concepts are *logically incompatible.* But let us deal with these one at a time.

First, a quick examination of language will show that the meaning of "human right" and the meaning of "central human capability" are not logically the same. This is because there is no contradiction in saying that one has a human right to x but is incapable of having x, whereas it is a contradiction to say that one is capable of having x but is incapable of having x. I can have a right to a long life, for example, but be incapable of having a long life. There is no contradiction in combining both statements. But if I am capable of having a long life, it makes no sense to add that I am incapable of having a long life. That is a contradiction, and what the contradiction shows is that human rights and central human capabilities are not the same sort of things. The point, moreover, is a general one, covering not just human rights but all kinds of rights and not just central human capabilities but all kinds of capabilities. Given any right, it is an open question whether I have the corresponding capability, and given any capability, it is an open question whether I have the corresponding right.

The second problem is that human rights are supposed to be *moral* rights (among other features). Capabilities, of course, are objective *properties* of beings; they are something beings *have*. If central human capabilities are coextensive with human rights, then human rights must also be properties of human beings. The problem is that capabilities in and of themselves are not necessarily moral. This should be evident alone when we take into account the fact that not just humans have central capabilities necessary for their flourishing but every biological species has them as well. But just because a plant or animal (and humans are animals for Nussbaum, following Aristotle and modern biology) has a central capability does not automatically mean that it has a *moral* claim and entitlement to exercise or satisfy that capability. A tiger, for example, has a central capability to eat animals like me for dinner, but that does not automatically mean that it has a moral claim and entitlement to kill and eat me. Similarly, a central capability of a mosquito is to suck blood out of the veins of animals like me, but that does not automatically mean that I am morally obligated or have a moral duty to stand there and wait until it is finished. It might be the case that plants and animals do in fact have natural moral rights based on their central capabilities, but certainly it would be an extremely odd moral universe, and for that reason alone something is wanted in the form of an argument, something substantial.

Nussbaum (2006) has a very long chapter (ch. 6, the last in her book) devoted to justice for nonhuman animals, in which she recognizes that every species has central capabilities and that there is "a wide range of types of animal dignity, and of corresponding needs for flourishing" (327). But does she attribute to them natural moral rights? The answer is that she does. She says, "The sphere of justice is the sphere of basic entitlements. When I say that the mistreatment of animals is unjust, I mean to say not only that it is wrong *of us* to treat them in that way, but also that they have a right, a moral entitlement, not to be treated in that way. It is unfair *to them*" (337).

But would it be unfair to plants? Nussbaum explicitly states that "We should not follow Aristotle in saying that there is a natural ranking of forms of life" (360). And yet she follows utilitarianism and accepts "the possession of sentience as a threshold condition for membership in the community of beings who have entitlements based on justice" (361–362). Although for theoretical purposes she adopts a "disjunctive approach" (sentience, or movement, or emotion, or reason), for practical purposes she accepts Aristotle's reasoning that sentience is going to be found in beings that have any of the other three disjuncts, so that in her view it is sentience that determines that "that creature has moral standing" (362). By "moral standing," moreover, Nussbaum does not simply mean being worthy of moral consideration. The concept, instead, is that of a *person*, of "the animal itself as an agent and a subject, a creature to whom something is due, a creature who is itself an end" (337). It is the individual animal, moreover, not the species, that has the moral standing, since, "as in the human case, the focus should be the well-being and dignity of the individual creature" (357).

Dignity, then, is the key difference for why plants do not have moral entitlements in her view but sentient animals do have them. But are sentient animals naturally entitled to equal dignity, not just within species but across species? *Dignity*, of course, is a difficult notion, involving many senses, including the sense of self-worth. But no matter, Nussbaum is attracted to *yes* to both questions, but does not commit to either, especially the latter, for political reasons, since she recognizes that her yes position is not going to gain a consensus among human cultures.

One can see here a fundamental tension in Nussbaum's thinking. On the one hand, as we have already seen, she wants to connect central human capabilities with universal human rights, as the best understanding of universal human rights. On the other hand, she wants to extend her capabilities approach to nonhuman animals, in fact to the sentient world as a whole inasmuch as that is possible, such that she "calls, in a very general way, for the gradual supplanting of the natural by the just" (400). The fundamental tension is that human rights, right from the beginning in the 1640s all the way to the Universal Declaration of Human Rights and related documents, were always supposed to be *human* rights, rights applicable only to humans. As Donnelly (2003) puts it with regard to this concept, "if one is not a human being, then by definition one cannot have human rights" (25). By trying to extend human rights to nonhuman animals, then, or by trying to conceive of human rights as a subset of animal rights, Nussbaum has lost sight of the ball.

Some of this is evident as a matter of internal inconsistency, as, for example, when Nussbaum refrains from an outright ban on the raising and killing of animals for meat, given that "nobody really knows . . . the extent to which such a [vegetarian] diet could be made compatible with the health of all the world's children" (402), or when she supports limited research on animals by admitting "an ineliminable residue of tragedy in the relationships between humans and animals" (404). In these and other cases, her speciesism seems impossible to square with what she recognizes as "basic animal entitlements" (405).

These inconsistencies indicate a deeper problem, however. The point and purpose of the human rights doctrine, from the Levellers to the Universal Declaration, is to reduce human conflict to an acceptable level. When human rights are understood as central capabilities, as Nussbaum herself recognizes, "if the threshold has been correctly set, any failure to secure a capability at a minimum level is a failure of justice, and we should work for a world in which those conflicts will not occur" (381). But one cannot extend this idea to the world of nature. The approach can only hope to work in the case of humans because humans are all of one species. But the world of nature is a world of roughly 30 million species. Most of those species are not sentient, granted, but the diversity among sentient species includes not only symbiosis but food chains and food webs, such that the imposition of what Nussbaum calls "justice" would have the effect of destroying the world of nature. As Heraclitus put it around 500 B.C., "War is father and king of all," "conflict is justice," and "harmony is opposing tensions, as in the bow and the lyre" (Fragments 53, 80, 51). One might disagree with this, and argue that nature is evil and needs to be transformed. But no matter. The debate points to a fundamental difference between universal natural moral rights confined to humans and universal natural moral rights extended to all species (or all animal species, or all sentient animal species). Reducing conflict *within* a species might be a good thing, but it does not necessarily follow that reducing conflict *between* species will be a good thing, too.

For political reasons, Nussbaum prefers to refer to the problem of equality across species, of "equal cross-species dignity" (384), as "a metaphysical question on which citizens may hold different positions while accepting the basic substantive claims about animal entitlement" (383). But philosophers cannot possibly leave the matter at that. To call an issue "metaphysical" is not to give free play to different opinions and feelings. For philosophers, metaphysical issues (real or so-called) are just as open to question and criticism as are any other.

At this point we need to back up and return to the issue of human rights alone, for there is a deeper metaphysical issue involved in Nussbaum's argument. What is needed, in short, if Nussbaum's approach to human rights is to work, is a *connecting link* between the concept of a central human capability and the concept of a human right, for the concepts are not the same, as pointed out above. To make her claim about human rights work, she has to provide that link, *and then* extend the argument to other species.

But it is difficult to see what the link could be. That an animal (human or otherwise) has a species-specific capability is one thing; that it has a moral claim and entitlement is another. In the consensus language of universal human rights, as argued earlier in this chapter, human rights are generally supposed to be objective moral properties that all humans have by virtue of being human. One might take the approach, as Jefferson and many others more recently have, that this is simply self-evident, that it is intuitively true. G. E. Moore (1903) held that moral properties exist objectively out there in the world, as simple (non-analyzable) non-natural properties of natural objects, processes, and events, that they supervene on the latter, and that the connections are in some sense necessary and universal connections. Many things are *good,* for example, and one can intuitively see this, such that of two identical things if one of them is good, then so is the other, but given that something is good, one cannot infer what the something is. Such is the nature of supervenience. Human rights theorists, however, can find little comfort in Moore's commonsense realism, and not only because human rights are not supposed to be supervenient (given that something is a human right, one can suppose that it is had by a human). The main problem is that Moore's approach is a form of intuitionism and an appeal to intuition is the end of argument, but argument is exactly what is needed when it comes to human rights. For if humans are capable of intuiting moral properties, human rights among them, it is surely a very grave difficulty to notice not only that human rights realists (including the most perspicacious among them) cannot agree on the scope of human rights, but that human rights talk began at a particular time and place only a few hundred years ago, as we shall see in the next two chapters.

Perhaps one could take the approach of Peter Railton (1986), who argues for moral realism as an inference to the best explanation, as the best way of explaining our moral behavior. But here again the problems outweigh the benefits, for as will be argued in Chapter 6, the best explanation of the human rights revolution, both its origin and spread, is the memetic explanation combined with the evolutionary psychology of fairness. For Nussbaum to make a compelling case against that argument, then, and in favor of central human capabilities, she would need an explicit argument that specifies the connection between a central human capability and a universal human right. But she has not done this.

Moreover, it would appear that she cannot do this, that in fact it cannot possibly be done, and this should become evident once we turn our focus to two key features of the consensus concept of universal human rights, namely, that they are *universal* and *equal.* As repeatedly emphasized throughout the present book, universal human rights are rights that *all* humans are commonly supposed to have *equally,* not some and some not, or all but more or less. They are rights that *all* humans are supposed to have and in the *same degree.* Nussbaum's central capabilities approach, however, is incompatible with these ideas and it is important to see why.

To begin, Nussbaum claims, as we have seen above, that her approach affirms "universalism." Moreover, the universals of central human capabilities are arrived at inductively, in an Aristotelian manner, not a priori or deductively. In other words, Nussbaum's (1997) approach focuses on individual cases and works toward the universals, the central human capabilities "enabling people to function in a fully human way" (222), the capabilities "of central importance in any human life" (223). As she puts it,

> Instead of asking "How satisfied is person A," or "How much in the way of resources does A command," we ask the question: "What is A actually able to do and to

be?" In other words, about a variety of functions that would seem to be of central importance to a human life, we ask: Is the person capable of this, or not? This focus on capabilities, unlike the focus on GNP, or on aggregate utility, looks at people one by one, insisting on locating empowerment in *this* life and in *that* life, rather than in the nation as a whole.... Indeed, this view denies that the most important functions are all commensurable in terms of a single metric and it treats diverse functions as all important, and all irreducibly plural. [222]

The problem now is the obvious one of marginal cases, the cases of severely defective human beings. As everyone knows, many humans lack the central human capabilities in Nussbaum's list or have them to an insufficient degree. To use the language of Aristotle, they have them neither actually nor potentially. For example, humans with Huntington's chorea do not have the capability of living beyond middle age, while those with Tay-Sachs disease do not live beyond the age of three. Some humans, either because of their genes or because of brain damage incurred at some point in their lives, do not have the capability of human reasoning at all or of human language, or have it to a degree that they are considered mentally retarded. Humans with 17α-hydroxylase deficiency, which is caused by a homozygous point mutation in a particular gene, never enter puberty and hence are incapable of reproduction. The list, of course, goes on and on. What the central capabilities approach to universal human rights requires is a justification or reason for why a human with Tay-Sachs disease, for instance, has a moral claim and entitlement to a long and full human life even though that human lacks the inherent capability.

If human rights *simply are* central human capabilities, then quite obviously *some* human beings are going to lack human rights (even though they are human) simply because they lack some of the central human capabilities. Human rights, then, are going to be neither *universal* nor *equal* human rights, so that Nussbaum's capabilities approach cannot be an elucidation or defense of the consensus concept. This is true whether we are talking about the right to a long life, to intellectual freedom and freedom of speech, to reproductive rights, or to any other rights that fall within the scope of the consensus concept of universal human rights. Those rights are supposed to be the rights that all humans have by virtue of being human, but there is nothing in this concept that requires each and every human to be inherently and equally capable of exercising those rights. Quite simply, the concepts are not the same.

Nussbaum, as we have seen, does not take an individualist or relativist approach to human capabilities. That would clearly be incompatible with the consensus concept of universal human rights. Her approach, instead, is universalist, and not in the sense of an abstract idealized conception of human beings but in the sense of an inductive generalization. As she puts it more recently (2006), her appeal is to "the species norm" (285), where the norm, moreover, is considered explicitly in terms of a "threshold": "for each important entitlement, there is some appropriate level beneath which it seems right to say that the relevant entitlement has not been secured" (291–292).

So what then is it that connects the central capabilities norm in the human species, conceived of as a threshold, with humans who not only temporarily but permanently (in any realistic meaning of the term) fall below the norm? Nussbaum does not take the approach that we have seen Griffin take in the previous section, which is to exclude those who fall below the threshold. But neither does she take Gewirth's approach examined in the section before it, which is to include defective humans by means of an "underlying similarity" to normal humans. Both solutions, as we have seen, are incompatible with the consensus concept of universal human rights. She also does not take White's approach, examined in the first section, which is simply to appeal to misfortune compared with personhood. In fact, her argument does not clearly appeal to personhood at all.[9] And she certainly cannot appeal to an underlying essence of the species, for Aristotelian essences died at the hands of Darwin.

Surprisingly, Nussbaum includes defective humans by appealing to "the very birth of a person into the human community" (285), by which she means simply "a person's existence as a human being." Hence in the case of Sesha, someone she knows with congenital cerebral palsy combined with severe mental retardation, such that the young woman is incapable of talking and reading and needs to be washed and fed, Nussbaum states that her "entitlements are not based solely upon the actual 'basic capabilities' that she has, but on the basic capacities characteristic of the human species," what she calls "the species norm" (285).

---

9. See Nussbaum's rejection of the concept of person found in Kant and Rawls in ch. 2 §5, which is based exclusively on reason, either the rational capacity to understand the categorical imperative (Kant) or the rational capacity to put oneself behind the veil of ignorance (Rawls). This concept of person, which categorizes nonhuman animals as "things," has a problem with humans whose rational capacity is severely retarded. On the other hand, Nussbaum states that "What is lacking in Rawls's account, as in Kant's, . . . is the sense of the animal itself as an agent and a subject, a creature to whom something is due, a creature who is itself an end. . . . the capabilities approach does treat animals as agents seeking a flourishing existence; this basic conception, I believe, is one of its greatest strengths" (337). This, it would seem, is to categorize animals, or at least higher animals, as *persons* without using the term, in a sense much wider than what is commonly found in philosophy and law. The problem remains, however, of extending distinctively human rights to mentally defective humans but not to dogs and cows and chickens, who also by her definition are persons.

The problem is that this solution cannot work. Granted, someone like Sesha should not be compared with a chimpanzee, for she could not possibly live "the life of a contented chimpanzee" (192). Instead she can flourish only in the context of human guardianship. But since Sesha lacks many of the central human capabilities that Nussbaum links with human rights, it is none but an arbitrary solution to extend human rights to her simply because she is a human. That is simply *speciesism,* giving preference over another simply because of membership in the preferred species.

Moreover, given that Nussbaum defines "to secure a right" as "to put them in a position of capability to function in that area" (287), it makes no sense to say that the complete set of human rights (whatever that is) extended to Sesha can be secured. According to Nussbaum, "Sesha's entitlements are not based solely upon the actual 'basic capabilities' that she has, but on the basic capacities characteristic of the human species. Even if she herself does not have the capacity for language, then, the political conception is required to arrange vehicles of expression for her, through adequate forms of guardianship" (285). But given that Sesha is incapable of language, it makes no sense to secure her right of free speech (taken to mean the right to say whatever one wants as long as one is not unjustly harming others). It is standard in ethics that *ought implies can*: it makes no sense to say someone ought to do something when that person cannot possibly do it. Similarly, it makes no sense to say that Sesha has the human right to free speech, a right that ought to be secured, when she is innately incapable of language.

Nussbaum's account also has a problem with the equality requirement of human rights. Her capabilities approach employs here again the concept of a threshold, such that, as she puts it, "for each important entitlement, there is some appropriate level beneath which it seems right to say that the relevant entitlement has not been secured" (2006, 291–292). The benchmark she stresses here in her section on equality is "human dignity," such that "the idea of dignity is spelled out from the beginning in terms of equality: it is the *equal dignity* of human beings that demands recognition." With "political, religious, and civil liberties," she says, such as voting rights and freedom of religion, they "can be *adequately* secured only if they are *equally* secured" (293). With other rights, however, the social and economic rights, such as health care and basic education, she holds that "what seems appropriate is *enough*" (293); a certain minimum in housing would be another example. For "equal human dignity" to be met here not everyone must be entitled to exactly the same, but only to whatever the minimum required to meet that basic level.

The problem here, however, should be obvious. What Nussbaum calls a "threshold of adequacy" (295), especially for the social and economic rights, is going to vary from human society to human society across the globe considered synchronically, and whatever the minimum average is going to be, it is not going to be static diachronically, over time, but is going to change as the average social and economic conditions of humans change over time. But this is not the concept of equal human rights that is part of the consensus concept, the concept enshrined in the Universal Declaration of Human Rights and related documents. As Donnelly (2003) accurately states the concept, "Human rights are equal rights: one either is or is not a human being" (10).

Nussbaum's central capabilities approach in itself is of great value for matters of national and international justice, but it should be clear by now that in attempting to provide a scholarly defense of universal human rights she has lost sight of the ball, in common with the rest of the scholarly approaches examined in this chapter.

Chapter 4

Getting the History of Human Rights Wrong

> One may thus think of the history of human rights as a journey guided
> by lampposts across ruins left behind by ravaging and insatiable storms.
> —*Micheline Ishay (2008, 3)*

WHEN DID THE MODERN CONSENSUS CONCEPT of human rights actually begin—the idea, and especially the belief, that humans have universal, equal, innate, and inalienable moral claims and entitlements? In other words, how far back does it go? It had to have a beginning in history at some time. And where did it begin? More likely than not it began in a particular place rather than independently at different places and times. In any event, when and where is a factual matter, and if one genuinely wants to get the facts of the matter right inasmuch as that is possible, then one needs to take history of ideas seriously, which means having a strong sense of history combined with a lot of attention to detail. A weak desire and sloppy thinking just won't do.

Many have claimed that the modern consensus concept of human rights is to be found in ancient or medieval sources, in this one or that, each person having their own favorite, even if their source lacks a corresponding term, or that this or that person was a precursor or forerunner of the concept. All of these claims are extravagant, and none of them would be surprising but for the fact that many of them have been made by professional scholars, people who should know better, people who are typically held to high standards in terms of logic and evidence.

This chapter is devoted to examining a representative sample of the claims of these scholars, to not only examining their claims but to seeing where and why they are mistaken. This is an important matter not only in itself, as a matter of historical knowledge, but also for helping to understand why the belief in universal human rights today is so widespread and strong. But more important, seeing where and why scholars went wrong on the history helps to prepare the way for the next chapter, where the case will be made for the actual origin of the modern concept and belief in universal human rights. But that is getting ahead of ourselves. What we shall see in the present chapter, using a variety of scholars as foils, is that ancient and medieval sources certainly had the concept of conventional rights, rights that can be given and taken away, along with various concepts of natural rights, duties, and virtues, but they did not have the modern consensus concept of universal human rights, the idea at the core of documents such as the American Declaration of Independence and the Universal Declaration of Human Rights, the idea that all humans have a set of natural and equal rights, rights they were born with and that cannot be given up or taken away. The idea just was not there.

The Bible

Western civilization is founded primarily on the Judeo-Christian and ancient Greek traditions. Given that the belief in universal human rights is a mainly Western phenomenon, it perhaps is not surprising that many have claimed that the concept is to be found in one or the other of these two sources. Let us begin with the Bible, both the Jewish part, called the Old Testament by Christians, and the Christian addition, called the New Testament by Christians.

The first thing to notice is that the Bible nowhere contains any explicit *language* of universal human rights. Everyone agrees about that. But is the concept implicitly there? And if not, does the Bible at least serve as a foundation for the concept? Many, indeed, have answered yes to one of these questions, if only vaguely. For example, in her book devoted to the history of human rights, Micheline Ishay (2008), Professor and Director of the International Human Rights Program at the University of Denver, after recognizing that "where does that history begin? ... is a politically charged question" (6), states that the central argument of her book is that "those human rights themes that survive the tests and contradictions of history provide in the long run a corpus of shared perceptions of universal human rights that transcends class, ethnic, and gender distinctions" and that "the history of human rights shows a clear dimension of progress" (12). Her approach is the politically correct, multicultural one. On the other hand, one of the people she quotes is the French UN delegate and law professor René Cassin, a major player in the drafting of the Universal Declaration of Human Rights (partly for which he later received a Nobel Prize), who claimed that "the concept of human rights comes from the Bible, from the Old Testament, from the Ten Commandments.... they [these principles] were often phrased in terms of duties, which now presume rights. For instance, Thou shall not murder is the right to life. Thou shall not steal is the right to own property, and so on and so forth. We must not forget that Judaism gave the world the concept of human rights" (19). While denying a necessary equivalence between religious injunctions and the modern concept of human rights, Ishay herself sees "the spirit of some religious injunctions in modern definitions of rights" (369n6), while in her reader (2007) she claims that "Some of these injunctions directly translate into later formulations of rights" (31)—that, for example, the injunction against murder "implies the right to secure one's life," the injunction against theft "implies a right to property" (xiii)—and that Judaism, along with Christianity and Islam, "preached universalism" (31).

It might be natural to think that if God commands us to honor and obey our parents, for example, then we have a duty to honor and obey them, and also that our parents have a right, a natural right, to be honored and obeyed by us, their children. The problem is that this assumes that duties logically imply rights. But do they? Certainly the answer must be no as a general principle, for as Alan White (1984, 85–86) points out, one can have a duty to do something that does not involve anyone else (indeed we sometimes talk of a duty to ourselves), one can have a duty to others who might be said to not have rights (such as animals), and one can have a duty to others who are capable of having rights but no rights are involved, as when (to use his example) a doctor's duty to not prescribe a drug wanted by a patient (say, Propofol) does not imply that the patient has a right to not have the drug.

But wouldn't God's commandments entail duties on our part and hence human rights? Not necessarily. As the legal scholar Louis Henkin (1990) points out, "The Bible ... knew not rights but duties, and duties were to God" (184). "The traditional ideal was not," he says, "individual autonomy, freedom, privacy—but conformity to God's will and to divine law." Thus the commandments in the Bible, as they are actually given, imply only duties to God, not rights of people. The commandment to not steal, for example, or to not commit murder, entails a duty to obey God, with the potential victims in the commandments each being "what we would call a third-party-beneficiary" (184). The same would follow for the commandment to honor and obey one's parents, each parent being a potential victim or beneficiary but not necessarily a rights holder. Henkin's claim is strengthened by looking at the context of the Ten Commandments (discussed in detail below), which is that God's chosen people have a duty to God as children to their parents, not that God's children have rights against each other, including natural rights, let alone rights against God.

A much more sophisticated argument in favor of human rights in the Bible is made by Nicholas Wolterstorff (2008), Noah Porter Professor Emeritus of Philosophical Theology at Yale University. Wolterstorff claims not only that "The conception of justice as inherent rights was not born in the fourteenth or the seventeenth century; this way of thinking about justice goes back into the Hebrew and Christian Scriptures" (xii), but that "inherent natural *human* rights were implicitly recognized in the moral vision of the writers of the Hebrew and Christian Scriptures," that that is where these rights "first gained recognition," the very same rights that received "general recognition" in the UN's Universal Declaration of Human Rights of 1948, and that the Bible "can now be used as a resource for articulating a grounding of such rights" (361).

Wolterstorff makes a useful distinction between natural rights, inherent rights, and human rights, but it needs some correcting. *Natural rights,* he says, are not necessarily inherent rights, since justice as natural rights might mean justice simply as the right order of things. *Inherent rights,* on the other hand, are necessarily "inherent in their bearers" (65). So not all natural rights are inherent rights. But inherent rights, it needs to be added, would have to be natural rights, since the opposite of natural rights is conventional rights, and conventional rights are not inherent rights but conferred rights, rights that are given and that can be given up or taken away. Hence the "natural" in "inherent natural rights" is redundant.[1] Human rights, he says, are not necessarily inherent in their bearers, since they possibly could be conferred, in the case of a global institution, for example, upon all and only human beings. But then they would be conventional human rights, not *human rights,* the sense of the modern consensus concept. One more point: when Wolterstorff claims that the concept of "inherent natural human rights" is found in the Bible, he fails to notice that the concept he has in mind is not the same as the modern consensus concept of universal human rights that I stress throughout this book, which is that of universal, equal, innate, and inalienable moral claims and entitlements that all humans have by virtue of being human.

---

1. So is the "universal" in "universal human rights" a redundancy, by the way. I retain it throughout this book, however, not only because one often hears the full phrase in human rights discourse, but also because it draws attention to the most important document in that discourse, the UN's Universal Declaration of Human Rights.

But even his concept of inherent natural human rights is not to be found in the Bible, or so I shall argue.

How does Wolterstorff argue that the modern concept of human rights is found in the Bible? Chapter 3 of his book is devoted to the Old Testament, and he begins by pointing out that the concept of justice in the Old Testament is one of impartiality, favoring neither the rich and powerful nor the majority but treating all alike, including the poor and resident aliens. Second, although only the Jews were given the Torah, the laws of God including the Ten Commandments, it is recognized in the Old Testament that people outside of the Jewish community are morally responsible and worthy of punishment, even before the issuance of the Torah to the Jews, given examples such as God's destruction of Sodom and Gomorrah because of their immorality. The Torah was given to the Jews as God's holy people, as part of his covenant with them, but was intended eventually to be given to the rest of the world. Next, God's commandments in the Torah are not a matter of justice simply because God commands them; instead God commands them because they are just. But more important to Wolterstorff's argument is his claim that "when we fail to do justice, we wrong God. We not only fail in our *obligations* to God. We *wrong* God, deprive God of that to which God has a *right*" (91). Hence the Old Testament often speaks of God's anger, which is justified when God's rights have been violated, and also of God's mercy and forgiveness, which again indicates that God has been wronged by injustice. But how did God get his rights? "God does not have these rights," says Wolterstorff, "on account of some norm that applies to him! They are not conferred upon God. They belong to God inherently; they come along with what God is and what God does" (94). In other words, "In that assumption by Israel's writers, that God has rights grounded in God's excellence, is to be discerned a recognition of inherent natural rights" (94).

So far the argument establishes only that, according to the Old Testament, God has inherent natural rights. What is needed next is a link from God to humans. Wolterstorff supplies this link by appealing to the *imago dei* of the Old Testament, the doctrine first found in *Genesis* that "in his own image God made humankind" (95). "Once one has said that God has worth," says Wolterstorff, "that that worth grounds God's right to worship and obedience, and that human beings likewise have worth, it proves impossible not to continue in this line of thought and hold that human beings have rights on account of their worth. The writer of Genesis took the first step down that road" (95). Thus, says Wolterstorff, "The proscription against murder is grounded not in God's law but in the worth of the human being. All who bear God's image possess, on that account, an inherent right not to be murdered."

But what does being made in the image of God mean? According to Wolterstorff, "The image of God ... consists of *resembling God with respect* to possessing the capacities necessary for exercising dominion" (349). The reference is to the first creation story in *Genesis,* in which God says to the first humans, "Be fruitful and multiply, and fill the earth and subdue it; and have dominion over the fish of the sea and over the birds of the air and over every living thing that moves upon the earth" (1: 28), a command that is repeated to Noah after the Flood (9: 1–3). But the connection with man's worth, according to Wolterstorff, is made most clearly in *Psalms,* in which it is said, "thou hast made him [mankind] little less than God, and dost crown him with glory and honour. Thou hast given him dominion over the works of thy hands" (8: 5–6).

Wolterstorff takes it as obvious that "no non-human animals bear it," the *imago dei,* since "none of them has the full set of capacities for receiving and exercising the blessing or mandate of dominion" (350). But not all humans have the necessary capacities either, since "Alzheimer's patients no longer possess them" (349), as well as those in a permanent coma, those born severely mentally retarded, and so on. They may be said to have human nature, but it is "malformed" (349), in many cases permanently malformed. So the *imago dei* is necessary but not sufficient, "not adequate, all by itself, for grounding natural human rights." The missing element is God's love: "being loved by God gives a human being great worth," and God loves human beings "equally and permanently" (352). So apparently this is what makes the "inherent natural rights" of humans not only equal but also universal and inalienable.

Wolterstorff has presented an undoubtedly interesting argument, and a quite sophisticated one compared with others reaching the same or a similar conclusion. But there are serious problems with his argument that make it highly implausible, some of them logical, some of them historical, and some of them a combination of both.

To begin, according to Wolterstorff's understanding of the Old Testament, the "great worth" of malformed humans would be not inherent but "bestowed" (353). But bestowed rights are not *inherent* rights, so in that alone Wolterstorff has lost sight of the ball, since the modern concept of universal human rights is that of inherent (innate) rights that all humans have, no matter whether individual humans are well-formed or malformed (a point I elaborated upon in the previous chapter).

One also has to wonder why God would be so egalitarian toward humans when Wolterstorff himself admits that a car of great worth is no longer of equal worth to others of its model if its engine is "beyond repair" (351). Is it simply because God's love is merciful? But then one would have to wonder why God is so unloving to nonhuman sentient animals and does not show them the same mercy, given a hierarchical system of nature with predation, parasitism, and starvation—along with *human dominion,* according to Wolterstorff and the Bible. In short, God's love would seem to be *speciesist* (especially if we include the issue of having souls), allotting preference and love based merely on species membership.

It is a leap, moreover, to claim that worth implies rights. To believe otherwise is to believe that everything that has worth, whether intrinsic or bestowed, has rights. But surely there is no contradiction in stating that something has inherent worth but no inherent rights, or inherent worth but no bestowed rights, or bestowed worth but no inherent rights, or bestowed worth but no bestowed rights. The life of a dog, for example, looking at the first disjunct in the list, surely has inherent worth to the dog, especially if it is an intelligent dog, but there is no contradiction in saying the dog has no inherent rights. Something else would be needed to make the implication from inherent worth to inherent rights, and the same point stands for the other three disjuncts in the list. Wolterstorff, however, has not provided the needed link.

There is also a problem with conflicting rights. God has the greatest worth, so God has the greatest rights, according to Wolterstorff on the Old Testament. Humans are at a level of worth below God, or below angels, but they have inherent natural rights nonetheless. Does that mean they have rights against God, rights that trump God's rights? Or do God's rights always trump human rights? Does the Old Testament have an answer either way? One would think it should if it has an implicit teaching of inherent natural rights.

All in all, Wolterstorff has violated his own principle of avoiding "going beyond what they [the Old Testament authors] actually say or assume" (87). To state the obvious, if those writers assumed that all humans have inherent natural rights, such as to not be murdered, why did they not say so? Wolterstorff himself claims that the Old Testament does include rights language, such as "the rights of all the destitute" and "the rights of the poor and needy" (*Proverbs* 31: 8–9), even though he admits that such language is used "infrequently" (91 and n26). But not even once do the Old Testament authors mention "the rights of all humans" or "human rights." This must strike one as highly significant.[2]

---

2. The point is only strengthened if O'Donovan (2009) is correct in his claim that "the use of the word ['rights'] in the plural *is not found in the ancient world*" (195). More specifically, he states that "Phantom 'rights' spring up liberally across pages translated from Hebrew, Greek, and Latin, corresponding to no plural noun in the original. The unwary may be led by the translators of the Revised Standard Version Bible to discover 'rights' in *Proverbs* 31: 8–9 and *Jeremiah* 5: 28, where the Hebrew noun in both cases is a singular" (197).

But even worse, the claim that Moses, the alleged author (or conduit) of the Pentateuch (*Genesis* and the four books following it), gave the world the modern consensus concept of universal human rights (or something close to it), or even more modestly that the Old Testament serves as part of the foundation for the concept (e.g., Ishay 2007, 2008), can be maintained only with a hefty dose of gerrymandering. Granted, in the Old Testament God is quoted as saying, "Let us make man in our image, after our likeness" (*Genesis* 1: 26), and he made them "male and female" (27). But in the second creation story he makes man first and only later creates woman as an afterthought, because among animals Adam could not find "a helper fit for him," even though that was their original purpose (2: 18–20). And as to make no mistake about the lesson of hierarchy here, God makes the first woman out of a rib taken from Adam and says, "she shall be called Woman, because she was taken out of Man" (23). The gender hierarchy that is blatantly evident in the Old Testament (and yet denied by so many Jewish and Christian believers today) is incompatible with the feature of *equality* in the modern consensus concept of universal human rights, which is expressed most notably in the American Declaration of Independence and the Universal Declaration of Human Rights, a point I elaborated upon in Chapter 2 and shall return to in the next.

The Ten Commandments fare no better. The first point that needs to be emphasized is that they were not given to mankind in general but to the Jews as God's chosen people, chosen "for his own possession, out of all the peoples that are on the face of the earth" (*Deuteronomy* 7: 6). Second, no reasons are given for obeying the Ten Commandments except paternal and practical ones. With regard to the former, the Commandments come from no less than God almighty, such that "as a man disciplines his son, the Lord your God disciplines you. So you shall keep the commandments of the Lord your God, by walking in his ways and by fearing him" (*Deuteronomy* 8: 5–6). The Commandments are also clearly practical ones, designed for social cohesion in the promised land given to the Jews by God following their exodus from Egyptian bondage. This lesson is repeated time and again in the context of the Commandments, "that your days may be long in the land which the Lord your God gives you" (*Exodus* 20: 12), "that you may live long in the land which you shall possess" (*Deuteronomy* 5: 33). This is explicitly given as "the meaning of the testimonies and the statutes and the ordinances which the Lord our God has commanded" (6: 20), that the Commandments are "for our good always, that he might preserve us alive" (24). There is no universalism here, let alone an implicit appeal to human rights. On the contrary, of the displaced peoples it is said, "you must utterly destroy them; you shall make no covenant with them, and show no mercy to them" (7: 2). Indeed, in another context God commands the wholesale slaughter of innocent men, women, and children, as with the destruction of Jericho and Ai (*Joshua* 6–8).

Slavery, too, is mandated from the perspective of the chosen people: "For they are my servants," says God, "whom I brought forth out of the land of Egypt; they shall not be sold as slaves.... As for your male and female slaves whom you may have: you may buy male and female slaves from among the nations that are round about you. You may also buy from among the strangers who sojourn with you and their families that are with you, who have been born in your land; and they may be your property. You may bequeath them to your sons after you, to inherit as a possession for ever; you may make slaves of them, but over your brethren the people of Israel you shall not rule, one over another, with harshness" (*Leviticus* 25: 44–46). In short, as God says right after he gives the Ten Commandments, "the slave is his money" (*Exodus* 21: 20).

Compounding the matter is the doctrine of inherited sin, which like the above neither implies nor is compatible with the concept of universal human rights. Certainly the sin of disobedience that all humans inherited from the original sin of Adam and Eve looks equal, but the weight of the sin is not equally distributed. Not only are the punishments for men and women different (it was the woman, after all, who sinned first), but the gender inequality is further emphasized when God says to Eve and to women in general, "your desire shall be for your husband, and he shall rule over you" (*Genesis* 3: 16). Indeed elsewhere in the Old Testament (Apocrypha) it is proclaimed that "From a woman sin had its beginning, and because of her we all die" (*Sirach* 25: 24). But even lesser sins get inherited. In the context of the Ten Commandments, right after the commandment to worship no other gods, God says, "for I the Lord your God am a jealous God, visiting the iniquity of the fathers upon the children to the third and fourth generation of those who hate me" (*Exodus* 20: 5; *Deuteronomy* 5: 9). Of this doctrine Thomas Paine, in his *Rights of Man* (1791), wrote that it is "contrary to every principle of moral justice" (668n). Paine is surely right, but only if we confine ourselves to our modern liberal concepts of moral justice.

When we turn to the New Testament, the picture becomes no better, and a great deal of presentism and gerrymandering are likewise needed to make it look otherwise. True enough, the gospel—"good news"—is now given to the world, not just the chosen few. As the fourth gospel puts it, "God so loved the world that he gave his only Son, that whoever believes in him should not perish but have eternal life" (*John* 3: 16). Indeed it is even said that "God is love" (*I John* 4: 8). Wolterstorff (2008) emphasizes Jesus's "no partiality" (128), in that he ate and drank with women, Gentiles, and horrible sinners, he included them in his message, and "Rather than avoiding the malformed as ritually unclean, Jesus touched them and healed them: the deaf, the dumb, the blind, the crippled, the paralytics, the possessed, those issuing bodily fluids—the whole lot" (125). To Wolterstorff all of this indicates a profound sense of universalism and egalitarian justice, even more than the Old Testament, given especially the gospel of forgiveness in the New Testament, such as "if you forgive men your trespasses, your heavenly Father also will forgive you" (*Matthew* 6: 14). His point is that "Forgiveness presupposes that one has been deprived of that to which one has a right. It presupposes the existence of subjective rights" (130). In short, according to Wolterstorff, "the gospel writers were assuming that human beings have inherent rights" (130).

All of this is quite a stretch and does not stand up to scrutiny. For a start, forgiveness does not presuppose the existence of rights, let alone subjective (innate or inherent) rights. What forgiveness presupposes, morally, is only that someone has been *wrongfully harmed,* which in turn presupposes a concept or theory of *moral wrong.* But unless one can successfully defend the radical claim that every concept or theory of moral wrong necessarily involves the concept of subjective rights, then forgiveness cannot be taken to presuppose subjective rights.

Nor do any of Jesus's teachings imply inherent human rights. The Ten Commandments, for example, are reduced by Jesus to just two: to love God above all others and to "love your neighbor as yourself" (*Matthew* 22: 37–39). Wolterstorff takes this to mean not that "one's love of oneself is to serve as a paradigm for one's love of one's neighbor," since "Human self-love is much too defective to serve as paradigm" (210). He prefers to read the passage in light of "This is my commandment, that you love one another as I [Jesus] have loved you" (*John* 15: 12), which he points out is prefaced by, "As the father has loved me, so I have loved you" (209). This connects with his reading of the Old Testament. And yet it is extravagant to read "love your neighbor as yourself" as an implicit recognition of universal human rights when it is clearly, instead, merely a version of the Golden Rule, for Jesus is likewise reported as saying, "whatever you wish that men would do to you, do so to them; for this is the law and the prophets" (*Matthew* 7: 12). Elsewhere Jesus is reported to have applied this rule in a specific situation. When the scribes and Pharisees bring to him a woman they are about to stone for being an adulteress, saying, "Now in the law Moses commanded us to stone such," Jesus replies, "Let him who is without sin among you be the first to throw a stone at her" (*John* 8: 5–7). The important point to notice is that Jesus does not defend her in terms of human rights, claiming that stoning her would violate her human right to life. Instead he uses the psychology of the Golden Rule, which is an entirely different matter, if anything an appeal to empathy.

The absence of the concept of human rights becomes equally apparent when we turn to the Sermon on the Mount, the core of Jesus's moral teaching. It is important to look at a number of these key Christian teachings. We are told, for example, that "Blessed are the merciful, for they shall obtain mercy" (*Matthew* 5: 7), "Blessed are the peacemakers, for they shall be called the sons of God" (9), "if any one strikes you on the cheek, turn to him the other also" (39), "Give to him who begs from you" (42), "love your enemies" (44), and as we have already seen, "whatever you wish that men would do to you, do so to them" (7: 12). In all of this and much more, no reasons are given in terms of anything like human rights. Instead these normative teachings are justified in terms of rewards to the doer. As Jesus says in the middle of the sermon, "Rejoice and be glad, for your reward is great in heaven" (5: 12).

Not only does Jesus in the New Testament lack the concept of human rights, but if he actually had the concept, he would have to be judged from the modern perspective as no respecter of human rights. This comes out especially clear in his teachings on divine judgment and punishment, which are strongly reminiscent of the Old Testament. For example, when sending out his twelve apostles to go to Jewish towns to preach the good news, he adds that "if any one will not receive you or listen to your words, shake off the dust from your feet as you leave that house or town. Truly I say to you, it shall be more tolerable on the day of judgment for the land of Sodom and Gomorrah than for that town" (*Matthew* 10: 14–15). And then of course there are his teachings on eternal hellfire (e.g., *Matthew* 25: 41–46; *Mark* 9: 47–48; *Luke* 16: 19–31).

The writings of Paul fare no better, and in what follows one must keep in mind that as a Roman citizen, as the foremost "apostle to the Gentiles" (*Romans* 11: 13), and as the author of more in the New Testament than any other, Paul was second in importance only to Jesus in the history of Christianity. First, there is what he wrote about women. In one of his letters, echoing *Genesis*, he wrote that "Neither was the man created for the woman; but the woman for the man" (*I Corinthians* 11: 9). In another letter he wrote, "Wives, submit yourselves unto your own husbands, as unto the Lord" (*Ephesians* 5: 22). Violations of this mandate he calls "blasphemy" (*Titus* 2: 5), a clear reference to God in the Adam and Eve story, which he further justifies by calling Eve the first "transgressor" (*I Timothy* 2: 14).

On slavery, there is absolutely no evidence in Paul's writings that he thought human slavery violated the natural right of humans to not be slaves. On the contrary, in one of his letters he sends a runaway slave back to his master, albeit in the hope that the master will free the slave, not in recognition that humans have a natural right to not be slaves, but because the slave had become a "brother …

in the Lord" (*Philemon* 10–18). Elsewhere he urges slaves to obey their masters much like wives their husbands and both toward Christ, in "singleness of heart" (*Colossians* 3: 22) and with "fear and trembling" (*Ephesians* 6: 5).

Paul might be defended in all of this by pointing out that he believed the end time was imminent, so he might have thought there was no point getting caught up in matters of social justice. But his doctrine of predestination clinches the case against him as not having a concept of human rights. In his letter to the congregation in Rome, Paul claims that God predestined, before they were born, some to righteousness—"predestined to be conformed to the image of his Son"—and others not (*Romans* 8: 29–31). He adds that for God "he has mercy upon whomever he wills, and he hardens the heart of whomever he wills" (9: 18). To the obvious objection, "Why does he still find fault? For who can resist his will?," Paul replies with the pottery analogy, comparing humans to pots and God to the potter: "Will what is moulded say to its moulder, 'Why have you made me thus?' Has the potter no right over the clay, to make out of the same lump one vessel for beauty [think of a flowerpot] and another for menial use [now a pisspot]?" (9: 19–21).

Clearly the Bible is no respecter of human rights, for the simple reason that the ancient Jews and Christians did not have the concept, so neither did the God that they fashioned in their image. Other ancient sources fare no better, although a surprising number of people want to believe otherwise.

Confucius, Cyrus, and the Koran

Confucius is a major example of a supposed ancient source on human rights, given his role as "arguably the most influential thinker in the history of the human race, and definitely so in China" (Ames and Rosemont 1998, 35). According to the Confucian philosopher Chung-Shu Lo, a special contributor to the 1947 UNESCO project on human rights,[3] "Chinese ethical teaching emphasized the sympathetic attitude of regarding all one's fellow men as having the same desires,

---

3. This was an attempt to find a common international and cross-cultural theoretical underpinning for the concept of universal human rights by canvassing famous intellectuals and statesmen from around the world. It was a colossal failure. Summarized by the French Thomist philosopher Jacques Maritain, although a broad consensus on what are the basic humans rights was obtained, the "ideological contrast [between rights theories] is irreducible and no theoretical reconciliation is possible" (quoted in Normand and Zaidi 2008, 183). The significance of the UNESCO project was further explored in the previous chapter.

and therefore the same rights as one would like to enjoy oneself" (quoted in Ishay 2008, 21). In the *Analects* Confucius does say that "Human beings are similar in their natural tendencies" (17: 2), and he gives a version of the Golden Rule: "do not impose on others what you yourself do not want" (15: 24). But there is no expression of human rights in any of this, not even implicitly. Instead, the reasoning given repeatedly throughout the *Analects* is the importance of social harmony, as when Confucius says, "if the common people do not have confidence in their leaders, community will not endure" (12: 7), or "the ruler of a state or the head of a household: Does not worry that his people are poor, But that wealth is inequitably distributed; Does not worry that his people are too few in number, But that they are disharmonious" (16: 1). His metaphor for social harmony was quite apparently music: "Much can be realized with music if one begins by playing in unison, and then goes on to improvise with purity of tone and distinctness and flow, thereby bringing all to completion" (3: 23).

It is interesting to contrast human rights readers here. According to Micheline Ishay (2007) in her section introducing readings from Confucius and others, she states that "Skeptics regarding claims of an Asian contribution to human rights will find pause for reflection in the writings of Confucius, Kautilya, Asoka, and various Buddhist texts" (23). According to the philosopher Patrick Hayden (2001), on the other hand, in his introduction to his selection from Confucius, "his ethical teachings place great stress on the hierarchical relationships of individuals in society and on the demands of obedience. In a virtuous state, Confucius emphasized that all people have a duty to contribute to its unity and harmony. Thus, Confucius cannot be considered an advocate of what we now think of as the human rights claims of individuals against governing authorities" (271).

Especially interesting in all of this is a book review of an anthology that resulted from a series of conferences on Confucianism and human rights. Marina Svensson (1999) observes that while none of the contributors argues that Confucian classics actually contain explicit human rights ideas, they nevertheless pick and choose passages that seem to imply human rights or that are human rights friendly. One problem with this, she rightly observes, is that "there is a difference between a language of benevolence and a language of rights which the authors tend to gloss over" (483). The difference, I might add, is one of reference, in that injunctions to benevolent actions by no means necessarily refer to *possessions* that we today call "rights," whether conventional or natural. Svensson also points out, interestingly, that the contributors "tend to forget, or ignore, other central tenets of Confucianism, such as its hierarchical nature, the low status of women, etc., which are at odds with contemporary human rights ideas" (483–484). The charge, of course, is that they gerrymander, which is to be expected when presentism is combined with ethnocentrism. At any rate, Hayden and Svensson would seem to have the objective assessment here. For example, in the *Analects* Confucius gives his daughter to one of his disciples for marriage and his niece to another disciple for the same purpose (5: 1–2), in each case apparently because he thought the men would make good husbands.

Another highly instructive example is Cyrus the Great. According to Lily Mazahery, for example, a human rights lawyer and political activist in Iran, Cyrus the Great was "the first messenger of the Universal Declaration of Human Rights, during his coronation as the Emperor of Persia (now Iran) in 539 B.C." ("Lily Mazahery Challenges Khatami"). Cyrus's proclamations were recorded on a stone cylinder, which was discovered in 1879 and now resides in the British Museum. Mazahery is not alone in her estimation of Cyrus. According to an entry in Wikipedia ("History of Human Rights"), Cyrus's cylinder is "recognized by many today as the first human rights document."

Clearly in the case of Cyrus, presentism is afoot, combined in many cases with ethnocentrism (it was two or three Persian students who one day after class politely first brought to my attention Cyrus on human rights). Among his proclamations, Cyrus gave his people religious freedom, abolished slavery, disavowed oppression, and allowed people to live and work wherever they wanted "provided that they never violate others' rights." Cyrus was truly great, but if we confine ourselves to the translations of his proclamations presented on Mazahery's website, we find not the concept of universal human rights but rather that of conventional rights, rights given and taken away. For example, he says if anyone oppresses others in his kingdom, "I will take his or her right back and penalize the oppressor."

Even more flagrant are attempts to see the concept of universal human rights in the Koran. According to the framers of the Universal Islamic Declaration of Human Rights, published in 1981, "Islam gave to mankind an ideal code of human rights fourteen centuries ago. These rights aim at conferring honour and dignity on mankind and eliminating exploitation, oppression and injustice." This claim is based on what is written in the Koran and in the Sunnah ("the example or way of life of the Prophet, embracing what he said, did, or agreed to"). More recently and definitely more interestingly, Riffat Hassan (1996), Professor of Religious Studies at the University of Louisville in Kentucky, claims not only that the Koran provides an "affirmation of fundamental rights which all human beings ought to possess" (371), in that "a large part of its concern is to free human beings from the bondage of traditionalism, authoritarianism (religious, political, economic, or any other), tribalism, racism, sexism, slavery or anything else ..." (370), but she also apparently thinks that the Koran is the earliest source of all these wonders, since she believes that the Koran is "the Magna Carta of human rights."

Hassan and all those who are like-minded are seriously mistaken on basically two counts. Beginning with the second count, the Magna Carta, ironically for Hassan's argument, was not a document professing human rights. First written in 1215 and modified over the next ten years, the Carta or Charta was written by rebellious English land barons against a cash-strapped King John, who wanted to tax them excessively. The signing of the Magna Carta by the king, forced into a corner by the capture of London, resulted in the forming of the English Parliament, which meant the subjection of the monarchy to English law. Interestingly, King John died a year after signing the Carta, and a year later, so as to gain support for the new monarch (his nine-year-old son, Henry III), the coverage of the document was changed from "any baron" to "any freeman," as in Article 1: "We furthermore grant and give to all the freemen of our realm for ourselves and our heirs in perpetuity the liberties written below and to have and to hold them and their heirs from us and our heirs in perpetuity" (www.archives.gov). The bottom line is that a document that purports to "grant and give" what are called "liberties" to a minority of people in one nation (in this case England) is not at all a document concerning universal human rights.

Second, the Koran does not contain the concept of universal human rights. (Taking the Sunnah into account will not change anything here.) Hassan claims that the Koran does contain the concept, that, for example, the Koran "upholds the sanctity and absolute value of human life" (371), such as where God declares human life "to be sacred" (6: 151) and where God confers "dignity on the children of Adam" (17: 70). There is a problem of translation here, as Hassan uses an English translation of the Koran that is slanted to suit her purposes. Looking at a different translation, a blatantly presentist one at that (Ali 2001), the two passages Hassan cites above read as "Do not take a life which God has forbidden" (6: 151) and "We have honored the children of Adam" (17: 70). These are hardly the same as proclaiming "the sanctity and absolute value of human life."

But aside from matters of translation (and Hassan's hyperbole), even if God in the Koran would proclaim that humans have inherent value and dignity, it would not be the same as proclaiming that humans have human rights. Logically the claims are different. This should be evident from the fact that there is no contradiction in claiming that human life is sacred and has dignity but humans were not born with moral claims and entitlements (human rights). This is evident alone in the case where humans are supposed to be the property of their maker and their maker is the only one with the rights, which is quite apparently the claim in the Koran. Not only did God create the universe from "nothingness" (2: 117) and later humans from earth (4: 1), but "all that is in the heavens and the earth belongs to God; and God is sufficient as guardian. He could take you away if He will, O men, and replace you with others: God has the power to do so" (4: 132–133). As with the Bible before it (from which Muhammad borrowed much), the only natural rights in the Koran seem to be God's, given also that "He cannot be questioned about what He does" (21: 23).

The same problems apply to other supposed human rights affirmations in the Koran, such as equality between the sexes, antislavery, and freedom of religion. One can find individual passages that seem to affirm these values (e.g., 3: 195; 2: 177; and 2: 256, respectively). But to maintain the facade, one has to do some serious gerrymandering. Beginning with the sexes, no one reading the Koran with an objective mind will see a lack of male chauvinism when the Koran itself is explicitly addressed only to men, when a man can have up to four wives (4: 3), when believing women have to wear veils (24: 31), when on reproduction "Women are like fields for you; so seed them as you intend" (2: 223), and when on inheritance "the share of the male is equivalent to that of two females" (4: 10, 176).

As for slavery, granted, it is sometimes said in the Koran that slaves are to be freed, but we have to be careful here. In one passage in the Koran it says, "free those slaves you possess who wish to buy their freedom after a written undertaking, if you know they have some goodness" (24: 33). The underlying claim is that human slavery is indeed permissible, not that slavery is wrong or that it violates human rights. All it says is that slaves should be freed if they want to be and if they are judged by their master as good enough to be freed. In another passage the Muslim reader is told to free a slave "who is a believer" when the master has killed a believer "by mistake" (4: 92). In yet another passage it is said that the "expiation" for breaking an oath, among other things, is "freeing a slave" (5: 89). In both of these passages the idea is one of penance, not at all that humans have a fundamental right to not be slaves.

It is even more difficult to see how the Koran offers freedom of religion when it has lines such as "your open enemies are the infidels" (4: 101) and "Cursed be the people who do not believe!" (23: 44), when true believers are instructed to "do away with" apostates (4: 89), possibly even "seize them and kill them wherever they are" (4: 91), and when it repeatedly threatens unbelievers with eternal hell punishment. My favorite passage is, "And those who disbelieve Our revelations shall be cast into Hell; and when their skin is burnt up and singed, We shall give them a new coat that they may go on tasting the agony of punishment" (4: 56). A later chapter adds that "They will live in it [hellfire] for ever, and will find no savior or helper" (33: 65).

By now the pattern should be familiar. It is presentism combined with gerrymandering motivated often by ethnocentrism widely conceived (taken to include not just ethnicity but also culture and religion). The belief in universal human rights has become so widespread, deep, and popular that the temptation is often irresistible, even to those who should know better (i.e., professional scholars), to think that one's preferred ancient or medieval source "must" have had the idea as well. Interestingly, presentism, gerrymandering, and ethnocentrism are kinds of thinking that actually help to further spread and strengthen the belief in universal human rights, such that each might in fact be an unconscious memetic strategy (memetics shall be discussed in Chapter 6), which might help to explain the sins of these professional scholars. But the fact remains that each of these kinds of thinking is a kind of bad reasoning, and it should be evident by now that there is enormous bad reasoning all around on the topic of human rights.

Ancient Greeks

According to the classicist Richard Bauman (2000), a Fellow of the Australian Academy of the Humanities, the ancient Greeks embodied the concept of human rights in their use of the term *philanthropia*. They used this term in a variety of contexts, such as goodwill from superiors toward inferiors, anyone's friendship or affection for another human being, the making of treaties, and as a "curb on brutality." In the case of Pericles's famous Funeral Oration as narrated by Thucydides, Bauman claims that "Thucydides gives only the substance of human rights, not the label" (11).

Something is curiously amiss in all of this, however. This is because the friendship love (*philia*) of humans (*anthropos*) is not at all the same concept as that of universal human rights. The latter is the concept of a particular kind of possession, namely, moral claims and entitlements that all humans have by virtue of being human. *Philanthropia,* on the other hand, is either an act or a possession, and even as a possession it is a very different kind of possession than that of human rights. This is because *philanthropia,* as a possession, is that of a *personal virtue,* which as such does not at all require or entail the possession of human rights on the part of those who benefit from philanthropic acts.

One can have the concept without the term, of course, but then one needs a greater amount of evidence to justify ascribing the concept to one who lacks the term. Looking at Bauman's example of Pericles's Funeral Oration, what we find is not at all the concept of human rights, but instead a long homage to the virtues of Athenians and their ancestors, such as their bravery, generosity, and lack of softness, all of which is prefaced by the claim that Athens was the first democracy, dedicated to "the multitude" and employing "an equality amongst all men in point of law for their private controversies" (Grene 1989, 109). In all of this there is no "substance" of human rights. There is not even a veneer. This should be sufficiently evident not only from the fact that Athenian democracy was extremely limited, including as citizens only adult males of a certain status, meaning roughly one-eighth to one-tenth of the total population (Hale 2001, 102; Dunn 2006, 35), but from the fact that women, children, and slaves were viewed basically as property, while barbarians (non-Greeks) were viewed mainly as inferior.

Bauman finds greater use of the term *philanthropia* in fourth-century Greece and during the Hellenistic period, but his evidence is simply a further extension of his presentism. The bottom line is that the ancient Greeks did not have the concept of human rights, either in thought or in practice. And we should not be surprised, given that their psychological presuppositions did not extend reason and dignity equitably to the human species.

Nor were ancient Greek philosophers much better in this regard, among whom the two most important were Plato and Aristotle. And yet selections of their writings are routinely included in human rights readers, not because they explicitly advocated human rights, but because they are seen as early "representatives of the natural law tradition" (Hayden 2001, 3), as strong advocates of the rationality of human beings (13, 24), and for having had "a profound impact on the development of the notion of justice and human rights" (Ishay 2007, 8).

Ishay (2008) goes further into specifics, stating that "Plato was among the first Western thinkers to assert that women had similar abilities to men, and that depending upon their individual capacities, they should be able to fulfill the same tasks as their male counterparts" (53). This, however, hardly "planted the seeds" (58) for later debates about human rights, in this case about equal human rights between men and women. Certainly Plato was far ahead of his time in having women in his ideal republic participate in leadership as "philosopher-kings" because of an equal share in reason and a corresponding capacity for knowledge (*Republic* V). Also in his dialogue on creation Plato has the Demiurge create all human souls, equal in number to the stars, and show them the timeless Forms. These non-embodied souls are then put into mortal human bodies (they are not to be gods, after all), all humans beginning as equals (*Timaeus* 41d–e). But that is where the rosy picture ends. The original human bodies are male bodies, and those souls that are unable to master themselves are reincarnated as women, or if really wicked, into lower levels, as animals of appropriate nature (42c, 76e, 91a). Women thus for Plato were the first major stage of degeneration below men (both psychically and physically), and this was reflected in his theory of reproduction: "they [men] sow the seed into the ploughed field of her womb" (91d). All of this merely adds to the argument that female rulers in Plato's best political system were not really thought by Plato to be equals to male rulers. The former were, instead, "manly souls" in female bodies, as a feminist scholar aptly puts it (Spelman 1994, 101).

Nor can one reasonably get out of Plato's concept of social justice any legitimate inspiration for the modern concept of universal human rights. In terms of social roles, Plato simply refused to give up the principle of assigning "different ways of life to different natures and the same ones to the same" (*Republic* 454b). What is rarely appreciated by those who read Plato is the real nature of the ideal political state that he develops in the *Republic*, which is summarized as "purely totalitarian" by Karl Popper in *The Open Society and Its Enemies, Volume I: The Spell of Plato* (1945, 169). Not only does Popper emphasize Plato's advocacy of extreme censorship in his ideal state, including religion, painting, poetry, and music, but he also focuses on Plato's advocacy of propaganda, most notably the "noble lie," the teaching that each person was born with one of four metals, this to reinforce the division of labor (414b–415d). The state is to be controlled by philosopher-kings, to be sure, those with the necessary knowledge and wisdom based on the eternal truths, the Forms, but the philosopher-kings are taken out of the military caste, which itself receives special education and selective breeding, and together they control the masses, the workers. The analogy Plato draws is to his theory of the just soul, in which the rational part combines with the spirited part to control the appetitive part. The psychology might appeal to common sense, but when compared to the political state, "control" becomes an ominous key word. As Popper (1945) puts it, "with all his uncompromising canvas-cleaning,... [Plato] was forced to combat free thought, and the pursuit of truth.... to defend lying, political miracles, tabooistic superstition, the suppression of truth, and ultimately, brutal violence" (200).

There is nothing like human slavery to highlight this point. According to Ishay (2008), "there was no discussion of the tasks of slaves in Plato's *Republic*, which led some to argue that Plato was implicitly calling for the abolition of slavery" (53–54). This is a naive statement at best, and grossly misleading at worst. Plato explicitly advocated slavery in the *Republic* (433d) and also in his later work, the *Laws* (777b–778a, 966b). As the eminent Greek scholar Gregory Vlastos (1981) puts it, "If he [Plato] wanted to abolish it [slavery], he would have argued—which he does not" (140), to which he adds that a possible reason Plato barely mentions slavery in the *Republic* is that he did not think of slaves as part of the *polis* (city-state) but only of the *oikia* (home) (141).

All of the above, combined with Plato's claim that democracy is the second worst of all political systems, a "diseased" form of government second only to "genuine tyranny" (*Republic* 544c), should make it obvious that not only did Plato not have the concept of universal human rights, but also to see him as a contributor to the concept is absurd. The bottom line is not simply that the letter of universal human rights is missing in Plato's concept of social justice, but most important that the spirit is missing as well.

With Aristotle the absurdity should be even more immediate. Aristotle is sometimes called "the father of natural law" (Shellens 1959, 72). Natural law theory (sometimes also called "common law" theory) is the family of theories that claim that divine rationality and moral law are woven into the very fabric of nature, including human nature, and that human reason is capable of discerning it. It is a law, moreover, held to be binding on all, no matter our conventional/political laws, such that the latter should attempt to correspond to the former as much as possible. That Aristotle was a natural law theorist, however, let alone the father of it, is highly questionable (Miller 1991).

Let us look at what is not questionable. In *Politics* (Barnes 1984) we are told by Aristotle not only that "man is by nature a political animal" (1253^{a}3) but also that "man is the only animal who has the gift of speech" (1253^{a}9), that man "alone has any sense of good and evil" (1253^{a}16), and that "man has reason,... and man only" (1332^{b}5). This looks good. But then there is Aristotle's theory of nature and hierarchy, which was that everything not only exists for a purpose but also that the lower exists for the sake of the higher. For instance, anticipating the idea of the Great Chain of Being or scale of nature (minus the creationism) that would dominate thought until the time of Darwin, Aristotle states that "we may infer that, after the birth of animals, plants exist for their sake, and that the other animals exist for the sake of man" (1256^{b}15). Again, he says, "in the world both of nature and of art the inferior always exist for the sake of the superior" (1333^{a}22).

This again looks good, until we notice that for Aristotle not all humans are equal, not psychologically or morally, even though we are all of the same basic (atomic) species. Some people are masters by nature, some are slaves by nature, each "from the hour of their birth" (1254^{a}22), the latter having "no deliberative faculty" (1260^{a}12). Hence masters are better off having slaves and slaves are better off having masters, it is best for both of them, since to live well a master needs others to provide the physical labor necessary for a good life (1253^{b}26) and a slave is incapable of being master of himself (1254^{b}22). A slave, instead, is "intended by nature to be governed" (1265^{b}25), such that he is not much better than a tame work animal (1254^{b}24), the latter of which are better off "when they are ruled by man; for then they are preserved" (1254^{b}11–12). But more than that, "a slave is a living possession" (1253^{b}32), so much so that "the slave is a part of the master, a living but separated part of his bodily frame" (1255^{b}11).

Women at best, for Aristotle, are roughly right in the middle of natural masters and natural slaves on the scale, since they have a deliberative faculty but "it is without authority." Children, at best (and they would have to be male), have an authoritative deliberative faculty but "it is immature." So, for Aristotle, "the freeman rules over the slave after another manner from that in which the male rules over the female, or the man over the child" (1260ª10–15). In all of this, Aristotle reminds us that "nothing which is contrary to nature is good" (1325ᵇ10).

But it does not stop there. Non-Hellenes, that is, barbarians, including non-Hellenic Europeans to a degree but especially Asiatics, are "a community of slaves, male and female," with "no natural ruler among them" (1252ᵇ6–7). In other words, "the people are by nature slaves," evident alone from the fact that they "do not rebel against a despotic government" (1285ª21–22). Hence Aristotle cites approvingly "the poets" who say, "It is meet that Hellenes should rule over barbarians," adding that it is "as if they thought that the barbarian and the slave were by nature one" (1252ᵇ8–9).[4]

Finally, Aristotle says, "the weaker are always asking for equality and justice, but the stronger care for none of these things" (1318ª4). Indeed for Aristotle the preeminent man, the vastly superior individual, "may truly be deemed a God among men," and he adds that for such persons there is no law, for "they are themselves a law" (1284ª10–14). So any city that has one, or a few of them, should make him or they "supreme over all," as a king or royal family (1288ª16–19).

Clearly, if Aristotle was the father of natural law theory, he was not at all a precursor of the theory of universal human rights, let alone a contributor to it. Far more interesting (and usually just as bad) are the attempts to see the concept of universal human rights in those who were clearly natural law theorists: in particular, Cicero and Ulpian, medieval scholars such as Huguccio and Ockham, or the Enlightenment thinkers Grotius, Hobbes, and Pufendorf.

---

4. All of this, interestingly, is despite Aristotle's apparent admiration for barbarian leaders such as Cyrus who "have given their country freedom"—this in the context of his claim that "royalty ranks with aristocracy, for it is based upon merit, . . . or on benefits conferred" (*Politics* 1310b33–36)—and that elsewhere he praises the Persian system of preserving wealth (*Economics* 1344ᵇ30). On the other hand, given that Aristotle thought that Asiatics were not capable of ruling themselves, he could not have thought that giving them their freedom would be a good thing. Moreover, Aristotle finds Persian rule "tyrannical," whether it is the father in the home, where he treats his sons as slaves, or the leader of the state (*Ethics* 1160ᵇ27–33, *Politics* 1313ª34–ᵇ10). "Tyranny" is defined by Aristotle as a "perversion" of government, as "a kind of monarchy which has in view the interest of the monarch only" (*Politics* 1279ᵇ7), whereas "true forms of government" are where "the one, or the few, or the many, govern with a view to the common interest" (1279ª27–28).

Ancient Romans

Richard Bauman (2000) claims not only that "the Roman model [of human rights] was the ancestor of modern human rights" (9), but that "the notion of human rights was well understood in Ancient Rome" (8). "The picture is admittedly clouded by the dark side," he adds, but then "so is the modern institution." Accepting the latter point, the former does not stand up to scrutiny. Bauman bases his claim largely on the concepts of *humanitas,* universalism, and natural law. The Latin term *ius humanum,* he says, was "an almost exact terminological equivalent for the modern 'human rights'" (21), the "closest equivalent to the expression 'human rights'" (28). In all of this the statesman, lawyer, and philosopher Cicero looms the largest in his argument, and it is important to see why Bauman is wrong about both Cicero in particular and ancient Rome in general.

According to Bauman, the term *humanitas* denoted "an attribute of the human race" (9) which, though it was an umbrella term, included meanings such as *clementia, moderatio,* and *pietas* (6). Cicero, he says, one of the earliest users of the term, used it some 150 times in his writings (137n1) and believed that "*humanitas* can only exist when founded on law" (47).

One problem with this concerns the meaning of *humanitas* itself. According to the classicist Christopher Francese (2007), *humanitas* referred to a moral virtue, "a disposition toward compassion and sympathy toward others" (227). Cicero added to the concept the modern idea of a liberal education, which he thought would promote the virtue of *humanitas* as traditionally understood (hence our modern meaning of the "humanities" in colleges and universities, the idea that a liberal education in the humanities will make us better persons and citizens). Whether the wide or narrow meaning, *humanitas* could not possibly have meant the same thing as "human rights," for the simple reason that a virtue is not the same sort of thing as a right. If I have the virtue of generosity, for example, that does not entail that you or anyone else has a right to the benefits of my generosity. Moreover, someone might have rights but no human virtues whatsoever, only vices. What seals the point of difference is that the term *humanitas* was used to refer to the treatment of or disposition not just toward humans but, as Francese points out, toward animals as well. Even Bauman quotes Cicero, using the term in reference to the treatment of humans and "dumb animals" (39). Clearly, then, *humanitas* could not have meant the same thing as "human rights."

Another problem with Bauman's thesis concerns the concept of *ius gentium.* The ancient Romans had two words for law. One was *lex,* which meant man-made laws that were part of a political system; hence what is today called "positive law" or "statutes." The other was *ius* (sometimes spelled *jus,* either way the root of our word *justice*), which had a much broader meaning, including not only *lex* but also unwritten laws, moral laws, laws given by the gods, and rights conferred by law (Zetzel 1999, xl). Hence you had *ius civile* ("civil law"), which could vary between states such as Athens and Rome, *ius gentium* ("law of nations"), which was universal or common legal practices among humans, and *ius naturale* ("natural law"), which was built into nature, including human nature, by the gods (more on this below). Bauman claims that *ius gentium* in Roman law was "virtually synonymous with natural law, and the latter in turn embraced human rights" (29). The synonymy was arguably Cicero's interpretation of Roman law along with many others, but that the concept of *ius gentium* "embraced human rights" is an enormous leap.

This becomes apparent when we focus on Cicero's use of *ius gentium*. According to Bauman, Cicero combined *humanitas* with natural law and was not the only one "to detect the link" (48). To be sure, even though Cicero was not technically a Stoic, Cicero borrowed heavily from the Stoic concept of natural law. What we shall see, however, is that he could not possibly have included the concept of human rights. One of Cicero's most complete statements on natural law occurs in Book 1 of his *De Legibus* (*On the Laws*; Zetzel 1999). According to Cicero, the gods gave humans, but not other animals, "a share in reason and thought" (§22), including a "soul," such that this created "a family relationship between us and the gods" (§24). Furthermore, says Cicero, "virtue is the same in human and god," all with the result that there are "common bonds among human beings" (§28). So what is the relationship between this universalism and justice? The relationship is *ius gentium*. Those who share reason share "right reason," he says, and that means "we humans must be considered to be closely allied to gods by law," to which he adds, "those who share law also share the procedures of justice" (§22). In short, Cicero defines *ius gentium* as "right reason in commands and prohibitions" (§33). Again he says, "law is the highest reason, rooted in nature, which commands things that must be done and prohibits the opposite" (§18). And again, this time in Book 3 of *De Republica* (*On the Commonwealth*; Zetzel 1999), he says, "True law is right reason, consonant with nature, spread through all people. It is constant and eternal; it summons to duty by its orders, it deters from crime by its prohibitions" (§33).

The problem here should by now be clear. Commands and prohibitions, along with duties and orders, are not the same concepts as rights, let alone universal human rights. What clinches this, in the case of Cicero, is his critique of democracy in Book 1 of *De Republica*, in which he states that "when everything is done by the people itself, no matter how just and moderate it may be, that very equality is itself inequitable, in that it recognizes no degrees of status" (§43). As Francese (2007) points out, the concept of equal dignity "was never contemplated in the ancient world." Cicero, he points out, "defines justice [in *De Inventione*] as a habit of mind that gives to each his *dignitas* while preserving the common good" (128). The "while" is key, for the common good among humans, according to Cicero, the object of "right reason," represented best in his mind by the *Pax Romana* of the Republic of Rome, requires *hierarchy*, and hence an *inequality* in dignity and privileges. This comes out clearly in Book 3 of his *De Oficiis* (*On Duties*; Griffin and Atkins 1991), which is about human duties with respect to natural law, and that for Cicero means the benefit of the common good. In a particularly telling passage, he says that in the case of starvation "the necessities of life should be transferred from an inactive and useless person to someone who is wise, good and brave, who, if he were to die, would greatly detract from the common benefit" (§31). Bauman's square peg fails to fit into the round hole after all. And the round hole largely explains what Bauman (2000) finds difficult to understand: why Cicero did not seriously object to "the slaughter at the games" and why "very few people objected to it" (44), and also why Cicero was "not a champion of slaves' rights" (37) and why slaves in ancient Rome were "both a human being and a piece of property" (115). The lack of an abolitionist movement against the games and against human slavery provides the most obvious reason for the most obvious conclusion, which is that the ancient Romans, Cicero among them, did not have the concept of universal human rights.

Cicero lived from 106 to 43 B.C. Another Roman lawyer and statesmen who is touted as being a pioneer of human rights, and who is in some ways a better candidate, is Ulpian, who lived from A.D. 170 to 224. Ulpian was born in Syria and became part of an inner circle of legal advisors and administrators to the Roman Emperor Septimius Severus, who himself was from North Africa (Tripoli) and was the first Roman emperor to be not entirely Italian. Severus, whose second marriage was to a woman from Syria, began a short dynasty that consisted mainly of himself and Caracalla, his oldest son from this wife. This dynasty marks a profound change in the Roman Empire in that Severus, continued by Caracalla, changed the Roman Empire from an Italian empire centered in Rome to a cosmopolitan society, with people of free birth in all the provinces receiving equal citizenship and rights with Roman citizens. For this purpose a cosmopolitan system of law was required. Ulpian, producing most of his works under Caracalla, wrote (by dictation) a massive survey and interpretation of Roman law, for the benefit of magistrates and citizens alike, in which he emphasized the egalitarian nature of Roman law. (Even Severus and Caracalla, who were officially above the law, were said by Ulpian to have put themselves under the law.)

Ulpian's influence was enormous, and it is perhaps no mistake to call him the most important of all Roman lawyers. Roughly 40 percent of Justinian's *Digest* was taken from Ulpian's writings. Justinian I was emperor of the Eastern Roman Empire from 527 to 565. He was responsible for what came to be called the

Corpus Juris Civilis (*Body of Civil Law*), a codification of Roman law from past
to present, which was created from 529 to 534. The second part of this work,
the *Digest,* consisted of a collection of Roman legal writings from the second and
third centuries. The influence of Justinian's *Corpus Juris Civilis* continued in the
East throughout the Middle Ages into the Renaissance and beyond, and also in
the West with the rediscovery of the *Corpus* in the late eleventh century.

According to Tony Honoré (2002), Emeritus Professor of Civil Law at Oxford
University, not only "By a process of osmosis Europe's view of law has been formed
more by Ulpian than by any other lawyer" (229), but also Ulpian was a major
"pioneer of human rights" (the subtitle of the second edition of his book but not
of the first), "the first lawyer who can ... properly count as the pioneer of the
human rights movement" (76). The word "pioneer," of course, can be taken in
a number of ways. For example, a pioneer of a concept might have contributed
to the eventual formation of the concept but not actually had it, or might have
contributed parts of a concept but not had the whole. Neither of these modest
claims, however, is Honoré's. Instead his claim is not only that Ulpian actually
had the modern concept of universal human rights but also that he was "the first
lawyer to champion human rights" (back jacket), "the first human rights lawyer"
(86), and that he did more to develop and promote the idea of human rights than
anyone else in antiquity. Here is how Honoré puts it in his Preface:

> Drawing mainly on the Stoic conception of natural law, his philosophy allows slaves
> the share in human dignity that is required by the belief that human beings are born
> free and equal. At present, when human rights are widely debated, it may promote
> a balanced view to see them in a perspective that goes back to antiquity. Human
> rights are not a product of the Enlightenment, still less of the twentieth century, as
> some otherwise well-educated people suppose. The values of equality, freedom, and
> dignity, to which human rights give effect, formed the basis of Ulpian's exposition
> of Roman law as the law of a cosmopolis. [ix]

There is a logical problem here right from the start. Assuming it is true that the
belief in human rights "give effect" to the values of equality, freedom, and dignity,
it does not automatically follow that the values of equality, freedom, and dignity
"give effect" to the belief in human rights. This is because the concepts are not
the same, as pointed out in the Introduction. Hence there is no contradiction in
Peter Singer, for example, as we have seen in Chapter 2 and shall further see in
Chapter 7, defending the values of human equality, freedom, and dignity but not
believing in the existence of human rights.

Of course, if Ulpian did in fact have the values of human equality, freedom,
and dignity, it is possible that he might also have had the belief in universal human
rights, including the core of the concept that constitutes the dominant moral

discourse of our world today. But are there good reasons to believe that he even had the concept?

In trying to answer this question, one should keep in mind a saying used by Carl Sagan in his video series *Cosmos,* when he turned to claims about the paranormal: "Extraordinary claims require extraordinary evidence." (I do not know whether Sagan originated this saying, but he provides the earliest expression of it as far as I know.) It would be extraordinary if Ulpian had the modern concept of universal human rights, when it can be shown, as we have already seen, that other proposed candidates in antiquity did not.

Certainly one cannot make the jump from natural law to universal human rights, given alone that, unlike the Stoics, "Ulpian asserts that natural law applies to all animals, whether domesticated or wild" (82). Honoré attempts to avoid this difficulty by stating that "respect for animals so far as they have reason ... is not the same thing as attributing rights to animals." This is true. But if natural law applies to all animals, in Ulpian's view, and if Ulpian's belief in natural law is the basis of his being "the first lawyer to champion human rights," which is Honoré's view, then it follows that whatever Ulpian had in mind cannot be close to what today is meant by "human rights," since the modern consensus concept of human rights does not apply to animals (they are called "*human* rights," after all). In other words, if belief in natural law is the basis of Ulpian's version of human rights, then he can hardly be a pioneer of the modern concept.

But there is more to the argument. According to Honoré, "These three values, freedom, equality, and dignity, are the essential elements of what we now term human rights," and Ulpian, he says, in elaborating on the new constitution of Rome that extended Roman citizenship to all the free people of the empire, "expounds Roman law as a law based on the view that all people are born free and equal and that all possess dignity" (76). Of course there is more to the modern consensus concept of universal human rights than that, much more, as I emphasize repeatedly throughout this book. But let us see whether Ulpian actually professed the three values named here, or whether Honoré is being both extravagant and presentist.

(i) All people are born free. As Francese (2007, 167) and many others have pointed out, including Honoré (2002, 86), the ancient Romans, particularly by Ulpian's time, thought that slaves were slaves only by convention, that they were slaves as a matter of bad luck rather than bad genes, as we would put it today. Hence it was not uncommon for slaves to lawfully gain their freedom and even become citizens of Rome. Ulpian himself went so far, as Honoré puts it, as to say that "Slavery is the prime example of an institution contrary to nature but recognized by the *ius gentium,* which 'encroached on' (*invasit*) the law of nature"

(80). In this way, says Honoré, Ulpian placed the law of nature above the law of nations, as "morally superior to it." But Ulpian's use of *invasit* does not automatically mean he believed that all humans have a "natural right" to not be enslaved, in line with the Universal Declaration of Human Rights (Art. 4), or even that slavery is immoral. He might have thought, like Cicero, that slavery is necessary for the common good. He could have simply meant, then, that slavery violates or attacks (*invasit*) the natural reason of slaves, much as it does animals, which we have seen Ulpian includes as partaking of natural law. In other words, his claim might have been merely descriptive rather than prescriptive.

Today, when human freedom is spoken of as a human right, it is broken down into a number of human rights, such as the right to freedom of speech and the right to freedom of religion; it is not simply the right to not be enslaved. It would be impressive if Ulpian, therefore, had something positive to say about these other freedoms as well, especially if he used the words *iura humanum*. But the evidence is lacking. In the case of freedom of religion, even just the minimal sense of freedom of conscience (which is the modern sense in human rights discourse), we don't find a positive statement. Honoré states that for Ulpian "A tolerant attitude to religious diversity, such as the *Augustan History* attributed to Alexander Severus, is not ruled out" (83). But the lack of a statement either for religious tolerance or against religious intolerance is hardly a statement in favor of religious tolerance. A positive statement is required. Otherwise we have the fallacy of *appeal to ignorance.*

(ii) All people are equal. According to Ulpian, "For though in civil law slaves are considered not to exist, it is different in natural law. So far as natural law is concerned, all men are equal" (88)—*quod attinet ad ius civile, servi pro nullis habentur: non tamen et iure naturali, quia, quod ad ius naturale attinet, omnes hominess aequales sunt*" (n110)—to which Honoré adds, "This is said in passing, as self-evident." But what does "equal"/*aequales* mean? Like "similar," it means very little unless a respect or sense is specified. It could mean that all humans are equal in species, equal in being sentient, equal in moral worth, or in the mathematical sense of counting as one. There may still be other possibilities, but the line does not necessarily mean equal in natural rights. That Ulpian might have meant the second possibility in my list is suggested by his statement that "If someone wrongs a slave, but not with a view to insulting the slaveowner, the magistrate must not let the wrong go unpunished, especially if the wrongdoer has beaten or tortured the slave. Obviously even a slave resents that" (87).

Honoré presents no evidence that by "all men are equal" Ulpian meant equality in moral worth, let alone in natural rights. When he does present a clear case of equality, it is between husband and wife, not master and slave. He says Ulpian's "regard for human equality emerges in two texts on the equality of husband and wife," one attacking the double standard in adultery (the wife could be charged with adultery but not vice versa), the other embracing the view that marriage should be for better or worse, which he says expresses a view "which is surely original in the ancient world" (101).

From that concession it is still a long road to the belief in universal human rights, especially given that Ulpian did not advocate the abolition of slavery, unlike genuine human rights theorists, such as Locke and Jefferson (as we shall see in the next chapter).

(iii) All people possess dignity. Here is where Honoré makes his most blatant mistake, a mistake that undermines his entire claim about Ulpian. He states that dignity "can be taken as the overarching value," that "It is in practice those forms of unfreedom and inequality that infringe human dignity that the law, then and now, takes account of and seeks, so far as is consistent with authority, to correct." But then he immediately tells us that "It is true that Ulpian recognizes degrees of dignity. Men have more than women. Married women have more than concubines. Slaves, by implication, often have less. All are equal in that they possess dignity but, in contrast with modern thinking, the degree of dignity varies from person to person" (85). The recognition was apparently not only descriptive, as a feature of Roman society, but prescriptive, given his line that "*maior dignitas est in sexu virili*" (n86)—a line that hardly needs interpretation, except for the word *maior,* a superlative meaning "size" or "degree" (Simpson 1968, 358), and the word *dignitas,* which means not only "worthy" and "worthiness," including "moral worth," but also "reputation," "prestige," and "honor" (Francese 2007, 127). Dignity was not a personal concept, as in "one's sense of dignity," which is often how we use the word *dignity,* but a social concept, one that applied not only to an individual human in relation to his or her society but also, for example, to a lion in his or her social world, whose loss of *dignitas* in old age could consist of indignities committed against it by inferior animals (Francese 2007, 127). Even something such as a building could have *dignitas* or the loss of it (Simpson 1968, 190). But clearly this is not at all the concept of dignity attached to the consensus concept of universal human rights in our modern belief system, according to which all humans possess equal dignity (moral worth, value) by virtue of being human.

When Honoré, therefore, states that in Ulpian's view the value of dignity was the overarching concept but varied in degree from person to person, it logically follows that the values of freedom and equality must have varied as well. If the average man has more inherent *dignitas* than the average woman, then in what sense are they both equal? They are both equal in the sense of being human, but that is trivial, since the man, in having more *dignitas* than the woman, has greater freedoms and also a greater capacity for being wronged. But none of this is consistent with the modern belief in human rights, which is that of universal, equal, innate, and inalienable human rights. Ulpian, then, we shall have to conclude, was no pioneer of the concept.

Medieval Scholars

Keeping with the theme of natural law, some scholars, medievalists, claim that the origin of the concept of universal human rights is not to be found in antiquity but in the late Middle Ages. Richard Tuck (1979), for example, Professor of Government at Harvard University, claims that "two important periods" need to be studied for our modern understanding of human rights. The first period "is clearly the period in which the language first appeared and developed into something close to what we see today," which spans the mid-1100s to the early 1400s. The second period, he says, "is the period of what can be termed the classic texts of rights theory, stretching from Grotius through to Locke" (2), which is basically the 1600s.

With the exception of Locke, I shall show that Tuck and other historians are guilty of the same kinds of errors we have seen already. This will require a look at their principal figures, some in more detail than others, namely, Ockham, Gerson, and Huguccio for the first period, Grotius, Hobbes, and Pufendorf for the second. In Locke (along with the Levellers before him), I shall argue in the next chapter, we find the first clear, unambiguous, and unequivocal expression of the concept of universal human rights and the probable birth of the modern idea. But it is the reason for this birth that shall turn out to be of the greatest interest and importance.

Beginning with the medieval philosopher William of Ockham, who flourished in the early 1300s, the neo-Thomist Michel Villey, in a series of writings published in French primarily during the 1950s and 1960s, argued that Ockham was the first to have a "clear and complete definition of subjective right" and hence was "the father of subjective right" (see Tuck 1979, 7–24; Oakley 2005, 95–100). Ockham is famous today primarily for the principle of parsimony named after him, Ockham's Razor, the idea that one should not multiply explanatory entities beyond necessity, and for his defense of *nominalism,* the idea that only individuals exist and not universals (Spade 1999). Villey argued that prior to Ockham, the word *ius* was used as "right" only in the "objective" sense, as something that is the right thing to do in a particular situation, not in the "subjective" sense of an individual possession. (One has to get used to this terminological distinction, as misleading as it is, for we shall see it again a number of times.) Ockham was embroiled in the then-current dispute over apostolic poverty, the poverty practiced by the early apostles of Jesus and by Ockham's own order of monks, the Franciscans. The Franciscans wanted to believe that they were free of property ownership, that in not owning property (either individually or collectively) they were being pure and true to the example set by Jesus and his apostles. The matter of apostolic poverty raised in stark relief the question of whether humans have a natural right to own property. The distinction was made between *dominium,* individual property ownership, and *utendi,* use but not ownership. The Franciscans took the position that man only has *utendi* (God only has *dominium*), while Pope John XXII determined that Adam, even before the creation of Eve, had *dominium* over the things of the world. Ockham, according to Villey, introduced into the debate the concept of *ius* or right as a *potestas* (a power to do or a power over something) and argued that man has *ius dominium* in the context of human judicial institutions, but only *ius utendi* in a natural state. The strategy apparently was to appease both the Franciscans and the pope; it was to conclude that humans can but need not have *dominium* in their possessions.

None of this about Ockham as the father of human rights is particularly convincing, given the ambiguities of the Latin terms. In fact Pope John XXII would seem the better candidate (Tuck 1979, 22–23), if not for the fact that he made no clear distinction between political rights and natural rights (Tierney 1997, 120–121). What is surely needed from Ockham (and also from Pope John XXII) is a clear claim that humans, all humans, have a natural right to own property as humans (and not as animals), whether inside or outside of a judicial context. That is our modern concept of the human right to property, a right that all humans have by virtue of being human, not by virtue of being part of a judicial system. Indeed the latter is a man-made right, not a natural right—to think otherwise is to confuse the distinction.

Tuck (1979) himself argues that the first clear statement of human rights comes a little later, that it was principally in the writings of the French nominalist Jean Gerson that "the transition was made to a fully fledged natural rights theory." In a book written in 1402, Gerson wrote that

> *Ius* is a dispositional *facultas* or power, appropriate to someone and in accordance with the dictates of right reason.... an entity has *iura,* defined in this way, equivalent to those positive qualities which constitute its identity and therefore its goodness. In this way the sky has the *ius* to rain, the sun to shine, fire to burn, a swallow to build its nest, and every creature to do what is naturally good for it.... So man, even though a sinner, has a *ius* to many things, like other creatures left to their own nature. [Tuck 1979, 25–26]

For Tuck, this was "the first time that an account of a *ius* as a *facultas* had been given. The idea of a *facultas,* an ability, had belonged hitherto mainly to non-moral discourse" (26).

But one has to be extremely careful here. As Tuck makes clear in the very first page of his Introduction, he is concerned to trace the origin of the concept of "human rights," and he laments the confusion that surrounds the modern concept. His view is that "there must be *something* to the language of rights" (1), and so his approach throughout his book is to engage in "something much more like the traditional history of ideas" (2). "Natural rights," however, does not necessarily denote the same concept as "human rights," so that we must resist the temptation to read into natural rights discourse what today is meant by "human rights."

In the case of Gerson, he is pretty clearly a natural rights theorist. Not only humans but also animals and even the sun and clouds have natural rights (and not just to exist but to do things). In the same work, Gerson states that "every creature has a *ius* directly from God to take inferior things into its own use for its own preservation. Each has this *ius* as a result of fair and irrevocable justice" (27). Natural rights according to Gerson, therefore, are God-given rights, and that, as we shall see in the next chapter, is the same foundation for the modern concept of human rights. But natural rights, even God-given ones, must not be identified or confused with human rights, even God-given ones. For our modern concept of human rights is that of *universal* human rights, rights that *all* humans have by virtue of being human. Moreover, according to the modern concept all humans have these rights *equally,* since we are all equally human. None of this is in the prime passages chosen by Tuck, and so I take it as a safe bet that they are not to be found anywhere in Gerson's writings.

What we have instead, then, in the case of Tuck on Gerson, is a case of presentism, reading the present into the past. Gerson accorded to humans natural rights, apparently even natural moral rights, but that does not automatically mean that he thought that all humans have them and have them equally. Nor is there any evidence, at least as presented by Tuck, that Gerson thought human rights are rights that humans can claim not only against each other but also against the state, against perhaps even God. Gerson wrote that "the humble have been given a right to all things which are to be possessed and held in *dominium,* not by civil law but by divine law," but this does not warrant us to say, as Tuck does, that "According to Gerson, men have rights against God as a result of God's promise to them" (30). Nor does it even warrant us to say that Gerson thought that humans have rights that they can claim equally against each other, for the term "the humble" does not necessarily mean that all humans are on a par, that no humans can have natural rights over other humans, such as property rights (slavery). Until we have that claim, we do not have the modern concept of universal human rights, and it is presentism to think otherwise.

All of this might be unnecessary, however. According to the medievalist Brian Tierney (1997), Bowmar Professor Emeritus in Humanistic Studies at Cornell University, the human rights talk of nominalists such as Gerson and Ockham before him was not a development from their nominalist philosophy, but instead was merely borrowed from earlier medieval scholars who provided commentaries or "glosses" on Gratian's *Decretum*. The *Decretum*, or *Harmony of Discordant Canons* (Christensen 1993), completed around 1140, was an attempt by a scholarly Italian monk named Gratian to synthesize and harmonize the discordant texts within Church law, going all the way back to the Bible. Shortly afterward, given the accidental rediscovery of Justinian's *Corpus Juris Civilis* in northern Italy around 1070, which reintroduced the work to the West, other scholars added considerations of Roman law to the *Decretum* as well as their own glosses, the latter of which were written into the four margins surrounding the main text of the *Decretum*. According to Tierney, none of these glossators—Rufinus, Ricardus, Huguccio, Alanus, and others, names that will not be recognized except by specialists in medieval studies—wrote a specific treatise on natural rights. Instead, "Their patterns of thought have to be reconstructed from scattered, sometimes laconic glosses on a variety of topics" (54). That by itself should begin to make one suspicious, given alone what we have examined in the case of Bauman and the ancient Romans.

I will cut to the chase, simply by focusing on Tierney's best evidence from one of the glossators whom he thinks most clearly expressed the concept of human rights, namely, Huguccio, who died in 1210. I say "human rights," for Tierney makes no distinction between "human rights" and "natural rights." The "idea of natural rights," he says, not only "first grew into existence" among the "medieval jurists," but is "a moral one.... rights that ought to be recognized in all societies because they are necessary for the fulfillment of some basic human needs and purposes" (5). Not only Locke and Jefferson, then, for Tierney, but at least some of the glossators of the *Decretum* had basically the same concept, too, and "not just some vague idea of a natural right, but many of the specific themes that we encounter in modern works on rights" (7).

Turning to Huguccio, then, who for Tierney of all the Decretists is "the greatest of them all" (64), Tierney tells us that Huguccio distinguished between different meanings of the term *ius naturale,* something Gratian had not done. One was "reason, namely a natural force of the soul," another was moral laws known by reason, such as the biblical rule "Do not do to others what you do not want done to yourself." But the two meanings, says Tierney, were not for Huguccio equally proper meanings of the term. "If audacity be granted," wrote Huguccio, "I will safely say that this [the latter of the two meanings] is improperly called *ius naturale.*"

Elsewhere he wrote that "The things set out here are not natural *ius* or natural *iura* but each is an effect of *ius naturale* or derives from it." For Tierney, then, "In his more lenient moods, Huguccio did acknowledge that *ius naturale* could mean a rule of conduct, a 'judgment of reason'; but this was a secondary, derivative meaning. For Huguccio, *ius naturale* in its primary sense was always an attribute of individual persons, 'a force of the soul,' associated with human rationality" (65).

That's it! The modern concept of human rights! Rights that all humans have equally by virtue of being human! Rights that all humans are born with and that cannot be given up or taken away! That Tierney is guilty of presentism here is evident alone from what he says about the Ten Commandments, such as the commandment not to steal: "To say that 'Thou shalt not steal' is a command of natural law is to imply that others have a right to acquire property, a point that medieval jurists clearly grasped" (33). We have seen earlier in this chapter that there logically is no such implication, that to think otherwise is in the very least an example of presentism. And it should be clear that Tierney does the same thing with Huguccio and natural law.

One could go on and on by looking at what Tierney does with the other Decretists in his list. But that would be to belabor the same point. Suffice it here to counterpoise medieval scholars against medieval scholars to in the very least produce a suspension of judgment on our topic. Ernest Fortin (1996), for example, at the time of his writing Professor Emeritus of Theology and Political Theory at Boston College and a highly respected medievalist, put the matter this way:

> If the information at our disposal suggests anything, it is that rights as the medievals understood them were subservient to an antecedent law that circumscribes and relativizes them.... these rights were by no means unconditional. They were contingent on the performance of prior duties and hence forfeitable. Anyone who failed to abide by the law that guarantees them could be deprived of everything to which he was previously entitled: his freedom, his property, and in extreme cases his life. Not so with the natural rights on which the modern theorists would later base their speculations, and which have been variously described as absolute, inviolable, imprescriptible, unconditional, inalienable, or sacred. [246–247]

Grotius, Hobbes, and Pufendorf

Failure to find a clear and unequivocal expression of the concept of universal human rights in the late Middle Ages brings us to what we have seen Tuck call the next relevant period in European history, the Enlightenment or Age of Reason. Although there are a number of thinkers from this period we could focus on, one of the most important in the earlier part of this period is the Dutch humanist and legal scholar Hugo Grotius (Huig de Groot), often called "the father of international law." In his most famous book, *De Iure Belli ac Pacis,* written in Latin and first published in 1625, Grotius certainly looks like he had the concept of universal human rights. But a problem immediately presents itself with the title of his book, which involves the key word *ius.* Because this Latin word, as we have already seen, ambiguously means either "right" or "law," *De Iure Belli ac Pacis* has been translated either as *The Rights of War and Peace* or *The Law of War and Peace.* While many have claimed that Grotius explicitly advocated the concept of universal human rights, and some go so far as to say that he was the first or at least the most important historically, we shall quickly see that it is more likely that he qualifies for none of those labels.[5]

Almost right from the beginning of the text of *De Iure Belli ac Pacis* (Campbell 1901), in the first chapter of Book 1, we find a problem, where Grotius elaborates on the various meanings of *ius.* One is simply the sense of "what is just" (§3). Referring to "the law of nature," he says "any thing is unjust, which is repugnant to the nature of society, established among rational creatures." But one should not assume that Grotius has in mind here our modern concept of justice as fairness. Explicitly following Aristotle (as did Cicero, as we have seen), Grotius accepts as a matter of justice that in human societies some people are equal and some are not, the former including relationships such as brothers, friends, and citizens, the latter including relationships such as "parents and children, masters and servants, sovereigns and subjects, God and men," so that there is the "right of equality" and the "right of superiority." There is no indication whatsoever that Grotius rejects this latter aspect of *ius.* In fact, as we shall see, it fits in with his overall scheme.

The second meaning of *ius,* the most important for our purposes, I shall save for last. The third meaning of *ius* is "the same meaning as Law, taken into its most extensive sense" (§9), rules that Grotius divides into man-made law, natural law, and divine voluntary law. The second of these is based on the familiar Stoic conception, natural law built into the structure of nature and human reason, while the third is revealed law, such as the Ten Commandments.

It is important at this point to examine Grotius's concept of natural law, or the law of nature, as it is central to his concept of human rights. In the Prolegomena

---

5. According to O'Donovan (2009), "Grotius never used the term 'rights' (*iura*) in the plural, except in quoting other authors or in speaking, in the classical manner, of legal acts" (201). This is a powerful point if true, but for the remainder of this section I shall ignore this matter of translation, as a convincing case can be made without it that Grotius did not have the modern concept of universal human rights.

to *De Iure Belli ac Pacis* (Tuck 2005), he explicitly connects "the law of nature" with "human nature" (1748). In the body of his book proper, he elaborates. For example, in a discussion on self-defense (I.2.§3), he states, explicitly following Cicero, that the law of nature "is not written, but innate," "the elements of it have been engraven in our hearts and minds," it "forms a part in the original complexion of our frames," to which he adds that self-defense "is founded on reasons of equity." Elsewhere, following his discussion on *ius* as law (I.1), Grotius elucidates on natural right (*ius,* which trades on the ambiguity between "right" and "law"), stating that "Natural right is the dictate of right reason, shewing the moral turpitude, or moral necessity, of any act from its agreement or disagreement with a rational nature, and consequently that such an act is either forbidden or commanded by God, the author of nature" (§10). Grotius even adds in the same section that although natural law was created by God, "the Law of Nature is so unalterable, that it cannot be changed even by God," for that would involve God in a "contradiction," like making two plus two equal to anything but four. Using the language of essentialism, and applying it to natural kinds, Grotius claims that "there are qualities inseparably connected with their being and essence." The idea here quite clearly is that human nature is a natural kind with an essence, so that if God would change the law of nature with regard to humans, the result would no longer be human nature. It is clear that Grotius considers humans to be essentially social, not solitary. As he puts it in the Prolegomena (Tuck 2005), human nature involves a "social instinct," but not just for any kind of community, but "one at peace, and with a rational order" (1747–1748). It is equally clear that Grotius includes "reason" as part of the human essence, as "that part of man, which is superior to the body," superior to "bare instinct" (I.2.§1). As such, reason is what primarily separates humans from other animals, from "brutes," who at most have "some shadow and trace of reason" (1.§23). Human reason is also the connection to the next meaning of *ius,* the sense of human rights. "For no beings," says Grotius, "except those that can form general maxims, are capable of possessing a right." Since it is obvious that God has "permitted wild beasts, fishes, and birds to devour each other for food," it is equally obvious that "they have nothing like justice, the best gift, bestowed upon men" (§11). In short, then, human nature for Grotius includes society, reason, and the law of nature.

This brings us to the second meaning of *ius* discussed by Grotius (I.1.§4), the meaning I have saved for last, which Grotius says is different from the first ("what is just") but arises from it. It is the meaning that gets presentists so excited (but shouldn't). Here, *ius* is "a moral quality annexed to the person, justly entitling him to possess some particular privilege, or to perform some particular act." Admittedly, not only does the use of *ius* here look like "a right" rather than "law," but it looks like the concept of human right, even universal human right. To this, one might add other passages, such as "the end of society is to form a common and united aid to preserve to every one his own" (2.§1), "Now all men have absolutely a right to do such or such acts as are necessary to provide whatever is essential to the existence or convenience of life" (§18), and "God has given life to man ... a right to the free enjoyment of personal liberty, reputation, and the controul over his own actions" (§2).

Hence Richard Tuck (1979), for example, in a book devoted ultimately to "the language of human rights" (1), claims that Grotius "is the most important figure in the history which we are tracing" (58). Knud Haakonssen (1985) likewise claims that while Grotius had precursors, he "transformed the concept of *ius* ... ius is seen by Grotius as something a person *has*." Thus in Grotius "The concept becomes 'subjectivized,' centered on the person," which is "one of the cornerstones of modern individualism in political theory ... something individuals have" (240). Benjamin Straumann (2009) similarly claims that Grotius was "the first of the natural lawyers to develop a fully fledged account of subjective natural rights" (58).

But though Grotius used *ius* in the second sense above as a subjective right, the sense of an individual right, the more one reads Grotius objectively and collectively, not with presentism and gerrymandering, the more it becomes obvious that by *ius* Grotius never really had in mind the concept of universal human rights at all. For a start, in the same section in which the second meaning of *ius* is found (I.1.§4), Grotius adds that "This moral quality, when perfect is called a Faculty; when imperfect, an Aptitude." The former, he adds, is a right "in its strict and proper sense," which includes (i) "the power ... we have over ourselves, which is called liberty, and the power ... we have over others, as that of a father over his children, and of a master over his slaves," (ii) it "likewise comprehends property," and (iii) "a third signification, which implies the power of demanding what is due." Here is the problem. According to R. J. Vincent (1990), by *facultas* Grotius meant "a jural claim," while by *aptitudo* he meant "a moral claim" (245). In other words, the former requires a political context, a state or government with a legal system, while the latter does not. The problem is that Grotius gave the former context priority over the latter. Not only in the above passage does he call the legal context of a human right "perfect" and the moral context "imperfect," but he claims that a human right in a legal context, a right in the sense of *facultas,* is a right in its "strict and proper sense." But moreover still, of this "strict and proper sense" of right he makes two divisions, the one "private, established for the advantage of each individual," and the other "superior, as involving the claims, which the state has upon the individuals, and their property, for the public good" (§6). In other words, then, state rights trump individual rights and both trump moral rights.

There can be little doubt that Grotius made these distinctions and claims because of his theory of human nature, which was that man is not only a "reasonable" but a "social being" (I.2.§1). As he elsewhere puts it, "man neither was, nor is, by nature, a wild unsociable creature. But it is the corruption of his nature which makes him so" (1.§12). And it is man's social being combined with his rational being that is the foundation of justice. As Grotius puts it, "any thing is unjust, which is repugnant to the nature of society, established among rational creatures" (§3).

Even more than being essentially social and rational, however, Grotius conceived of human nature as essentially hierarchical. And this is necessary for understanding his concept of justice, and ultimately his concept of human rights. We can see this in his discussion on parents and children. By the mere act of "generation" (procreation), he says, "parents, both father and mother, acquire a right over their children" (II.5.§§1–5). This right extends for as long as the children have not yet developed their rational capacity, in the sense that a child "cannot rule himself." And if there is a difference between the "commands" of the parents, "the father's authority is to be preferred in regard to the dignity of the sex." The right of patrimony even extends so far that "may a father naturally, and where the civil law does not obstruct it, pawn his child, and sell him too," to which he adds the qualification, "if there be a necessity for it, and no other way of maintaining him."

This brings us to Grotius's discussion on slavery and on sovereignty in general (I.3.§8). Following Aristotle, Grotius argues not only that some people are "naturally slaves" but that "In the same manner some nations are of such a disposition that they are more calculated to obey than to govern."[6] In some societies even, he claims, what is warranted for "its peace and existence" is "the absolute government of a single person." Moreover still, on "the rights of sovereignty," Grotius claims that the very meaning of "sovereignty" entails "any share in which the people are excluded," for whether monarchy, aristocracy, or democracy, "there never was any government so purely popular, as not to require the exclusion of the poor, of strangers, women, and minors from the public councils." Grotius even argues against the view that "the sovereign power is vested in the people," against the view that the people have "a right to restrain and punish kings for an abuse of their power," against the view that a king may necessarily be "deposed" because of "mismanagement," against the view that individuals or states have a "natural right" to fight for their "independence" (II.22.§11), and he argues for the view

---

6. Granted, elsewhere Grotius adds, on the topic of slavery, that "It does not follow that, because any one is fitted for a particular condition, another has a right to impose it upon him" (II.22.§12). But as we shall see below, this creates a new problem for seeing Grotius as a human rights theorist.

that "the state or the sovereign who represents it, can use that property ['The property of subjects'], or destroy it, or alienate it, *not only in cases of extreme necessity,* which sometimes allow individuals the liberty of infringing upon the property of others, but on all occasions, where the public good is concerned" (III.20.§7). Such even is the importance of the public good that the right of self-defense, which is a right based on the "law of nature" (II.1.§4), is not an equal right, since although one has the right to kill someone who threatens one with lethal force, either explicitly or implicitly, one does not have the right if the person making the threat is "the person of the Sovereign," the one "whose person is rendered sacred and inviolable by all divine, human, and natural laws" (§9). Indeed in a number of places Grotius seems to confine the right of self-defense to "equity" (I.2.§3) or "equality" (III.20.§32).

The "public good," then, not the individual, is the key to understanding Grotius's concept of human rights. Grotius defines the state as "a perfect body of free men, united together in order to enjoy common rights and advantages" (I.1§14). But we have to read this objectively, not with modern eyes. He says "free men," not "humans," and "perfect" does not mean "equal." For Grotius, the fundamental purpose of the state is not to protect the human rights of its citizens, which is our modern concept, but instead to maintain its "peace and existence" (I.3.§8). And peace he conceives of as "the only end for which hostilities can be lawfully done" (III.25.§2). Hence the title of his book, *The Rights (or Law) of War and Peace.* Given this fundamental purpose of the state, Vincent (1990) concludes that for Grotius "all human rights were so conditioned that they did not bind in cases of extreme necessity" (246).

I would agree that for Grotius all human rights are conditional, but not because of extreme necessity (as the quotation in the second previous paragraph shows), nor even because state rights for Grotius trump individual rights. Instead, what logically makes Grotius's concept of human rights conditional rather than unconditional is his view that individuals could give up their human rights. In other words, not only for Grotius are human rights not equal, but they are *alieanable,* not *inalienable.* Recall Grotius's definition of *liberty,* given in his discussion of *ius* as an individual right, which is "the power we have over ourselves." Grotius later argues that while liberty belongs to "all men and states" as a "right of nature," the "law of nature" does not preclude choosing a life of slavery, since "no one can be called free, if nature leaves him not the privilege of chusing his own condition" (II.22.§11). Elsewhere he states that if an individual "might engage himself in private servitude to whom he pleased," so might "a whole people ... completely transfer their sovereign rights to one or more persons" (I.3.§8), to which he adds that people might do this, might "make an unqualified surrender of themselves and their rights," in order "to avoid greater evils" (§11).[7] The confusion here is that human rights, logically, are not the sort of thing that one can choose to give away. I can give away possessions such as my property, even my liberty, but I cannot possibly, in the logic of human rights, give away my human rights while still remaining human. That is what is at the heart of the difference between human and other rights. Other rights can be given up, given away, or taken away, but not human rights, not while one remains human.

All in all, Grotius's concept of human rights turns out not to be the concept of universal human rights as we understand it: inalienable rights, rights that all humans have by virtue of being human, rights that all humans have equally, rights connected with the dignity of man, rights that normally should not be violated by other individuals or by states. Indeed, arguably, Grotius's concept of human rights is really that of universal human *state* rights, rights that states have by virtue of being sovereign states, rights that all sovereign states have equally.

If Grotius did not have the concept of universal human rights, neither did the next big name on the list, Thomas Hobbes, considered by many to be "the greatest English political philosopher" (Tuck and Silverthorne 1998, xxxiii). Hobbes's main work in this regard, *Leviathan* (Curley 1994), named after the sea monster mentioned in the Bible, was first published in English in 1651 and later in Latin in 1668, although it is unclear whether it was originally written in English or in Latin.

There is no end to the praises of Hobbes as an early and important human rights theorist, even as the originator of the modern concept. According to the political scientist Leo Strauss (1953), Hobbes produced an "epoch-making change" (169) in morality and politics. Prior to Hobbes, says Strauss, rights were based on duties, ultimately on natural duties, but Hobbes "squarely made an unconditional natural right the basis of all natural duties"(182). The shift is profound, according to Strauss, not only is it an "epoch-making change" (169) in perspective, but also in action, since "Men can more safely be depended upon to fight for their rights

---

7. What also seems to make human rights conditional for Grotius is his claim not only that God gave humans their natural rights but also that God can take them away. He says God "has sovereign dominion over our lives and substance, as being his gift, which he may take away from any one, whenever he pleases, without assigning his reasons" (II.21.§14). To this one might oppose the passage we examined earlier, in which Grotius says, "the Law of Nature is so unalterable, that it cannot be changed even by God himself," that for God to do so would imply a "contradiction" (I.1.§10). But then Grotius adds that if God would take away someone's life or property it would not be a crime because God "is the sovereign Lord of our lives and of all things" (ibid.). Clearly one cannot have it both ways, nonconditional and conditional human rights, but that exactly is the corner into which Grotius painted himself.

than to fulfil their duties" (183). Hence Hobbes was "the founder of liberalism" (182). The political scientist Ian Shapiro (1986) likewise claims not only that the concept of human rights was at the "heart of Hobbes's political theory," but also that in Hobbes's writings one finds "its earliest recognizably modern form" (23). The professor of political philosophy Norberto Bobbio (1993) claims that "Scholars agree unanimously . . . The theory of natural rights is born with Hobbes. There is no trace of it in Grotius" (154). Not quite as extreme, the philosopher Gary Herbert (2002) claims that Hobbes's *Leviathan* contains "the first fully-modern account of individual (subjective) natural rights" (101). And Micheline Ishay (2008) finds it interesting that being "one of the first realists in international politics [Hobbes] was also a human rights advocate. His assertion of a right to life [which she characterizes as 'fundamental' and 'inalienable'] would ultimately be echoed in many international bills of rights" (85). Elsewhere (2007) she claims that Hobbes "opened the door to three hundred years of debate over what would become the liberal basis of human rights" (102).

These views are rather easily dismissed. But first we have to set up the contrary position. For a start, great importance is usually placed on the fact that Hobbes considered all humans as basically equal in terms of their faculties. As Hobbes puts it in *Leviathan,* "Nature hath made men so equal in the faculties of body and mind that . . . the difference between man and man is not so considerable as that one man can thereupon claim to himself any benefit to which another may not pretend as well as he" (I.13.§1). The physically weakest human can kill the strongest while the latter's guard is down, such as while sleeping, or when in league with others. As for mental faculties Hobbes found even "a greater equality" (§2), since not only do our inflated egos judge us as superior to others, but the development of our mental faculties is mainly due to time and experience, not to differences in innate endowment. Hobbes also thought women the equal of men here, since "whereas some have attributed to the man only, as being of the more excellent sex; they misreckon it" (II.20.§4), which is further emphasized by his acceptance of women as monarchs (§7). All of this is what Hobbes means when he states that "all men are equal" (15.§21). Hence, says Herbert (2002), "Hobbes's theory opens the way to acknowledging equally the natural rights of all people, regardless of race or sex" (100).

The second key feature of Hobbes's theory is his account of the state of nature, which according to Strauss (1953) "became an essential topic of political philosophy only with Hobbes" (184). The state of nature is the state that humans naturally fall into when they are under no supervening government or authority. Being by nature individuals rather than social parts, and driven by greed, safety, pride, and fear of others, the natural state of man is that of "war," with "every man against every man" (I.13.§8). This state of war does not mean perpetual fighting, however, but the "disposition" to fight, "peace" existing only when there is an "assurance to the contrary" (an assurance that is not going to exist in the state of nature). Living in perpetual fear of others, there is no sense of time in the state of nature, no arts and humanities or science, no commerce or industry. The constant state of man against man results in a life that is "solitary, poor, nasty, brutish, and short" (§9). During this relatively brief time there is "no propriety, no dominion, no *mine* and *thine* distinct, but only that to be every man's that he can get, and for so long as he can keep it" (§13).

Natural rights talk starts at the beginning of the very next chapter, in which Hobbes calls it a "Right of Nature" that each man has "for the preservation of his own nature, that is to say, of his own life, and consequently of doing anything which, in his own judgment and reason, he shall conceive to be the aptest means thereto" (14.§1). Hobbes shortly afterward adds that "as long as this natural right of every man to everything endureth, there can be no security to any man (how strong or wise soever he be) of living out the time which nature ordinarily alloweth men to live" (§4).

According to Herbert (2002), "The fundamental fact of the Hobbesian state of nature is that natural right creates a condition that precludes *recognition* of natural rights" (97). Herbert also claims that to fully understand "the founding of the modern account of natural right," "the first full development" (90), which we have seen he (along with a number of others) attributes exclusively to Hobbes, we have to understand his physics, particularly in opposition to that of Descartes. It may well be that a full understanding of Hobbes's theory of human rights requires an understanding of his physics, but we cannot afford to ignore the immediate context of his human rights talks, particularly his definitions. In that context is to be found the fatal problem with thinking of Hobbes as a human rights theorist at all.

For a start, Hobbes argues that in addition to being driven by passions such as fear of death and a desire for a full life, humans are driven by rational thinking, and "reason suggesteth convenient articles of peace," which he calls "the Laws of Nature" (I.13.§14). He then follows with two chapters that elaborate on these laws, but we have to keep in mind that the two chapters together are a prelude to Hobbes's solution to the state of nature, which is the social contract, the political state. The two chapters, 14 and 15, make sense only in that context. The laws of nature, then, are not really *laws of nature,* nor do they have anything to do with natural or human rights as we understand them.

Beginning with "The Right of Nature, which writers commonly call *jus naturale,*" by which he clearly means "natural right," Hobbes defines it as "the liberty each man hath to use his own power ... for the preservation of his own nature, that is to say, of his own life, and consequently of doing anything which, in his own judgment and reason, he shall conceive to be the aptest means thereunto" (14.§1). *Liberty* is the key concept here, which Hobbes defines simply as "the absence of external impediments" (§2). Defined as such, a natural right is simply the lack of external obstacles to self-preservation, nothing more.

A Hobbesian law of nature is a little more complicated. The very phrase "law of nature" naturally suggests that Hobbes was referring to the state of nature, but one has to be very careful here. "A Law of Nature (*lex naturalis*)," says Hobbes, is simply "a precept or general rule, found out by reason, by which a man is forbidden to do that which is destructive of his life or taketh away the means of preserving the same, and to omit that by which he thinketh it may best be preserved" (§3). In a state of nature, a human can discover by reason these laws of nature, but as we shall see they do not apply to the state of nature so much as to the political state, Hobbes's solution to the horrible state of nature. In other words, the "laws of nature" are conclusions of rational human beings in the state of nature that will lead them to join with other rational human beings into a social contract. Hobbes gives some nineteen or twenty of these laws, and a few examples should make the point clear. The first law, says Hobbes, is that "*every man ought to endeavour peace, as far as he has hope of obtaining it, and when he cannot obtain it, that he may seek and use all helps and advantages of war*" (§4). The second law is "*that a man be willing, when others are so too, as far-forth as for peace and defence of himself he shall think it necessary, to lay down this right to all things, and be contented with so much liberty against other men, as he would allow other men against himself*" (§5). The fifth law is "*that every man strive to accommodate himself to the rest*" (15.§17), while another law is "*that they that are at controversy, submit their right to the judgment of an arbitrator*" (§30).

These and the rest of the laws are preludes to Part II of the *Leviathan*, which deals with the commonwealth, which is begun by a social contract (if not by conquest). The laws of nature, then, are what a person in a state of nature would come to see in the sense of rational self-interest. What makes this especially evident is the distinction Hobbes draws between a right and a law—the distinction between "*jus* and *lex* (*right* and *law*)"—which he says is normally confounded. "Right," he says, "consisteth in liberty to do or to forbear, whereas Law determineth and bindeth to one of them; so that law and right differ as much as obligation and liberty" (14.§3). Grotius would count as someone who made this mistake, given Hobbes's distinction, for, as we have seen, Grotius defined *ius naturale* "in a way which makes it a command or prohibition" (Curley 1988, 79n4).

Hobbesian laws of nature, then, are not commands or rules, they are not "binding" in the sense of morality or justice. They are not really laws. Instead, as Hobbes later puts it, "These dictates of reason men use to call by the name of laws, but improperly; for they are but conclusions or theorems, concerning what conduceth to the conservation and defense of themselves, whereas law properly, is the word of him that by right hath command over others" (15.§41).[8]

Possibly Hobbes used the phrase "laws of nature," as Bobbio (1993) claims, "only to pay homage to tradition" (44). I don't know; it's a mystery to me. But whatever the truth, we also need to recognize that a Hobbesian natural right is similarly not really a right, in the sense of morality or justice. In what should be the definitive passage for interpreting Hobbes on human rights, he says, "To this war of every man against every man [the state of nature], this also is consequent: that nothing can be unjust. The notions of right and wrong, justice and injustice, have there no place. Where there is no common power, there is no law; where no law, no injustice" (I.13.§13). And as if to avoid any confusion, Hobbes immediately adds that "Force and fraud are in war the two cardinal virtues. Justice and injustice are none of the faculties neither of the body, nor mind. If they were, they might be in a man that were alone in the world . . . They are qualities that relate to men in society, not in solitude." The last man alive in the world would still nevertheless be a man. If he would have *human* rights before his solitude he would have them still. But not according to Hobbes, because any rights that he has in the proper sense of *subjective* or *individual rights* exist for him only when he is part of a political state.

_____

8. Hobbes immediately adds that "if we consider the same theorems, as delivered in the word of God, that by right commandeth all things; then they are properly called laws." Oakley (2005) is inclined to take "Hobbes's more theological moments seriously," so that he takes "Hobbes's definition of law in general as the result of an efficient cause and the mandate of a sovereign will to extend also to natural law, the efficient cause in that case being the omnipotent creator God and the obligating prescription of that law being the mandate of his sovereign will" (93). The fundamental question, then, would seem to concern Hobbes's theism, whether it was sincere or, as many have thought, a politically needed veil to hide his atheism (see Berman 1988, 64–69). I am inclined toward the latter. But either way it does not matter, since Oakley's conclusion does not follow. Even if we are to take Hobbes's theism seriously, God in his account would not be the "efficient cause" of the laws of nature. He would, instead, be the supreme reason that sees their truth. Hobbes's laws of nature do not require God for their existence or for their nature. Their status as laws "properly called" would only be *in addition* to their fundamental status as "conclusions or theorems." This conclusion finds further support in the fact that in the Latin edition of *Leviathan* Hobbes omitted the passage about God quoted at the beginning of this note (Curley 1994, xxxi). It is also to be noted that just before Hobbes's two chapters on the laws of nature, chapters 14 and 15, he states that "reason suggesteth convenient articles of peace" (13.§14). As Bobbio (1993, 45) points out, a suggestion is logically not the same as a command. All in all, then, the conclusion most warranted is that each of Hobbes's laws of nature is really nothing more than, as Curley puts it, a "hypothetical imperative," in the sense of *if you want this (and you do), then you ought to do that.*

What I have called above "the definitive passage" should alone make it clear once and for all that Hobbes was not a human rights theorist even remotely similar to our modern understanding of the phrase, but surprisingly only a few modern scholars have drawn this conclusion (e.g., Yolton 1993, 278; Tierney 1997, 340–341).[9] The modern concept of human rights is that of moral claims and entitlements that all humans have by virtue of being human, *not* by virtue of being part of a social contract. And yet the misunderstanding persists that Hobbes was a human rights theorist, even the founder of the modern concept.

One problem, raised by Kinch Hoekstra (2007, 120), is that elsewhere Hobbes defines "injustice" as breaking a contract and "justice" as everything else. The particular passages reads as follows: "Injustice is no other than *the not performance of covenant*. And whatsoever is not unjust, is *just*" (15.§2). This definition, by itself, implies that everything in the state of nature, no matter what, is just. But the definition is not by itself. It is immediately preceded with the words, "But when a covenant is made, then to break it is *unjust*; and the definition of Injustice is …" The principle of charity requires that we take Hobbes's definition of "injustice" in its context, not out of context. Taken out of context, his definition involves him in a contradiction, but not when it is in context. Taken in context, it should be clear that Hobbes's meaning is that justice is keeping a contract, not that everything in the state of nature is just. In fact, at the very end of the next section Hobbes states very clearly that "the nature of justice consisteth in keeping of valid contracts" (§3). It follows that where there are no valid contracts, there is no justice—or injustice.

A further problem, again raised by Hoekstra (2007, 120), though garbled with the previous, is that if we grant that Hobbes does confine justice to contracts or covenants (and we have just seen that he does), Hobbes also allows that contracts or covenants can sometimes occur in the state of nature without removing the state of nature. For example, Hobbes says that "Covenants entered into by fear, in the condition of mere nature, are obligatory" (14.§27). This again would imply that Hobbes contradicts himself, for it follows that there might never actually be a state of nature with no justice or injustice. But again the principle of charity is needed here. Taken literally, yes, Hobbes contradicts himself (justice both can and cannot exist in the state of nature), but that should not be taken as an invitation to interpret him as a natural or human rights theorist. Justice and injustice, along with right and wrong, have no place in the state of nature

---

9. This is all the more surprising since the same basic point was famously made by Pufendorf in the latter part of the 1600s (see Tuck 1979, 159–160). I shall return to Pufendorf at the end of this section.

for Hobbes because covenants are not the norm in the state of nature but the exception. And as the exception, the state of war remains in the state of nature, defined not as the constant battle of one human against another, driven by fear of death, competition, and vanity (the three main causes of the state of war in the state of nature, says Hobbes), but as the ever-present *disposition* to "war of all against all." As Hobbes puts it, "the nature of war consisteth not in actual fighting, but in the known disposition thereto during all the time there is no assurance to the contrary" (13.§8). Small covenants can crop up here and there between individual humans, but they do not remove the disposition to war that is the norm in the state of nature. In other words, the possibility of a covenant struck between a few people where the rest of the people in the region are themselves in a state of nature does not remove the danger of losing one's life. As Hobbes puts it, "covenants without the sword are but words, and of no strength to secure man at all" (II.17.§2). For the latter kind of covenant, we need the state, the commonwealth, the "artificial man" Hobbes calls in his Introduction "Leviathan" (§1). Indeed, Hobbes makes all of this clear at the beginning of his second chapter on laws of nature. There he says, "injustice actually there can be none till the cause of such fear be taken away, which, while men are in the natural condition of war, cannot be done.... there must be some coercive power to compel men equally to the performance of their covenants" (I.15.§3).

By focusing on isolated passages, then, Hobbes can seem to contradict himself on whether there can be justice or injustice in the state of nature. But that should not be taken as an open door to interpreting him as a natural or human rights theorist. The principle of charity requires otherwise. It is therefore remarkable that the majority of Hobbes scholars have read Hobbes as such a theorist. The evidence overall suggests that they should not. In our modern view, rights entail duties and obligations, either in the sense that something is demanded of us (sometimes called *positive rights* or *active rights*) or in the sense that we are required to refrain from doing something (sometimes called *negative rights* or *passive rights*).[10] For example, if I have a child and that child has a right to be nourished by its parents (positive/active right), then I have a duty or obligation to provide the child with nourishment. If I have a right to a particular piece of property (negative/passive right), then you have a duty or obligation not to occupy it or use it. If I have a right to life (negative/passive right), then you have a duty or obligation not to kill me. And so on. In other words, our modern concept of human rights is a

---

10. For a further discussion on these distinctions (which are not entirely adequate for a number of reasons, including the connotations of the terms), see, for example, White (1984, 17–19), Donnelly (2003, 30–31), and Mahoney (2007, 74–75).

moral one, such that the violation of a human right, no matter when or where or by whom, is normally a matter of injustice. But there is absolutely none of this in Hobbes's concept of rights in the state of nature. The only thing in common with the modern concept is the name, "rights." In the state of nature, for Hobbes, there can be no violation of human rights as we understand them because in the state of nature there are no such things as human rights in the moral sense. The only way one can have rights is to remove the state of nature by creating the social contract, the state or Leviathan.

All in all, then, we should not be fooled by Hobbes's line that in the state of nature "every man has a right to everything, even to one another's body," that there is a "natural right of every man to everything" (I.14.§4). The tendency is to read into Hobbes's use of "right" what today is meant by "rights," much as reading our meaning of "sporting person" into the use of the phrase a hundred years ago (which, unlike our use, referred to someone who frequented bars and whorehouses and who gambled a lot). Supporting evidence is then highlighted, while negative evidence is either ignored or argued away. By "natural right" Hobbes simply means the liberty to do what we want, most importantly to defend ourselves and to procure what is necessary for our existence. His meaning is not a moral one or a matter of justice, and hence is nothing like what is meant today.

This becomes even more evident when Hobbes turns to his social contract theory, where he provides a second meaning of "rights," closer to our modern meaning but still no cigar. He says, in a number of places, that when we enter into a social contract it is "as if every man should say to every man *I authorise and give up my right of governing myself to this man, or to this assembly of men, on this condition, that thou give up thy right to him [also], and authorize all his actions in like manner*" (II.17.§13). Again he says, "The mutual transferring of right is that which men call Contract" (I.14.§9). And again, "From this institution of commonwealth are derived all the *rights* and *faculties* of him, or them" (II.18.§2). The very fact that these so-called rights by Hobbes in a state of nature can be *given up* or *transferred* indicates once again that Hobbes's concept of human rights is not at all like the modern one. Following the American, French, and UN Declarations as the leading documents, human rights are supposed to be "inalienable."[11]

---

11. There is, however, something of the inalienable in Hobbes's discussion on rights. For example, he says that "there be some rights which no man may be understood by any words or other signs to have abandoned or transferred. As, first, a man cannot lay down the right of resisting them that assault him by force, to take away his life" (I.14.§8). He then gives as examples surrendering oneself to wounds, chains, and imprisonment. But we have to look at Hobbes's reasons here. The barrier to abandonment or transference of these rights is not that by giving up or transferring these rights one would cease to be human and one cannot do that, but instead that one

At this point we need to look at Hobbes's "absolutism," a term that in the seventeenth century was at the center of a variety of political theories (Sommerville 1991), and no one doubts that Hobbes's theory was one of them. For Hobbes, because everyone who enters into a social contract enters voluntarily, it follows that "every subject is by this institution author of all the actions and judgments of the sovereign instituted." In other words, it follows that "whatsoever he doth, it can be no injury to any of his subjects, nor ought he to be by any of them accused of injustice." Consequently, "he that complaineth of injury from his sovereign complaineth of that whereof he himself is author, and therefore ought not to accuse any man but himself; no nor himself of injury, because to do injury to one's self is impossible. It is true that they that have sovereign power may commit iniquity, but not injustice, or injury in the proper signification" (II.18.§6). Elsewhere he adds that the sovereign is "sole legislator, and supreme judge of controversies" (20.§3; see also 21.§7). Hobbes's reasoning is not only that the state is an "artificial [man-made] man" in which "the *sovereignty* is an artificial soul, as giving life and motion to the whole body" (Introduction §1), but that the absolutism of the sovereign is necessary to prevent the worst scenario, which is the state of nature: "And though of so unlimited a power [the sovereign] men may face many evil consequences, yet the consequences of the want of it, which is perpetual war of every man against his neighbor, are much worse" (20.§18). This is why although Hobbes allows that the sovereign could be an assembly of persons, he clearly favors that the power be put in the hands of one person only (II.19).

Because of Hobbes's absolutism, Herbert (2002) claims that "Hobbesian natural right does not take us to a complete and reliable recognition of rights" (101). This is true, but not because Hobbes had the concept of human rights and combined it with the concept of the absolute sovereign. Instead it is because Hobbes never had the concept of human rights in the first place (or if he did, he rejected it).

We turn next to the German lawyer and political theorist Samuel Pufendorf, who was originally a follower of Grotius but broke away to develop his own natural law theory, which combines elements from the thinking of both Grotius and Hobbes. His major work in this regard is *De Jure Naturae et Gentium* (*On the Law*

---

would be committing a self-contradiction. Immediately preceding this passage, in the context of entering a social contract, Hobbes says that "it is a voluntary act, and of the voluntary acts of every man the object is some *good to himself.*" We enter into the contract for "the security of a man's person, in his life and in the means of so preserving life as not to be weary of it" (§8). As rights, as native liberties, we cannot ever really lose them or give them up, for then we would be at odds with ourselves. Other rights, other native liberties, however, such as to take from or to kill others, these we can indeed transfer to the sovereign, who may in turn take from or kill us with impunity.

of Nature and Nations), published in 1672, which he rewrote in a condensed form the following year as *De Officio Hominis et Civis Juxta Legem Naturalem* (*On the Duty of Man and Citizen According to Natural Law*). It is this latter work I shall refer to. Pufendorf has been called "the first philosopher of modern politics" and is credited with playing "a decisive role ... in establishing the juridical form of modern thought" (Tully 1991, xx, xxiv), and he has also been included among the "human rights visionaries" (Ishay 2008, 80). Although I cannot possibly examine them all, he is the last I shall show was not really a human rights theorist.

There are passages, of course, that seem to suggest otherwise. Pufendorf believed in the equality of the human species, not only because "we are all descended from the same stock" (I.7.§2), but in the combined sense that "Human nature ... belongs equally to all" (§1) and that with regard to fellow humans "one must practice the precepts of natural law towards another and one expects the same in return" (§2). By "natural law" Pufendorf simply means "The laws of ... sociality, laws which teach one how to conduct oneself to become a useful member of human society" (3.§8). These laws were created by "the author of the universe" (2.§6) and are "dictates of reason" accessible by "the innate light" (3.§10). Pufendorf can also be found referring to what are commonly thought to be human rights, such as property. "Ownership," he says, "is a right" (12.§3) that "was introduced by the will of God, with consent among men right from the beginning and with at least a tacit agreement" (§2). This right, moreover, includes "that man may use other creatures for his own benefit, and that he may in fact in many cases kill them ... even though they die in pain" (§1).

The harmony of thought in the idea that Pufendorf was a human rights vision-ary, however, quickly slides into disharmony, in fact into a loud dissonance, once other passages are examined.

The key is the Thirty Years' War in Europe, which was resolved by the Treaty of Westphalia in 1648, in effect a collective constitution for the European states. Among other things, the Treaty recognized religious diversity within and between states and recognized each European state as an autonomous entity within a "family of nations." As James Tully (1991) puts it in his Introduction to *On the Duty of Man and Citizen According to Natural Law*, Pufendorf's project was to construct "a natural law theory of this complex configuration," one that would take into account both the religious and political dimensions of the Treaty (xviii) and that would seek to preserve "peace and order" (xxiv). It should come as no surprise, then, that Pufendorf's fundamental concern was not really with human rights but rather with human duties, namely, duties to God, duties to oneself, duties to other humans, and duties to the state. "Duty" he defines as "human action in conformity with the commands of law on the ground of obligation" (I.1.§1), where "law" is defined as "a decree by which the superior obliges one who is subject to him to conform to the superior's postscript" (2.§2)—in other words, "Laws necessarily imply a superior" (3.§10)—and "obligation" is characterized as being "introduced into a man's mind by a superior, by one who has not only the strength to inflict some injury on the recalcitrant, but also just cause to require us to curtail the liberty of our will at his discretion" (§5).

Already one might have a feeling for what is to come. But let us work into this gradually. One of the interesting consequences of Pufendorf's framework concerns one's duty to oneself, specifically the duty of "self-preservation." "If two men," he says, "are in immediate danger of both perishing, one is allowed to do anything to hasten the death of the other (since the other would perish anyway) in order to save himself" (I.5.§21). One would think that if one believed in the human right to life, then no one should have the moral right to shorten someone else's life in order to save their own. In the modern case of abortion, of course, many today argue that the right to life of the mother trumps the right to life of the fetus if bringing the fetus to term threatens the life of the mother. More generally it is claimed that one's right to life means that one can kill another in self-defense if no other option is available. But none of this falls under Pufendorf's claim here. His claim, instead, is that I morally can shorten someone's life whose life is no threat to me if this means saving my own life. One of the examples he gives is when two men are being chased by an enemy intent on killing them. Either one of them, he says, "may leave the other in danger of his life, either by closing a gate behind himself or by breaking down a bridge, if both cannot be saved together." This hardly seems to be a case with an underlying *moral* claim and entitlement, let alone one that a person has by virtue of being human. It seems merely, instead, to be of the nature of a Hobbesian right in the state of nature.

Another odd claim of Pufendorf's involves the relations between men and women, in particular with regard to marriage. He says, "the husband should be the head of the family," and this is because of "the natural condition of both sexes," which means that "the man's position should be superior" (II.2.§4). Whatever one takes "the natural condition of both sexes" to be, inequality in marriage is not at all what one would or should expect from someone who actually believes in *human* rights, since men are not more human than women but both are equally and fully human.

Another interesting consequence concerns human slavery. Pufendorf recognizes that human slavery probably began by humans "offering themselves out of their own free will," either to escape severe poverty or because they realized they were too stupid to take care of themselves (I.4.§1). He also recognizes that many slaves are the product of war, where slavery is the price paid by the defeated in return for their lives being spared. In either case, Pufendorf does not argue against slavery. Instead, he asserts that the slave "has no goods of his own" and "his body belongs to the owner" (6.§11). Moreover, not only can the slave "not be allowed to leave his servitude against the master's will," but "the offspring of slave parents is itself of servile status, and belongs, as a piece of property, to the owner of the mother" (§6). Of course, Pufendorf reminds the reader that "since humanity bids us never to forget that a slave is in any case a man, we should by no means treat him like other property, which we may use, abuse and destroy at our pleasure" (§5). But no matter, Pufendorf is clearly lacking the concept of human rights here. This is not only because human slavery violates what is commonly supposed to be one of the most basic of human rights, the right to liberty, but also because a human right is logically not something that one can give to another, whether willingly or not, for the simple reason that one cannot possibly give up one's membership in the human species to another.

Next, one has to take into account Pufendorf's view of the citizen toward the state. The "good citizen," he says, is "one, in fact, who believes nothing to be good for him unless it is also good for the state" (II.5.§5), and his duty to the state "is that its safety and security be his dearest wish; that his life, wealth and fortune be freely offered to preserve it" (18.§4). But there is more. The state, he says, when conceived out of a social contract, becomes a "composite moral person," such that it is "separated and distinguished from all particular men by a unique name; and has its own special rights and property, which no one man, no multitude of men, nor even all men together, may appropriate apart from him who holds the sovereign power or to whom the government of the state has been committed" (6.§10). Part of what this means is that "those who have once consented to peace and mutual help for the common good must be prohibited from dissenting thereafter, whenever their own private good seems to be in conflict with the public good" (§3). What it also means is that "Sovereign authority ... has its own particular sanctity. It is therefore morally wrong for the citizens to resist its legitimate commands. But beyond this even its severity must be patiently borne by citizens in exactly the same way as good children must bear the ill temper of their parents. And even when it has threatened them with the most atrocious injuries, individuals will protect themselves by flight or endure any injury or damage rather than draw their swords against one who remains the father of their country, however harsh he may be" (9.§4).

There is no need to continue any further. It should be obvious by now that Pufendorf was primarily a duty theorist, not a human rights theorist, with the duty to the state trumping our duty to others or even to ourselves. Accordingly in Pufendorf we do not find at all the modern concept of universal human rights, the concept of moral claims and entitlements that all humans have by virtue of being human and that they can make not only against other individuals but also against the state. For the origin of that concept, and for the origin of the belief in it, we have to look in a different direction, to a different time and place.

Chapter 5

Getting the History of Human Rights Right

> ... small sparks do oftentimes occasion great fires.
> —*Edward Sexby, "England's Miserie and Remedie" (1645)*

THE END OF THE PREVIOUS CHAPTER brings us to a contemporary of Pufendorf's, born in the same year even, the English philosopher John Locke, father of British empiricism and certainly one of the preeminent thinkers of the European Enlightenment, who according to Strauss (1953) deserves the label of being "the most famous and the most influential of all modern natural right teachers" (165). With Locke, unlike with Grotius, Hobbes, or Pufendorf, it is generally agreed that we clearly find the modern concept of universal human rights. There are some exceptions to this belief, which I shall deal with in the section on Locke, but the point that needs to be emphasized here is that Locke was not the first. For that we need to go back to the events that motivated Hobbes's writing of *Leviathan,* the English Civil Wars, and in particular to the rise of the English Levellers among the various radical movements. From them was born the idea that has taken over the modern world, spread via the writings of Locke decades later to America, then to France, and then to the United Nations (to make a long story short).

I recognize that the title of this chapter rubs the wrong way; it still gives me pause when I look at it. Can anyone really get history right, especially where so many others got it wrong? Is this not an arrogant title? And then there are the

professional historians, who as Pauline Maier (1997) puts it, "have a way of weary-
ing people by insisting that virtually any subject is too complex for simple answers"
(xix–xx). This chapter should definitely not be read as a dogmatic proclamation
or as a simple answer. It is born, however, out of the belief that it is sometimes
possible to get history basically right in complex and conflicting matters, such
as who killed JFK (Bugliosi 2007) and Darwin's species concept (Stamos 2007).
One will have to decide for oneself in the present case. A just thinker will see,
it is my hope, that the evidence is remarkably strong, providing one keeps one's
eyes on the ball, which is the consensus concept of universal human rights that I
stress throughout this book. This chapter, in league with the previous, lays out the
preliminary evidence for a bold explanatory hypothesis developed in the following
chapter. Should the analysis provided in the present chapter be fundamentally
sound, then the profundity of the origin and spread of the belief in universal
human rights cannot be overstated, given especially the intimate connection with
genuinely democratic beliefs and values. But that is the topic of the next chapter.
For the present we need to go back to the beginning.

The English Levellers

The belief that humans have universal, equal, innate, and inalienable human rights,
remarkably enough, was not born from the brain of any major thinker in human
history, but instead has a humble origin, the brains of a group of commoners
caught up in the storm of a most troubled time. Made up mainly of merchants,
apprentices, and soldiers, the Levellers (not their own label, but given to them
as a term of abuse) were a radical political movement in England that emerged
and swelled into many tens of thousands during the latter part of the first of the
English Civil Wars of the 1640s, what would prove to be one of the most defining
decades in all of human history. From 1629 to 1640 King Charles I had ruled
England without a Parliament (House of Lords and House of Commons). Over
the next two years the two Houses attempted a compromise with the king but
failed. Charles was a firm believer in the divine right of kings, the doctrine that
kings were accountable to no one but God. Accordingly he levied taxes at will,
forced loans to the government and imprisoned those who refused to pay, censored
the press, and imprisoned and executed political opponents. Many rightly feared
that he was attempting to gain for himself absolute power, which was against the
English tradition established by the Magna Carta of 1215. On top of it all he
was a Roman Catholic sympathizer, having married a French Catholic princess
and having made a High Anglican the Archbishop of Canterbury. But to make

the matter worse, he imposed religious conformity throughout his kingdom. The inevitable result was the first Civil War, which erupted in August 1642. With the king eventually surrendering in June 1646 to the New Model Army (the military force created by Parliament in 1645) led by Sir Thomas Fairfax and Oliver Cromwell, and the country now in an economic depression, Parliament in turn began its own tyranny. It tried to disband the New Model Army, it failed to pay soldiers their arrears, it wanted to send many of the soldiers to Ireland to subjugate the Irish, and it began instituting religious intolerance, which included a proposed blasphemy law (eventually passed in May 1648) that would enforce the Presbyterian style of worship and punish nonconformists with imprisonment, branding on the left cheek with a B, and ultimately hanging. Playing both sides against each other, the king eventually brought in the Scottish army to bolster his royalists and thus instigated the second Civil War in the summer of 1648. The New Model Army won again, resulting in Cromwell's purging Parliament of both the House of Lords and the Presbyterian majority in the House of Commons (leaving it the so-called Rump Parliament). In the very least, this allowed Cromwell to put the incorrigible Charles on trial and to gain a conviction. A few days later, on the thirtieth day of January 1649, the king lost his head, literally.

The Levellers, emerging as a recognizable group in 1645, asserted the fundamental equality of all people under God, they wanted religious liberty, and they wanted political power to be in the hands of the people, an "agreement of the people," with the vote extended to the poor. For a time they supported Cromwell (many of the Levellers were members of the New Model Army), even though he supported a much more restricted vote, only to have him turn on them in 1649 and effectively crush them.

Leveller thinking was eclectic and was never collected into a single systematic treatise. Instead it was spread out among numerous pamphlets written by its leaders. The content varied in tone and approach from Leveller to Leveller and to the specifics of the politics they were reacting against (Sharp 1998, xxxi). Nevertheless, they represented the sparks of genuine democratic beliefs and values (a point I shall elaborate upon in the next chapter) and were the first to espouse universal human rights.

Part of the problem was that they faced impossible odds: permanently abolishing the monarchy and the House of Lords went against English tradition, most of the English people believed in God-given political inequality rather than equality (Sharp 1998, xix), and the Levellers could claim neither Cromwell nor Fairfax as one of their own. But arguably a greater part of the problem was that they lacked a systematic philosopher and truly great thinker. Looking at their upper echelon, John Lilburne, their main leader, known by his admirers as "Freeborn John," was a lieutenant colonel in the New Model Army who previously had been a clothier apprentice and then became active in Calvinist sectarianism. He was self-educated, author of more than eighty pamphlets, high-spirited, and enormously courageous—his story, with its numerous imprisonments, episodes of torture, and legal trials in the name of liberty, would make for an exciting movie—but he was after all primarily a man of action, not a theorist. The other Leveller leaders could not claim much more. William Walwyn was a successful London clothing merchant who was active in ward politics and petitioning before becoming a Leveller. Richard Overton was a professional actor and part-time playwright and printer who previously had been a religious refugee in Holland and possibly before that an undergraduate at Cambridge University. John Wildman was a young lawyer or law student who shortly after the first Civil War became a soldier and later an officer in the New Model Army. Thomas Rainborough was a colonel in the New Model Army who before his association with the Levellers had been an officer in the king's navy. Edward Sexby was a private and agitator (a regiment representative for the General Council of the New Model Army). Thomas Prince was a successful London cheese merchant. Being all of the "middle sort," as Lilburne characterized the Levellers (Brailsford 1961, 10, 314), they lacked theoretical might and consequently never managed to get their ideas lodged into the heads of the higher sort.

Nonetheless, with these first sparks of genuine democratic beliefs and values there also occurred the first sparks of genuine belief in universal human rights. In "An Agreement of the People" (October 1647), their most famous manifesto, which is of unknown authorship (although historians agree that the Leveller leadership must have had a hand in writing it), they refer to "grounds of common right and freedom" (Sharp 1998, 92) and "our common rights and liberties" (93), they often refer to "our native rights" (95, 97, 101), and they state that "*those whom yourselves shall choose* shall have power to restore you to, and secure you in, all your rights" (96). According to the historian David Wootton (1991), "An Agreement of the People" is "the first proposal in history for a written constitution based on inalienable natural rights" (412). They also used phrases such as "the property right and title that every man has to what is his own" (Sharp 1998, 161), used by Lilburne and three other Leveller leaders (Walwyn, Prince, and Overton) in "A Manifestation" (April 1649), written while they were imprisoned in the Tower of London for high treason. Two weeks later, in "An Agreement of the Free People of England" (May 1649), the same four leaders would write of the choice of political representation as a "natural right" (170). Almost four months later, while still in the Tower, Lilburne in "The Young Men's and the Apprentices' Outcry" (August 1649) would write of "the native rights of the people" (180) and "our native liberties and freedoms" (192).

It is possible to interpret many of these phrases, of course, particularly the ones that include the word "native," as referring not to the natural rights of all of mankind but to the ancient rights and liberties of the English people, as they the Levellers understood them. But this interpretation, as plausible as it might be in itself, becomes overshadowed when more evidence is taken into account. Most important here are the writings of Richard Overton, arguably the first person in history to have the concept of human rights and to coin the term. In his satirical pamphlet titled "The Arraignment of Mr. Persecution" (April 1645), Overton writes of "the general and equal rights and liberties of the common people ... their native and just liberties in general," while in a pamphlet titled "An Appeal ... to the Free People" (July 1647), he writes of "our natural human rights and freedoms."[1] Overton's most important pamphlet on human rights, however, written and published while he sat in prison, is his "An Arrow Against All Tyrants and Tyranny, Shot from the Prison at Newgate into the Prerogative Bowels of the Arbitrary House of Lords and All Other Usurpers and Tyrants Whatsoever" (October 1646). (The title is actually much longer, usually briefly referred to as "An Arrow Against All Tyrants," but I reproduce the first quarter of it here for its flavor and effect.) Right at the beginning, in the first two paragraphs, Overton claims that "every one ... has a self-propriety, else he could not *be* himself," to which he adds, "by natural birth all men are equally and alike born to like propriety, liberty and freedom" (Sharp 1998, 55). Again he refers to this as "a natural, innate

---

1. These references are found in Stassen (1992, 148, 153). In his chapter titled "The Christian Origin of Human Rights," Stassen credits Overton with originating both the concept and the term "human rights." Stassen claims that the explanation for this origin lies in (i) Overton's deep Christian convictions, his interdenominational experience (part of which was in Holland, at the time a model for toleration), and his biblical grounding, (ii) the battles and rapid change that occurred during the English Civil Wars, and (iii) the "Christian struggle for liberty, justice, and peace for all" (139–158). Stassen is Professor of Christian Ethics at Fuller Theological Seminary in Pasadena, California, which explains his Christian slant on the matter, a slant that is akin to ethnocentrism. Objectively, there are good reasons for rejecting primarily theological explanations of Leveller beliefs. As Wootton (1986, 54–56) points out, Walwyn's favorite source on true Christianity was the skeptic Montaigne, such that he was accused (with good grounds) of atheism, as was Overton, who did not believe in life after death except (possibly) for conditional immortality, while Wildman thought that natural reason could not establish the existence of God and Sexby preferred to cite Roman sources, such as Livy and Pliny. For a fuller discussion, see Wootton (1991, 434–442). Overton's particular religious background, then, placed in the context of the first Civil War, does not really explain. To my mind, instead, the key to understanding the rise of belief in universal human rights in the Levellers is the rise in them of genuinely democratic beliefs and values, for which I make my case in the next chapter.

freedom and propriety" and also uses the phrases "natural right and freedom" and "birthright and privilege." This natural self-propriety or ownership over oneself he apparently takes to be the origin of private property. "Mine and thine cannot be," he says, "except this [self-propriety] be." To this he immediately adds, "No man has power over my rights and liberties, and I over no man's," such that if I violate this rule then "I am an encroacher and an invader upon another man's right—to which I have no right." He also claims that it is "nature's instinct to preserve itself from all things hurtful and obnoxious," and that "from this fountain or root all just human powers take their original." Of these "just human powers," he says, "originally God has implanted them in the creature, and from the creature those powers immediately proceed and no further." Human rights, then, according to Overton, are part of human nature. They do not proceed "immediately from God (as kings usually plead their prerogative) but mediately by the hand of nature, as from the represented to the representers." Moreover, human rights are inalienable: "For as by nature no man may abuse, beat, torment, or afflict himself, so by nature no man may give that power to another, seeing he may not do it to himself."

All of this—arguably the first clear expression of human rights as universal, plural, equal, innate, and inalienable—stands in sharp contrast to what we have seen in the previous chapter. But at this point we need to take a look at what are now known famously to political historians as the Putney Debates. Held at Putney Church by the New Model Army in the fall of 1647 during its disputes with Parliament, chaired by Cromwell, and recorded by a military clerk who developed a kind of shorthand, these remarkable debates were over the future constitution of England. Although they were supposed to be focused on the proposals contained in two recent documents, "The Heads of the Proposals" presented to the imprisoned king and "The Case of the Army Truly Stated" presented to Fairfax, the focus quickly switched to the proposals contained in "An Agreement of the People," which apparently was designed specifically for these debates. What needs to be kept in mind is that many and perhaps even most of the soldiers and officers were either Levellers or Leveller sympathizers, which helps to explain why civilian Levellers were allowed participation in the debates. The key debate for our purposes was held on the second day, October 29, over the nature of political representation in the new constitution, specifically voting rights for the "General Representative." Henry Ireton, Cromwell's chief lieutenant and son-in-law, who was also his main voice in the debates, wanted to confine voting rights to those with "fixed property," those who owned rent-producing land or a corporation (a business with a fixed location), while the Levellers, as the Leveller Colonel Thomas Rainborough put it (Sharp 1998, 111), wanted "property in the franchise" extended to the poor, not only soldiers, servants, and apprentices but also beggars (Wootton 1991, 428–429).

Ireton replied that "if you make this the rule, I think you must fly for refuge to an absolute right and you must deny all civil right" (Sharp 1998, 103). More specifically, he claimed that "if this [extended suffrage] be allowed (because by the right of nature we are free; we are equal; one man must have as much voice as another), then show me what step or difference there is why I may not by the same right take your property, ..." (108–109). Again he says, "You infer this to be the right of the people, of every inhabitant, because man has such a right in nature, ... By the same rule, show me why you will not by the same right of nature make use of anything that any man has, ... Show me what you will stop at, wherein you will fence any man in a property by this rule" (114).

It is not clear whether Ireton had read Overton's "Arrow" pamphlet quoted above, but it is clear that he was performing what he believed to be a *reductio ad absurdum* against what he took to be the general Leveller position. The *reductio* might seem to work because Overton and other Levellers lacked a clear theory of property (of what makes something private property) and hence of property rights. Interestingly, Rainborough, Ireton's main interlocutor, staunchly denied the charge that the Levellers were for "anarchy" and appealed not to human rights but to the Bible, to the commandment "Thou shalt not steal" (109–110), which he took to be not only a divine sanction of property ownership but a divine check against Ireton's *reductio*. The fact remains, however, that the Levellers did not have a clear and convincing theory of property. Locke would later supply the much-needed theory, which he was fully aware was both highly original and enormously consequential (Laslett 1988, 101, 288n). As he stated in the last year of his life, "Property I have nowhere found more clearly explained, than in a book entitled, Two Treatises of Government" (quoted in Laslett 1988, 3).

We shall return to Locke below. Also of interest is the repeated use among the Levellers of phrases such as "lives, limbs, liberties, properties, and estates," used in "An Agreement of the Free People of England" (May 1649), or "lives, liberties, and properties," used a little later by Lilburne in "The Young Men's and the Apprentices' Outcry" (August 1649). Lilburne explicitly refers to a "remarkable speech" to Parliament given by John Pym in 1641 (not a Leveller, Pym was the leader of Parliament against the king), from which he (Lilburne) apparently borrowed the phrase. In that speech Pym claimed that "Your honours, your lives, your liberties and estates are all in the keeping of the law. Without this, every man hath a right to anything" (Sharp 1998, 184, 193n35). Locke would later use "life, liberty, and estate," which Jefferson changed to "life, liberty, and the pursuit of happiness."

The intellectual connection was not merely in phraseology. But before we look at that connection, again it must be emphasized that the sparks of universal human rights talk, significant as they were among the Levellers, never ignited into a flame. The ideas were not coherent, they were not systematic, and they were not developed with anything that might be called intellectual rigor. What was needed was someone to bring the ideas together into a cohesive and powerful system of thought, someone with intellectual stature who commanded respect. That someone was supplied roughly thirty years later in the person of the Oxford-educated John Locke.

Locke

According to Peter Laslett (1988, 22), there is no direct evidence that Locke ever read any of the Levellers' literature. Nevertheless, there is no question that he was directly connected with the Levellers in a number of intriguing ways. For a start, Locke owned a copy of James Harrington's *The Art of Law-Giving,* published in 1659, which explicitly quotes and critically discusses the constitutional proposals of the Levellers in their "An Agreement of the Free People of England" (May 1649). (The key passages in Harrington's book are reproduced in Wootton 1986, 410–415.) Harrington was well familiar with this pamphlet and the main issues that surfaced before it in the Putney Debates. In writing his *Two Treatises of Government,* which was eventually published in 1689, Locke used Harrington's book and, as Jacqueline Stevens (1996) puts it, "the language Locke uses and the problems he discusses in the *Second Treatise* are remarkably consistent with those of James Harrington in *The Art of Law-Giving*" (424). Secondly, concurrent with the time of writing the *Two Treatises* was Locke's close association with his patron and friend the earl of Shaftesbury, whose circle of political friends included a number of former Levellers, among them Major John Wildman. Locke had in fact become good friends with the former Leveller leader, and there is strong evidence that Locke was involved in a series of conspiracies, headed largely by Shaftesbury, to remove and even assassinate the king in the early 1680s. Wildman was one of the co-conspirators, as was another former Leveller, Colonel Richard Rumbold, whose house served as the proposed scene for the infamous Rye House Plot. The most important work in all of this is Richard Ashcraft's *Revolutionary Politics & Locke's Two Treatises of Government* (1986). Not only does Ashcraft examine in detail Locke's life as a political conspirator, but he meticulously brings Locke's *Two Treatises* down from the abstract heights of political and philosophical theory and places it in the flesh-and-blood world of the revolutionary politics of Locke's life and times. In doing so he places "Locke in much closer proximity to the Levellers and to the radical political theory they developed than has previously been supposed," and he also shows that "the radical Whig political tracts of the 1680s . . .

suggested to contemporaries that the Shaftesbury-led Whigs were attempting to revive the Levellers' movement" (164).

Locke, it should be noted, did not begin with a liberal or radical mind-set. In his earlier years he was not much into politics. All the more interesting is it, then, as Laslett (1988) tells us, that although Locke "could have proceeded either in the authoritarian or in the liberal tradition," he "was brought back into the tradition which they [the Levellers] began by an unexpected turn in his personal life" (22).

That "unexpected turn," of enormous significance for the history of ideas, was the chance beginning of Locke's association with an aristocrat by the name of Anthony Ashley Cooper, who would later become the first earl of Shaftesbury, one of the richest, most politically powerful, and most intellectually astute men in England at the time, and who would prove to be the greatest influence on Locke's life and thought. In the summer of 1666, the future earl came to Oxford to drink the spring water, in the hope of improving his health. It was not his Oxford physician, however, who brought him the water, but a close friend of the latter, a former medical student at Oxford named John Locke. It was the beginning of what would quickly become a close and important friendship. During the spring of the next year, Locke became a member of Shaftesbury's household, having his own apartment, an arrangement that he would have for the next eight years. With Shaftesbury as his patron, Locke provided medical advice, tutoring to his son, and intellectual conversation, writing parts of what would become his most famous book, *An Essay Concerning Human Understanding*. In July 1668, Shaftesbury was suffering horribly from an abscess on his liver. Locke suggested and supervised a radically new operation, which saved the man's life. With the friendship as good as it could be, Shaftesbury did everything he could to secure Locke's fame in the medical profession (Locke was made a Fellow of the Royal Society in November of that year). Shaftesbury also employed Locke in a variety of well-respected offices. Shaftesbury, however, was quite the liberal and revolutionary: formerly one of Cromwell's ministers and later an opponent; following the restoration of the monarchy, the leader of the movement for constitutional reform; effectively the founder of what would become the Whig Party; and through it all an untiring champion of religious freedom. His politics eventually would bring upon him and his associates the full wrath of the king, Charles II. Shaftesbury had in fact been arrested by the king in 1681, accused of treason, and after temporarily managing to avoid prosecution he fled to Holland in exile, where he died in January 1683. Locke remained in England, where he almost certainly was involved in the Rye House Plot, a failed attempt in March 1683 to assassinate Charles and his brother James (Ashcraft 1986, 370–390). With the plot later uncovered, Locke fled to Holland in August 1683, fearing the same accusation of treason that had earlier forced Shaftesbury to flee. In November 1684, Locke's faculty position at Oxford, a medical Studentship (which guaranteed him a tenured stipend), was terminated by the university, not only because of its political traditionalism, but because of a royal order motivated mainly by the discovery of Locke's close association with English revolutionaries living in exile in Holland. Indeed, Locke's alma mater would continue the ban not only on Locke but also on his works well into the beginning of the next century, rejecting one of the greatest of its sons by far.

In an ironic twist of history, then, in a roundabout way occasioned by an abscessed liver in a future earl, the development of Locke's political thought brought him close to that of the Levellers before him, even though his education was of a thoroughly different and higher standing. As Laslett (1988) puts it, "without Shaftesbury, Locke would not have been Locke at all" (27). The basic principles of human equality and participatory justice, central to the Levellers and now much of the world, were also central to Locke's political theory, and for the first time in history were fully integrated with and reinforced by the concept of universal human rights.

Turning then to Locke's writings, the central document is his *Two Treaties of Government*, first published in 1689 (Laslett 1988). In the *Second Treatise*, right at the beginning, Locke claims that in the state of nature all humans are not only in a "*State of perfect Freedom*" but they are in a "*State* also *of Equality*" (2.§4). This means "all the Power and Jurisdiction is reciprocal, no one having more than another." This follows—"there being nothing more evident" (Jefferson would later use "self-evident")—from the fact that "Creatures of the same species and rank promiscuously born to all the same advantages of Nature, and the use of the same faculties, should also be equal one amongst another without Subordination or Subjection." Again he says, echoing Hobbes, "The State of Nature has a Law of Nature to govern it, which obliges every one: And Reason, which is that Law, teaches all Mankind, who will but consult it, that being all equal and independent, no one ought to harm another in his Life, Health, Liberty, or Possessions" (2.§6). Locke also adds the view that humans are the special workmanship of God, but I will save that for below.

Within this framework, all the descendants of the first man, Adam, have an "equal Right to the use of the inferior creatures [animals]" (9.§87). Man, on the other hand, "has a *Property* in his own *Person*. This no Body has any Right to but himself" (5.§27). Moreover, "The *Labour* of his Body, and the *Work* of his Hands, ... are properly his" (§27). This, then, is the extremely important origin of the right to private property in Locke's view. Since nature was given to "Mankind in common" (§25), it is made into private property when one "mixed his Labor" with it (§27). Indeed labor, thought Locke, gives "a Right of Property" (§45), providing only that the private property is not made from the private property of others. The term "property" is used ambiguously by Locke, partly in the sense that we use it, particularly throughout his chapter "Of Property" (ch. 5), the sense of things owned, but throughout most of the *Second Treatise* "property" is used in an expanded sense (Laslett 1988, 102), namely, "Property, that is, his Life, Liberty and Estate" (7.§87). Hence not just the restricted but the expanded sense of property involves the transgression of others against our property. Locke took it as obvious to "Reason," not only that against "Whosoever uses *force without Right*" everyone has "a *Right* to defend himself" (19.§232), but that "the State of Nature has a Law of Nature to govern it," which is that "no one ought to harm another in his Life, Health, Liberty, or Possessions" (2.§6).

The "Law of Nature," as with Hobbes before him, was a set of conclusions or theorems in a particular set of circumstances, not something innate in human nature, as Strauss (1953, 229) rightly points out. (In the *Essay* Locke argued strenuously that there are no innate ideas.) But unlike Hobbes, Locke was a real natural rights theorist, applying universal human rights to the state of nature. Hence Locke adds that "every one has a right to punish the transgressors of that Law to such a Degree, as may hinder its Violation" (II.2.§7), and only victims have a "particular Right to seek Reparation" (§10). Punishment, in this view, however, including reparation for damages, must be "proportionate to his Transgression" (§8). This includes the crime of murder, which Locke views as a "declared War against all Mankind," so that a murderer "may be destroyed as a *Lyon* or a *Tyger,* one of those wild Savage Beasts, with whom Men can have no Society nor Security" (§11).

With regard to women and children, Locke took great exception to the view, expressed most famously in his time in Sir Robert Filmer's *Patriarcha,* that God in *Genesis* gave Adam a supreme and unlimited dominion over Eve and their children (Filmer used this to defend the divine right of kings). According to Locke, "God, in this Text, gives not, that I see, any Authority to *Adam* over *Eve,* or to Men over their Wives" (I.5.§47). Instead, marriage is a "conjugal contract" and "personal" (9.§98), a contract between two persons with "common Interest and Property" (II.7.§82), the husband has "no more power over her Life, than she has over his," and the wife has a "natural Right" (qualified by "in many cases") to separate from her husband, whether the marriage contract "be made by themselves in the state of Nature, or by the Customs or Laws of the Countrey they live in." Locke also implies that men and women as human kinds have an equal share of reason, since during pregnancy it is "from her" that the child "receives the Materials and Principles of its Constitution," including "the rational soul" (I.6.§55). Keeping with the topic of parenthood, the Bible "set up the *Mother* equal with him ['*the*

Father'], and injoyn'd nothing but what was due in common" (I.6.§61), "one common Right belonging so equally to them both, that neither can claim it wholly, neither can be excluded."[2] With regard to their children, parents have a "right to their Subjection" (II.6.§71), which is not an "Absolute Power of Life and Death" (I.6.§51), of "*exposing or selling* their Children" (§55), but an obligation of "Care" (§56), "the Obligation ... to *bring up* their Children" (§72), while children have a "Right to be nourish'd and maintained by their Parents, till they are able to provide for themselves" (II.7.§78) and have "a Title, and natural Right of Inheritance to their Fathers Goods" (I.9.§89).

Also important is Locke's theory of slavery. He defines "slavery" as "*the State of War continued, between a lawful Conqueror, and a Captive*" (4.§24). Although, he says, the "Natural Liberty of Man is to be free from any Superior Power on Earth" (§22), "Captives taken in a just War, are by the Right of Nature subjected to the Absolute Dominion and Arbitrary Power of their Masters" (7.§85). Since the captives were engaged in an unjust war, they "forfeited their Lives, and with it their Liberties, and lost their Estates." And because they "are not capable of any Property," they "cannot in that state be considered as any part of *Civil Society*; the chief end whereof is the preservation of Property." Nevertheless, it does not seem to be Locke's view that they lost their basic human rights, but instead that those rights have been trumped (i.e., they are inalienable but not absolute). Elsewhere he says, "But granting that the *Conqueror* in a just War has a Right to the Estates, as well as Power over the Persons of the Conquered; which, 'tis plain, he *hath* not: Nothing of *Absolute Power* will follow from hence, ..." (16.§193). Moreover, if in this state of slavery, he says, an agreement is reached "for a limited Power on the one side, and Obedience on the other," then "the State of War and *Slavery* ceases, as long as the Compact endures" (4.§24). All of this is in line with Locke's theory of punishment in the state of nature, which we have seen above, that everyone in the state of nature has the right to punish a wrongdoer, which Locke admits "will seem a very strange Doctrine to some Men" (2.§9). What needs to be appreciated is that Locke's theory of slavery is of a piece with that very same doctrine, and as such puts him far ahead of his time, certainly far ahead of his near contemporaries such as Grotius and Hobbes, whom I have argued were not really universal human rights theorists at all.

---

2. There is, of course, much more to Locke on women, including especially what has come to be known as "Locke's ambiguity." See, for example, the collection of essays in Hirschmann and McClure (2007). The papers especially by Melissa Butler and Jeremy Waldron support my contention that in Locke the foundation of modern inclusiveness was there, both in terms of human rights and democracy.

Nor can a person, says Locke, willingly give himself up to slavery. If a person sells himself to hard labor, "'tis plain, this was only to *Drudgery, not to Slavery*" (§24). Since liberty, says Locke, "is so necessary to, and closely joyned with a Man's Preservation, that he cannot part with it," and since (for reasons we shall see below) a man cannot rightfully "take away his own Life," it follows that he "cannot give another power over it," that he "*cannot,* by Compact, or his own Consent, *enslave himself,* to any one" (§23).

Indeed with Locke, as with Overton before him, human or natural rights are inalienable rights. And as with Overton before him, Locke's claim is equally theological. Locke believed that we are all God's property and therefore cannot do with our lives as we will. As he put it in the *Second Treatise,* "Men being all the Workmanship of one Omnipotent, and infinitely wise Maker; ... they are his Property, ... made to last during his, not one anothers Pleasure" (2.§6), to which he later adds, "he that cannot take away his own Life, cannot give another power over it" (3.§23).

Locke cannot, then, be rightly thought of as subscribing to the concept of natural slave, contrary to so many others before him and during his time. Nor is there any evidence that he excluded human races from the human species, from "men" or "man." True enough, he thought that American Indians, for example, lived mostly in the state of nature. The "wild *Indian,*" he says, "who knows no Inclosure, ... is still a Tenant in common" (5.§27), and "in the beginning all the World was *America,* ... for no such thing as *Money* was any where known" (§49). (See also §45, 7.§87, and 8.§10.) But the very fact that he would include American Indians in his discussion on the state of nature indicates alone his inclusion of them in his concept of human being. The point is clinched, moreover, when he includes them as having a natural right to property. "The Fruit, or Venison, which nourishes the wild *Indian,*" he says, "must be his, and so his, *i.e.* a part of him, that another can no longer have any right to it" (§26), and that "Thus this law of reason makes the Deer, that *Indian's* who hath killed it; 'tis allowed to be his goods who hath bestowed his labour upon it, though before, it was the common right of every one" (§30). Nor did Locke think it impossible that American Indians could enter into contracts. He is perfectly comfortable with the thought of a European and an Indian making a compact. "The Promises and Bargains for Truck," he says, "between a *Swiss* and an *Indian,* in the Woods of *America,* are binding to them, though they are perfectly in a State of Nature, in reference to one another." His point is simply that "'tis not every Compact that puts an end to the State of Nature between Men, but only this one of agreeing mutually to enter into one Community, and make one Body Politick" (2.§14).

So far what we have examined in Locke involves mainly the state of nature. We have yet to examine his political theory. The state of nature, says Locke, despite its many rights and freedoms, is "full of fears and continual dangers," in that "the enjoyment of the property he has in this state is very unsafe, very unsecure" (9.§123). Hence at various times and places throughout history people formed a social contract, meaning that by "mutual consent" they erected a government—variously called by Locke a "Civil Society," "Political Society," "Body Politick," or "Commonwealth"—meant to exercise "the will and determination of the majority" (8.§96), the "great and chief end" of which is "the Preservation of their Property" (9.§124; also 7.§85). Indeed Locke calls it "this Fundamental, Sacred, and unalterable Law of Self-Preservation, for which they enter'd into Society" (13.§149). Hence if one or more private individuals are the victims of "unlawful acts done by the Magistrate," they "have a right to defend themselves, and to recover by force, what by unlawful force is taken from them" (18.§208). And if a government should ever overstep its proper bounds, such as enslaving some of its citizens or raising taxes without the consent of the people, in other words if it should transgress on their natural rights, then the people "have a Right to resume their original Liberty" (19.§222) and rise up in "Rebellion" (§226; also §243). Indeed for Locke, again, the fundamental purpose of government is to protect human rights: "Government being for the Preservation of every Mans Right and Property, by Preserving him from the Violence or Injury of others, is for the good of the Governed" (I.9.§92).

The connection with genuine democratic beliefs and values is also sufficiently clear in Locke's *Two Treatises*. But that is a topic I want to reserve for the next chapter, for that is where we shall examine the profound significance of the connection.

At this point we need to examine some criticisms of the above interpretation of Locke. A chain of argument is only as strong as its weakest link, after all, and if the interpretation of Locke presented in this chapter is weak, it would make the entire argument of this book weak.

For a start, Jack Donnelly (2003), for example, on the one hand admits that Locke is "the seminal figure in the strand of liberalism that grounds the commitment to equal liberty on natural, or what we today call human, rights" (47). On the other hand, however, he also claims that "Locke clearly envisioned a political world of propertied Christian men. Women, along with 'savages,' servants, and wage laborers, were never imagined to be holders of natural rights" (60). I think we have seen already, however, from the passages quoted above, that this interpretation is far from charitable or accurate.

In another line of criticism, it might be thought that Locke did not really have the modern concept of universal human rights after all, since he seemed to believe that some human rights can be given up or are transferable. For example, in the *Second Treatise* Locke claims, as we have seen, that in the state of nature every individual human has the natural right to punish a wrongdoer against the "Law of Nature." But he also claims that when humans enter into a social contract they transfer this right, the right to "punish the Offences," to the state, for "there, and there only is *Political Society,* where every one of the Members hath quitted this natural Power, resign'd it up into the hands of the Community in all cases that exclude him not from appealing for Protection to the Law established by it. And thus ... the Community comes to be Umpire" (7.§87). Again he says, "he has given a right to the Commonwealth to imploy his force" (§88). Locke adds that the intention behind the transference has remained the same, "the better to preserve himself his Liberty and Property" (9.§131). But no matter. If a right is transferable, then it cannot be a *human* right, for one cannot transfer one's humanity.

There is no question that there is a problem of inconsistency here. The problem, however, affects not only Locke but also many modern democracies based on the belief in inalienable human rights, for example states that alienate the right to vote from prisoners or states that alienate the right to life by means of capital punishment. *Inalienable,* of course, does not automatically mean *absolute,* as pointed out in the Introduction. Moreover, it is possible to conceive of human rights as innate and inalienable and yet *context dependent,* for example as being latent in the state of nature but manifest in a political context or vice versa. But the point perhaps can still be made that many modern democracies are not perfectly consistent in the way they deal with human rights. And yet that does not mean that they do not believe in universal human rights. For all of the above reasons, then, I do not think it follows from possible inconsistencies in Locke's writings that he was not a genuine human rights theorist, specifically that he did not have an early version of the modern consensus concept.

Much more troubling is the argument developed by Jacqueline Stevens (1996). In line with her argument that attempts to show that Locke indeed believed in majority rule in a just state (a matter taken up in the next chapter), she attempts "to show Locke's rejection of natural rights doctrine altogether, once a majority has inaugurated political society" (453n4). In other words, she attempts to show that all human rights according to Locke are lost once one enters into a political state, that what matters for Locke is only "'the people's' rights en masse (or, rather, as a majority)" (434). There is much to be said against this interpretation of Locke as a *communitarian* in this sense of the term. Suffice it here to say not only that it goes against the consensus of Locke scholarship, but also that there are passages in Locke's *Two Treatises* that clearly swing toward the interpretation of Locke defended in this chapter. For one, Locke clearly states that "Government being for the Preservation of every Mans Right and Property, by preserving him from Violence or Injury of others, is for the good of the Governed" (I.9.§92). The word "every" here is key, for it is clearly inconsistent with "en masse" or "majority." Another key passage is Locke's discussion on divorce. As we have seen already, Locke claims that a wife has a "natural Right" to divorce her husband, "whether the Contract be made by themselves in the state of Nature, or by the Customs or Laws of the Countrey they live in" (II.7.82). The word "whether" here is key and makes it clear that Locke did not think this natural right was lost once one enters into a political state. In the next chapter we shall look more closely at Locke's theory of property in connection with his democratic beliefs and values, but the above should be sufficient to deflate interpretations of Locke as a communitarian rather than as a genuine human rights theorist.

Or rather it should deflate the *above* sense of "communitarian." Matthew Kramer (1997) develops and defends a very different interpretation of Locke as a communitarian, where the term is defined "roughly as the moral/political prioritization of collective needs over any individual's needs" (ix). Kramer rejects the traditional interpretation of Locke as a radical liberal in favor of Locke as a communitarian, not only with regard to the political state but even with regard to humans in a state of nature. Kramer takes seriously not only Locke's theology but also his statement in the *Second Treatise* that "in the State of Nature ... *Mankind are one Community,* ... one Society distinct from all other Creatures" (9.§128). It is Locke as the state-of-nature communitarian that explains Locke's theory of human rights both generally and in particular, such as the natural right of anyone to punish a transgressor in the state of nature (2.§7, 9.§128) and the limitation on the natural right to private property to "where there is enough, and as good left in common for others" (5.§27). As Kramer puts it, "Efficiency-oriented reasoning can account for the bestowal of rights of property on the earliest human agents, *not* because such rights were integrally promotive of the welfare and wishes of every agent, but because the rights were integrally promotive of the welfare of humankind. In other words, such reasoning assigns people their rights as functions of collective goals and demands" (126). The same reasoning applies to humans in a political state. Again as Kramer puts Locke's thinking, "Rights of property, like rights to liberty and security, did not disappear or come to be overridden and null; but their boundaries were tightened in order to make the operations of government feasible" (225). Kramer has a very attractive interpretation of Locke in all of this, one that explains much that has hitherto seemed rather odd. But is Kramer's interpretation of Locke compatible with the interpretation of Locke that I defend in this and the next chapter, according to which the purpose of government is the protection of human rights and human rights can be claimed against the state? In a personal communication, Kramer has confirmed to me that, to use Dworkin's (1978) distinction between *policy* and *principle* (22)—where the former is about "an improvement in some economic, political, or social feature of the community" and the latter is about "justice or fairness or some other dimension of morality"—majority rule in a just society for Locke determines only "matters of policy"; it does not and cannot determine "matters of principle," since "the latter matters involve the basic rights of individuals" (pers. comm. 2010).

Jefferson to the Present

From this beginning in Locke—the first major thinker in history to have the concept of universal human rights—we can trace the spread of universal human rights thinking to the rest of the world, which not coincidentally was on the back of the spread of democratic beliefs and values.

It is now generally agreed that Locke did not write the *Two Treatises* in order to justify the "Glorious Revolution" of 1688 (more on this in the following chapter), but that the majority of it was written almost a decade prior, during a year or two sometime between 1679 and 1683, primarily to justify and promote an insurrection, with only some of the parts of the *Second Treatise* having been written concurrently with the Glorious Revolution or shortly following it (Milton 1994, 14–15). But whatever the facts, there should be no surprise that when the British colonies in America began seriously contemplating independence from the British monarchy, some of the most influential of their thinkers turned largely to the writings and ideas of Locke.

The line from Locke to Jefferson, of course, was not "monocausal" or "single-track" (Haakonssen 1991, 42–52). During the early and mid-eighteenth century, moral theory as taught in American colleges and universities was heavily influenced by moral theories of the English and Scottish Enlightenment, including human rights as well as natural law and "moral sense" theories (the latter accounting for "self-evident" moral truths). The beginning of the second paragraph of the Declaration of Independence as penned by Jefferson clearly reflects this influence: "We hold these truths to be self-evident: that all men are created equal; that they are endowed by their creator with inherent and inalienable rights; that among these are life, liberty, & the pursuit of happiness: that to secure these rights, governments are instituted among men, deriving their just powers from the consent of the governed; ..." (Peterson 1984, 19).

Immediately a problem arises. For what did Jefferson mean by "men"? A common criticism, expressed by Richard Primus (1999), for example, is that the use of "human rights" in the Universal Declaration of Human Rights of 1948 "represented the rise of a new concept" (191), that "what modern Americans mean by 'human rights' differs from what Locke and the Founders meant by 'natural rights'" (192), that "Natural rights theorists often excluded non-whites, women, and other groups of people from the population of rights-bearers, but human rights theorists insist that all people everywhere bear the same rights." "The vocabulary of 'human rights,'" he adds, "emerged during the 1940s as a way of articulating the anti-totalitarian political creed that all people had certain rights, no matter where or under what kind of law." Moreover still, he says, "the American Constitution was written long before the rise of 'human rights' as a term and as a concept" (195), and the "'inalienable rights' of Americans in 1776 certainly did not include rights against racial or sexual discrimination" (196). The Declaration of Independence is mainly "poetry" and "was of course not intended to operate as a legal code" (197).

There is much to be said for these statements, and also much to be said against them. Certainly many in Jefferson's day read "men" in the Declaration the way Primus claims. And certainly America at that time was rife with racism and sexism. But we need to distinguish between *principle* and *practice*. I submit that the principle of modern inclusiveness was already there, even though the practice was not and would take many more years. We have already seen the principle quite clearly in Levellers such as Lilburne and Overton and also in Locke. When they used the terms "men" or "man" in the context of natural rights, they were using them in the gender-neutral sense, not in the gendered sense.

And there were many in Jefferson's day who read the Declaration of Independence in the very same way. Thomas Paine, for example, despite the title of his *Rights of Man* (1791), read the "Revolutions of America and France" as "a renovation of the natural order of things" (Foner 1995, 537), such that "all men are born equal, and with equal natural rights" and "*the unity or equality of man*" clearly referred in his mind to "male and female" (463).

What Jefferson himself thought, of course, is also extremely important. In a letter to Paine written in 1792, in reference to Paine's *Rights of Man,* Jefferson gives him his full endorsement, calling himself a "votary" (Peterson 1984, 992).

But there is more. It is surely significant that years later, in a letter written in 1825, on the topic of "the object of the Declaration of Independence," Jefferson would claim that

> Not to find out new principles, or new arguments, never before thought of, not merely to say things which had never been said before; but to place before mankind the common sense of the subject, in terms so plain and firm as to command their assent, and to justify ourselves in the independent stand we are compelled to take. Neither aiming at originality of principle or sentiment, nor yet copied from any

particular and previous writing, it was intended to be an expression of the American mind, and to give to that expression the proper tone and spirit called for by the occasion. All its authority rests then on the harmonizing sentiments of the day, whether expressed in conversation, in letters, printed essays, or in the elementary books of public right, as Aristotle, Cicero, Locke, Sidney, &c. [Peterson 1984, 1501]

For all the claim to "the harmonizing sentiments of the day," however, and "the expression of the American mind"—Jefferson clearly was not claiming that the American mind was original here, but rather was referring to the general *state* of the American mind—the single most important influence was clearly that of Locke. In a letter written much earlier, in 1789, Jefferson would declare "Bacon, Locke, and Newton ... the three greatest men that have ever lived, without any exception," as having laid the foundation of "the Physical & Moral sciences" (Peterson 1984, 939–940). And of these three Locke is really the only one who is relevant to the "moral sciences."[3]

Moreover still, Jefferson was commissioned to write the Declaration of Independence by the Committee of Five, of which he was a member, which itself was commissioned by Congress to draft a "declaration of Independency [*sic*]." It is surely significant not only that the Committee of Five submitted Jefferson's draft to Congress virtually unchanged (Maier 1997, 122), but also that both Jefferson's friends and political opponents recognized Locke's influence in the Declaration. Richard Henry Lee, for example, who drafted and submitted his Resolution for Independence to Congress on June 7, 1776—which was ratified, by the way, on July 2—and who was a friend of Jefferson's and a fellow Virginian statesman, was given by Jefferson a copy of his draft of the Declaration that was submitted to Congress. Lee responded to Jefferson that the Declaration had been "copied from Locke's treatise on government" (124). A few decades later certain members of the Federalists had a repeat experience of Lee's impression and tried to minimize Jefferson's authorship by claiming that he "stole" various ideas from Locke (171).

---

3. Jefferson's statement might seem to conflict with what he thought of Jesus. Although Jefferson apparently rejected the concept of the Trinity and was a "deist" only in the sense in which he defined the term—literally, *mono*theism (Peterson 1984, 1124, 1468–1469)—he considered himself a Christian "in the only sense he [Jesus] wished any one to be; sincerely attached to his doctrines, in preference to all others; ascribing to himself every *human* excellence; & believing he never claimed any other" (1122). (See also what is known as Jefferson's Bible.) So did Jefferson believe that Jesus taught human rights? Apparently, if only in spirit, since Jesus's "system of morals ... if filled up in the true style and spirit of the rich fragments he left us, would be the most perfect and sublime that has ever been taught by man" (1125). By "the three greatest men that have ever lived," then, Jefferson, given the principle of charity, should be taken to mean "the three greatest *systematic philosophers* that have ever lived."

That Jefferson's contemporaries recognized the influence of Locke should not be surprising. Again, Locke's political theory had been widely taught in American colleges and universities. But not only that, as James Hutson (1991) points out, it was Locke's, and not Hobbes's, concept of the state of nature that "began appearing in American writing less than thirty years after the publication in 1690 of Locke's *Two Treatises*" (71), such that "From one end of the colonies to another, Americans after 1774 considered that the actions of George III [the king of England] had reduced them to a state of nature" (73). In other words, it was mainly Locke's theory of human rights that provided the ideas behind the American Revolution. As Hutson argues, from the time the English Parliament imposed the Stamp Act in 1765 on the American colonies, involving a variety of taxes without consent and trial without jury, both in violation of the Magna Carta, to most notably the Coercive Acts of 1774 (so called by the British but called the Intolerable Acts by the Americans), a series of four remarkably severe laws passed in response to the Boston Tea Party, which were supported by the king's call for a military response to American resistance, the colonists turned from the British Constitution to natural law theory as their source of rights. As one of the colonists put it, "by the Revolution [Americans] have regained all their natural rights" (70). Except for the poor choice of the word "regained," this is clearly the message of the Declaration of Independence.

We can also clearly see the echo of Locke's *Two Treatises* (as Jefferson and many of his contemporaries must have understood it) not only in the Declaration but in related ideas subscribed to by Jefferson. For example, although not found fully explicit in the Declaration, Jefferson often wrote of "expatriation being a natural right" (Peterson 1984, 9, 36, 374–375, 702). And while in the Declaration he wrote that "to secure these rights [the 'inherent and inalienable rights' of man], governments are instituted among men, deriving their just powers from the consent of the governed" (19), he also elsewhere in the context of expatriation wrote of the new republic's being founded on "democratic principles" (36). He similarly wrote that "the will of the majority, the Natural law of every society, is the only sure guardian of the rights of man" (491).

Moreover, Jefferson clearly did intend to include all humans under the label "men" (just as Locke did before him). As he points out in his *Autobiography* (1821), not only did he fight for the emancipation of slaves as early as 1769 (5), but he also included a passage in the Declaration censuring slavery, as a "cruel war against human nature itself, violating its most sacred rights of life and liberty" (22), which was struck out by Congress for fear that the Declaration would not be signed by a number of states such as Georgia (18) (unity against Britain, after all, was at that time the prime expedient). He would later write that "the day is not distant when it [the public mind] must bear and adopt it [an amendment against slavery], or worse will follow. Nothing is more certainly written in the book of fate that these people are to be free" (44).[4] As for American Indians, Jefferson stated in his *Notes on the State of Virginia* (1781) that "They astonish you with strokes of the most sublime oratory; such as prove their reason and sentiment strong" (266). He would later state, in his Second Inaugural Address (1805), that "The aboriginal inhabitants ... [are] Endowed with the faculties and the rights of men" (520). And as regards women, Jefferson wrote in *Notes on the State of Virginia* that (much like Locke) "It is civilization alone which replaces women [compared with barbarous people] in the enjoyment of their natural equality" (185–186).

There are yet further interesting points of comparison between Locke and Jefferson. For example, although in his *Two Treatises* Locke surprisingly did not explicitly include freedom of religion and freedom of expression (which would entail freedom of the press) in his various discussions on human rights (Laslett 1988, 86), both were deeply important to him. The former he had previously included as an "absolute and universal right" (as we shall see in the next chapter), while later in life he explicitly advocated for the "liberty to print whatever he would speak," subject only to laws against libel and sedition (Goldie 1997, 329–339). Likewise Jefferson, although he did not mention freedom of religion or of expression in the Declaration of Independence, clearly included freedom of religion among the "natural rights of mankind" (Peterson 1984, 285, 348), and wanted "freedom of the press" included in the Constitution (71) limited only by "commission of private injury" (344), which he defended as late as his Second Inaugural Address in 1805 (522). Jefferson even seems to have shared Locke's circumscription of human rights in terms of society rather than the individual (as per Kramer's interpretation of Locke examined in the previous section), in that he is "convinced" that man "has no natural right in opposition to his social duties" (510).

Returning to the Declaration of Independence, it was not written by Jefferson simply as "poetry." He was commissioned to write it, such that it served primarily as a "constitutional document ... one that concerned the fundamental authority of government" (Maier 1997, 126). It is also surely significant that the all-important

---

4. See also Griswold (1991). All of this stands despite the lamentable fact that Jefferson advocated the segregation of blacks and whites into separate countries, by "emancipation and deportation peaceably and in such slow degree as that evil [slavery] will wear off insensibly," as he put it in his *Autobiography*, the former slave-labor jobs in America eventually to be filled by "free white laborers" (Peterson 1984, 44). For an elaboration on his reasons, which indeed leave much to be desired, but none of which denies blacks as bearers of human rights, see Query XIV of his *Notes on the State of Virginia* (264–270).

second paragraph—the one with the statement that "all men are created equal; . . . they are endowed by their creator with inherent and inalienable rights"—remained fundamentally intact as the Declaration went through eighty-six alterations (Hunt 2007, 18) from Jefferson's own alterations to the final version ratified by Congress. The most notable difference is that "inherent and inalienable rights" in Jefferson's "original rough draft" ultimately ended up as "certain inalienable rights" at the hands of Congress (Maier 1997, 134), evidently because "inherent" was thought to be redundant. No doubt the *practice* was still some time in coming, but I submit that the *principle* of modern inclusiveness was there, as it had been in Locke and the Levellers before him.[5]

In all of this, then, I think it is safe to say that it is as if a torch had been passed from Locke to Jefferson. The "as if" is an important qualification, for the ideas from Locke were already in the American air by the time Jefferson sat down to write the Declaration of Independence. But the Declaration was the crucial document, the most crucial following Locke's *Two Treatises*. And from Jefferson's paragraph on human rights in the Declaration the flame continued to spread. State constitutions followed with their own declarations of human rights. For example, in 1779 John Adams, who himself served as Chair of the Committee of Five, wrote the Constitution for the state of Massachusetts—eight and ten years, respectively, before the drafting of the federal Constitution (1787) and the Bill of Rights (1789), the first ten Amendments to the Constitution—the first Article of which states, "All men are born equally free and independent, and have certain natural, essential, and unalienable rights, among which may be reckoned the right of enjoying and defending their lives and liberties; that of acquiring, possessing, and protecting their property; in fine, that of seeking and obtaining their safety and happiness"

---

5. The influence of Locke on Jefferson has been seriously challenged notably by Wills (1978). But the challenge has been sufficiently refuted, to my mind, by Maier (1997, esp. pp. 124–125 and 134–137), who also defends (as does Wills) the above interpretation of "all men" and "equal" as meaning all humans. Jefferson was mainly a funnel, a sieve, a conduit—which is not to diminish his importance—who even quoted in one of his later writings Colonel Richard Rumbold, an English Leveller to the last, who with a noose around his neck made a Leveller motto famous just before he was hanged in 1685 for treason: "I am sure there was no man born marked of God above another; for none comes into the world with a saddle on his back, neither any booted and spurred to ride him" (Maier 1997, 125; quoted in full in Sharp 1998, vii). Given the many complexities of the history, I shall continue to write, for the sake of simplicity and not naively, of Jefferson as the "author" of the Declaration of Independence (which Jefferson himself instructed to be on his gravestone), keeping in mind that my focus is on the all-important second paragraph and that Jefferson did not write independently. In fact, that he did not write independently only strengthens my case.

(Thompson 2000, 298). This draft became a model for other state constitutions and for the federal Constitution itself (despite the latter's lack of a preamble on human rights). And it is interesting and important to add here that in a previous writing, titled "A Dissertation on the Canon and Feudal Law," written in 1765, Adams defines "rights" in terms of "the populace," stating, "RIGHTS, for such they have, undoubtedly, antecedent to all earthly government,—*Rights,* that cannot be repealed or restrained by human laws—*Rights,* derived from the great Legislator of the universe" (Thompson 2000, 22).

From the American Revolution the idea of universal human rights spread to the French Revolution. In the French Declaration of the Rights of Man and of the Citizen, published in 1789 under the "auspices of the Supreme Being," as the Declaration puts it, and written "most likely with Jefferson's help" (Hunt 2007, 16), it states that "Men are born and remain free and equal in rights" and that "The aim of every political association is the preservation of the natural and inalienable rights of man. These rights are liberty, property, security, and resistance to oppression" (Hayden 2001, 350). In France, it should be noted, although they invented the phrase "rights of man," this wording was not only common prior to 1789 but also was commonly used alongside the phrases "rights of humanity" and "rights of the citizen," thanks mainly to the popularity of Rousseau's *Social Contract* of 1762, which uses both phrases interchangeably (Hunt 2007, 23–24).

The nineteenth century experienced a backlash against the concept of universal human rights, as the historian Lynn Hunt (2007) puts it, "an explosion in biological explanation of difference" (186). But the backlash did not come simply from "new forms of racism, anti-Semitism, and sexism." Nationalism and colonialism received enormous support from creationist biology, to be sure, the latter including the likes of Georges Cuvier, Robert Knox, and Louis Agassiz, but some of the backlash came from the implications of Darwinian evolution, evident in the writings of "Darwin's Bulldog," T. H. Huxley, such as his essays "On the Natural Inequality of Men" and "Natural Rights and Political Rights," both published in 1890. And while another source of the backlash was the rise in communist thinking (Marx and Engels), we can also add the rise in utilitarian thinking (Bentham and Mill). (There will be more on both of these in the following chapters.)

Perhaps the peak in the backlash during the 1800s was the debate over slavery in the days during and preceding the American Civil War. As Abraham Lincoln put it in a letter dated April 6, 1859, with reference to contemporary American politicians and the second paragraph of the Declaration of Independence, "The principles of Jefferson are the definitions and axioms of free society. And yet they are denied, and evaded, with no small show of success. One dashingly calls them 'glittering generalities'; another bluntly calls them 'self evident lies'; and still others insidiously argue that they apply only to 'superior races'" (Fehrenbacher 1989, 19). Lincoln himself was convinced that not only Jefferson but also the rest of the Founding Fathers took "all men" in the Declaration to mean all human beings, not just whites (57, 213), and that they intended to set the institution of slavery in America "in the course of ultimate extinction" (38, 141).

Given these different strains in the opposing forces of the nineteenth century, it should probably come as no surprise that the next major landmark in human rights talk came not after World War I but after World War II, in the form of the Universal Declaration of Human Rights, framed by the United Nations in 1948. WWI resulted in the deaths mainly of soldiers, around 14 million, whereas WWII resulted in far more deaths, upwards of 60 million, and mostly civilians (Hunt 2007, 200–201). But even more significant, the Universal Declaration was in obvious response to Adolf Hitler's attempt to take over the world, which included the world's greatest case of genocide (if not in numbers, then certainly in mechanization), and also to the impending Cold War, as Stalin had rejected the UN as an effective body (Norman and Zaidi 2008, 152). People wanted no more, they wanted hope, they wanted a new world order, and the window of opportunity was slim indeed.

Two features of the Declaration are of special interest. One is the lack of any reference to God or to a Creator. This was in deference to the Soviet camp, resulting in Saudi Arabia's abstaining largely because the Declaration was secular, which set a pattern for later critiques (Normand and Zaidi 2008, 187, 193). What we find, instead, is the claim that "all members of the human family" have "equal and inalienable rights" (Preamble) and that "All human beings are born free and equal in dignity and rights. They are endowed with reason and conscience and should act towards one another in a spirit of brotherhood" (Art. 1).

The second interesting feature is the long list of specific human rights, given in thirty Articles. Among them are: "Everyone has the right to life, liberty and security of person" (Art. 3); "No one shall be held in slavery or servitude" (Art. 4); "Everyone has the right to a nationality" (Art. 15); "Men and women of full age, without any limitation due to race, nationality or religion, have the right to marry and to found a family. They are entitled to equal rights as to marriage, during marriage and at its dissolution" (Art. 16); "Everyone has the right to own property alone as well as in association with others" (Art. 17); "Everyone has the right to freedom of thought, conscience and religion" (Art. 18); "Everyone has the right to take part in the government of his country, directly or through freely chosen representatives" (Art. 21); "The will of the people shall be the basis of the authority of government; this will shall be expressed in periodic and genuine elections which shall be by universal and equal suffrage and shall be held by secret vote or by equivalent free voting procedures" (Art. 21); "Everyone, without any discrimination, has the right to equal pay for equal work" (Art. 23); "Everyone has the right to form and to join trade unions for the protection of his interests" (Art. 23); "Everyone has the right to rest and leisure, including ... periodic holidays with pay" (Art 24); "Everyone has the right to a standard of living adequate for the health and well-being of himself and of his family, including food, clothing, housing and medical care and necessary social services" (Art. 25); "Everyone has the right to education. Education shall be free, at least in the elementary and fundamental stages" (Art. 26); "Parents have a prior right to choose the kind of education that shall be given to their children" (Art. 26).

Since the Declaration by the United Nations in 1948, there has been a proliferation of declarations in the form of various Conventions, Covenants, Charters, Declarations, and Drafts, among them the European Convention for the Protection of Human Rights and Fundamental Freedoms (1953), the United Nations International Covenant on Economic, Social, and Cultural Rights (1966), the International Convention on the Elimination of All Forms of Racial Discrimination (1969), the United Nations Declaration on the Rights of Disabled Persons (1975), the Helsinki Declaration on Principles Guiding Relations Between Participating States (1975), the Convention on the Elimination of All Forms of Discrimination Against Women (1979), the African Charter on Human and Peoples' Rights (1981), the Universal Islamic Declaration of Human Rights (1981), the United Nations Convention on the Rights of the Child (1989), the Vienna Declaration and Programme of Action (1993), the Declaration on the Rights of Persons Belonging to National, Ethnic, Religious, or Linguistic Minorities (1993), the Draft Declaration on the Rights of Indigenous Peoples (1994), and the Draft Declaration of Principles on Human Rights and the Environment (1994).

In all of this, from the core of beliefs begun by the Levellers and furthered by Locke, to the American and French Revolutions and then to the UN and beyond, though much has been added to the core from the beginning, the spread of the concept of universal human rights bears an uncanny resemblance to the spread and evolution of a bacterium or virus in a host population, or rather the spread and evolution from one population to other populations that make up the species. Our next question is how to successfully account for this.

Chapter 6

Explaining the Human Rights Epidemic

> Modern representative democracy has changed the idea of democracy almost beyond recognition. But, in so doing, it has shifted it from one of history's hopeless losers to one of its more insistent winners.
>
> —*John Dunn (2006, 20)*

Memetics

FOLLOWING THE BIOLOGIST RICHARD DAWKINS, who coined the term in his classic *The Selfish Gene* (1976, ch. 11), a *meme* is a unit of cultural inheritance (*meme* is taken from the Greek word *mimeme,* which means "that which is imitated"). Much like genes, memes are units of information carried in a physical medium (at this preliminary stage we shall confine ourselves to human brains). In common with genes and with information in general, memes behave as if their prime directive were to make more and more copies of themselves (hence the metaphor *selfish,* just like *selfish genes*). This is a truly revolutionary idea. As Dawkins puts it, "What we have not previously considered is that a cultural trait may have evolved in the way that it has, simply because it is *advantageous to itself*" (200). We typically think of people as having ideas, but memetics requires us to turn this upside down and think of ideas as having people. From this perspective the success of a meme is the number of people who carry copies of the meme in their brains. Since each human brain can store a limited amount of memes, since there are a limited number of human brains in the world, and since many memes are incompatible with one another, memes compete against other memes in a Darwinian struggle for existence, all of which means that memes are subject to the evolutionary processes of mutation, natural selection, drift, and symbiosis.

Another part of memetic theory is that our bulbous, metabolically greedy brains evolved in large part to be what Dawkins calls "meme machines" (Dawkins 1976, 201; Blackmore 1999, 235), not only in the sense that we can store a lot of memes and are fairly good at copying them, but also that we are built to spread them and in many cases will even defend them, sometimes with our very lives. This is the memetic perspective on ideologies, and it helps to illuminate E. O. Wilson's (1975) claim that "Human beings are absurdly easy to indoctrinate—they *seek* it" (286).

The overall picture, then, is that while many memes function simply as ideas, many other memes function as behavioral programs, providing the appearance that they are controlling the behavior of their hosts. This is particularly true of memes that are not grounded in evidence, such as religion memes, examined in vivid fashion in Bill Maher's documentary *Religulous*. There should be no surprise, then, that religion has been the subject of repeated memetic analyses (e.g., Lynch 1996, ch. 5; Blackmore 1999, ch. 15; Stamos 2008, 177–184). Unlike science memes, which contra thinkers such as Kuhn and Foucault spread mainly or ultimately because of the force of evidence, religion memes seem to proliferate in a virus-type fashion, with thousands of meme complexes evolving and competing for hosts.

What I shall argue in this chapter is that memetics provides the best explanation of the origin and spread of the belief in universal human rights, or rather, that it best explains the origin and spread of the *content* of the belief. At the end of this chapter I shall then employ evolutionary psychology to help explain the psychological *force* of the belief.

Before we get into the application of memetics, however, I want to deal with what are perhaps the two main criticisms against it. Partly because it is so new, and partly because it seems so counterintuitive, memetics is highly controversial, not only in its particular applications but in itself, with many doubting that it is a legitimate science at all, and many questioning the nature and even the very existence of memes (see, e.g., Aunger 2000, 2002, 2007; Laland and Brown 2002, ch. 6; Distin 2005; Richerson and Boyd 2005). Most prefer explanations in terms of cultural, economic, political, and intellectual forces. Before I apply memetics to the topic of universal human rights, then, I need to address the main criticisms against it, if only to open the reader's mind to the central argument of this chapter.

One of the problems that many people have with memetics is that the analogy between memes and genes seems a poor one. Memes, it is said, have too low of a copying fidelity. Genes, after all, are digital (life on Earth involves a four-letter genetic code), with little noise in their reproduction. Point mutations, the most common of all mutations, consist of a single change in one of the four letters in a gene, and are relatively rare when copies of genes are made. Memes, on the other hand, are analog, not digital, which is to say they exist as patterns rather than as quantitative bits of information. Moreover, they have a high ratio of noise in their reproduction and are capable of a substantial amount of blending.

Despite these differences, however, it should be obvious enough that memes (we shall keep it simple and confine ourselves to ideas) do seem capable of having *enough* copying fidelity to function as replicators in an evolutionary process, to be capable of sufficient longevity to produce a population of recognizable copies and to be subject to processes such as mutation (alteration), natural selection (nonrandom differential reproductive success), and drift (sampling error). Even the most stubborn skeptic, I would think, should at least be able to admit that some ideas seem to spread simply for their own sake, simply because there is something about them that increases their spread from one human brain to another. It is common knowledge that a catchy tune, for example, which began, say, with one person singing the tune on TV, can be stuck in your head before you know it, and then you hear someone humming it in an elevator or whistling it on a sidewalk, if not outright singing it, too. At any rate, the lesser fidelity of memes compared with genes, along with their ability to blend, has the consequence that memetic evolution is generally going to occur much faster than genetic evolution, not that it has no evolution at all.

There is a further important feature that memes have in common with genes. None but the unreflective think of genes as physical things, as segments of DNA or RNA. Biologists often talk of genes as physical things, but when they do they are talking loosely and it is not what they really mean. The eminent biologist George C. Williams (1992) makes this abundantly clear when he writes of genes as units of "information," that "DNA is the medium, not the message. A gene is not a DNA molecule; it is the transcribable information coded by the molecule" (11). To anyone who has studied the standard genetic code, the matching of sixty-four codons (triplets of RNA letters) to twenty amino acids (the building blocks of life on Earth), this should be obvious, given that the code involves (as it must) a great deal of synonymy (redundancy). Since different strings or sequences of DNA and RNA letters can carry the exact same genetic message (and even other kinds of molecules could conceivably do so as well), it follows that genes, as with information in general, supervene on their mediums and so are not reducible to them. In much the same way, memes are not physical either, but are units of information carried in different mediums. The mediums are not DNA or RNA but instead brains, and more recently books, magnetic tapes, CDs/DVDs, and computer hard drives. As such, memes supervene on their different mediums and accordingly are not reducible to them. (To help get this point across, when you buy a book, such as this one, you are not paying mainly for the paper and ink but for the information it carries, which was produced by a brain and originally carried in a hard drive and can be carried by still other physical mediums.)

The second main difficulty that people have with memetics has to do with the concept of *copying*. Genes are genuinely copied. In DNA replication, for example, when the double helix is uncoiled, each helix serves as a template for the production of a complementary strand by DNA polymerases, resulting in two identical DNA molecules (barring mutations). With memes, however, there is no direct copying from brain to brain. (I'm leaving aside books and related mediums for the sake of simplicity.) One brain does not have direct access to another, from which it copies its memes from a template. Instead, memes are copied only in a loose sense, if they are copied at all, as the process is an indirect one involving a number of stages from one brain to the next brain. In the first brain there is an idea, which is carried via a set of signals from the brain to the mouth in the case of verbal communication, resulting in a set of linguistic utterances. Those utterances are then perceived by another human, which involves a set of signals going to its brain, resulting (though not necessarily) in a corresponding idea. This process is so complicated and so indirect, with an enormous potential for change in the information between the one brain and the next, that many do not want to call the process "copying" at all, but rather, at best, "reproducing" or "re-creating." And if that is an accurate description of what is really going on, then it would seem that memes do not really exist, given the definition of *meme* as "a unit of cultural transmission, or a unit of *imitation*" (Dawkins 1976, 192).

This criticism, however, as powerful as it might seem, needs to be put into perspective to better appreciate memetics. For a start, if we simply confine ourselves to ordinary language, it should be clear that copying is no less copying if the copying process is not direct but involves intermediate processes. When a student copies an answer from another student during an exam, for example, the answer, a string of information, begins in one brain and ends up in the second brain via a long sequence of intermediate processes. And yet no one would think of absolving the second student of cheating because the intermediate processes were too long and complicated to count as genuine copying. The same goes for when one copies a document using a photocopier. The copying machine is not misnamed because of all the intermediate processes involved, no matter whether the machine is an excellent one like the ones of today or the horrible ones in the library way back when I was an undergraduate. There is a problem, of course, with how much similarity is required for something to be rightly considered a copy of something else, but the fact remains that the way we ordinarily talk provides no barrier to our rightly saying that a copying process has gone on even when it involved many intermediate processes. Ordinary language is not the be-all and end-all of meaning (a point elaborated upon in Chapter 3), but until a good reason is provided for why ordinary language should not be followed when it comes to the word *copying,* the criticism against memetics based on intermediate processes lacks force.

There is even more that needs to be said against this criticism. Many might object, of course, to the comparison of photocopiers with humans, viewing it as a bad or false comparison, for it may be said that humans are not machines after all. Nevertheless, modern science gives us plenty of reasons to think of humans as rather good copying machines, even as excellent ones. One reason is *neoteny* in human evolution, the evolution of juvenile characteristics into adulthood. Few if any biologists doubt anymore that this occurred in human evolution. If you take the face of an adult human and compare it with the face of an adult chimpanzee and a juvenile chimpanzee, by far the closest similarity is between the face of the adult human and the face of the juvenile chimpanzee. For whatever reason, humans, unlike our primate relatives (or to a far greater degree), evolved neotenously. We are, in the words of Stephen Jay Gould (1981), "permanent children," and he puts it this way: "In other mammals, exploration, play, and flexibility of behavior are qualities of juveniles, only rarely of adults. We retain not only the anatomical stamp of childhood, but its mental flexibility as well.... Humans are learning animals" (333). What Gould should have added is that juvenile mammals, at least among primates, are generally more imitative than adults, and that this would be an adaptive trait necessary for their greater learning curve. As the anthropologist Barry Bogin (1990) points out, in primates "most imitative learning occurs between females and their offspring" (20). A juvenile chimpanzee, for example, learns which foods are good to eat and how to get them by imitating its mother, which is the way it also learns how to interact with other members of the group. Learning is something more than merely imitating, of course, but imitating is among the early stepping stones to learning. In all of this we need not go the whole hog and argue that memes in early humans drove neoteny in human evolution all the better to spread themselves (a pet hypothesis of mine, to which I give very little weight), with the human brain reaching virtually adult size when its body has reached only 40 percent of its adult size, but whether a product or by-product of evolution, a greater ability to imitate is part of the adult human repertoire.

A further reason to believe that humans are remarkable copying machines comes from neuroscience, specifically the discovery of what are called *mirror neurons* (Rizzolatti and Fogassi 2007). First discovered in two specific regions of the brains of macaque monkeys, these neurons function to imitate observed behaviors, in the case of macaque monkeys "hand mirror neurons" for goal-oriented hand actions and "mouth mirror neurons" for mouth actions, with a small subset functioning as "communicative mouth mirror neurons" for imitating behaviors such as lip-smacking and tongue protrusion. Also interesting in all of this is that roughly one-third of the mirror neurons are "strictly congruent" and roughly two-thirds are "broadly congruent" in their copying fidelity. In the case of humans, brain-imaging studies have located the same systems but also more, including mirror neurons for non-goal-oriented behaviors, such as a meaningless arm movement, and an "echo mirror neuron system" for speech sounds. Equally interesting with the latter is the discovery that one of the mirror neuron systems in the macaque brain corresponds to the mirror neuron system in the posterior region of Broca's area in the left hemisphere of the human brain, which is one of the two areas in the human brain responsible for language. Human language comprehension in the sense of meaning involves much more than imitation, of course. Even so, the early stepping stones are there in the form of mirror neurons. But it turns out that there is much more to mirror neurons in humans. This is not only because the core of the mirror neuron systems in the human brain is found in the frontal and parietal regions of the neocortex (the frontal lobe is responsible for the higher cognitive functions), but also because a number of recent experiments have indicated that certain mirror neuron systems in the human brain play a central role in understanding the intentions of others and in predicting their actions. (The implications of mirror neurons for understanding autism alone are enormous; see Gazzaniga 2008, 180–181.)

On top of all of this is the fact that humans, very much unlike other animals, are highly capable of copying correction, analogous in a loose sense to DNA repair mechanisms in cells. We can exercise self-criticism to see whether we got an idea right from someone else, and as parts of social groups we often experience criticism from others when we appear to have gotten an idea wrong. All of this is possible in us, and so different from other species, not only because of our intelligence but also because of our ability for *language*—real, complex language, not just in the sense of symbols and meanings (*proto-language*), but also in the full-fledged sense of language as understood by professional linguists, which is that of a system of sentence-forming rules (syntax) combined with a set of symbols (semantics). It is this full-fledged sense of language that catapulted our species far above all others, such that we not only adapted to our environment but also adapted our environment to us and accordingly have taken over the world.

Language was probably the latest substantial stage in human biological evolution. But human cultural evolution elevated our ability as copying machines to an entirely new level with the advent of writing. The negative of this was recognized by Plato, which he expressed in an imaginary dialogue between the pharaoh of Egypt and Thoth, the god who invented writing: "If men learn this," said the pharaoh, "it will implant forgetfulness into their souls; they will cease to exercise memory because they rely on that which is written, calling things to remembrance no longer from within themselves, but by means of external marks" (*Phaedrus* 275a). It is well known that in ancient times human memory did seem much better than today, with many able to recite all of Homer's *Iliad* or the Bible. Plato was not a complete technophobe, however, for he did recognize that one's own writings will serve a useful function when one gets old, "as reminders for himself … and for everyone who wants to follow in his footsteps" (276d). Even so, Plato clearly did not imagine the situation from the point of view of memes, which is understandable given that Darwinian thinking did not yet exist and was quite a ways off. From that point of view, writing seems very much a godsend, in the very least an extremely fortunate cultural invention, for writing took the ability to store, retrieve, and copy information to a whole new level, far surpassing that of human memory. In a way, one can view writing as frozen memes, waiting to be unfrozen and spread to brains equipped with the necessary machinery for reading and understanding. In another way, one can view writing as the phenotype of memes, as a cultural adaptation that carries and preserves memes and vastly increases their level of fitness (defined as in biology, in terms of reproductive success), increasing not only their fidelity and longevity (despite matters of interpretation) but also their fecundity to a level that far surpasses human brains. Computer technology was the next stage, and the Internet the latest stage of all, giving memes more opportunities for spreading and finding hosts than ever before.

Putting all of the above into an overall perspective, it may well be that Darwinian models of cultural evolution do not necessarily require memetics. Perhaps something like the "population thinking" approach of Richerson and Boyd (2005) captures much of the real world. Rather than natural selection operating on a pool of cultural replicators, they argue that cultural variation is the norm among human groups and that cultural transmission and change occur due to a variety of different mechanisms, such as patterning behavior after a single charismatic leader, or those of a higher economic status, or the common type in the population, or allegiance to inherited ethnic values. They even argue that cultural change may actually help shape human biological evolution. All of this might in fact capture a lot of the nature of cultural evolution, including part of the nature of human evolution, but it does not automatically follow that no cultural evolution is memetic. All that the argument in this chapter needs—and all that memetics needs—is the recognition that *some* cultural evolution *can* be memetic. Similarly, it may well be that memes are not discrete enough for particulate inheritance, which is partly why Richerson and Boyd and others reject memetics, but it does not automatically follow that memes cannot have sufficient fidelity, fecundity, and longevity to function as replicators in cultural evolution. In other words, the key feature of memetics need not be a concept of memes as discrete and particulate, but rather a concept of memes as "reasonable facsimiles" sufficient enough to function as replicators and to be selfish, in the sense that they behave and evolve as if their only goal is to make more and more copies of themselves. Grant these concessions to memetics along with the looser definition of *meme* above, and the door swings open for a memetic explanation of universal human rights.

What we shall see in the remainder of this chapter is exactly how memetics helps to explain the origin and spread of the belief in universal human rights as well as the resistance to its spread. In this sense it is akin to doing epidemiology in medicine. This application of the theory, it should be added, has never been done before, and so is not only original but risky. The application, however, is strengthened by showing that memetics is not only successful in helping to explain the origin and spread of the belief in universal human rights but that it is contrastively better than competing explanations. If the argument should prove to be a strong one, then it would have the interesting effect of increasing the credibility of memetics. Successful explanation, of course, does not prove the truth of that which does the explaining, the *explanans,* but it does provide a presumption in its favor. In this way, with repeated and varied applications, a theory could indirectly become confirmed.

In short, to follow and appreciate the argument in the rest of this chapter, one does not have to take memetics fully seriously as a convert, but only seriously enough and provisionally enough. Hopefully the rather difficult theoretical and technical discussion provided above will be sufficient to have allayed preliminary objections in the mind of the reader. All that is asked is that one tentatively accept the possibility of memetic evolution long enough to follow the argument and hopefully to see the power of its explanation.

The Democracy Connection

We begin, then, by looking at the idea of universal human rights as a meme or, more properly, a meme complex, a core set of memes (that humans have universal, equal, innate, and inalienable moral claims and entitlements by virtue of being human) surrounded by particular human rights memes (such as the right to freedom of religion). This central core may have been produced by mutation and recombination a number of times and places independently in history, but there is only one clear example of it and its spread, and that is its origin and spread from Europe beginning during the dawn of the European Enlightenment. From the English Levellers and through the writings of John Locke, the meme complex spread to the American and French revolutions, then to the United Nations, and then to much of the rest of the world, with the core remaining basically the same.

The time span here is particularly revealing. Human rights activists, such as the law and sociology professors Normand and Zaidi (2008), are not far off when in their enthusiasm they write that "The speed with which human rights has penetrated every corner of the globe is astounding. Compared to human rights, no other system of values has spread so far so fast" (8). This may rightly be called a "rights revolution" (Ignatieff 2007), and we may rightly be said to live in "the age of rights" (Henkin 1990).[1] But we need to recognize that the human rights meme complex did not spread so fast and so wide because of the force of empirical evidence (since that is seriously lacking) or because the meme complex is self-evidently true (since it most assuredly is not to the soberest of modern minds, and was totally lacking in the ancients). Instead, it bears all the marks of a virus of the mind.

From the viewpoint of the individual, there is deep psychology at work here, unlike with, say, fashion memes. Michael Ignatieff (2007) is surely right when he states that human rights talk has worked its way "deep into our psyches" (2), and he is also surely right when he states that human rights are "a residual system of entitlement that people have irrespective of citizenship, irrespective of the states in which they happen to find themselves. Human rights are the rights men and women have when all else fails them" (36). The latter statement largely explains the former. But none of this entails that universal human rights are objectively real. Evidence alone that there is deep psychology afoot here rather than logic or evidence is the look one gets when one states that human rights are not real, that they are a modern myth—looks that murderers, pedophiles, and neo-Nazis

---

1. Fagan (2009) claims that this view is a myth (33), primarily because of widespread human rights abuses by "all states" (46) and the lack of effective mechanisms of redress. But this misses the point. The Age of Enlightenment in Europe, to draw a useful comparison, was no less an age of enlightenment even though none of its countries were ruled primarily by reason. It was an age of enlightenment in contrast to what preceded it, known as the Age of Belief or the Dark Ages. Similarly in the case of human rights, the history of the belief from its humble origin in 1640s London to its explosive spread to most of the world—with the Universal Declaration of Human Rights, human rights institutions, human rights lawyers, and so much more—indicates a major change not only in language but in mind-set. It is also deserves to be called "the rights epidemic," as we shall increasingly see.

can largely relate to. There clearly is a powerful behavioral force at work here. Memetics alone, I believe, cannot explain that power. Something else is needed, something that is reserved for the final section of this chapter. On the other hand, whatever the deep psychological attraction of the idea of universal human rights, that attraction alone, that deep hold on so many modern minds, cannot in itself explain the rise and spread of the meme complex itself, nor of the resistance to its spread. For that we need to turn first to democracy.

What is surely significant, particularly from the viewpoint of memetics, is that the universal human rights meme complex did not originate and spread independently but rather in *symbiosis* with the spread of the democracy meme complex. The word "democracy" is not to be confused with what is being said here. As the political historian and theorist John Dunn (2006) points out, the word itself not only "never travels alone" but "has travelled in fine company," including "human rights" and "material prosperity" (24). What I am saying instead is that the group of ideas constituting the *concept* of universal human rights evolved in an intimate and reciprocal union with the group of ideas constituting the *concept* of democracy, one that makes perfect sense from the memetics point of view.

We can see this if we return to our ancient sources and look back at the history of democracy. *Demokratia* in ancient Athens did not spark a human rights revolution, because it was essentially a direct democracy, not a representative democracy, with citizens spending a portion of their time in the Assembly and Law Courts, deciding matters of war, legislation, and court cases. Decisions were made by the majority of citizens in attendance, granted, and the citizens were equal before the law, but such a direct democracy could not possibly involve the will of the people, the *demos*, not even close. This is because the citizenry was composed of a small portion of the people, one-eighth to one-tenth of the total population (Hale 2001, 102; Dunn 2006, 35), and an unrepresentative portion at that: native-born males who did not work for others (employees, women, slaves, and resident foreigners were excluded), many of whom lacked the necessary wealth and leisure for the demands of direct participation to rarely if ever make it to the Assembly or courts. At bottom, the foundation of modern inclusiveness was just not there, given especially the deep-seated beliefs about women, natural slaves, and non-Greeks— "Slave-dependent, women-excluding, unabashedly ethnocentric," as Dunn puts it (2006, 197n56). Because of this, ancient Athenian democracy would better be termed a *proto-democracy* (in analogy with *proto-language* in linguistics)—I shall attempt to define "democracy" below in this section.

It is sometimes said that ancient Rome had a full-fledged democracy, in the sense of a representative democracy, hence a democracy truly capable of expressing the will of the people. If this is true, then according to my thesis a rights revolution should have sparked there into a flame. But the political system of ancient Rome, not only of the Principate but of the Republic before it, was not really a democracy. As E. T. Salmon (1968) puts it, "Even in republican times the participation of the lower orders in politics [the mass of freeborn citizens—the *plebs*—and below them the freedmen—the *libertini*] had been more nominal than real" (58; see also Dunn 2006, 54–57). Hence human rights talk did not spark in ancient Rome, let alone burst into a flame, even among its most progressive adherents, such as Cicero, who himself favored a mixed constitution of monarchy, aristocracy, and democracy (Zetzel 1999, xv).

In the case of Grotius, as we have seen in Chapter 4, the evidence of human rights talk is stronger, but still equivocal at best. It is surely of great significance that Grotius wrote his *De Iure Belli ac Pacis* during the Thirty Years' War, a series of wars from 1618 to 1648 that began between the emperor of the Holy Roman Empire and a number of German Protestant states and that developed into an all-out war between Catholic and Protestant states for control of Europe. Since the war lacked any supervening authority, Grotius tells us in the Prologue to his *De Iure Belli ac Pacis* that his main motive for writing the book was to help resolve such wars between states (Tuck 2005, 1753). As the title of his book itself suggests, his main interest was not to help protect individuals against state oppression. In fact, Grotius was open to absolute monarchy (Tuck 1979, 63–64, 77–79), possibly even more than open, like Hobbes shortly after him (Bull 1990, 85). Democracy, to the mind of Grotius (much like Cicero and Aristotle before him), went against human nature. Hence there should be no surprise that his emphasis was not on human rights but on state rights, international law, and just war as it pertained to states, as it was with Pufendorf after him.

When we turn to the political setting in England during the same century, however, the connection between democracy and human rights becomes evident. Indeed, this is where and when it all began, the sparks that ignited the modern flame of democracy and human rights. The first Civil War in England broke out in 1642, between the forces of King Charles I and Parliament, with the latter winning in 1646 and again (after a brief second Civil War) in 1648, eventually resulting in a "crowned" republic established under Oliver Cromwell, really a military dictatorship with Cromwell ruling openly as the self-styled "Lord Protector" from 1654 to 1658. It was during this period that Hobbes wrote *Leviathan*, first published in 1651, and *De Cive* (*On the Citizen*) before it, first published in 1642, both while living in exile in France because of his extreme support for the king. In his writings Hobbes advocated absolute power of the "sovereign" (preferably in the form of one person), as the only guarantee against falling back into the state of nature, represented in his time by the English Civil Wars. There should be no surprise, then, as we found in Chapter 4, that he was not an advocate of democracy or of human rights.[2]

But a movement genuinely advocating both democracy and human rights did emerge in this setting, the movement known as the Levellers. In the previous chapter I focused on the origin of the belief in human rights among the Levellers, as the first expression in history of genuine belief in universal human rights. Here I want to focus on their belief in democracy, as the first expression in history of genuinely democratic beliefs and values.

Looking collectively at their two constitutional manifestos, "An Agreement of the People" (October 1647) and "An Agreement of the Free People of England" (May 1649) (Sharp 1998, 92–101, 168–178), we find that there is to be no monarchy or House of Lords. Instead, "the supreme authority of England" is to be a "Representative of the People," based on "that power and right of the people in their representatives" and consisting of "*those whom yourselves shall choose.*" The first "Agreement" is vaguely a document of universal male (adult) suffrage, while the later "Agreement" limits the vote to males twenty-one and older and excludes servants and beggars (notably, neither of the latter in England was considered a permanent position). Anyone eligible to vote could also run for office as a representative. The size of the parliament is to consist of "four hundred persons," representatives with a distribution "proportionable to the respective parts of the nation," in accordance with "the number of the inhabitants," a parliament voted in every one or two years, with no one representative being in office for two consecutive terms. The idea here is that of "an especial means to avoid factions and parties." But the ultimate purpose of these parliaments is clearly to "remove your burdens and secure your rights," and it is interesting that the Levellers saw these major constitutional reforms as being "the only effectual means to settle a just and lasting peace."

---

2. In *De Cive* (Tuck and Silverthorne 1998), Hobbes states that "When men have met to erect a commonwealth, they are, almost by the very fact that they have met, a *Democracy*" (7.§5). But one must put this into perspective. Hobbes fled England for Paris just before fighting broke out because of his support for the king against Parliament. And he likewise supported Cromwell during his Protectorate. Moreover, in both *De Cive* and *Leviathan* Hobbes clearly prefers absolute monarchy over any other kind of sovereign so as best to avoid a return to the state of nature. In the state of nature, moreover, as we have seen in Chapter 4, Hobbes's concept of natural rights is not a moral one, not a matter of justice or injustice. As Hobbes states in *De Cive*, "it is by natural right that an animal kills a man, it will be by the same right that a man slaughters an animal" (8.§10). Natural rights in the state of nature for Hobbes are simply liberties, not moral possessions. There are no such things as human rights on Hobbes's account in any way similar to our modern understanding.

The laws established by each parliament are to be made "equal," designed for the "safety and well-being of the people," such that "the laws shall bind all alike, without privilege or exemption," meaning that the representatives "shall be in a capacity to taste of subjection as well as rule." But in none of this is the purpose or power of the parliaments to "level men's estates, destroy propriety, or make all things common."

With regard to "criminal cases," they are to be tried by juries of peers and no one is to be punished "for refusing to answer to questions against themselves." Nor is the state to imprison "any person for debt of any nature." Punishments are to be "equal to offenses," and injured parties are to receive compensation "according to the conscience of his [the malefactor's] jury."

Conscription into the military had hitherto targeted the poor, but in the new commonwealth there is to be no forced conscription: "your native freedom from constraint to serve in war, whether domestic or foreign, shall never be subject to the power of parliaments—or any other." Instead, "every man's conscience ... [is] to be satisfied in the justness of that cause wherein he hazards his own life, or may destroy another's." The military is not to be separate from the civil power, moreover, and "no forces shall be raised but by the Representatives for the time being."

Concerning "matters of faith, religion, or God's worship," the state is to leave it up to "every man's conscience." Furthermore, the state shall not have the power "to impose ministers upon any of the respective parishes," and it also cannot force "tithes."

In all of this it is difficult not to see the Levellers as the first real democrats in history, even though they never used the word "democracy" as a label for their views—"As it entered the eighteenth century, democracy was still very much a pariah word" (Dunn 2006, 71). That the Levellers really do deserve the label of the first democrats requires, of course, an acceptable definition of "democracy." I take it that one can make out a *consensus definition,* such that *democracy* is the government "of the people, by the people, for the people" (Lincoln), in accordance with the principle of "one person, one vote" (Douglas, *Gray v. Sanders*), involving free and uncoerced voting in periodic elections preceded by discussion and debate, all of which means that decisions of the state are ultimately determined by the majority of adult citizens who themselves represent the interests of the majority of the population. This definition allows for democracy to be either direct or representative and also a matter of degree, while the last part of it allows for a threshold between proto-democracy and democracy proper.

One can, of course, readily find claims about genuine democracies predating the time of the English Levellers, aside from examples such as the ancient Greeks and Romans. One example is the Iroquois Confederacy, with its "Great Law of

Peace," which some claim began as early as 1142, was "the oldest living participatory democracy on Earth," and provided the blueprint for the Fathers of the American Constitution. Much plays into this belief: American Indian ethnocentrism, white guilt, romantic Noble Savage pseudo-anthropology, but not a single shred of solid historical evidence, especially given that the earliest documentation of the Great Law of Peace dates to almost one hundred years *after* the drafting of the American Constitution (Jensen 1991). Another common example is the early Swiss cantons (semi-autonomous districts), particularly the original three of the Old Swiss Confederacy, which supposedly amalgamated with the Federal Charter of 1291 and had an annual *Landsgemeinde* (popular assembly and vote). Accordingly, many have called Switzerland "the world's oldest democracy." But the problem here is the same, in that there is not a shred of solid evidence for the existence of genuinely democratic beliefs and values in the early history of Switzerland, whether in terms of going beyond a mere collective mentality (Scott 1995, 108), in terms of most of the males getting to vote (Sablonier 2008), or in terms of women being regarded as the mental and moral equals of men (Head 1995, 551). The same is true of the supposed "early modern democracy" during the 1500s of a Swiss mountain canton known as the Grisons (Boone 1997; Von Freideburg 2001). In all of this, the belief in Switzerland as the world's oldest democracy is the stuff of myth, intense national pride, and poor scholarship. It is really no better than the belief in William Tell, the "first Confederate," a myth that most Swiss still believe in but that is rejected by professional historians (Popham 2007), who in turn are denounced by the Swiss public as heretics (Scott 2009).

All of these claims, it will be noticed, share much in common with claims about ancient and medieval expressions of universal human rights, many of which were examined in Chapter 4. In each and every case, evidence is lacking in accordance with the principle of proof beyond a reasonable doubt, such that expressions of the principles or foundation of modern inclusive democracy, I suggest, are to be found nowhere prior to the English Levellers, but only expressions of proto-democratic beliefs and values at best.

Keeping all of this in mind, some have questioned whether the Levellers themselves really expressed genuinely democratic beliefs and values, claiming that the ascription is an example of presentism. It is crucial for my thesis to address this matter head-on, as an argument is only as strong as its weakest link.

David Wootton (1991), as a good example, refuses to see the Levellers as democrats, "but nearly so" (442), because "they did not see the right to vote as inalienable" (433). This is because they conceded to changes in the right to vote between "An Agreement of the People" (October 1647) and "An Agreement of the Free People of England" (May 1649). In the first "Agreement," and in other writings at that time and prior, the Levellers wanted to extend the vote to all adult males, including servants and beggars (Wootton 1991, 428–429). Following the Putney Debates in late October 1647 (which debated the first "Agreement," among other matters), the General Council of the Army resolved that "all soldiers and others, if they be not servants or beggars, ought to have voices in electing those which shall represent them in Parliament, although they have not forty shillings per annum in freehold land" (429). In the later "Agreement," written by Lilburne, Walwyn, and Overton while imprisoned in the Tower of London by Cromwell for treason, the proposed franchise is "(according to natural right) all men of the age of one-and-twenty years and upwards (not being servants, or receiving alms, or having served the late king in arms or voluntary contributions)" (Sharp 1998, 170).

The problem here with Wootton's "nearly so" is a much too narrow definition of "democrat" or "democracy," given that, as noted in *The Economist* (November 3, 2009), "In 48 American states and seven European countries, including Britain, prisoners are forbidden from voting in elections. Many more countries impose partial voting bans (applying only to prisoners serving long sentences, for instance). And in ten American states some criminals are stripped of the vote for life, even after their release." Clearly it would be excessive to claim that these states are not genuine democracies, even though they take away the right to vote from some of their citizens, and many states, such as Canada, recently changed their laws in this regard. The cases are not the same, of course, since with the later "Agreement" the Levellers were attempting a political compromise with Cromwell. But still, by parity of reasoning it is excessive to claim that the Levellers were not genuine democrats.

Alan Craig Houston (1993) provides a direction of interpretation of the Levellers even further away than Wootton's "nearly so" interpretation. For Houston, the key to understanding the Levellers is not democracy and the vote but rather monopolies, for the Levellers in his view were fundamentally anti-monopolists, primarily with regard to religious worship, to trade and commerce, and to politics and law. The ultimate reason for this was the peace, freedom, and prosperity of the nation, and Houston is impressed with "the intelligence with which they [the Levellers] confronted the present" (420). In other words, without using the term, Houston views the Levellers primarily as communitarians of a sort. All of this would seem to explain their various strategies: supporters of and members (many) in the New Model Army, then mutineers against the Army; rejection of economic equality and disapproval of the Diggers when that movement arose (more on them below); waffling on male suffrage; the exclusion of women from the vote.

As intriguing as this theory is, however, it fails to explain the commitment of the Levellers (or at least that of their leaders) to universal, equal, innate, and inalienable human rights, a commitment we have seen in the previous chapter.

Houston claims that the only legitimate sense of "Leveller" that the Levellers accepted for themselves, "this principle only" (407), was equality before the law. But this is not true. They were also *levellers* in the sense of human rights, and this was fundamentally a matter of principle for them, not merely a matter of policy: it, too, was a matter on which they were not willing to fundamentally change. Both Houston and Wootton seem to converge on this point, though indirectly, on the principle of religious freedom. Houston (1993) notices that, to his surprise, "the first monopoly condemned by Lilburne was not economic but religious" (387), that the same seems true of Walwyn and Overton, and that "it is here, with their defence of religious freedom, that we must pick up the first threads of their identity as a political and intellectual movement" (388). Wootton (1991) claims that "the principle of freedom of conscience ... much more than the franchise, was an issue of principle in the eyes of the Levellers" (434). What both seem to miss is that the Levellers wove freedom of religion, human rights, and the franchise all into one fabric. Richard Overton, in his "An Arrow Against All Tyrants" (October 1646), which was directed not only against the House of Lords but also against the Presbyterian clergy, stated that from "nature's instinct," which is "most reasonable, equal and just," "all human powers take their original—not immediately from the hand of God (as kings usually plead their prerogative) but mediately by the hand of nature, as from the represented to the representers. For originally God has implanted them in the creature, and from the creature those powers immediately proceed and no further" (Sharp 1998, 55). Walwyn, Wildman, Lilburne, and Overton similarly combine the three elements in "An Agreement of the People" (October 1647), which includes a section on "matters of religion" and "our consciences" (94), such that "your principle right most essential to your well-being is the clearness, certainty, sufficiency, and freedom of your power in your representatives in parliament" (96). And again, "*those whom yourselves shall choose* shall have power to restore you to, and secure you in, all your rights" (96). To say that the Levellers held freedom of religion as a matter of principle but not the vote, or human rights for that matter, is, it would appear, to entirely miss the point.

Others, such as Andrew Sharp (1998), do indeed see the Levellers as "liberal democrats" (xiii) and as proposing "that the franchise would be vastly extended" (xvi), but they do not see beyond the program of "universal male suffrage" (xv). For the same reason some see the Levellers as forwarding only "proto-democratic ideas" (e.g., Robertson 2007, xi).

The problem here is that, much like the American and French Revolutions and constitutions that would follow more than a century later, but very much unlike earlier so-called democracies, such as those examined above, Leveller democracy contained the foundation of modern inclusiveness, including female suffrage and female politicians. This is not only because the Levellers had female activists among them as well as female preachers, which was particularly rare for that time, but also because they believed in the mental and moral equality of men and women (Brailsford 1961, 317–318; Sharp 1998, xix, 205). As John Lilburne, their foremost leader, put it in "Postscript to The Freeman's Freedom Vindicated" (June 1646), in reference to Adam and Eve—the "earthly, original fountain"—and "all and every particular and individual man and woman that ever breathed in the world since," they, he said, "are, and were by nature all equal and alike in power, dignity, authority, and majesty—none of them having (by nature) any authority, dominion or magisterial power, one over or above another" (Sharp 1998, 31). The spirit of the times obviously made any hope of success for the idea of female suffrage politically unrealistic (that was yet far to come), such that one can hardly blame the Levellers for not including the idea in their political program. They fancied themselves political realists after all. But clearly the foundation of modern inclusiveness was there.

It is safe to say, then, not only that the Levellers were the first to express genuinely democratic beliefs and values, but also that they were the first in history, as argued in the previous two chapters, to express genuine belief in universal human rights, particularly in the writings of Richard Overton. In all of this, however, the sparks never erupted into a flame, not even (arguably) among the Levellers themselves as a whole. But the flame was soon to come.

With the monarchy restored in 1660, establishing Charles II as king, a second great war erupted in England in 1688, called the Glorious Revolution, between the forces of the Catholic King James II (brother of Charles II) and the Dutch Protestant Prince William of Orange (whose wife, Mary, was James's eldest daughter), the latter invited by Parliament to replace the king. Parliament won again (this time the king's forces retreated without any bloodshed), crowning William in early 1689 and enacting the English Bill of Rights, which mentions "true, ancient and indubitable rights and liberties of the people of this kingdom" (Hayden 2001, 342). This was not a document of universal human rights, but basically, as Clapham (2007) puts it, a "political settlement" (6). Locke, favoring the side of William and Parliament, returned to England from his exile in Holland. His *Two Treatises,* written mostly a decade before, was now published, thereby injecting into the scene, with great intellectual force, clear talk of universal human rights mixed with genuinely democratic beliefs and values: in short, that the purpose of government is to express the will of the people and to protect their inalienable human rights.

At this point, just as with the Levellers, we need to take a closer look at some of the democratic beliefs and values in Locke's thought. I shall do this only partially here, however, reserving the rest for a little later in this chapter when I turn to the topic of explanation. For just as with the Levellers, what needs explaining is the connection in Locke between democracy and human rights, and not just any explanation will do.

In the *Second Treatise* Locke claims that "the *Legislative*" or Parliament should be "the *supream power* of the Common-wealth" (11.§134), that the "divers Persons" who constitute the legislative assembly should be "themselves subject to the Laws, they have made" (12.§143), that the legislative assembly should be "made up of Representatives chosen for that time by the People" and "this power of chusing must also be exercised by the People, either at certain appointed Seasons, or else when they are summon'd to it" (13.§154).[3] As for the executive power, possibly put into a single person, a king for example, "though *Oaths of Allegiance* and Fealty are taken to him, ... *Allegiance* being nothing but an *Obedience according to Law,* which when he violates, he has no right to Obedience, ... the Members owing no *Obedience* but to the publick Will of the Society" (§151). And if the king should enforce his will against the legislative assembly in any way, such as by using force "to hinder the *meeting* and *acting of the Legislative*" when it is required (§155), or when he "enforces new Laws" or "subverts the old" (29.§214), then he has made himself "a single private Person" (13.§151) and put himself into "a state of War with the People" (§155), such that "the People have the right to remove it [the executive] by force."

Read widely in the Western world and regarded highly, in Locke the sparks of human rights talk erupted into a flame along with genuine democratic thinking. The flame would eventually spread to the American and French Revolutions in the late 1700s, as these were democratic revolutions that not coincidentally borrowed heavily from the writings of Locke, particularly through the Declaration of Independence, penned mainly by Thomas Jefferson.

From the American and French Revolutions human rights talk spread with the expansion of democracy, leading eventually to the Universal Declaration of Human Rights, drafted by the United Nations in 1948. This had its immediate origin in the United Nations Declaration drafted during World War II, at the beginning of 1942, which was signed, in order of importance, by the United States, Great Britain, the Soviet Union, and China (Normand and Zaidi 2008, 92–93). The

---

3. Unlike the Levellers, Locke was basically ambiguous on the vote, whether on individual or general elections, but he can hardly be said to have exercised "silence" on the matter, let alone an "extremely significant" silence, contrary to Marshall (1994, 271–272), who takes Locke's supposed silence to mean that his theory of representation should be viewed "not as being democratic."

Declaration had a Preamble which mentioned "to preserve human rights," but it was principally a document of military alliance, of a united front, against the Axis forces led by Hitler.

The 1948 Declaration, on the other hand, was written as an expression of the worldwide hope that the horrors of WWII, including especially the Holocaust, would not be repeated. In a sense, then, Hitler and the Nazis served as the "catalyst" for the Declaration (Morsink 1999, ch. 2). Nazism and the basic principles of democracy were antipodes, so it is not surprising that democratic principles were debated and made their way into the 1948 Declaration. Not only is the inclusion highly implicit, with references to "freely chosen representatives," "periodic and genuine elections," and "universal and equal suffrage" (Art. 21), but it is also fully explicit in the reference to "the general welfare in a democratic society" (Art. 29).

The driving force here was both political and ideological. Although the membership of the Human Rights Commission was very international, its members representing eighteen states, the leadership of the Commission, including those involved in the Drafting Committee, was mainly Western in one way or another (Glendon 2001). American former first lady Eleanor Roosevelt was Chair of the Commission and leader of the entire process; the Canadian international law expert John Humphrey, though not an actual member of the Commission, wrote the preliminary draft; the French delegate and law professor René Cassin (who was of Jewish descent) added the Preamble and gave an organic structure to the list of rights provided by Humphrey (Cassin would receive a Nobel Peace Prize in 1968 for his work on human rights); Charles Malik of Lebanon was Greek Orthodox and got his Ph.D. under Alfred North Whitehead at Harvard University, after which he returned to Lebanon to teach at the American University of Beirut; Peng-Chun Chang, the Chinese delegate and Vice Chair of the Commission, got his Ph.D. under John Dewey at Columbia University (China, it should be noted, had not yet been completely overtaken by the Red Army of Mao Zedong). As Normand and Zaidi (2008) put it, "There is little room for debating the simple historical fact that the Universal Declaration was based largely on western philosophical models, legal traditions, and geopolitical imperatives" (195). In the words of the American Secretary of State John Foster Dulles, the Universal Declaration was America's "Sermon on the Mount" (195).

It is also interesting to notice that even though the Human Rights Commission was originally given the task of framing a universal declaration along with devising means for its implementation (Glendon 2001, 32), the document ended up excluding mention of any means of enforcement, as this was the only way it could gain even the appearance of "unanimous" approval (Norman and Zaidi 2008, 196). Even so, out of the fifty-six states that made up the United Nations at that time, which constituted roughly four-fifths of the global population (Glendon 2001, 50), no state cast a negative vote, while eight chose to abstain, namely, South Africa, Saudi Arabia, and the Soviet bloc (Morsink 1999, ch. 1.4; Normand and Zaidi 2008, 141, 190–196).

The question is how best to explain all of this, both the rise and spread of genuine human rights thinking.

Competing Explanations

Theorists on the rise of explicit human rights talk usually do not emphasize the rise of democratic beliefs and values in England and elsewhere in Enlightenment Europe. They tend to emphasize, instead, one or more of the following: the rise of mercantilism, the emergence of a middle class, the scientific revolution, the dawn of capitalism, a shift in the discourse of power, or even the popularity of the epistolary novel.

According to Micheline Ishay (2007), for example, "These developments [the first three] stimulated the expansion of Western power, even as they created propitious circumstances for the development of modern conceptions of human rights. They ultimately shattered feudalism and delegitimized appeals by kings to divine rights" (xxiii).

Similarly, Donnelly (2003) claims that the demand for human rights sprang not from "traditional societies" but from the "social conditions" of "modern markets and states," which alone explains for him why the West "got a jump on the rest of the world in developing the response of human rights" (78).

In the case of Hobbes, Strauss (1953) looks to the rise of the scientific revolution, which was a "nonteleological science" (166), and in the case of Locke, whom he regards as "The most famous and the most influential of all modern natural rights teachers" (165), the further social influence was the rise in "the spirit of capitalism" (246).

Shapiro (1986) likewise connects the modern conception of human rights to "the emergence of capitalism in England" (23), though he relates this force a little earlier to Hobbes's political theory.

Michel Foucault (1977), in his neo-Nietzschean fashion, according to which "truth" and "will to power" are coterminous, meaning that "truth" is really a matter of power politics, suggests that during the Middle Ages "The monarchy presented itself as a referee, a power capable of putting an end to war, violence and pillage ... one whose limits it naturally began to overstep," such that "Sovereign, law, and prohibition formed a system of representation of power which was extended during the subsequent era by the theories of right" (121). For Foucault, then, the language of natural rights would be a matter of power conflict, specifically during the seventeenth and eighteenth centuries, between the monarch and the people.

Finally, in a very different vein, the historian Lynn Hunt (2007) argues that the origin of human rights talk coincided chronologically with the rise of the epistolary novel in Europe, which "surged as a genre between the 1760s and 1780s" (40), novels made up of letters that evoked empathy in the readers and made them recognize autonomy in diverse people including women, slaves, and tortured prisoners, thereby accounting not only for the emergence of human rights talk but for the claim of self-evidence as well. In her view, then, "'imagined empathy' serves as the foundation of human rights" (32).

The devil is in the details, however, and none of these correlations really explain. Beginning with the last, while the psychological nature of the belief in human rights is a topic reserved for the last section of this chapter, it needs to be noticed at this point that human rights talk did not spark and ignite into a flame in the second half of the eighteenth century. Instead, as we have seen in the previous chapter, the sparks began with the English Levellers and ignited into a flame in the writings of John Locke, roughly three-quarters of a century before Hunt's chronology. As intriguing as her theory is, it just doesn't fit the evidence. Epistolary novels and related mediums such as pictures in public exhibitions might have helped fan the flame into a conflagration, centered in the American and French Revolutions, but those mediums do not help to explain the origin of the flame itself. Something very different is needed.

A shift in the discourse of power doesn't fit the evidence either. It is true, of course, that the language of monarchical power included the "divine right of kings," a language that meant that the king's right to rule came from God rather than from the people, so that the king was answerable only to God (absolutism). This had become part of natural law theory, particularly at the hands of Sir Robert Filmer in his *Patriarcha*, first published in 1680 but probably written before the first of the English Civil Wars. According to J. N. Figgis in his classic study of the subject (1896, 38–51), the theory of the divine right of kings arose in the thirteenth century out of the power conflict within the Holy Roman Empire between the papacy (which claimed supreme authority over the Christian commonwealth) and the emperors (who in return claimed their own divine right of supremacy over the papacy). As the Holy Roman Empire gradually lost its hegemony over its component kingdoms, the theory of the divine right of emperors was followed by the theory of the divine right of kings (against the popes and the emperors). In England, the most famous defender of the theory was James I (father of Charles I and famous also for the King James Version of the Bible). James I gained the throne of England in 1603, following the rein of Elizabeth I, but the theory of the divine right of kings had clearly made its way into England well before his ascension to the throne (Wootton 1986, 29–31, 91–127; Salmon 1991, 246–249; Sommerville 1991, 355–361). From all of this it is attractive to view the origin of the language of human rights in the Levellers as nothing more than the language of rebellion against the king (Charles I in their case), as part of the attempt to shift the power in the king (the "divine right of kings") to the people (the divine rights of the people, "human rights"), the new would-be sovereign. This seems to be the sort of thing that Foucault was suggesting (minus the specifics). As Foucault (1977) puts it in the same context quoted above, "political theory has never ceased to be obsessed with the person of the sovereign" (121).

As intriguing as this theory may be, it can be tested, using the evidence of history. The theory allows us to predict that, for example, the leaders of the New Model Army, those who were *not* part of the Levellers, should have appealed to some other of fundamental rights, something somewhere between the divine right of kings and human rights. But they did not make such an appeal, or did not mainly, which is evident in the Putney Debates (Sharp 1998). Cromwell and Ireton, for example—although Ireton can occasionally be found appealing to a "ground of right" (126) and a "birthright" as "the most fundamental part of your [England's] constitution" (121)—appealed fundamentally to tradition, to "what was originally the constitution of this kingdom" (104), and to "justice and reason and prudence" (121), meaning "the safety of the kingdom" (123), "the public interest of the kingdom" (124). Cromwell himself was willing to extend the vote (male), but not to the point of including "servants" and "he who receives alms" (129). Ireton was less willing to bend, and wanted the vote (likewise male) confined to those with a "permanent fixed interest in this kingdom" (103), meaning a minimum ownership in land or in a corporation (a business with a fixed location). A "more equal" representation by borough, as Ireton would allow, including a lowering of the standard property ownership requirement from forty shillings (net) per annum in rent, as he would also allow, but still confined, as he insisted, to those with a "permanent fixed interest," meant a change in representation from roughly 2.5 percent to not much more than 10 percent of the total population (xxi, 112–114), while extending the vote to all males in England but not to servants and beggars (or of course criminals) meant extending the vote to roughly 16 percent of the total population (Davis 1968, 174). The fundamental point is that rights talk hardly played a role in either proposed shift in sovereignty.

Equally interesting are the so-called Diggers or True Levellers (the latter their preferred label for themselves), the first true communists in English history, led mainly by Gerrard Winstanley. This radical movement began its activities on

April 1, 1649, a few months after the execution of King Charles I, and lasted slightly more than a year as the result of a series of persecutions by local landowners aided by the military. Having probably not more than one hundred members at its peak, the movement was named for digging up common and uncultivated land for farming purposes and for wanting to rid society peacefully of all hierarchy and property ownership. According to Christopher Hill (1983), Winstanley seemed to advocate in his early writings "an anarchical form of communist society, without state, army or law" (41), while according to David Wootton (1991), "by gathering support they hoped slowly to deprive the propertied economy of its labour force" (425). There was a principle of sovereignty here, allied with a principle of human equality. As Winstanley put it, "man had domination given to him, over the beasts, birds and fishes; but not one word was spoken in the beginning, that one branch of mankind should rule over another. And the reason is this, every single man, male and female, is a perfect creature of himself; and the same spirit that made the globe dwells in man to govern the globe" (Hill 1983, 77). Not surprisingly, then, Winstanley can occasionally be found appealing to "an equal right to the land with you [landowners] by the righteous law of creation" (100). He can also be found appealing to conventional right, in the sense that "we have paid taxes, given free-quarter and ventured our lives to preserve the nation's freedom as much as you, and therefore by the law of contract with you, freedom in the land is our portion as well as yours, equal with you" (104). But all of this rights talk is really quite minor in his writings and is found in only a few places in his earlier writings. Moreover, the concept of *individual* rights is just not there. Winstanley distinguishes between "righteous property" and "particular property," the latter of which we today call "private property" or "individual property," and the latter, he says, is "that disturbing devil" (100), "the cursed thing ... which is the cause of all wars, bloodshed, theft and enslaving laws, that hold the people under misery" (107). Elsewhere he distinguishes between "property on the one hand" and "community on the other hand" (268).[4]

The point is that looking just to revolutionary England in the 1640s, arguably the most important time and place for the subsequent political history of the world, there is no general correlation between natural rights talk and a shift in

---

4. This is not to say he thought that all things should be held in common, such as husbands, wives, children, and personal items such as home or furniture. In his very last writing as a True Leveller, his "The Law of Freedom in a Platform," which was written in late 1651 as advice to Oliver Cromwell, Winstanley refers to the above (home, children, etc.) as "proper to himself" (twice) and "proper to themselves," never once as rights, and in the interest of "the law of peace" (Hill 1983, 303–304).

the discourse of sovereign power. Winstanley's main appeal was not to rights but to the opposition between "self-love" and "universal love," the former manifested chiefly in monarchy, aristocracy, clergy, army, lawyers, and private property, the latter in the Diggers, genuine community, and above all in Jesus, "the head Leveller" (Hill 1983, 204). We get the same result (I suspect), no general shift in the language of rights, if we look to those who rebelled against kings and privilege in other countries during this era. Certainly in seventeenth-century England there was no general correlation in rights talk. With the Levellers, however, they appealed to human rights in line with their attempt—the first in history—to make the people the sovereign power of the nation. The explanation that appeals simply to the power politics of natural rights language ultimately fails to explain this remarkable correlation.

The correlation with the scientific revolution will not do either, as it needs to be noted only that the ancient Greeks had a scientific revolution, too, in fact the first in world history, beginning in Asia Minor, that was furthered by the Romans. At its core it undermined traditional religious authority and the authority of the state, and part of the revolution included a nonteleological universe (principally the ancient atomists), but nowhere did it spark a human rights revolution, not from the time of its beginning around Thales to its demise marked by the burning of the library at Alexandria. The scientific revolution of the Renaissance, of course, with atomism at its core, subverted the teleological view of the universe that dominated the Middle Ages, and hence served to undermine the belief in natural law (the idea that we traced from the Stoics in Chapter 4). Natural law theory, however, did not die during the Renaissance and Enlightenment (most of the thinkers, of course, were not natural scientists), far from it, and it needs to be noted only that both Leveller leadership and Locke believed in natural law. But even if natural law theory would have died at that time due to the scientific revolution, there is no logical or psychological or philosophical or theological reason—let alone a scientific one—for why natural rights theory would rise to take its place.

With regard to mercantilism, while it did not exist until the modern nation-state, where *mercantilism* is taken to mean government regulation of imports and exports so as to increase the nation's wealth, international trade nevertheless was big in the time of the ancients, some of it with a supervening authority such as the Roman Empire, and much of it without, as with the heyday of the Phoenicians and beyond. But in all of this there was no talk of international law or human rights, and it is not at all clear why or how international trade or mercantilism would create pressure for the development of human rights talk specifically, whether in ancient times or during the Enlightenment.

Finally, as regards capitalism, wealth in ancient Rome included capitalism, with a middle class and a lot of upward mobility, and even a stock exchange (Carpocino 1941, 79–88), while many ancient societies, such as the ancient Egyptians (Manning 1995), allowed citizens to have private ownership of land, not just high status groups or royalty, but none of this sparked a human rights revolution. In reply it might be said that what matters is the *size* of the middle class, that human rights talk is the product of the majority struggling to acquire property ownership and capital. But the size of the middle class in seventeenth-century England no more fits this description than that of ancient Rome.

The key factor, instead, would seem to be the rise of genuinely democratic beliefs and values. This is especially important when we look at the *details* of those who first started advocating universal human rights. At the time of the English Civil Wars, it was not the owners of land and capital who were advocating universal human rights. As we have seen in this and the previous chapter, Cromwell and Ireton and the majority of the English revolutionaries resisted the idea. Instead, it was advocated by the English Levellers (or at least their leaders), all of whom wanted the voice in elections to be radically extended to include the poor (or the working poor), people *without* land and capital. As the Leveller Colonel Thomas Rainborough put it in the Putney Debates, in words that strike a chord as powerfully today, "I am a poor man, therefore I must be *oppressed*?" Instead, he said, "I think that the poorest he that is in England has a life to live as the greatest he," so that "every man that is to live under a government ought first by his own consent to put himself under that government" (Sharp 1998, 109, 103).

Locke is an even more troubling case for those who would connect the rise of belief in universal human rights with the rise of capitalism. Granted, in joining with Shaftesbury, Locke went from "the *petite bourgeoisie* to the *haute bourgeoisie*," as Laslett (1988, 43) puts it, and Locke certainly did not pass up the opportunity to make profitable investments. But on the other hand, as Laslett also points out, Locke "profoundly mistrusted commerce and commercial men," and "he shared Shaftesbury's contempt for lawyers." He was instead a medical man–cum–philosopher, "middle class" primarily in the sense, as Laslett puts it, that he was "an independent, free-moving intellectual" (44).

But more to the point was his politics. It was not what one would expect from someone who was a cork bobbing on the rising tide of capitalism. This is because, much like the Levellers before him, he argued that political power must be radically extended beyond the owners of land and capital to the working poor (not explicitly the vote, but not explicitly not either). This is evident from the *Second Treatise*. "For the preservation of Property being the end of

Government," he says, "and that for which Men enter into Society, it necessarily supposes and requires, that the People should *have Property*" (11.§138). This would have to refer not just to his expanded sense of property ("life, liberty, and estate") but in particular to his restricted sense of property ("goods," things owned), where "*Labour*, in the Beginning, *gave a Right of Property*," a "natural common Right" (5.§45). The key for Locke is not landownership, or capital, but *labor*. As we have seen in the previous chapter, he claims that when I mix the common property of nature with my labor it becomes my private property. This is true whether of land or of acorns. The addition of business and money and government does not fundamentally change this, since, as Locke puts it in the *First Treatise*, "*Justice* gives every Man a Title to the product of his honest Industry, and the fair Acquisitions of his Ancestors descended to him" (4.§42). The most that just laws and governments can do, then, returning to the *Second Treatise*, is "regulate the right of property" (5.§50).

Hence for Locke, given his labor sense of property, political representation must extend to the majority of the people, including the working poor, rather than be restricted to the privileged few, the landowners and capitalists. As Locke puts it in the *Second Treatise*, not only is the "*Legislative*" the "*supream power* of the Common-wealth" (11.§134), but "in well order'd Commonwealths, where the good of the whole is so considered, as it ought, the *Legislative* Power is put into the hands of divers Persons who duly Assembled, ... they are themselves subject to the Laws, they have made" (12.§143). Representation, Locke further adds, must be "fair and *equal*," such that "whenever the People shall chuse their *Representatives upon* just and undeniably *equal measures* suitable to the original Frame of the Government, it cannot be doubted to be the will and act of the Society" (13.§158). Moreover, Locke himself seems to have favored a mixed constitution (monarch, lords, and commons; see Yolton 1993, 41–42), but in making the legislative assembly the supreme power of the commonwealth, not the executive, and in placing the original and continued power of it in the people, Locke clearly helped lay the foundation of the modern inclusive sense of democracy. (His theory of human nature, moreover, examined in the previous chapter, lends itself to this interpretation.) What further aids this view is Locke's claim, as we have already seen, that "there remains still *in the People a Supream Power* to remove or *alter the Legislative*, when they find the *Legislative* act contrary to the trust reposed in them" (13.§150). And this power, as he earlier states in the *Second Treatise*, resides in the majority, in "the people" (a term he never qualified), that "When any number of Men have so *consented to make one Community* or Government, they are thereby presently incorporated, and make *one Body Politick,* wherein the *Majority* have a Right to act and conclude the rest" (8.§95).[5]

There are some problems of interpretation, however, that still need to be addressed, as they might seem to impair the interpretation of Locke as a genuine democrat. In the previous chapter I made a case for Locke as a genuine human rights theorist, which in the previous section I connected to the modern inclusive sense of democracy. It is important in the present section to continue that line of argument, though now with the focus being on the connection between Locke's theory of property and his theory of government.

The first problem concerns whether Locke in the *Two Treatises* defends the property rights of *individuals* against the state. The consensus in Locke scholarship is that he does. Explicitly against this consensus, Stevens (1996), as we have seen in the previous chapter, argues that Locke defends only "'the people's' rights [to possessions] en masse (or, rather, as a majority)." Her conclusion more fully is that Locke defends the property rights only of the majority "against being expropriated by an illegitimate minority running the government," *not* that "individuals have rights to their economic assets that trump the prerogative of majorities" (434). In other words, Locke defends only "the properties of the majority" (436).

Against this view are a number of key passages in the *Second Treatise,* such as "The *Supream Power cannot take* from any Man any part of his *Property*

---

5. See also the discussions in Laslett (1988, 110), Stevens (1996, 426, 458n50), and especially Ashcraft (1986, 582–584; 1992, 759–761, 767–768; 1994, 250–251). Shapiro (1986), for example, is entirely wrong when he states that "there is nothing in Locke's writings remotely approaching a doctrine of democratic participation" (117). To the above should be added Locke's definition of "perfect democracy": "The Majority having, as has been shew'd, upon Mens first uniting into Society, the whole power of the Community, naturally in them, may imploy all that power in making Laws for the Community from time to time, and Executing those Laws by Officers of their own appointing; and then the *Form* of the Government is a perfect *Democracy*" (10.§132). From the context of the passage it is sufficiently clear that Locke did *not* mean by "perfect democracy" a *direct* democracy, without representatives. Instead, it is sufficiently clear that for Locke an *imperfect* democracy would be one with a mixed constitution, such as one with a hereditary monarchy and nobility and an elected parliament, which was precisely, as mentioned above, Locke's own preference. It would still be a democracy, only not a *pure* one, just so long as the elected parliament was in fact and practice "the *supream power* of the Common-wealth." Locke goes on in §133 to not limit a "commonwealth"—"*any Independent Community*"—to a perfect democracy or to any other particular form of government, but combined with what else we have seen, the balance of evidence is in favor of the view that Locke indeed held genuinely democratic beliefs and values. And as Ashcraft shows (1986, 585–589; 1992, 763–765, 739–741), that is exactly how his contemporaries read the anonymously authored *Two Treatises of Government.*

without his own consent" (11.§138). (Elsewhere Locke writes: "property … The nature whereof is, that *without a Man's own consent* it *cannot be taken from him*" [16.§193].) Following Ashcraft (1994), I take it that Locke's reasoning here is that "if someone could take 'any part' of my property without my consent, he could take it all, and then it could not be said that I have any property at all" (236). Ashcraft goes on to make the point, focusing on Locke's discussion on taxation, that Locke never bothers to make clear his solution to the problem of how much a just state may confiscate (tax) the private property of its citizens, the problem of limits, only that the amount should ultimately depend on the will of the majority of the people.

Stevens (1996) also comments on the contrast between Locke's "enlightened Dr. Jekyll side and his darker Mr. Hyde" (451) when he was a Commissioner for Trade in the mid-1690s, noting that he drafted "some absolutely brutal recommendations on policies toward the poor, including the working poor" (463n103). But Locke's 1697 "Report to the Board of Trade on Poor Relief" is not hard evidence that Locke was a "majoritarian, not individualist." As Woolhouse (2007, 396–397) points out, Locke distinguished between the poor who are incapable of working and the poor who are capable but lazy. Toward the former he was always quite generous and supportive, while toward the latter, the only ones he regarded as social parasites ("living unnecessarily upon other people's labor"), he came down hard, thinking of them as a kind of criminal. As for the working poor, he penalized them only if they had more children than they could support, recommending that the children be sent to "working schools" where they could learn a trade.

David Wootton (1992) likewise focuses on Locke's "Report" of 1697 as well as on his role in the "Fundamental Constitutions of Carolina," first written in 1669, to argue against what he calls "the Ashcraft thesis," which is that "Locke and Shaftesbury were committed to … egalitarian principles" (79). In 1663 Charles II gave control of the English colony in Carolina to eight "Lords Proprietors," in exchange for ownership of one-fifth of the land and a portion of revenues. Locke's patron, Anthony Ashley Cooper, the future earl of Shaftesbury, was one of these Lords Proprietors. By 1669 the colonists were deeply in debt, so the debts were partly forgiven and a constitution was drawn up as a way of starting again. Locke was employed from 1669 to 1675 as secretary to the Lords Proprietors and played a role in the making of the first draft of the "Constitutions." What alarms Wootton is that the document "provided not only for slavery, but also for hereditary serfdom" combined with an "entrenched, powerful aristocracy" and that although the document is famous for affirming religious freedom, even for slaves, it involves a "complete rejection of any notion of inalienable individual legal or political rights" (82).[6]

The first main problem with all of this is that it amounts to circumstantial evidence, none of which would stand up in a court of law. Locke, after all, was an employee, albeit a highly valued one, and there is no direct evidence of whether he contributed to or supported the passages in the "Constitutions" on slavery and serfdom, or on whether he supported the political powers the document gives to the Lords Proprietors.[7] But secondly, no matter how much he supported this form of government, the fact remains that we have direct evidence of his views in the *Two Treatises,* most of which was written (all are now agreed) sometime between 1679 and 1683. If Locke did not believe in fundamental human rights and in democratic participation in legislative government during his years as secretary to the Lords Proprietors, we have every reason to believe that he did by the time he came to write the *Two Treatises.* What happened in the meantime is anyone's guess. But something must have happened to produce such a change of mind, if there was in fact a change.

All in all, then, despite the reservations examined in the previous two pages, it would seem fair to view Locke, in line with the consensus interpretation of him, as having genuinely maintained in the *Two Treatises* a deep connection between his labor theory of property and his democratic theory of government, with the legislative being the supreme power of government representing the interests of the majority *and* the purpose of government being to protect the human rights of its constituent individuals.

Inference to the Best Explanation

The cause of the rise of democratic beliefs and values in Locke and in the Levellers before him is an interesting question in itself. Clearly the nature of the English

---

6. The "colonial" reading of Locke's *Two Treatises,* which views it not only as a political document justifying insurrection but also as justifying colonialism, is developed in detail by David Armitage (2004).

7. The proposal, after all, was partly democratic, involving a parliament consisting of the eight Lords Proprietors (or their deputies) who owned one-fifth of the land, the land barons under them who owned another fifth, and an elected representative for each precinct, with elections every two years, "every member" of parliament getting "one vote" (Goldie 1997, 174). Debates in parliament, nevertheless, were to be confined to measures approved by the Lords Proprietors.

monarchy and Parliament and the friction between them culminating in the Civil Wars, with each side in its turn producing a tyranny over the people, played a central role. The nature and sacrifices of the New Model Army also need to be added here (neither mercenaries nor conscripts but volunteers, with officers promoted from within the ranks, all fighting for the good of their country). Finally, certain religious beliefs need to be added to the mix along with technology in the form of the printing press (though most of the commoners were illiterate, political pamphlets were meant to be read aloud).

I wish to resist, however, the modern contextualist trend in professional history writing, which sees ideas not as products of preexisting ideas or even of unique minds, but instead predominantly as products of their social-cultural environment. I prefer, instead, to view the history of ideas much as a Darwinian views the history of organisms, as a history involving not only environmental changes and processes, such as natural selection, but also purely internal processes, such as spontaneous mutation. There is an interesting comparison here. From Darwin's younger contemporary A. R. Wallace to the present there is a tradition in evolutionary biology that views natural selection and other environmental processes as acting on *preexisting* variation. Darwin himself, however, held the view that a single small change in the hereditary material of an individual organism could possibly alter an evolutionary outcome. This view also has its more recent exponents in evolutionary biology, such as H. J. Muller and G. C. Williams. Interestingly, the Darwinian view of evolutionary history has been vindicated during the past two decades using computation simulation studies and long-term studies on populations of *E. coli* made from the same clone, both kinds of studies demonstrating the importance to evolutionary trajectories of spontaneous mutation and mutational order (see Stamos 2010).

I suggest that the same kind of thinking return to the professional history of ideas, which in the present case must include both the origin of belief in inclusive democracy and the origin of belief in universal human rights. Each should not be viewed necessarily as inevitabilities but possibly instead as spontaneous mutations, originating in unique minds (and possibly recurring in others), ideas that went on to have unpredictable effects and to spread in interesting ways.

The question of order is not what primarily concerns me here. We will probably never know which came first and in whom, the belief in inclusive democracy or the belief in universal human rights. But what we do know, what I believe I have shown, is that there is a remarkable correlation between the two beliefs. That striking correlation is the real *explanandum*, the fundamentally important point that requires an explanation.

I suggest that memetics provides the best explanation of this correlation, in the sense of *inference to the best explanation*. This kind of explanation has become

popular in the debate in philosophy of science over the nature of scientific explanation. As Peter Lipton (1990) puts it, at the very heart of inference to the best
explanation is *contrastive explanation,* explaining why this rather than that. To
use Lipton's example (252), if I am going to argue that Kate has the best entry in
an essay contest, it will do no good for me to focus only on the merits of Kate's
essay. I also have to show why Kate's essay is better than those of the other finalists.
The thesis in this chapter is that the rise of the belief in universal human rights
provides a prime field for memetic explanation not only as a genuine explanation but also as the best explanation in contrast to competing explanations. The
historical/philosophical analysis presented in this and the previous two chapters
was absolutely essential for this purpose, for it was necessary to show that the
rise of the belief in universal human rights, contrary to the very many scholars
who claim otherwise, coincided with the rise of genuinely democratic beliefs and
values, particularly in the cases of Overton (possibly the first to have the concept
of universal human rights) and Locke (who got the concept off the ground). The
connection with democratic beliefs and values is not the only key, as shall be argued
in the final section of this chapter, but it is for the memetic part of the analysis.

From the memetic point of view, the democracy meme complex evolved a
natural and deep symbiotic union with the universal human rights meme complex because the union increases the spread of each complex. The key concept
here is *symbiosis,* which is a central concept in biology. A symbiotic relationship,
narrowly conceived as *mutualism,* is one where the fitness levels of each of the
symbionts are increased by the relationship (where *fitness* is defined in terms of
survival and reproduction). Some of these relationships are obligatory, where
the symbionts cannot exist on their own, and some of them are not obligatory.
Either way, it is the increase in fitness levels that explains the evolution of the
symbiotic relationship. A classic example is discussed by Dawkins (1998, 229),
that of termites and the microorganisms in their guts. The termites need the
microorganisms to digest the wood they feed on, while the microorganisms,
rarely found anywhere but in the guts of termites, need the termites to find the
wood and to chew it into little pieces for them. No matter the example, it is
important to notice that symbiosis is not an alternative to competition in nature,
but rather a result of it as a further competitive strategy. As the biologist Peter
Price (1991) succinctly puts it, "mutualistic associations are commonly antago-
nistic to a third species" (263).

Returning to the democracy and human rights meme complexes, memetics
explains their coevolution as symbionts in a highly competitive world of political
beliefs and ideas, in that the individual fitness levels of the component memes
in each of the two main meme complexes are raised to a higher level than what

their fitness levels would be without the symbiotic relationship. As with termites and their digestive microorganisms, it is important to see precisely how this is so.

Beginning with the human rights meme complex (the idea that all humans are born with a set of equal and inalienable moral claims and entitlements), the benefit conferred to this system of ideas by the democracy meme complex is very direct and simple. Democracy is the only political system that is conducive to the spread of the human rights meme complex, a government that is for the people and by the people, one that expresses the will of the majority of the people rather than a minority (such as landowners), one that is devoted to protecting the rights of the people. Other political systems would favor different belief systems, such as the divine right of kings or the fundamental interests of the collective. In doing so they would actually confer resistance to the human rights meme complex. In fact it is difficult to imagine any political system favoring the belief in universal human rights except democracy.

Turning now to the democracy meme complex, the benefit conferred to this system of ideas by the human rights meme complex is a little more complicated. Democracy, in the very least, is the only political system that by definition puts the people first. Universal human rights also puts people first, although it is not the only moral system to do this. Democracy itself is also furthered, both in terms of the value of the individual vote and the value of the majority vote, by a strong sense of dignity and moral equality inherent in the people, along with a sense of individual freedom, and this is precisely what the human rights meme complex delivers, possibly better than any other moral system of ideas.

Indeed, the two meme complexes seem pre-adapted to each other, a perfect fit. If one should already firmly have the belief in genuine democratic beliefs and values, then universal human rights seem "self-evident." And similarly if one should already firmly have the belief in universal human rights, then democratic beliefs and values seem the obvious way to go. The two meme complexes are entirely different in content, but they make a remarkably complementary pair.

It is hardly a coincidence, then, from the memetic point of view, that genuine democratic beliefs and values and belief in universal human rights originated at the same time and place and involved the same persons, most notably the Leveller Overton and the philosopher Locke a few decades afterward.

There is yet another and very important way that the human rights meme complex furthers the spread of the democracy meme complex, and so would be expected to coevolve with it from the memetic point of view. The fundamental flaw of democracy, the greatest internal hindrance to its spread, is what Alexis de Tocqueville and John Stuart Mill after him famously called "the tyranny of the majority," Tocqueville in his *Democracy in America* (1835) and Mill in his

On Liberty (1859). As a young aristocratic lawyer traveling through the United States in the early 1830s, Tocqueville came to reflect on the nature and value of democracy, especially as it existed in that country, and came to see the tyranny of the majority as the greatest of all dangers to democracy both in America and in general. As he puts it, "If America ever loses its liberty, the fault will surely lie with the omnipotence of the majority, which may drive minorities to despair and force them to resort to physical force. This may lead to anarchy, but to an anarchy that will come as a consequence of despotism" (I.2.§7). Tocqueville also emphasized the effect that the tyranny of the majority has on the mind, in stifling independence of thought and free discussion. As he puts it, "In America, the majority erects a formidable barrier around thought. Within the limits thus laid down, the writer is free, but woe unto him who dares to venture beyond those limits" (§7). Similarly Mill recognizes that "the people ... *may* desire to oppress a part of their number," and that the tyranny of the majority "leaves fewer means of escape, penetrating much more deeply into the details of life, and enslaving the soul itself" (90–91).

Their solutions to this problem, however, miss the historicity of the situation. Quoting Thomas Jefferson and James Madison in support, Tocqueville claims that the tyranny of the majority is best checked by having various levels and branches of government with different functions and by having an independent judicial system, partly because lawyers and judges tend to have an aristocratic frame of mind and so are not prone to follow the whims and prejudices of the majority, but also because lawyers function primarily as professional advocates for individuals and small groups (I.2.§§7–8). What is particularly odd is that he fails to see the role of rights, in particular human rights. He claims Jefferson as "the most powerful apostle that democracy has ever had" (I.2.§7) and that he knows "of no idea more beautiful than that of rights" (§6), but he utterly fails to connect the dots. Jefferson was not only an apostle of democracy but also an apostle of human rights. And lawyers "today constitute the most powerful barrier against the excesses of democracy" precisely because they defend the rights, including the supposed human rights, of their clients. As such, then, as Jefferson was an apostle of human rights, lawyers are their high and low priests (judges and defense attorneys, respectively; prosecutors, being restricted mainly to applying the law, are in effect the representatives of the majority).

Moreover, the Founding Fathers were well aware of the importance of rights in the protection of minorities against the majority. Jefferson himself, for example, in a letter to James Madison (1787) about the Constitution, laments "the omission of a bill of rights" (Peterson 1984, 915), while in another letter to Madison (1789), again on the need of a bill of rights, he warns of the "tyranny of the legislatures" as "the most formidable dread" (944). And through to the time of his First Inaugural Address (1801), he recognized that "though the will of the majority is in all cases to prevail [which he calls 'this sacred principle'], that will to be rightful must be reasonable; that the minority possess their equal rights, which equal law must protect, and to violate would be oppression" (492–493). But it was Madison who was most important in this regard, as the principal framer of the American Constitution and the Bill of Rights (the first ten Amendments to the Constitution). In arguing for the latter, Madison was well aware of the dangers in a republic of an "over-bearing majority" (Rakove 1999, 160), of an unchecked "tyrannical will" of "the majority of the Community" (421), of "the majority against the minority" (446). Against this "great danger" he proposed not only a separation of executive and legislative branches of government, regular elections, and an independent judiciary among the necessary checks and balances, but also a "bill of rights," and that "*absolute* restrictions in cases that are doubtful, or where emergencies may overrule them, ought to be avoided" (422). But interestingly it was not necessarily natural rights that he had in mind. Freedom of religion and freedom of speech, to name two important examples, were such, but "Trial by jury," he wrote, "cannot be considered as a natural right," as "one of the pre-existent rights of nature," but instead is "a right resulting from the social compact which regulates the action of the community, but is as essential to secure the liberty of the people" (445–446). (The significance of this distinction will be revisited in Chapter 7, where I discuss the importance of basic rights.)

Mill, as the greatest proponent of utilitarianism after Bentham, placed his hope not in rights but in the utilitarian calculus. He argued that a society that protects minorities against the tyranny of the majority will be happier (all other things being equal) than a society that does not. As he put it in *On Liberty*, "I regard utility as the ultimate appeal on all ethical questions; but it must be utility in the largest sense, grounded on the permanent interests of a man as a progressive being" (95). The latter, Mill argued, requires not only access to education, but most important, freedom of conscience and thought, which must be protected from the beliefs of the majority. The only limitation Mill put on the individual for freedom of thought and action was harm to others. This has come to be known as the *harm principle*. As Mill puts it, "Over himself, over his own body and mind, the individual is sovereign" (95) and "the only purpose for which power can be rightfully exercised over any member of a civilized community, against his will, is to prevent harm to others" (94). Mill could not acknowledge the existence and role of human rights, because as a utilitarian he could not believe in the reality of human rights. For him, human rights talk is only "clothing" (I will have more on Mill and Bentham on human rights in the next chapter) and the utilitarian calculus alone should be the arbiter of right and wrong, justice and injustice. Because of this, he failed to perceive the role of human rights talk in checking the excesses of democracy, not only in individual cases, such as disputes over property rights, but also more generally in the context of religious, racial, and other minorities (and also for the other half of the people itself, women).

From a memetic point of view, the historical and ongoing connection between democracy and human rights talk makes perfect sense. What belief in universal human rights accomplishes vis-à-vis democracy, or at least when those rights are protected, is protection for minorities against the rule of the majority. The tyranny of the majority is the fatal flaw, the Achilles' heel, of democracy. Excess of power in the majority threatens the very existence of any democracy, not only because tyrannized minorities contain the seeds of revolution (which may bring an end to the democracy), but more important, because the excess undermines the fundamental democratic values of individuality and liberty, values that are essential for the life of any genuine democracy. When those values get eroded, the democratic value of one-person-one-vote and the necessary respect for the will of the majority get eroded too. Belief in universal human rights and mechanisms for their protection, then, provide a fundamental check and balance against the excess of power in the majority. Together, in a deep symbiotic relationship, democracy memes and universal human rights memes increase each other's spread.

This fundamental idea, quite interestingly, finds close expression today in Ronald Dworkin's idea of rights as trumps against the majority. In his highly influential *Taking Rights Seriously* (1978), the Frank Henry Sommer Professor of Law at New York University characterizes rights, including what he calls "individual human rights" (vii), as "trumps over collective goals" (xv), as a "protection ['an individual is entitled to'] against the majority even at the cost of the general interest" (146), as "the majority's promise to the minorities that their dignity and equality will be respected" (205), as "a claim to a trump over the general welfare for the account of a particular individual" (364), as "an individual trump over decisions justified collectively" (366). Dworkin says his defense and characterization of rights "does not presuppose any ghostly forms," it "does not suppose that rights have some special metaphysical character," but instead he conceives of them as purely "formal" (xi). Again he says he does not think of rights as "spooky sorts of things that men and women have in much the same way as they have non-spooky things like tonsils." He does not make "ontological assumptions of that sort," he says, but instead only thinks of them in the formal sense of being "a special, in the sense of a restricted, sort of judgment about what is right or wrong for governments to do" (139). All of this even though he believes that "many rights are universal," properly called "human rights," in the sense that "arguments are available in favour of these rights against any collective justification in any circumstances reasonably likely to be found in political society" (365).

It is doubtful that Dworkin (1978), as he thinks, is really taking fully seriously the concept of human rights accepted by "the present United States Government" (184), the concept enshrined in the Declaration of Independence and the Universal Declaration of Human Rights, which is that of human rights as *possessions*, as *moral facts* about humans. His non-ontological "formal" conception of human rights is something different. (A similar point was made in detail in Chapter 3 in the section on Beitz.) Nevertheless, quite remarkably, what Dworkin says makes much sense from a memetic point of view (for democracy and human rights, but not for the divine right of kings). It is also important to notice how widespread his view of rights as trumps has become (whether taken to be formal or as possessions). Michael Ignatieff (2007), for example, states that "Interests can always be traded, but rights cannot. . . . We think of them as trumps. 'Give me my rights' is not an invitation to compromise. It's a demand for unconditional surrender" (17).

Looking back to Locke, it is sometimes noted with surprise that nowhere in his political writings does he provide for a mechanism to protect minorities against the tyranny of the majority (e.g., Strauss 1953, 233n104; Shapiro 1986, 116; Stevens 1996, 434–450). Instead, it is claimed, his focus was on the good of society and of the individual, or just on the good of the majority. Against either claim it might be pointed out that over half of the text of Locke's *Two Treatises* has been lost (Laslett 1988, 77). But putting aside the principle of charity, what needs to be recognized is that a memetic analysis does not require the hosts of a new meme or meme complex to be consciously aware of what Blackmore (1999) calls "memetic tricks" (192–193). This is because most of what goes on inside our minds is at the subconscious level. Competition between memes for a place in our minds, mutations in the memes that we do have or that we spread, the joining of memes into meme complexes, and the symbioses of meme complexes should all be expected to occur subconsciously for the most part. Likewise my analysis of the rise of the belief in universal human rights, focused as it is on Locke and the Levellers before him, does not require any of them to have been fully aware of the role of human rights talk in relation to the rise of democratic beliefs and values. The full awareness could have come later or not at all. Without the full awareness the symbiosis could still have evolved much the same. (Indeed, host brains do not have to have conscious awareness at all of what their meme parasites are really doing for those parasites to do their tricks.)

But it so happens that Locke was in fact well aware of the problem of the tyranny of the majority, as were the Levellers before him. One of the fundamental issues in England during their time was religious freedom: the right of minority modes of religious worship, such as Catholics, Quakers, Baptists, and Jews, in the face of the dominant Church of England. Not surprisingly, religious freedom was a major theme in the writings of both the Levellers and Locke. Overton, for example, was a Baptist and possibly for a time a Mennonite before becoming a Leveller. In his pamphlet on human rights examined in the previous chapter, "An Arrow Against All Tyrants" (October 1646), much of the pamphlet is a defense of "matters of conscience" against the religious tyranny of the Presbyterian clergy that dominated the House of Commons (Sharp 1998, 64), a tyranny that involved "hanging, burning, branding, imprisonment, etc." (65) for the purpose of "tithes, oblations, obventions," and "the prohibition of all to teach God's word but themselves" (66). Freedom of religion, indeed, was a major theme in Leveller writings, such as Overton and Walwyn's "A Remonstrance of Many Thousand Citizens" (July 1646), Walwyn's "Toleration Justified and Persecution Condemned" (January 1646), and their constitutional proposals, "An Agreement of the People" (October 1647) and "An Agreement of the Free People of England" (May 1649), the former protecting "matters of religion and the ways of God's worship" based on "our consciences" (94), the latter stipulating that "we do not empower or entrust our said Representatives to continue in force or to make any laws, oaths or covenants, whereby to compel by penalties or otherwise any person to anything in or about matters of faith, religion, or God's worship; or to restrain any person from the profession of his faith or exercise of religion according to his conscience" (173).

Locke himself was mainstream, an Anglican committed to the Church of England (Marshall 1994, xix, 9–12, 371–372; Woolhouse 2007, 51, 53). But even so, in his "An Essay on Toleration," written in 1667 and showing clearly the influence of Lord Ashton (later the earl of Shaftesbury), Locke states that "speculative opinions and divine worship, are those things alone which have an absolute and universal right to toleration" (Goldie 1997, 136). His only qualifications or limits on these are, first, that they "be done sincerely and out of conscience to God," and second, that they "do not tend to the disturbance of the state, or do not cause greater inconveniences than advantages to the community" (140). (Locke at this time, by the way, drew the line against Catholics and some Protestant fanatics over this latter limit.) Similarly in his much longer "A Letter Concerning Toleration," published in 1689 but written while in Holland in 1685, Locke states that "liberty of conscience is every man's natural right, equally belonging to dissenters as to themselves; and ... nobody ought to be compelled in matters of religion, either by law or force" (Wootton 1993, 417), where "natural rights ... are not forfeitable upon account of religion" (432). Locke, nevertheless, did not extend religious tolerance to atheists, not only because "Promises, covenants, and oaths, which are the bonds of human society, can have no hold upon an atheist," but also because atheism provides "no pretence of religion whereupon to challenge the privilege of a toleration" (426).

All in all, then, what should be surprising is not that Locke and the Levellers before him had nothing to say about the tyranny of the majority over minorities, for as we have just seen they were very aware and sensitive to this issue. Rather, they both had little or nothing to say about the emancipation of women and of slaves. In their defense, success requires not trying to do everything at once, since ideas play themselves out in concrete social and political contexts. Nor can anyone be expected to completely slough off and transcend all the prejudices of their time. Hypocrisies and contradictions inevitably remain.

And they have remained in democracies to the present day (without ceasing to be democracies, I should add). But while the hypocrisies and contradictions of the West in human rights talk were and continue to be many, one must not miss the proverbial forest for the trees. Democratic nations were and continue to be the principal hosts of the universal human rights meme complex, while so-called communist countries (not to mention dictatorships, theocracies, and aristocracies) represented and continue to represent the strongest resistance to it.

Resistance to the Human Rights Epidemic

The reason for the resistance of communist countries (or rather countries with a communist ideology) traces back principally to the writings of Karl Marx. In his essay "On the Jewish Question," which was published in 1843 and focuses mainly on the French Declaration of the Rights of Man and of the Citizen (Tucker 1978, 42–45), Marx argues that the concept of universal human rights fails to recognize man as a "species-being," as a social and political species, but instead construes him as the "egoistic man," as a "self-sufficient monad." The problem, for Marx, is that "the *political community*" is reduced to "a mere *means* for preserving these so-called rights of man." For Marx it should be the other way around: the individual should exist for the community, in the Marxist utopia, the collective. The individual is the means, the collective is the end. For Marx, human rights talk, with its proclamation of a natural right to individual freedom, to freedom of religion, to private property, and so much more, is a social construction born of a false consciousness. Instead of providing what is best for its citizens—for Marx we need to be freed "from religion," "from property," "from the egoism of business"—human rights talk virtually guarantees conflict in a society, and therefore represents a major obstacle to the utopian society Marx envisaged (no classes, no conflict, natural cooperation among its members, a society wherein everyone's needs are met), made possible only with his theory of human nature (man as naturally a member of a collective, but not as innately hierarchical, exploitative, greedy, or lazy). Many years later, in a letter written in 1875 and given the title "Critique of the Gotha Program" by Engels, Marx reiterates the slogan of the communist utopia—"From each according to his ability, to each according to his needs!"—and rejects the concept of "equal rights" as "obsolete verbal rubbish" (531).

Not only this hook to the individual (everyone's needs met), but mainly Marx's inversion of the individual and society (combined with the Marxist theory of human nature), more than anything else, explains the resistance of communist countries to the human rights ideology, beginning with the Russian revolution to the present (see Courtois et al. 1999, 437, 752–753). Looking just to the framing of the Universal Declaration of Human Rights itself, Andrei Vyshinsky, the USSR's Deputy Foreign Minister and head of the Soviet delegation (famous for being the prosecutor in Stalin's purge trials), claimed explicitly that rights "could not be conceived outside the State," that "the very concept of right and law was connected with that of the State," and that rights not created and protected by the state were "empty illusions, easily created, but just as easily dispelled" (Normand and Zaidi 2008, 194). Similarly, Alexei Pavlov, the Soviet delegate who was part of the Drafting Committee, repeatedly rejected the drafts because they would "violate the principle of sovereignty of states," and instead wanted qualifiers added to political and civil liberties such as "in accordance with the law of the State" or "except as determined by national legislation" (Glendon 2001, 110, 113). Vyshinsky added that in the communist state "there could not be any contradiction between the government and the individual, since the government was in fact the collective individual" (Morsink 1999, 22). In short, the human rights ideology, in an important sense, places the individual over the collective, and that idea can never mix with communism, except on the surface as a political expedient, which is what we see in the case of international agreements.

The Marxist ideology, then, as a meme complex that places the collective over the individual, must compete for mind/brain hosts against the democracy meme complex, which places the individual over the collective. The latter evolved symbiotically with the universal human rights meme complex because together they further the spread of their component memes, while the former evolved with an altogether different meme complex, Marx's theory of human nature.

It is interesting to notice at this point that Marx derived much of his inspiration from G. W. F. Hegel, who in his *Outlines of the Philosophy of Right* (1821) rejected democratic individualism in favor of the state, which in a rational society represents the best interests of the individuals that belong to it. In a letter to Feuerbach, Marx wrote that Hegel provided "a philosophical foundation for socialism" and praised Hegel for bringing the concept of human nature down from "the heaven of abstraction to the real earth" (Tucker 1978, 53). But Marx clearly went much further than Hegel, who recognized some individual human rights—or rather, *person* rights, since "The highest thing for a human being is to be a person" (§37)—such as "the absolute *right of appropriation* which human beings have over all 'things'" (§44), the right to "private property" (§46), and the right to "my life and my body," to which he adds that animals "have no right to their life, because they do not will it" (§48).

Hegel's socialism brings us to John Rawls, James Bryant Conant University Professor Emeritus at Harvard University prior to his death in 2002. Considered by many the greatest political theorist of our time, Rawls is most famous for his *A Theory of Justice* (1971), in which he bases the concept of justice as fairness on his *veil of ignorance* thought experiment. Interestingly, Rawls (1993) attempts to defend a minimalist conception of human rights, not only one confined to basic human rights but also one that "does not depend on any particular comprehensive moral doctrine or philosophical conception of human nature, such as, for example, that human beings are moral persons and have equal worth, or that they have certain particular moral and intellectual powers that entitle them to these rights" (68). Rawls, then, it would seem clear enough, does not conceive of human rights as *possessions,* but instead defines them purely in terms of *function* or *role,* in the sense of specifying "the outer boundary of admissible domestic law of societies in good standing in a just society of peoples" (71). And he emphasizes that this conception is "politically neutral" (69), in that it cannot be rejected for being "ethnocentric or merely Western" (79). In fact he claims that his conception would satisfy political systems from Western democracies to "hierarchical societies," such as Hegel's brand of socialism (69–70, 79–80), with the obvious exception of "outlaw regimes," such as Nazi Germany (72).

Much like Dworkin's formalist approach to human rights as trumps, then, Rawls's functionalist approach is not really a defense of the modern consensus concept of human rights either. In this they are not alone but have some company (as we have seen in Chapter 3). Suffice it here to say that Rawls's approach makes much sense from the viewpoint of memetics as well. Dworkin's approach captures the memetic trick of symbiosis as argued in this chapter, but Rawls's approach is a memetic trick of a very different kind, specifically a *memetic compromise* designed to spread the human rights meme complex in environments where the doctrine of human rights is commonly viewed with suspicion as an ethnocentric product of the West. The memetic trick can also be viewed as largely destined to fail, not only because (looking only now at the case of Marxism) the Marxism meme complex cannot possibly evolve a symbiosis with the human rights meme complex without losing its identity (as Marx was sufficiently aware), but also because, according to Marxism, the communist utopia cannot be established without the intermediate stage of a socialist dictatorship, and Rawls's minimalism explicitly does not extend to "tyrannical and dictatorial regimes" or to "expansionist states" (78–79).

The case of Marx on human rights points to a mainly ideological resistance to the spread of the human rights meme complex, whereas the case of Rawls on human rights points to cultural resistance as well. It is important at this point to see how culture alone can come into conflict with the belief in human rights.

The term *culture*, of course, suffers from a variety of definitions with little if any consensus, but whatever the definition it should not be confused with *ideology*. The latter is a system of ideas, social and political in nature, that drives and constrains an individual or group, to the point of dutiful slavery to the ideology, which typically includes lies, fallacious reasoning, little or no reflective critical reasoning, and sometimes even murder and suicide in the name of the ideology, while *culture* is a much more expansive term, involving ways of living, particular mannerisms, art and fashion, a language or dialect or lingo, and a shared body of beliefs and values. Hence we speak of Marxism as an ideology but not a culture, while we speak of Jamaican as a culture but not an ideology. At any rate, given Dawkins's definition of *meme*, examined at the beginning of this chapter, both ideologies and cultures would have to count as meme complexes. And much as an ideology can confer resistance to the spread of the universal human rights meme complex, so, too, can a culture.

I shall focus on just one example. Claude Ake (1987), a former professor of political science in Nigeria, argues that the Western conception of human rights is largely inapplicable to Africa and that this explains why Africans for the most part have been indifferent to the concept. Part of the reason is culture, in that throughout Africa the cultural emphasis is on the family, the tribe, the ethnic group. Foreign is the idea that the individual can morally make claims against one's group. But that, of course, is precisely what the Western concept of human rights involves. Donnelly (2003, 78–79) adds that even where African cultures have allowed for personal rights against one's government, focusing now on evidence from traditional, precolonial African societies, the claims were based on criteria such as age, sex, achievement, and hierarchy, not on being human. Whatever the historical situation, the current situation in Africa of mass poverty, starvation, disease, illiteracy, and domestic political oppression requires, according to Ake (1987), that the Western concept of universal human rights be modified so as to apply to the concrete situations faced by Africans in the current age. For him that means mainly extending the concept to include "collective human rights for corporate social groups such as the family, the lineage, the ethnic group" (114).

The problem now, of course, is that we no longer have the concept of universal human rights, rights that all humans have by virtue of being human, but something else. In other words, group rights are not and cannot be human rights, for the simple fact that *a group of humans is not a human.* (Put another way, if a particular group of humans has rights that the rest of humans do not, then those rights cannot be *human* rights.) As long as we accept this as a fact, then the concept of human rights, of rights that each and every human has by virtue of being human, has some plausibility. But the second we go further, into group rights, the concept begins on a path toward self-destruction. One reason is that the concept of group rights easily descends into nonsense, its own *reductio ad absurdum*, since it clears the way for any group whatsoever to claim its natural rights to this or that. Another reason is that the concept of group rights is a mutated concept, one that has mutated into a form that no longer makes it recognizable with its predecessor. It has become, then, a new species. And as a new species, it cannot possibly hope to enjoy the benefits of the environmental niche that its predecessor enjoyed. In the present case, that means the possible loss of symbiosis with the democracy meme complex (plausible because group rights cannot confer the needed check and balance against the tyranny of the majority, for the majority can now claim its own group rights, too), which in turn threatens the very survival of the democracy meme complex itself.

From this perspective alone it can be predicted that the concept of group rights as human rights will never become popular in genuine democracies.

Evolutionary Psychology and Fairness

Even if it should be agreed that memetics provides a powerful explanation for the origin and spread of the modern consensus concept of universal human rights, and also for the resistance to that spread, the question of explanation is still not complete. For it might still be asked, "How is it possible that so many people worldwide, including millions of intelligent and educated people, could believe so strongly in this myth?" It is not simply an *idea* to them, but to use the distinction developed by David Hume (1739) in an entirely different context (I.3.§7), it is a *belief,* an idea with the "force and vivacity" of a sense impression. Thomas Jefferson used the phrase "self-evident" when he penned the Declaration of Independence, the very same phrase used today by many, such as a former president of the American Society of International Law, Louis Henkin (1990, 2), as well as the Eugen Weber Professor of Modern European History at the University of California (Los Angeles), Lynn Hunt (2007, 214), while others such as the historian and Professor of Government at Harvard University, Richard Tuck (1979), claim that "there must be *something* to the language of rights" (1). One or the other is the sentiment of almost everyone I have ever discussed this topic with (outside of academia) and seemingly every journalist, politician, and lawyer on the tube. The reason cannot simply be, as Richard Primus (1999) puts it, that much of human rights talk is "outcome-driven" (194), concerned not with foundations or justification but with consequences. There has to be more to it.

Following Hume's extremely important and useful distinction between beliefs and ideas, memetic analysis, it would seem, can take us only so far. It cannot explain the "self-evident" nature of the belief in universal human rights, why people, including deeply thinking and highly educated people, so many and so widely, fail to question the reality of human rights and take them as a given, so much so that anyone who questions the reality of universal human rights is viewed with deep suspicion, even as malevolent or pernicious. For that we need something more.

Ultimately what is required is a twofold explanation common in biology, namely, genetic/evolutionary on the one hand and environmental on the other, one providing an explanation of the origin and spread of the idea of universal human rights (environment), the other providing an explanation of the strength of the belief (genes/evolution).

It has been argued in this chapter that the environmental explanation for the existence of the idea is satisfied by memetics. The universal human rights meme complex evolved symbiotically with the inclusive democracy meme complex, since together the memes of each are more fit, more likely to survive and reproduce, than if they were apart.

The genetic/evolutionary explanation is no less interesting. What is wanted is an explanation of what Ignatieff (2007) quite appropriately alludes to when he claims that "rights have worked their way deep inside our psyches" (2). What is also wanted is an explanation of what Ignatieff also correctly claims, which is not only that rights entail obligations but that it is "the reciprocal character of rights … [that] makes them social" (32).

As contrastively the best explanation, I suggest that the psychological strength of the modern belief in universal human rights is rooted in an evolved instinct for *fairness*. This might seem counterintuitive, since there is so much unfairness in the human world, both past and present. But humans are much more complex than the dichotomy fair-or-unfair suggests, and two powerful lines of theory and evidence support the conclusion that human nature, in addition to involving instincts for hierarchy and division of labor and so much more, also involves a powerful instinct or two for fairness (where *instinct* is taken to mean a behavior that evolved biologically as an *adaptation,* not a by-product, which means that the behavior evolved by natural selection because it increased survival and reproduction).

The first line of argument involves the theory of *reciprocal altruism,* the evolution of an instinct for altruism between non-kin. (Altruism between kin is easily explained by kin selection, but up until a few decades ago altruism between non-kin has been something of a dilemma for evolutionary biologists.) An instinct for reciprocal altruism is expected to evolve in tight-knit social groups with a fair amount of intelligence and memory capacity for remembering who did what to whom. In short, it goes like this: I'll help you even if it has no immediate payoff to me, but if I find out that you're a cheater, that you won't return the favor in similar circumstances, then I'll no longer be willing to help you. The sociobiologist Robert Trivers proposed this theory in his revolutionary paper, "The Evolution of Reciprocal Altruism," published in 1971 in the *Quarterly Review of Biology* (which according to the journal's website is the most cited article in its history). In his introduction to the reprint of this paper in his volume of collected essays (Trivers 2002), Trivers suggests that "a sense of fairness would evolve as a way of regulating reciprocal tendencies, a way of judging the degree to which other people were cheating you (and you them!)" (17). There is evidence that this evolved sense (assuming such) goes back in evolutionary time and is shared, by degree, with other primates. The primatologist Frans de Waal (1996, 159–160), for example, has observed it among chimpanzees when it comes to food sharing. A chimpanzee will readily share food with another chimpanzee in its group, but will no longer share with that chimpanzee once it realizes that the favor is not returned, and will even exhibit "moralistic aggression" toward the cheater.

Trivers (2002, 17) claims that it is not plausible that our sense of fairness came from interactions with close kin, since these do not normally require a return benefit, let alone of equal proportion. But this is not entirely correct. A sense of fairness also relates to early childhood family dynamics, where although parents rarely if ever treat their offspring completely fairly, it would be adaptive for offspring to have an evolved sense of fairness to execute alternative strategies in the competition with siblings for parental resources (food, attention, etc.). This might explain why offspring are normally highly sensitive to unfair treatment (Sulloway 1996, 90–93).

And again, there is evidence of this other kind or sense of fairness in primates. In his most recent book, de Waal (2009, 183–187) calls this other kind of fairness *egocentric fairness,* a sense of fairness based on resentment. De Waal and one of his students taught a group of capuchin monkeys to barter pebbles for pieces of cucumber, a watery fruit the monkeys happily munched on. At a later time, while feeding them cucumber this way in pairs, de Waal and his student introduced a variation. Instead of giving cucumber to both monkeys in each pair, they gave one of them grapes in return for a pebble, a sugary fruit that is one of the favorite foods of capuchin monkeys. In each case, the monkey in the pair that did not get the grapes threw a temper tantrum, typically throwing away its pebbles and pieces of cucumber. Capuchins are highly trainable and are possibly the most intelligent of all monkey species, such that their temper tantrums in de Waal's experiments are not what should have happened if these monkeys were motivated simply by self-interest.

Both kinds or senses of fairness might involve the very same neural circuitry, or they might involve different circuitry. It doesn't much matter (to my argument). What matters is that we can readily see the same kinds of fairness in human behavior.

Humans, of course, unlike other primates, have in addition a higher sense of fairness, what might be called *universal fairness*. Against de Waal's position that the "building blocks" of human morality can be found in primates and other highly social species, Philip Kitcher (2006) replies that humans are not "wantons" (136), driven simply by their impulses, but have a capacity for impulse control as well as an ability for ethical judgments as "impartial spectators" (134). Similarly, Peter Singer (2006) replies that only humans are capable of taking "an impartial perspective, which leads us to consider the interests of those outside our own group" (144), and he emphasizes that ethics distinctively involves the human capacity for reason, with which "we can abstract from our own case and see that others, outside our group, have interests similar to our own" (145). Steven Woolcock (1999), against evolutionary ethics in general, argues that ethics is not a matter of following our feelings or instincts but instead involves claims that are universal (they apply to everyone), are categorical (no ifs, ands, or buts), and are backed up by reasons or justification. As he puts it, "Justification does not collapse into explanation, nor do reasons collapse into causes" (291).

The higher sense of fairness that humans have might well be the consequence of the human capacity for reason, which itself (along with the capacity for language) is after all an evolved capacity, not a divine dispensation from the gods. We might also have what Michael Ruse (2002) calls "a collective illusion of the genes, bringing us all in (except for the morally blind)" (659), an evolved instinct for thinking that our moral beliefs are objectively and absolutely true. But more important, what the critics above (and many others) are missing are a number of important insights into the nature of ethics, points that I have argued elsewhere (Stamos 2008, 170–173).

I shall focus here on two. First, as Darwin and Aristotle long before him well knew, most moral behavior in humans is not reasoned out beforehand but is reasoned out only afterward, if at all—it is "post hoc," as de Waal nicely puts it (2006b, 178).

Second, if one examines the various normative theories in philosophy, the various moral theories in philosophy of what we should do, one is left with the impression that ethics is a field without a foundation. All that one gets are conflicting theories. But if one takes evolution seriously, then a very different way of looking at these theories presents itself. In philosophy of religion, what is sometimes appealed to in defense of religious pluralism is the Buddhist parable of the elephant and the blind Indians, in which each blind Indian felt and described a different part of the elephant but thought he felt and described the whole. Human morality, I submit, is the elephant, the product of our evolutionary past (much of which is shared with other species, either as homologies or as analogies). Aristotelian virtue ethics, the psychological egoism of Hobbes, the sentimentalism of Hume and Smith, the utilitarianism of Bentham and Mill, the deontologies of Kant and Ross, Rawls's veil of ignorance, and more recently feminist ethics and environmental ethics, collectively describe the elephant, but each of the descriptions or theories is typically given by a blind Indian, each thinking that he or she has captured the whole when in fact each has captured only a part.

So what has this to do with universal human rights? The doctrine of universal human rights appeals to a very real part of the elephant, but not in the sense that there really are human rights. Instead, it appeals to the deep sense (or senses) of fairness that humans innately have and that many have come to extend to all humans. As Henkin (1990) aptly puts it more widely, human rights "reflect a common sense of justice, fairness, and decency" (2). Human rights advocates such as Thomas Jefferson and Eleanor Roosevelt represent that higher sense of fairness that I have labeled *universal fairness,* but most *claims* of human rights represent that lower sense of fairness that de Waal labels as *egocentric.* This sense of fairness is aptly captured in Ronald Dworkin's characterization of rights (including human rights) as trumps against the majority.

If the above is basically correct, it would go a long way in explaining the psychology of the modern belief in universal human rights. Memetics alone explains remarkably well the origin and spread of the idea, but it cannot explain the "force and vivacity" of the belief. Evolutionary psychology is needed to complete the picture. If there is a deep sense of fairness in our psyches, rooted in human nature and possibly earlier, that deep sense would act as a *pre-adaptation* in humans for the belief in universal human rights.

That pre-adaptation would then have to be combined with certain background beliefs, as part of the necessary environmental conditions. One would be the belief that humans as a kind are not only innately special but are morally superior to animals. Human rights, after all, are supposed to be exclusive to humans, as a special and elitist kind of club, one that excludes nonhuman animals. Another requirement would be the belief that all humans are of the same species, meaning the same basic kind. Without this belief, with some humans belonging to the human genus but not necessarily to the human species, some humans could be excluded as bearers of human rights, and so human rights would not be universal.

With these two backgrounds beliefs, along with a sense of egocentric fairness built into our brains, all that would be further needed is the trigger, the very *raison d'être* of the belief in universal human rights. That further and final requirement, if the argument presented earlier in this chapter is basically correct, would be the emergence and evolution of the belief in inclusive democracy.

The question then becomes, "What do we do if, after all, the belief in universal human rights is not only unfounded but false?" That is the focus of our next and final chapter.

Chapter 7

Evolution, Ethics, and Justice

> Be a philosopher; but, amidst all your philosophy, be still a man.
> —*David Hume (1748, §1)*

Bentham and MacIntyre

Jeremy Bentham (1789) wrote the following in response to the famous "inalienable rights" passage penned by Jefferson in the Declaration of Independence: "Who cannot help lamenting, that so rational a cause should be rested upon reasons, so much fitter to beget objections, than to remove them?" (17.§29n). As for the concept of natural law upon which the concept of human rights is based, Bentham had this to say: "the pretended *law of nature*; an obscure phantom, which, in the imaginations of those who go in chase of it, points sometimes to *manners,* sometimes to *laws*; sometimes to what law *is,* sometimes to what it *ought* to be" (17.§27n). A few years later, in 1796, Bentham wrote an essay against the French Declaration and its aftermath titled "Anarchical Fallacies," which was not published until 1816, in French, and then not in English until 1834, two years after his death. In that essay Bentham wrote words that would become famous to those familiar with the history of controversy over human rights. Of the concept of "natural rights," which he clearly took to mean human rights, the "rights of man" in the French Declaration, the concept is "simple nonsense," he said, and of "natural and imprescriptible [not changeable or removable] rights," the "natural, inalienable and sacred rights" in the French Declaration, the concept is "rhetorical

225

nonsense,—nonsense upon stilts" (Bedau 2000, 263). For Bentham, the concept of law and the related concept of rights make sense only in a political context, as the rules of state authority, and the rules of state authority, and of morality in general, should according to Bentham be based on a firm foundation. As a legal reformer known now as the father of utilitarianism, Bentham (1789) took that firm foundation to be the only genuinely self-evident truths about morality and justice, which are that humans are placed by nature "under the governance of two sovereign masters, *pain* and *pleasure.*" From these we get "the standard of right and wrong," they alone "point out what we ought to do" (1.§1), which basically is to act, and to judge actions, in accordance with the "*principle of utility*" (§2), which is solely concerned with whether an action or law produces more happiness than unhappiness in the sum of those affected by it.[1]

Much more recently, the philosopher Alasdair MacIntyre (1981, 67–69) argued not only that rights presuppose "the existence of a socially established set of rules," but also that the concept of natural rights, of human rights, is vacuous. "Every attempt to give good reasons for believing that there *are* such rights," he says, "has failed." Consequently, philosophers have fallen back on an "emotivist use" of human rights, but this he says "is precisely what one would expect if the philosophical projects had all failed." Similarly, when philosophers defend human rights as "self-evident truths," as intuitively obvious, "the word 'intuition' by a

---

1. It is standard for utilitarians to not believe in human rights (although it is uncommon for them to be as forceful about it as Bentham). J. S. Mill, for example, states clearly near the end of his introductory chapter in *On Liberty* (1859) that "I forego any advantage which could be derived to my argument from the idea of abstract right, as a thing independent of utility. I regard utility as the ultimate appeal on all ethical discussions." In *Utilitarianism* (1861), Mill shows that he is perfectly comfortable with using the language of rights, but it is clear in his discussion on justice that rights talk to his mind is merely the modern means by which two central ideas concerning justice "clothe themselves" (5.§24), namely, the idea that an individual has been harmed and another individual must be punished. As clothing only, Mill defends human rights talk from the viewpoint of "general utility," in that a society that secures individual rights satisfies "the most vital of all interests," that of "security," which he calls "this most indispensable of all necessaries, after physical nutriment" (§25). Most recently, Peter Singer, despite his support for rights talk in *The Great Ape Project* (Cavalieri and Singer 1993), repeatedly makes it clear in his writings that he regards rights talk, explicitly following Bentham, as "a convenient political shorthand," in other words "a shorthand way of referring to protections that people and animals morally ought to have" (Singer 1975, 8). This is repeated in his reply to the argument by de Waal (2006b, 75–80) against ape rights and lawyers for apes, in which Singer (2006) states, "I find claims about rights unsatisfactory.... That's because rights are not really the foundation of our moral obligations. They are themselves based on concern for the interests of all those affected by our actions" (154).

moral philosopher is always a signal that something has gone badly wrong with an argument." Because of the failure of the project, and because human rights talk began only "near the close of the middle ages," MacIntyre concludes that "there are no such rights, and belief in them is one with belief in witches and in unicorns."

Interestingly, MacIntyre makes a similar argument against Bentham, Mill, and the principle of utility. Just as with human rights, utility is a "fiction" since, given the many complicated features of humans and the satisfaction of their desires, "the notion of summing them either for individuals or for some population has no clear sense" (70). MacIntyre, instead, defends a version of virtue ethics that he believes to be fundamentally Aristotelian, arguing that beneath the surface variation of beliefs in human virtues found in different cultures there is a common core of human virtues that is necessary for a civilized society to flourish.

Virtue ethics, too, has its own serious problems (see, e.g., Rachels 2003, ch. 13). But so does the whole field of ethics in philosophy. As I pointed out at the end of the previous chapter, a fundamental problem with the field is that each normative theory is typically advocated as best answering the question of what we ought to do morally and how we ought to be morally. In so doing, it makes the student of ethics either an advocate of one theory against the rest or it leaves the student with a deep sense of disillusionment, with the strong impression that ethics is just a bunch of competing theories with no solid foundation whatsoever, that it is ultimately all just a matter of opinion. In other words, the field of philosophical ethics unintentionally fosters postmodernism, particularly among students.

The Elephant and the Blind Indians

At the end of the previous chapter I applied the Buddhist parable of the elephant and the blind Indians to normative theory in philosophy, such that the advocates of each theory may be viewed as blind Indians. Each theory captures a part of the whole but its advocates typically think it captures the whole (feminist ethicists tend to be the exception here). Morality *does* involve virtues and vices (virtue ethics), we *do* often instinctively act in our own best interest (psychological egoism), not only is there nothing inherently immoral about self-interest but it *is* sometimes morally what we ought to do (ethical egoism), we *do* need to apply sympathy and empathy to moral situations (sentimentalism), pleasure *is* basically good and ought to be maximized for the greatest number (classical utilitarianism) while pain *is* basically bad and ought to be minimized (negative utilitarianism), moral objects should *not* be treated merely as things (Kant), we *do* have prima facie duties and when they conflict one of them takes priority over the other (Ross), we *do* need to think more objectively about others and not look at matters of justice only from our own point of view (Rawls), we *do* need to think more in terms of fairness and stop being so unfair (human rights), we *do* need to make an effort at being more caring and nurturing and at fostering relationships built on trust and loyalty (feminist ethics), and we *do* need to take the environment into account and not treat it with reckless abandon (environmental ethics).

Each of these normative theories derives its power as an intuitive force from one or another of the parts of our evolved moral nature, which explains why in different practical situations we can feel pulled in different moral directions, or even in multiple directions at the same time. Take, for example, an intriguing thought experiment provided by Bernard Williams (1973, 99). Jim is a foreign botanist traveling through a small town in South America. Upon entering the middle of the town he finds, to his utter shock, that twenty blindfolded native Indians are about to be shot to death by a firing squad. Seeing Jim, the captain calls him over, informs him that the Indians were protesting government oppression, and that in honor of his visit he'll let nineteen of the Indians go if Jim shoots any one of them to death; otherwise he says he'll have all twenty of them shot to death. Jim is horrified. The crowd of villagers is crying and pleading with him to accept the offer. But what ought Jim morally to do?

A utilitarian would probably say that Jim should aim for the forehead of the oldest of the Indians and shoot him to death. Williams himself thinks that Jim should maintain his moral integrity by sticking to his principle of never killing an innocent person and should not accept negative responsibility for the deaths of the twenty Indians (negative in the sense of refraining to act). But if Jim is a relatively normal human being, I think the most important lesson of the thought experiment is that Jim is going to be traumatized by the experience no matter what he does and will feel guilty for a very long time to come. Why would that be? If he shoots any one of the Indians, he will have saved nineteen of the twenty Indians and will therefore have reduced an awful lot of pain, suffering, and killing, and accordingly will have gained the praise of the crowd, but the action will do violence to his senses of sympathy, empathy, fairness, and treating what he recognizes to be a person, a moral object, not merely as a thing. And if he doesn't shoot any one of the Indians, he will have satisfied his need to never treat a person merely as a thing, but he will have failed to do what he alone could have done to reduce an awful lot of pain, suffering, and killing, and accordingly will have gained the censure of the crowd, and his choice may again do violence to his senses of sympathy, empathy, and fairness. Given that Jim is not in a position to shoot the captain, he could, of course, simply run away from the situation, which might satisfy his sense of self-interest, but he would feel like a coward, and even if he didn't his conscience would probably haunt him for the rest of his life.

Jim, it would seem, was morally in a no-win situation, given that the main normative theories of ethics that were relevant to the situation did not converge on the same answer, each of them rooted, according to the present theory, in a different part of the elephant and collectively pulling him in different directions (this is where the analogy with a single elephant breaks down). The thought experiment speaks to the fundamental nature of ethics, not only that the main normative theories of ethics, given any particular topic in applied or practical ethics, need not necessarily converge on the same answer, but that when they do not converge we get genuine and apparently intractable moral debates. On the other hand, when they do converge, or at least most of them, in a kind of consensus or majority, such as on the proscription against rape, they collectively provide an apparently very powerful argument, at least for most people, and that power comes, arguably, from the elephant as a whole, so to speak, from our evolved moral nature.

Human rights, of course, were not included in the thought experiment. This is not because human rights theory is not one of the main normative theories in ethics (it is), but because it cannot be maintained in light of this book. In the previous chapter I argued that the part of the elephant it unknowingly refers to is the deep sense (or senses) of fairness that evolved in us and other intelligent, highly social animals, and *that* is what was included in the thought experiment.

Unlike the other main normative theories in ethics, the theory of universal human rights itself, if the argument of this book is correct, must be regarded as a *myth*, as a life-guiding fictional story believed by many in defiance of critical reasoning. It is sometimes said that we no longer live in the age of myth. But this is not true, and what makes it not true is not the fact that the majority of people in the world are religious to some degree and believe in one or another supernatural agency if only vaguely. What makes it true is that in this modern age of reason, where science and law and business and so much more are dominated by the values of logic and evidence, the majority of people, including the majority of educated people, at least in the West, believe strongly and fully and unthinkingly in universal human rights, so much so that this belief system has made its way into the very core of our political and legal systems and our ethical debates.

The whole of our conceptions of ethics and justice need to be *demythologized*.[2] Many will be skeptical of this approach. At the extreme is the view expressed by Leo Strauss (1953), who claims that "The contemporary rejection of natural right leads to nihilism—nay, it is identical with nihilism" (5). A much less extreme view is

---

2. I borrow the term from the Protestant scholar Rudolf Bultmann (1958), who argued that we can no longer rationally accept the myths of the Bible, so that if we believe that the Bible has a deeper meaning "concealed under the cover of mythology," then we must "de-mythologize" it to preserve that deeper meaning (18).

elaborated by the political scientist Stephen Lukes (1993), who in a series of thought experiments contrasts five imaginary countries based on "five doctrines or outlooks that are dominant in our time" (20), none of which are nihilistic but only one of which fully recognizes universal human rights, the one he thinks is comparatively the best (Egalitaria, not Utilitaria, Communitaria, Proletaria, or Libertaria).

Strauss's extreme view does not follow, and Lukes's thought experiment is missing a possible major contender, which might be called Naturalia. This is because both views fail to take evolution seriously. Against the Standard Social Science Model, according to which there is no such thing as human nature, that what we call "human nature" is simply the product of contingent social and cultural forces, we need to apply an evolutionary view of human nature conceptualized in a statistical rather than essentialistic sense as the behavioral part of the human genotype. By *bringing out* human nature thus conceived, the picture of morality and justice that emerges is not one that would lead to nihilism at all. Instead, demythologized of theological and natural rights elements, it would arguably be even better than Egalitaria.

The problem now, if this is agreed, is how to bring out human nature into a coherent and justifiable normative theory of ethics, including justice. The sociobiologist E. O. Wilson (1975) famously proclaimed that "the time has come for ethics to be removed temporarily from the hands of the philosophers and biologized," and his own solution was what he called "innate moral pluralism," by which he meant that "no single set of moral standards can be applied to all human populations, let alone all sex-age classes within each population" (288; see also Wilson 1978). While selfishness, for example, is generally not an acceptable moral standard for adults, it is evolutionarily adaptive for young children, such as the "terrible twos," and it would be maladaptive to force on them a moral standard that so deeply goes against their nature.

But Wilson's solution, for all of its merits, runs afoul of what in moral philosophy is known as the *is-ought fallacy*, that one cannot genuinely infer a moral "ought" from a nonmoral "is," a value from a fact, more specifically an evaluative statement from a purely descriptive one. (I shall have more to say about this fallacy in the next section.) And surely we do not want to say, the is-ought fallacy aside, that what is adaptive is necessarily good and should be promoted. For after all, if rape is an evolved reproductive strategy in the DNA of the males of humans and many other animal species, as some have argued (e.g., Ghiglieri 2000), it surely doesn't necessarily follow that we should strive to make rape legal. Nevertheless, if ethics is to be grounded in human nature, it most certainly has to be biologized in some way, and more recent years have seen an explosion in books and essays attempting to accomplish this task (see, e.g., Ruse 1986, 2002; Rachels 1990; Nitecki and Nitecki 1993; Thompson 1995; Maienschein and Ruse 1999; Broom 2003; Joyce 2006). What one typically finds in these discussions, however, is a lot of theory but very little if any *applied* theory, what might be called *naturalized normative ethics*, a thoroughly naturalized theory of ethics applied to help settle controversies in the field formally known as *applied* or *practical ethics*, such as abortion, capital punishment, and euthanasia. (Rachels 1990 is an exception, but he has no normative theoretical *method* that he applies.)

My presentation of what I call Naturalia attempts a balance between theory and application—which since it is the anticlimax of the book must be confined to no more than the final chapter—a balance that is required if one wants to argue, as I do, that there is a much better way of dealing with matters of ethics and justice than appealing to human rights. In doing so I shall attempt to show how the problem of the is-ought fallacy is to be avoided, as well as the problem of postmodernism when the standard theories in normative ethics are taken either as a whole (with the exception of human rights theory, of course) or individually in a partisan manner (which is the norm in moral philosophy).

Naturalized Normative Ethics

What would Naturalia be like, with its naturalistic conception of ethics and justice? I can only provide a sketch in the present and next section, which I shall then apply to half a dozen examples routinely dealt with today in terms of human rights. The contrast is not merely a matter of words, and it should help to give us a good glimpse of Naturalia.

The first thing to do is to focus on the prime moral facts of human nature. What the utilitarians got fundamentally right is that pleasure is basically good and pain is basically bad and that they are fundamental motivators. From an evolutionary point of view, of course, pleasure and pain are *adaptations,* meaning that the mechanisms for these experiences evolved because they increased survival and reproduction. Evolution itself, of course, is arguably morally neutral, but there is nothing morally neutral about pleasure and pain in themselves, for they are clearly *subjectively* good and bad, respectively. And that is what makes them morally significant, as recognized not only by utilitarians but also by philosophers as ancient as Plato, Aristotle, and Epicurus, who premised morality on happiness (hence the label *hedonism,* which should not be confused with the popular meaning of the term).

Pleasure and pain, however, are not the only facts of our moral existence. Another is our evolved capacity (likewise shared with many other animal species) for *kin altruism,* self-sacrificing *behavior* and (in our case at least) self-sacrificing *motives* toward close kin. We also have an evolved capacity for *reciprocal altruism,* as discussed in the previous chapter, which likewise is of enormous moral significance. Equally significant also is that we come equipped with well-developed capacities for sympathy and empathy. These need to be distinguished from each other. *Sympathy* is a fellow feeling or resonance maintained from a separate point of view, as when I feel bad for you when you are sad or in pain or I feel happy for you when you are overjoyed. *Empathy*, on the other hand, is when I slip into your shoes, so to speak, whether deliberately or not, when I temporarily lose myself in your perspective and look at matters from your particular point of view and imagine your happiness or pain.

Interestingly, sympathy and empathy have been making a comeback in moral theory (although usually in a blind Indian way). In recent decades *feminist ethics* has become prominent in normative theory (e.g., Baier 1987; Held 1998), much of which is an ethics of care based on concrete relationships involving trust, loyalty, nurturance, love, sympathy, and empathy (although the latter two are not mentioned in the literature as often as one would expect). Feminist ethicists view care ethics either as completing traditional ethics—with its male-dominant left-brain emphasis on abstract rules (such as the utilitarian calculus of Bentham and Mill and the categorical imperative of Kant) and its typical exclusion of so-called female virtues from the list of human virtues (Aristotle)—or as being more important than considerations of justice and impartiality, or as replacing traditional ethics altogether. Recently, the philosopher Michael Slote, in his *The Ethics of Care and Empathy* (2007), takes feminist ethics a step further and argues that all of morality and justice can be adequately explained and justified by an appeal to an ethics of care based on sympathy and empathy, while the primatologist Frans de Waal (2009), based on his studies of primates (including the fifth ape, humans), argues for what is captured in the title of his book *The Age of Empathy* (2009).

I used the word "comeback" above, for it needs to be mentioned that the Scottish Enlightenment is the principal source of what is now called the *moral sentimentalist* tradition in ethics. Francis Hutcheson (1728), the first major thinker in this tradition, argued that human morality is not reducible to or based on self-love or reason but instead on what he called a "moral sense," a sense analogous to the external five senses, in that it is not mediated by a chain of reasoning or dependent on our will. Instead, it is a part of human nature that makes "publickly useful Actions and kind Affections *grateful* to the Agent, and to every Observer" (II.§1), to which he adds, "without any view to private Happiness" (II.§0). Connected with the moral sense are a number of "*publick Passions* about the *State of others*." Among them are "Pity or Compassion" and "*Congratulation*," in that "We have *Aversion* to any impending Misery; we are *sorrowful* when it befalls any Person, and *rejoice* when it is removed" (I.3.§4).[3]

---

3. See Hutcheson's extended discussion on compassion in Hutcheson (1725, II.5.§8).

David Hume, often regarded as the greatest philosopher of the English-speaking world, took Hutcheson's thesis a major step further, by emphasizing sympathy.[4] Observe, Hume (1739) wrote, "the force of sympathy thro' the whole animal creation, and the easy communication of sentiments from one thinking being to another" (II.2.§5). This is especially true in man, he claimed, who "has the most ardent desire of society." Indeed, "the minds of men are mirrors to one another, not only because they reflect each other's emotions, but also because those rays of passions, sentiments and opinions may often be reverberated, and may decay away by insensible degrees." So much is this part of human nature that a solitary human, given omnipotence, "will still be miserable, till you give him some one person at least, with whom he may share his happiness, and whose esteem and friendship he may enjoy." Elsewhere Hume (1740) likened sympathy to a kind of resonance: "As in strings equally wound up, the motion of one communicates itself to the rest" (3.§1). But especially important is the role Hume accorded sympathy to morality. Not only is sympathy "that principle, which takes us so far out of ourselves, as to give us the same pleasure or uneasiness in characters which are useful or pernicious to society, as if they had a tendency to our own advantage or loss," but "sympathy is the chief source of moral distinctions," an "original instinct" that is part of "human nature" (§6). He thought that once a society establishes a system of law and justice that is advantageous to both the society and the individual, "it is *naturally* attended with a strong sentiment of morals; which can proceed from nothing but our sympathy with the interests of society" (§1).[5]

Adam Smith (1759), Hume's younger friend and a former student of Hutcheson's, took the tradition yet a step further, and perhaps in the most interesting way. For Smith, the fundamental feature of morality is indeed our capacity for sympathy, which he defines as an act of imagination, since "we have no immediate experience of what other men feel" (I.1.§1). "By the imagination," then, "we place ourselves in his situation," and sympathy is "our fellow-feeling with any passion whatever." But sympathy is much more than a mirroring or resonance, for Smith, since we can feel horrible for the happy person who has lost his reason, or for a deathly sick child whose pain is only in the present, or even for a dead person. Sympathy, then, is an act of imagination that "does not arise

<hr/>

4. In what follows it needs to be noted, as pointed out by Slote (2007), that "the term 'empathy' ... didn't exist in English till the early twentieth century, when it entered the language as a translation of the German word *Einfuehlung*" (13). Hence we need to keep in mind that Hume used the word "sympathy" ambiguously, to mean both sympathy and empathy, as did Smith and Darwin after him, as we shall see.

5. See also Hume (1751), which Hume considered to be his finest work.

so much from the view of the passion, as from that of the situation that excites it." But there is more. Our sympathies are often dulled by a variety of personal biases and prejudices, and are sometimes completely shut off by a "paroxysm" of emotion or distress. Sympathy, then, by itself, cannot be the basis of moral judgment. However, we are by nature social creatures, not fit for a solitary life, such that when we do harm to another, particularly out of passion, and then cool down and begin to reflect on what we have done, if we are not motivated by sympathy toward our victim, we are motivated by sympathy toward our fellow humans, our society, such that "by sympathizing with the hatred and abhorrence which other men must entertain for him, he becomes in some measure the object of his own hatred and abhorrence," which is "the nature of that sentiment, which is properly called remorse" (II.2.§2). But there is still more. Sympathy, combined with our instinctual need for society, actually allows us to attain *objectivity.* Not only does sympathy make us more conscious of how others view us, such that it must "humble the arrogance of his self-love, and bring it down to something which other men can go along with," but when after an act of injustice to another, when we have cooled down from "the heat and keenness with which our peculiar situation inspires us, ... we can enter more coolly into the sentiments of the indifferent spectator," the "severe eyes of the most impartial spectator," an ideal judge who views a situation with sympathy but without bias or prejudice. This "judge within" is the ultimate form of sympathy, and as such is the foundation of conscience and of "the general rules of morality" (III.3–5).[6]

It should not go unnoticed that this sentimentalist tradition was given moral support, one might say, by none other than Charles Darwin, who in addition to discovering evolution by natural selection and so much more was the first pioneer of what today is called *evolutionary ethics.* In *The Descent of Man* (1871), Darwin devotes an entire chapter (ch. 3) to what in humans he calls the "moral sense or conscience," which he derives from what he calls the "social instincts" (more on this below), an important component of which is sympathy, which in the context of quoting Hume and Smith he argues is an "instinct," whatever its origin, since "it will have been increased through natural selection; for those communities, which included the greatest number of the most sympathetic members, would flourish best and rear the greatest number of offspring" (82).

Today much of evolutionary ethics is devoted to following Darwin's lead, to understanding human morality and ethics from an evolutionary point of view. The consensus, basically, is that morality evolved in humans (or rather was further

---

6. For more on the moral theories of Hutcheson, Hume, and Smith, including some important differences between them, see Turco (2003).

evolved in humans), along with a greater reasoning capacity and a universal grammar, because it increased group cohesion in a world of competition. We did not begin in cities and towns supported by farming, but rather evolved ever so gradually from an ancestral species that we share with modern chimpanzees and bonobos from around 5 million years ago. From that one species evolution went blindly in at least two and possibly more directions, one of them resulting in a number of modified lineages consisting of small hunting-gathering groups, of which our own species is the last and only remaining. A division of labor would have had to have evolved in all of those small hunting-gathering groups, with males doing most if not all of the hunting and the fighting against other groups and predators and females doing most if not all of the gathering and the taking care of offspring. The evidence for this division of labor is abundantly obvious in ourselves, not only in our physiology (such as the statistical differences between the sexes in physical size, strength, facial hair, and hormones) and in our behavior (such as the statistical differences between the sexes in empathy, caring, talkativeness, multitasking, and violent aggression), but also in the studies by anthropologists over the past century or more of the rapidly dwindling groups of humans still living the hunting-gathering lifestyle, such as the Kalahari Bushmen and the Eskimos. It is also evident in our close cousins, not just the chimpanzees who sometimes go on brutal war campaigns against other chimpanzee groups (in each case the attackers are exclusively males), but more interestingly in our recently extinct sibling species the Neanderthals, in that almost all of the male skeletons have broken bones (paleoanthropologists have concluded that Neanderthals did not throw their spears but ran right up to their massive prey).

From the viewpoint of evolutionary ethics, then, morality is not a veneer or clothing but is encoded in our very DNA. Those groups that had more of morality, along with more intelligence and language and more of a division of labor, tended to survive better and have more reproduction among their members (the bottom line is always the spread of genes). There is no need for the theory of group selection here, however. In the very least, those individuals in a group that displayed more sympathy and empathy and altruism toward their fellow members would probably have been more attractive than not to the other sex, which is still the case today (Buss 2003, 102–104).

At some point in our past, possibly around 12,000 years ago, some of us evolved the cultural innovation of domesticating plants and animals, a cultural innovation that spread relatively rapidly to other parts of the world (and possibly independently in a number of cases). With that innovation, group after group eventually settled down and gave up the nomadic way of life, creating villages, then towns, cities, and eventually countries, to the point where we now have pretty much a global community.

With the spread of the cultural innovation of the urban way of life, our moral instincts naturally extended their reach to those who previously would have been considered outsiders. With the identification no longer confined to the small group or tribe, but with the country or international world as a whole, we became distinctively civilized and modern.

And we also got ethics as we now know it, ethics that involves not only moral behavior toward strangers but also universal moral principles, such as the utilitarian calculus and Kant's categorical imperative. And of course we got the belief in universal human rights. All of these can be viewed as extensions of our moral instincts, as natural and in many cases rational extensions of instincts that hitherto were confined to small groups. For Darwin (1871), indeed, "there is only an artificial barrier to prevent his [man's] sympathies extending to the men of all nations and races," and even to "the lower animals" (100–101).

Ethics also got increasingly demythologized, in the sense that its normative principles ceased to have a theological basis. Virtue ethics, beginning with Aristotle, has always focused on the nature of virtues and vices as they pertain to human nature. The sentimentalist tradition focuses on the moral sense, in particular sympathy and empathy. Utilitarian ethics is based on the subjective nature of pleasure and pain, as self-evidently good and bad, respectively. Kantians place morality on the foundation of reason, in the sense of avoiding self-contradiction. Rossians appeal to our enlightened intuitions about prima facie duties and absolute duties in the situations where the former conflict. Rawlsians attempt to be objective by applying the veil of ignorance to matters of justice. Feminist ethics focuses on context rather than rules and emphasizes concrete relations and caring. In none of these has theology been given a foundational place, even though many philosophers and others who subscribe to one or another of these ethical systems are and have been religious.

What remains is the doctrine of universal human rights. While virtue ethics and the sentimentalist tradition never had it and still do not, the concept of universal human rights has played and continues to play an ancillary role in the Kantian, utilitarian, and Rawlsian systems, and in many cases it is much more than ancillary in feminist ethics (which is understandable given the history of oppression against women). And of course human rights have become central in domestic and international law.

Ethics, then, along with law, needs a yet further round of demythologization. In the end what is needed is a *collective and thoroughly naturalistic approach* to dealing with matters of morality and justice, akin to the naturalization of epistemology appropriately known as *naturalized epistemology* (Kornblith 1994). What that approach must include, however, is not just a full account of an evolved morality in humans, but also a full recognition of the fact that the human species includes evolved mechanisms that function to dampen or even turn off our moral instincts and moral reasoning. In other words, evolutionary ethics must take into account the *anti-moral* in human nature, just as (to continue the comparison) evolutionary epistemology needs to take into account the *anti-epistemological* in human nature (see Stamos 2008, 27–33), between which there is some overlap.

What exactly is the anti-moral in human nature? The research here is fascinating and ongoing, but it arguably goes back to Darwin (as with so much else). In *The Descent of Man* (1871), Darwin argued that we can see in individual animals not only instinctual behaviors that have their only real explanation in natural selection, but also that, in the very same animal, instincts can pull against each other. One of his examples is the mother swallow with a late brood of chicks, the parental instinct to take care of them pulling her in one direction, the migratory instinct to fly south for the winter pulling her in another. Darwin used this basic lesson to explain human conscience, and it is a brilliant example of the idea of moral and anti-moral instincts pulling against each other, with one of them winning at least for a time. On the one hand we have the older instincts, the selfish instincts, such as "self-preservation, hunger, lust, revenge" (89). On the other hand we have the newer instincts in our evolutionary history, "social instincts," such as "a tendency to be faithful to … comrades," "obedience to the leader of the community," and "sympathetic feelings" (anyone lacking this is an "unnatural monster"), the latter accounting for phenomena such as our "love of praise" and "the still stronger horror of scorn and infamy" (85–86). The social instincts are "ever present and persistent" (89), but occasionally they will be temporarily overpowered by one or more of the selfish instincts, resulting in antisocial (immoral) behavior. Once gratified, however, and the normal state returns, "when past and weaker impressions are contrasted with the ever-enduring social instincts, … Man will then feel dissatisfied with himself, and will resolve with more or less force to act differently for the future. This is conscience; for conscience looks backwards and judges past actions, inducing that kind of dissatisfaction, which if weak we call regret, and if severe remorse" (91).[7]

Equally if not more interesting are the results of modern empirical psychology. Solomon Asch (1955), for example, observed that out of 123 test subjects (all of them male college students, put into groups of seven to nine peers) only one-quarter of them consistently went with the plain evidence of their senses against

---

7. Darwin clearly owes much to Hume and Smith here, particularly the latter. What Darwin added was mainly an *ultimate* explanation for the *proximate* explanations provided by Hume and Smith. For more on this distinction in biology, see Mayr (1988, 28).

the unanimous answers of the rest of their group (the other members of each group were plants and purposely gave a false answer). The remaining three-quarters of the test subjects, finding themselves a "minority of one," changed their answers to conform with their group with varying frequency, some of them going with the majority nearly all the time. (Although all answers were declared publicly, the group situation involved no direct peer pressure. In the business world, on the other hand, where there is enormous pressure to conform, the result is known as *groupthink*.) In a follow-up study, Bogdanoff et al. (1961) found that those who did not change their answers but consistently went against the group suffered various degrees of anxiety, including one subject who was dripping with sweat. Recent evidence using fMRIs suggests that our brains reward us with a "dopamine kick" when we socially conform (Klucharev et al. 2009).

Much more sinister in its implications are the studies conducted independently by Stanley Milgram and Philip Zimbardo. In a series of experiments conducted in the early 1960s to test obedience to authority, Milgram found that almost two-thirds of his test subjects delivered the maximum electric shock to a person strapped in an electric chair in the next room, despite that person's horrific screams (unknown to the test subjects, it was a good actor). Instead of acting upon their natural senses of sympathy and empathy, they transferred their sense of responsibility to the authority figure. Milgram (1974) called this *the agentic state*, by which he meant "the condition a person is in when he sees himself as an agent for carrying out another person's wishes," which he contrasted with *autonomy*, "when a person sees himself as acting on his own" (133).

In 1971, in a makeshift prison constructed in the basement of a building at Stanford University, Zimbardo divided twenty-four male university students evenly into prisoners and prison guards to study the psychology of imprisonment. What was supposed to be a two-week experiment was stopped after six days due to various degrees of descent into abuse on the part of the guards, including sadism. He would later dub this the *Lucifer effect* (Zimbardo 2007).

There is much more of the anti-moral in humans that would have to be taken into account, of course, such as the phenomena of psychopathy and autism, the effect of discovering cheaters in reciprocal altruism, stereotyping, us-and-them thinking, the effect of anger and aggression on sympathy and empathy, and gender differences in empathy, including a shut-off effect in males when they are in competitive situations (Baron-Cohen 2007, 216–218; de Waal 2009, 214–218), all of this on top of the horrible spectacles of rape, murder, war, dehumanization, and genocide (Ghiglieri 2000; Buss 2005a; Smith 2007, 2011). All in all, we humans really are bipolar as a species, capable of enormous kindness on the one hand and enormous cruelty on the other, of making both heaven and hell here on Earth.

If we put all of this together, the moral as well as the anti-moral in human nature, then what each of the normative systems has to offer from an evolutionary point of view, as well as the evolved mechanisms that work against them that I briefly just outlined, what we get as a whole, despite some tensions in the details and applications, is a very powerful framework for dealing with matters of ethics and justice. And the beauty of it all is that we do not have to appeal to any fictions. Pleasure and pain are as real as real can be, and subjectively there is no doubt that they are perceived by us (or rather the vast majority of us) as good and bad, respectively. Sympathy and empathy are clearly moral virtues for humans, fitting into Aristotle's scheme of happiness and unhappiness (though now not just focused on the individual) and having a mean between too much and too little. They are also capable of being *rationally extended,* beyond their naturally evolved limits, as are altruistic behavior and care. Moral objects, too, whether defined as persons, are treated by us as ends-in-themselves, not merely as means, and this, too, can be rationally extended beyond its original boundaries. All of this is our common human experience. At one extreme are the psychopaths, who totally lack the capacity for sympathy and empathy (and also guilt, remorse, and conscience), they are the morally blind, while one can easily imagine the other extreme, the excessively morally sensitive and altruistic, who become dysfunctional because of too much sympathy, empathy, and caring.[8] Between the two extremes is the morally full and complete human being. All of this should be obvious to us, as part of our collective moral experience. We should also collectively take it as obvious not only that pain is fundamentally bad but also that unnecessary pain, suffering, and killing is wrong and something ought to be done about it. This might not seem obvious to the individual until it is allied with our natural instincts for sympathy and empathy. The former is simply the unimpeded extension of the latter.

These natural instincts, then, these moral instincts, are the fundamental foundation of our moral experience. From an evolutionary point of view, there can be no other foundation. As Michael Ruse (2002) puts it, morality in humans is a "biological adaptation" (658), a "shared adaptation" (661), evolved by natural selection as are all biological adaptations, in this case for group cohesion. To many, of course, this will seem unsatisfactory. We feel it in our bones, as massively obvious, that winding up and throwing a baby against the wall, for example, is not only

---

8. According to the psychopathy experts Babiak and Hare (2006, 19–24), the lack of moral traits is not only a matter of degree (something we all know), but full-fledged or "true" psychopaths constitute roughly 1 percent of the human population. I do not know whether there is a similar statistic established for the opposite condition, but it surely must exist, given that biology is statistical.

wrong but absolutely and horrendously wrong, in and of itself wrong, that it is wrong even if there are others who do not agree that it is wrong. And so we try to find the foundation and justification of morality outside of this world, outside of humans and human nature, in the wisdom of gods or God, or in Platonic eternal Forms, or in the transcendence of logic and reason. But all of that, too, speaks to the shared adaptation, to the part that Ruse calls "the collective illusion of the genes" (659). It is none other than a part of the elephant, the highest part, the brain, without which the elephant would not live and would not have evolved.

None of this is to deny the enormous cultural variation in human moralities both synchronically and diachronically, the variation emphasized by earlier cultural anthropologists, such as Ruth Benedict, and by many who read history. But that variation is easily explained as surface variation, the result of differences in beliefs and social conditioning and in physical environments, analogous to Chomsky's relegation of natural languages to surface variation above the Universal Grammar. The Universal Morality of the human species would no doubt be statistical, varying between individuals and between geographical groups, and allowing for probably more variation than Chomsky's Universal Grammar, but the idea is basically the same (appropriately Darwinized, of course).

In addition, a naturalized approach to ethics provides what is arguably the only legitimate answer to the question repeated throughout the history of ethics, the question that has occupied center stage in the cogitations of thinkers as diverse as Plato, Aristotle, Kant, Mill, and Nagel. It is the question, "Why should I be moral?" Plato and Aristotle focused their answers on happiness. According to Plato (*Republic* IX), an immoral soul is a disordered soul and a disordered soul cannot achieve happiness because it is not in control of itself. But there is no reason you could not have a rational psychopath, one who uses his reason in conjunction with the spirited part of his psyche to control his appetites, all the better to exploit people for his own gain and happiness. Aristotle (*Nichomachean Ethics* I, II) argued that only the virtuous soul can be happy and that the list of moral virtues is a matter of human nature. But a rational psychopath will not be convinced by this argument either, simply because he has a different nature than what Aristotle thought is human nature and he looks down on human nature as weak. Immanuel Kant (1785, 72–81) thought we should be moral so as to avoid self-contradiction, which can occur when a personal maxim of action is universalized. (If my maxim is to treat persons merely as things whenever it is to my advantage, then I'm going to be treated merely as a thing if everyone lives by the same maxim, and I don't want that.) But a rational psychopath will simply reject the premise that reason requires universalization and therefore the conclusion that he should universalize his maxims. Jeremy Bentham (1789, ch. 1) and J. S. Mill (1861, ch. 4) thought we should seek the greatest happiness of the greatest number because we seek our own happiness and avoid our own pain. But there is no logically compelling reason that will convince a rational psychopath of why he should extend his own pursuit of happiness to the greatest number of people or sentient beings, except only as a means to his own happiness. Thomas Nagel (1986) takes it as "self-evident" (160, 162) not only that "pleasure is a good thing and pain is a bad thing" (261), each "in itself" (158), regardless of their evolutionary functions, but that basic pain gives us an objective—"agent-neutral"—reason to be altruistic to others, "a reason to want any pain to stop, whether or not it is his own" (159). But the self-evidence is only because he is a normal human being, with sympathy and empathy. To a psychopath, a person wholly devoid of sympathy, empathy, and other moral instincts, it is equally self-evident that only his pain matters, that he has no objective reason whatsoever to reduce someone else's pain.

To one who takes evolution seriously, there can really be only one answer to "Why should I be moral?" and that is: "Because you are a human being." Or rather: "Because you are a *normal* human being." To a psychopath—and they can be as sane, rational, and intelligent as anyone—there can be no logically compelling argument for why he should be moral, only for why he should *pretend* to be moral. Psychopaths are the morally blind, after all, totally lacking in the very stuff of morality (with the exception of intelligence). But for the rest of us, the answer to why we should be moral stems from the norm of our humanity. It is the elephant, in its fullness. It is the same as if one were to ask a bird, "Why should you fly?" The answer can only be: "Because I am a bird." There can be no other justification. Evolution is the only justification.

It is at this point that many will scream "bloody foul!," charging that the argument commits the *is-ought fallacy*, the fallacy of trying to genuinely derive a moral "ought" from purely "is" premises (premises that in themselves are neither moral nor evaluative), or more generally a value from a fact.[9] The word "genuinely" here is important and preferable over the word "logically," for as Richard Joyce (2006,

---

9. It is routine, even among philosophers, to confuse Hume's (1740) *is-ought fallacy* with Moore's (1903) *naturalistic fallacy*, but neither the fallacies nor the philosophies behind them are the same. Hume thought that so-called moral facts are projections onto the world by our emotions and imagination, so that a moral "ought" conclusion cannot be deduced (he uses the word "deduction") from purely "is" premises. Moore thought that moral facts really are out there in the world, as non-natural properties, so that moral predication, as in "pleasure is good," is fine just as long as the copula used is the "is" of predication, but not when it is the "is" of identity, since moral properties supervene on a disjunctive set of nonmoral properties, relations, and objects. There is a resemblance between the two fallacies, in that both say that given any number of factual/natural/descriptive premises it is still an open question what we ought to do or what is good, but the resemblance is superficial only. For complementary discussions see Joyce (2006, 146–152) and Stamos (2008, 156–158).

153) points out, one can indeed *logically* derive a moral "ought" statement from an "is" statement. One way is by using the law of logic known as *addition*: if "p" is true, then "p or q" is true by addition, since the truth of a disjunction requires only that one of the disjuncts be true, and in this case "q" could be a moral "ought" statement. Any argument with this form is logically valid and could also be sound (logically valid with true premises). Another way is by using the law of logic known as *simplification*: if "p and ~p" is true, then "p" is true and "~p" is true by simplification, since the truth of a conjunction requires that both conjuncts be true; if "p" is true, then "p or q" is true by addition; and if "p or q" is true, then "q" is true by *disjunctive syllogism* (from "p or q" and "~p"), where again "q" could be a moral "ought" statement. Any argument with this form could not be sound (since "p and ~p" is a contradiction and therefore cannot be true), but it would be logically valid. Both arguments, it will be noticed, completely stall if Bertrand Russell's (1940) claim is true that there are no extra-mental disjunctive facts (83–84), which would mean that the law of addition could not be used in trying to deduce a value from a fact.

What "genuinely" really means, therefore, in saying that one cannot genuinely derive a moral "ought" from purely "is" premises, what is really behind the is-ought fallacy, is that one cannot logically derive a moral "ought" conclusion from a set of non-disjunctive, noncontradictory, and nonmoral "is" premises, and that this is because values are a very different sort of thing than descriptive facts.

One possible reply to the charge of committing the is-ought fallacy is to appeal to some form of *noncognitivism* (e.g., Ruse 2002, 659–661), which is to say that moral statements are not really statements expressing beliefs about the world, that they are statements only in form, that they do not really have descriptive content and so are neither true nor false. But this ignores what Mackie (1977) calls the "apparent authority of ethics" (33), the "claim to objectivity" (35), what Joyce (2006) calls the "convention-transcendent practical clout" of ethics (63), the "practical oomph with which moral values and imperatives are imbued" (176). What this means is that when we make moral judgments, we normally think not that we are saying something merely subjective or intersubjective, but (with the exception of psychopaths) that we are saying something fully objective about the world combined with, as Joyce puts it, a "call for action or for the refraining from action" (192), all of which transcends our personal desires or anyone else's, as when we say, to use Joyce's example, "No, slavery is really, truly *wrong!*" (167). We can exercise our philosophical skepticism, but as Hume (1748) put it in a wider context, which includes moral skepticism, "as soon as they [the principles and arguments of extreme skepticism] leave the shade, and by the presence of the real objects, which actuate our passions and sentiments, are put in opposition to the more powerful principles of our nature, they vanish like smoke, and leave the most determined sceptic in the same condition as other mortals" (12.§2).

Moral beliefs, then, even if they are rooted in our human and even prehuman evolution, are still arguably *beliefs*, inasmuch as religious beliefs, even if they are likewise rooted in our human and even prehuman evolution (e.g., Hamer 2004; Wade 2009), are no less beliefs: they are referentially either true or false. And unlike many other beliefs rooted in evolution, such as mathematical beliefs or the belief in physical objects, the evolutionary basis of moral beliefs, granting such, as with the evolutionary basis of religious beliefs, gives us a particularly salient reason to question the verity of those beliefs, for the neurological basis of each might not have evolved as calibrations to the environment, the world of nature that was inhabited by our distant ancestors, but only for the purpose of social or group cohesion, which raises the possibility that they each could be what Joyce calls "a useful *fiction*" (163).

Another possible way of avoiding the is-ought fallacy, one that embraces cognitivism as a feature of our moral language, is to appeal to some form of *moral realism* (e.g., Moore 1903; Railton 1986), which is to say that in addition to nonmoral facts the world is also made of moral facts and both are connected in numerous but objective ways. This approach, however, faces seemingly insurmountable problems (Mackie 1977, ch. 1), especially from an evolutionary point of view (Joyce 2006, ch. 6), not the least of which is Ockham's Razor, in that it is explanatorily luxurious, or that it certainly doesn't follow from an evolutionary view of the biological world.

To cut to the chase, the approach I favor is to grant cognitive status to moral statements (they express beliefs that correctly or mistakenly refer outwardly to the world), to reject moral naturalism (there are no moral facts apart from sentient experiences and mental states), to accept the is-ought fallacy as a genuine fallacy in reasoning (some don't, but I think they are mistaken), and to view a moral argument as a *consistency argument,* one with at least one moral or evaluative premise (hence no violation of the is-ought fallacy).

To the question, then, "Why should I be moral?," the proper reply from an evolutionary point of view is: "Because you value sympathy, empathy, fairness, and altruism and because you think that unnecessary pain, suffering, and killing is wrong and something ought to be done about it." If the premises are true (they would not be true for a psychopath), then the conclusion logically follows. And it is to be noticed that the values and beliefs in the consistency argument are not arbitrary ones: they were not picked out of the air but instead are fundamental moral values and beliefs that are rooted in our evolved human nature. They are objective, then, inasmuch as our species exists objectively, but they are not absolute, not timeless truths and values that apply to all moral agents in the universe past, present, and future. From an evolutionary point of view, this is realistically the most that one can hope for.

This answer to the question "Why should I be moral?," however, which can only in this chapter be a sketch, needs an important qualification. Our moral instincts evolved along with what I have above called *anti-moral* instincts, mechanisms for dampening and shutting off or overpowering our moral instincts. Each evolved for a reason, as adaptations in the struggle for survival and reproduction. What needs to be added is that what is adaptive in one environment can be maladaptive in another. This is standard in evolutionary theory. Our propensity for foods high in sugar, salt, and fat, for example, was adaptive in our hunting-gathering nomadic past (this is why the Happy Meal has the "Happy" in it), but is maladaptive in the land of plenty known as modern civilization, with its high rate of obesity and corresponding health problems such as heart disease, diabetes, and cancer (the Happy Meal should really, then, be called the Happy Maladaptive Meal). The same is true for our anti-moral instincts. They served us well in the environment we evolved in, but they serve us very little in modern civilization and in fact are usually contrary to modern civilization, especially as it has become an international community with the potential for total annihilation. In modern civilization, no matter how we look at it, the anti-moral instincts are maladaptive more often than not, resulting generally not in happiness but in unhappiness. To the question, then, "Why should I be moral?," the complete answer would be, "Because I am a normal human being living in civilization."

In Naturalia, the moral instincts would be embraced, while the anti-moral instincts would be fought against by a variety of means. In a twist on a phrase by Richard Dawkins (quoted in the closing section below), we can and must go against the tyranny of our genes that code for anti-moral behavior. Arguably the future of our world, or at least the future of civilization, depends on it. One way is to foster sympathy, empathy, care, and altruism in early childhood education. Pets would be very useful here. They have an innocence that children can readily relate to, and they tend to be amplifiers of love and affection, giving far more than they take. But not only pets and other animals serve to teach and improve us. Epistolary novels would also be important (Hunt 2007, ch. 1), along with live drama (especially participating in live drama) and the visual power of TV and the Internet (evidence the recent earthquake in Haiti). Each of these add a new twist to Marshall McLuhan's (1964) "the medium is the message," in that they each help to bring out sympathy, empathy, and concern for others. Laws would also be designed to punish and deter anti-moral behavior and possibly also to reward moral behavior (such as tax breaks for pet owners and charity donations). But laws and institutions would also be designed with much more in mind.

At this point we need to take a closer look at Naturalia, in terms of specifics. In particular, we need to contrast Naturalia with our modern world, where much in ethics and law is settled in terms of universal human rights.

Naturalia

Keeping in mind the naturalized ethics outlined in the previous section, our first question is: "What would Naturalia be like in terms of laws and institutions?" For a start, it would be a democracy, "the worst form of government except all those other forms that have been tried from time to time" (Churchill). For this reason, and also because the people in it would be far from perfect, Naturalia would not be a utopia. Far from it. But it would be, I daresay, all other things being equal, a country better than any other country that has ever existed.

Rights would exist in Naturalia, and they would be taken very seriously. But none of them would be thought of as human rights, which would be regarded as a myth and delusion. Many of the rights in Naturalia would, however, take the place of what today are thought to be human rights, such as the right to food and shelter. They would be called *basic rights*. Henry Shue (1980) defines the term as "everyone's minimum reasonable demands upon the rest of humanity" (19). They are basic also in the sense that "enjoyment of them is essential to the enjoyment of all other rights." Shue calls basic rights "the morality of the depths" (18) and argues that there are basically three: subsistence, security, and liberty. It might be better to define them more specifically in terms of the first two levels of Abraham Maslow's five-level hierarchy of needs (Maslow 1943), the first level being basic needs (food, water, sleep, sex, etc.) and the second level being security needs. Security needs cannot be happily satisfied without the former, so that there would be some hierarchy in basic rights. As for liberty, it is an awfully vague concept, although Mill's harm principle should probably be taken as the standard, as vague as it is, and added to the second level of need. Most important, basic rights in Naturalia, unlike as Shue conceives of them, would not be thought of as a subset of human rights but would be extended beyond humans (more on this in the following section). They also would not be thought of as absolute but would be thought of as prima facie, following the distinction by Vlastos (1962) discussed in the Introduction. Neither would they be thought of as innate: they would not be the rights *of* humans, but instead would be rights *for* humans (and in many cases not just for humans). At any rate, rights in Naturalia, including especially basic rights, would largely function as a check and balance against the possibility of a tyranny of the majority (and also against any tyranny of a minority). Naturalia would also cooperate with other nation-states in securing international rights, but as an autonomous nation-state it would still refuse to subscribe to any of them as *human* rights.

The difference between human rights and basic rights as here conceived is not simply a difference in words, as the cynical often like to characterize matters. Instead it marks a profound difference in both actions and consequences. To give an example from my home country, Canada, in 1970 the then prime minister, Pierre Elliott Trudeau, invoked the War Measures Act in what is now known as the October Crisis. This came at the height of a growing insurrection involving a decade of bombings, arsons, and armed robberies by a group of Quebec separatists known as the FLQ, the height marked by the kidnapping of two government officials. Taking into consideration the request of the mayor of Montreal, the request of the premier of Quebec, and the uncertain intelligence from the Royal Canadian Mounted Police on the size of this terrorist group, Trudeau brought in the military and rounded up approximately four hundred suspected members of the FLQ. Human rights advocates in Canada continue to this day to vilify Trudeau for what he did, but in the context of the situation he did the right thing considering what was known at that time (see Trudeau 1993, 130–152; English 2009, ch. 3). From the viewpoint of *human rights,* of course, or rather in the eyes of many, it is always wrong, no matter what, to violate or temporarily suspend human rights. But there is no problem here from the viewpoint of *basic rights,* when the democracy and the safety of the community is threatened, and Naturalia would follow those like Trudeau in this matter.[10]

In addition to having a constitutional set of basic rights, it hardly needs to be said that Naturalia would be a country based in law. But the laws would not be based on an original position of rational self-interest. Legislators, instead, would frame laws based on the values and moral instincts of a fully developed human in a civilized context, which would include a desire to reduce pain and suffering and death as much as possible and to maximize empathy and care without going to irrational extremes. In all of this, legislators would take very seriously the implications of evolutionary psychology for law (e.g., Jones 2005).

---

10. It is interesting to note that the Canadian Charter of Rights and Freedoms, a major part of the Canadian Constitution framed under the leadership of Trudeau and passed in 1982, makes no mention of *human* rights. In fact in Article 1 it states that the Charter "guarantees the rights and freedoms set out in it subject only to such reasonable limits prescribed by law as can be demonstrably justified in a free and democratic society." Among the rights and freedoms protected are "freedom of conscience and religion" (Art. 2) and "the right to life, liberty and security of the person" (Art. 7).

The justice system would not be the justice-is-blind "rule of law" approach commonly advocated today. Instead, it would be a more flexible approach tempered by considerations such as empathy. This would apply not only to judges but also to lawyers. The conception of the lawyer as the pure advocate, with a mandate to do anything within the boundary of the law to win the case, would have no place in Naturalia. Instead, lawyers would be moral agents, bearing some of the responsibility for any of the harm they cause (Cohen 1985). The relation between prosecutor and defense attorney, moreover, would be less adversarial and more cooperative (Taylor 1971), involving not only extensive deliberation between them but also with the client (Gutmann 1993). In all of this, the presumption of innocence would have center place, meaning that evidence of guilt would be required beyond a reasonable doubt. Judges but also jury members would have the most responsibility here, and accordingly could be held accountable for not taking logic, evidence, and objectivity seriously enough.

This last point ties back to laws and public education. As Aristotle recognized so well in his *Nichomachean Ethics* (II.§3, X.§9), a just society will focus on laws and on childhood education designed to promote good habits and not bad, virtues and not vices. Naturalia will follow Aristotle's advice, though with a much wider list of human virtues, wider for both moral and epistemic virtues (for the latter, science education will be mandatory).

The moral and legal concept of person in Naturalia, moreover, will include not just *moral agents,* those worthy of moral praise and blame, but more widely *moral objects,* the latter defined as all those worthy of moral concern. Moral objects will be treated as ends-in-themselves, never merely as means, and in this would consist their dignity, following the Latin word *dignitas,* which means "worth" or "worthiness." This worth will be based mainly on sentience (more on this below).

Naturalia will also apply the latest and most powerful evidence from psychology, in particular on how empathy and other moral senses are increased and decreased (see, e.g., Silk 2007; Baron-Cohen 2007; Slote 2007; de Waal 2009) and also on their absence (see, e.g., Hare 1993; Babiak and Hare 2006). Accordingly, to give but one example with regard to the latter, people in power in Naturalia, from the president on down, will have been screened beforehand by psychologists with expertise in Hare's Psychopathy Checklist. This will include not only politicians and judges but also people with important positions, such as CEOs and generals. Since in Naturalia human rights are believed to be a delusion, a virus of the mind (Naturalia's education system, from preschool to postsecondary, is very evidence- and science-based), no one will object to these tests.

All of this is merely a sketch. We shall finish this chapter now by looking at six concrete examples of how the method of naturalized normative ethics developed in this chapter would handle issues often dealt with today in terms of universal human rights, the first four commonly falling under the heading of practical or applied ethics, the last two commonly falling under the heading of international relations. By a series of such examples, the question should be sufficiently answered, "What would you put in place of human rights?"

Abortion, Affirmative Action, Same-Sex Marriage, the Treatment of Animals, Waterboarding, and Political Regime Change

Abortion is a good topic to begin with, not only because it is a central topic in practical or applied ethics, but also because it provides a sharp contrast between the different approaches of Naturalia and Egalitaria. In our society today the debate over abortion is often phrased in terms of human rights. The supposed right to life of the fetus is pitted against the supposed right to personal autonomy of the mother. Debating in terms of human rights, each side easily becomes entrenched. Those on the so-called pro-life side see the fetus's right to life trumping the mother's right to choose (e.g., Noonan 1970; Foster 2005), while those on the so-called pro-choice side see the reverse (e.g., Thomson 1971; Warren 1989).

From the viewpoint of a fully naturalized normative ethics, however, there is no impasse. To be sure, there can be genuine moral dilemmas using this approach, which occur in particular situations when moral instincts pull in different directions in the same individual (i.e., to add to Darwin, it is not just the moral and anti-moral instincts that can pull against each other). But in the case of abortion there is little if any real conflict. On the one hand, it is quite evidently a human virtue to take life seriously and not frivolously, and that would have to include fetal life (Hursthouse 1991). On the other hand, however, that abortion should be legalized is obvious from the viewpoint of utilitarianism. As long argued by Henry Morgentaler (e.g., Morgentaler 1996), the doctor who spearheaded the legalization of abortion in Canada, a society in which abortion is illegal is going to be a much less happy society than one in which it is legal (all other things being equal), given that when illegal there will be more unwanted children both in homes and in orphanages (and hence more child abuse, more juvenile crime and later adult crime, and so on), more careers of women will be either set back or ruined, and abortions will still be performed, though usually by unqualified people, often resulting in serious damage to the mother or even death.

One also needs to look at the issue from the perspective of empathy. Granted, abortion might be said to take away not only the life of the fetus but also the future life that the normal fetus possesses, the life of a full human being, a "future-like-ours" (Marquis 1989). But it is highly questionable whether a future is the sort of thing that anyone can properly be said to *possess*, and hence that it is something of which a human at any stage can properly be said to be deprived (McInerney 1990). What is certain, as Michael Slote (2007, 16–19) points out, on the topic that got him "started on empathy," is that early fetuses look more like fish or salamanders, they lack brains or at least brain activity, and babies but not fetuses cry, all of which explains why empathy is more easily evoked in us for babies and adults than for fetuses.

But I would go further than Slote, especially given that for him "caring about and even empathy with plants, the environment, and the biosphere may not be *completely* out of the question." We all (barring psychopaths) can readily empathize with a pregnant woman, many of us to a remarkably high degree (even if we've never been a mother), not only with the physical handicap of pregnancy but with the emotions and fears involved. But we cannot *rationally extend* empathy to the fetus, especially not for the first trimester. As Singer points out (1993, 164–165), although the average fetus exhibits brain activity after eight weeks, it is not until at least eighteen weeks that the synaptic connections in the cerebral cortex are sufficiently developed to receive signals of any kind, including pleasure and pain, and it is probably not until around thirty weeks that it could possibly have conscious awareness (before that it would be in a state of sleep). If this is basically correct, one could then no more rationally empathize with a fetus in its first trimester than with a turnip, while in its third trimester a fetus is probably less sentient or conscious than the average fish.

Legislation on abortion, then, balancing these and the previous considerations together, and wanting to play it safe, might make abortion perfectly legal up to the first eighteen weeks and then require increasingly serious medical reasons as time goes on.

Another interesting topic is affirmative action, or "reverse discrimination" as it is sometimes pejoratively called. Ronald Dworkin (1978, ch. 9), for example, discusses the case of a Jewish student named Marco DeFunis, who in 1971 was denied acceptance to the University of Washington Law School. His test scores and grades were not enough to get him accepted unless he was a member of a visible racial minority, since the school was implementing a program of affirmative action. DeFunis took his case all the way to the Supreme Court, where he argued that the university's law school violated the Fourteenth Amendment to the United States Constitution, which provides equal protection under the law.

It should be noted at the outset that this was not simply a civil matter, for basically two reasons. First, Article 7 of the Universal Declaration of Human Rights states that "All are equal before the law and are entitled without any discrimination to equal protection of the law," while Article 26 states that "higher education shall be equally accessible to all on the basis of merit." Second, as Dworkin (1978) puts it in a different context, "Our [the American] constitutional system rests on a particular moral theory, namely, that men have moral rights against the state" (147).

In the case of DeFunis, the Supreme Court decided that the case was moot, since a lower court had already decided in his favor and the university consequently accepted his application with the guarantee that he would be allowed to graduate even if the Supreme Court decided against him. Justice William O. Douglas, however, dissented against the neutral position of his colleagues and argued that the Court should have upheld DeFunis's argument on the basis of its merits. (The case, after all, was a *hard case,* one that did not fall under a clear rule of law and was therefore open to establishing a precedent.) Dworkin himself (1978) argues in favor of the university's original position, and hence against DeFunis and Douglas, in that although the affirmative action program of the university did not defend DeFunis's "right to *equal treatment,*" he did not have the right to equal treatment in the first place, since "legal education is not so vital that everyone has an equal right to it" (227). What really matters, according to Dworkin, is "the right to *treatment as an equal,*" and the affirmative action program of the university did defend this right; it was attempting to produce a "more equal" society, and for Dworkin "a more equal society is a better society even if its citizens prefer inequality." Hence for Dworkin any admissions program "is justified if it serves a proper policy that respects the right of all members of the community to be treated as equals, but not otherwise" (239).

The basic problem with this approach, of course, is what if the right to treatment as an equal does not in fact exist, that it is not a right that all humans have by virtue of being human? Or rather, to use Dworkin's own language instead of the language of possessions, what if it is not true that "arguments [good arguments] are available in favour of these rights ['human rights'] against any collective justification in any circumstances reasonably likely to be found in political society" (365)? In the context of his discussion on "constitutional law and moral theory," Dworkin claims that lawyers "must recognize that law is no more independent from philosophy than it is from these other disciplines [sociology and economics]" (149). But if we add evolutionary biology to these other disciplines, no matter how one frames the questions above, the result is devastating for the belief that all humans have equal human rights, whether the right to treatment as an equal or anything else. The case of DeFunis, however, and others like it, would not face this difficulty if appeals to human rights were replaced with a fully naturalized approach to normative ethics. Granted, as Dworkin is at pains to show, the consequences of affirmative action programs in terms of utilitarianism are by no means clear-cut, but what about other aspects of a naturalistic approach to ethics?

Certainly it cannot be defended as a moral virtue to discriminate against others on the basis of nonmoral features, which is precisely what straightforward discrimination does in the cases of race and gender, for example. But it might be taken to be a moral virtue to attempt to level the playing field; fairness is arguably a human virtue, after all.

An empathic approach is even more decisive. Clearly we cannot empathize with a minority group, or a nonminority group such as women, that has been subjected to discrimination and oppression. This is because one cannot logically empathize with a group at all, since a group does not have a mind. (In this sense, an empathic approach overlaps with minimalist approaches to human rights, since the latter do not recognize group rights.) What one can do, however, is empathize with particular individuals, and from there make comparisons. In the case of DeFunis, I can empathize with how he must have felt. The rejection of his admission to the law school, but the acceptance of a number of others with equal or lower test scores and grades than his own, must have excited his innate sense of egocentric fairness. But I can also empathize, say, with a black student who was accepted to the school because of affirmative action, and my empathy for that student makes me defend the affirmative action program of the university against DeFunis. This is because DeFunis, as a member of the Jewish community in America, would not have a sense of discrimination and oppression and disenfranchisement that would come even close to the sense of discrimination and oppression and disenfranchisement of the student who is a member of the African-American community. (Keep in mind that the comparison is confined to a particular context, namely, the history of treatment toward Jews and African-Americans *in the United States*.) An empathic approach, then, by itself, although it would probably find aid in utilitarian and virtue ethics approaches, would in many cases defend affirmative action programs.

Another interesting topic often debated in terms of human rights is same-sex marriage. Looking at my hometown of Toronto, for example, Tim Ryan, a Roman Catholic priest, wrote an editorial published in the *Toronto Star* (February 29, 2004) in which he argues on behalf of same-sex marriage as a matter of "human rights" and states quite interestingly—in line with Dworkin's trumps and in a polite capuchin monkey way—that "fundamental human rights simply cannot be left at the mercy of majority political opinion." The Canadian bishops had been campaigning energetically against the direction of the Canadian courts and government on this matter. Ryan had been an activist for the "full minority rights" of "gays, lesbians, and other sexual minorities" in the Church stretching back for thirty years, but when he finally went public with his support for the Canadian government and courts against the Church on the legalization of same-sex marriage, he was punished by being defrocked. More recently, in an article published in the *Toronto Sun* (November 12, 2009), it was announced that in two days Karl Clemens, a sixty-nine-year-old retired Catholic priest, would be marrying his partner, Nick. He is reported as saying, "I'm leading the way, or pioneering, as it were, in something that I think is very important. It's a human right." He is also reported as saying that he intends to keep his vow of celibacy and that "If I was any more celibate I don't think I'd be alive," to which he adds, "Openly gay life can be interpreted in many ways" (LifeSiteNews.com, February 12, 2009). No matter; Father Clemens was also defrocked.

Not that it is the ultimate arbiter of such matters, a kind of paper pope, but it is important to look at the Universal Declaration of Human Rights here, since for believers in human rights this is the most important document of them all. Article 16 states that "Men and women of full age, without any limitation due to race, nationality or religion, have the right to marry and to found a family. They are entitled to equal rights as to marriage, during marriage and at its dissolution. Marriage shall be entered into only with the free and full consent of the intending spouses. The family is the natural and fundamental group unit of society and is entitled to protection by society and the State."

There is nothing here stating that same-sex marriage is a human right, and nothing stating that it is not. The document is not explicit either way. For gay rights to be human rights, of course, whether marriage rights or anything else, they would have to be subsumed under a general right that all humans have (not just a subgroup of humans), such as, in the Universal Declaration, "All are equal before the law and are entitled without any discrimination to equal protection of the law" (Art. 7). But this interpretative and implicative approach can just as easily be used against same-sex marriage as a human right, given that the Universal Declaration also states that "In the exercise of his rights and freedoms, everyone shall be subject only to such limitations as are determined by law solely for the purpose of securing due recognition and respect for the rights and freedoms of others and of meeting the just requirements of morality, public order and the general welfare in a democratic society" (Art. 29). What this passage implies for our topic is that positive law based on a majority opinion of morality and general welfare would be within the bounds of universal human rights to exclude same-sex marriage as a legal right. We then have one implication of the Universal Declaration possibly playing against another.

A common criticism against same-sex marriage, of course, is that if it is legalized then there is nothing to stop the legalization of polygamous marriage, either polygynous (one husband with more than one wife) or polyandrous (one wife with more than one husband). There is a real slippery slope here. If same-sex marriage is a human right, then there is no reason polygamous marriage would not also be a human right. One could complain, of course, that if polygamous marriage is practiced widely in a society, then it is likely going to leave a lot of people with a right to marriage that they won't be able to exercise (this is unless polygynous and polyandrous marriages would be roughly equal in number). The same could be said if a society has more gays than lesbians or vice versa. But this now is a practical matter, not a matter of rights per se.

If one does not believe in human rights, of course, then the entire debate is pointless. What matters, instead, and what would matter for Naturalia, is whether same-sex and polygamous marriages are innately harmful and in a utilitarian sense. Barring that, there would be no legislation against them. Empathic concerns would also seem to point to the same conclusion, that as long as no one is being harmed, there should be no legislation against someone who wants to enter into a same-sex or a polygamous marriage.

Naturalia, however, would have to do some more thinking than that. It would have to take into consideration relevant evidence from sociology, anthropology, and psychology. Historically, polygamy has been quite prominent. According to the cultural anthropologist Marvin Harris (1989), for example, each of the variations in marriage "is as 'natural' as the other, since each represents a socially constructed pattern of mating dictated by prevailing social and natural conditions, rather than by specific genetic instructions" (196). Evolutionary psychology, on the other hand, paints a quite different picture. In the animal world, polyandrous mating systems are quite rare, especially among primates, and polyandrous marriages are found in almost no human societies, whereas polygynous mating systems are quite common in the animal world, including primates, and polygynous marriages are found in over 80 percent of human societies (Buss 2003, 178–179; Schmitt 2005, 260–268; Low 2007). This reflects the basic male need for numerous mating partners, an asymmetry between human males and females that is routinely recognized in evolutionary psychology. Given these underlying asymmetries, then, including the fact that sexual jealousy tends to be far more violent in males than in females (Buss 2003, 125–141), it is not obviously the case, from an evolutionary point of view, that the legalization of same-sex marriage should be taken to entail the legalization of polygamous marriage. The former implies no harm to women, while the latter, given human nature, implies increased competition between males for females and a great deal of harm to women. And if that is the case, then a just society would have sufficient reason to not legalize polygamous marriage even though it has legalized same-sex marriage.

Clearly we could go on and on with topics in practical or applied ethics that are often dealt with in terms of human rights, such as aboriginal rights, worker rights, freedom of religion, euthanasia, the right to being fat, and so much more. I shall deal with one more, what I think is the most important of them all, before turning to two topics that are of concern in terms of international relations. It is the question of our treatment of animals, which is sometimes dealt with in terms of animal rights, as we have seen in Chapter 3, but usually in terms of the lack of anything like human rights at all. For example, the Anglican Archbishop Desmond Tutu (1996), in his Preface to an anthology exploring religion and human rights, claims that the Bible "came to be the foundations [*sic*] of the culture of basic human rights," that "Both creation narratives in Genesis 1–3 assert quite categorically that human beings are the pinnacle, the climax, of the divine creativity" (ix), that "Nearly all major religions envisage a *post mortem* existence for human kind that far surpasses anything we can conceive" (xi), and that humans are "persons created in God's image" such that "That is what invests them with their preciousness and from this stems all kinds of rights" (xiii). More recently the Catholic theologian Jack Mahoney (2007) states quite approvingly that "what human rights reveal is that humanity forms a single moral family, all of whose members are united in human solidarity and thus owe to each other a mutual moral respect based on their shared dignity as awe-inspiring human beings" (ix).

All of this is pretty standard thinking, and it is all well and good if one is a human being. But to be truly awe-inspiring we need to look beyond the pomp and circumstance of human rights talk and ask a simple, humbling question, "What about the rest of sentient beings?" Sentient beings are, after all, the only legitimate objects of sympathy and empathy. So why not make the capacity for sentience that which unites us all into a single moral family?

As we have seen, in its early history the belief in universal human rights was justified mainly by an appeal to theology (and still is in many quarters). We have also seen that the belief in universal human rights has spread to the secular domain in the fields of ethics, politics, and law, with various justifications, such as appeals to human nature, to language, and to an international normative consensus or practice. What one cannot help but notice in all of this is that the myth of universal human rights has replaced a major function of an older myth, the myth of immortal human souls. One of the functions of the older myth was not only to provide hope for heaven (along with fear of hell punishment), but also to create and maintain a moral divide between humans and animals to justify the enormous pain, suffering, and killing inflicted on the latter by the former—in a word, to put it mildly, *exploitation*—including at its worst the horrendous practice of vivisection. Judaism has always considered the children of Abraham to be God's "chosen people" (keyword "people") (*Genesis* 18: 18–19; *Deuteronomy* 7: 6), or more specifically the children of his grandson Jacob (Israel) (*Genesis* 32: 28), not the descendants of his children and of his goats, for example, while according to Christianity Jesus came to save any human who would believe in him (*Romans* 10: 9; *John* 3: 16), which clearly excludes the animal world. In neither of these traditions do animals exist as ends-in-themselves, but merely as means, justified by the "dominion" God gave mankind over animals (*Genesis* 1: 28) and also by their lack of souls, for God only made "man"—"male and female"—in his own "image" (*Genesis* 1: 26).[11]

As the belief in immortal human souls waned with the rise of modern science (since the more we know about the brain, the more obvious it becomes that immortal souls are a myth), the belief in universal human rights has risen to take its place. In fact it has become the new secular religion, the new anthropocentric faith, the new Dividing Link in a revived Great Chain of Being, the reincarnation of the belief in an enormous moral gulf between humans and animals. Singer (2003) estimates that tens of millions of animals are used annually as research subjects in laboratories and that in 2002 "ten *billion* birds and mammals were raised and killed for food in the United States alone" (216). This is a silent holocaust occurring around us every day, one that makes the Holocaust perpetrated by the Nazis pale in comparison.[12] Hitler and the Nazis used racism in the form of the myth of Aryan supremacy (along with Christianity) to justify the Jewish Holocaust, while people more widely use speciesism in the form of the myth of universal human rights to justify the animal holocaust. In both cases, people have to take a share in the responsibility for what they support (a dollar spent, after all, is a kind of vote).

With regard to what he called "the insuperable line," Bentham (1789) put it perfectly when he wrote, "the question is not, Can they *reason*? nor, Can they *talk*? but, Can they *suffer*?" (17.§4n). It is fundamentally that capacity, and no other—to experience pain and pleasure, unhappiness and happiness, suffering and joy—that is or should be the very foundation of dignity, of moral worth. But the issue requires a closer look, including the so-called dignity of man.

Prior to Darwin, the dignity of man was based mainly on the *imago dei* of the Bible, which not only set animals apart from man but also made animals part of the dominion of man, for their use. In that sense of the dignity of man, as Rachels (1990) argues, Darwinism "leads inevitably to the abandonment of the idea of

---

11. Eastern religions never shared this metaphysical belief, that humans but not animals have postmortem souls, and accordingly practiced a very different ethic toward animals.

12. I make this comparison not to diminish let alone to trivialize the horror of the Jewish Holocaust (far from it), but instead to emphasize an even greater horror.

human dignity ... by taking away its support," and he calls this the "main argument" of his book (172).

Darwin, along with the modern science of biology, which he helped found, certainly proved that the history of life on Earth is such that "I have no need of that hypothesis [God]"—to use what Laplace famously stated to Napoleon about explanations in physics—since heritable variation and natural selection along with a few other physical principles fully explain the evolution of life on Earth. But Darwin himself (1859) took this to mean, looking now to all life, "When I view all beings not as special creations, but as the lineal descendants of some few beings which lived long before the first bed of the Silurian system was deposited, they seem to me to become ennobled" (489). Rather than lower the dignity of man, then, Darwin thought that evolution raised the dignity of life. But clearly this will not satisfy most people, to think they share the same dignity with, say, a turnip, no matter how much dignity the latter is supposed to have.

There is a third way to approach the matter of dignity, however, which is arguably superior to the previous two. Darwinism has eventually made it clear that most species of animals are sentient beings, which by the very nature of sentience means they literally have interests. Given that this is what our own sense of dignity boils down to, when it is shorn of its metaphysical and religious fancies—having our interests, especially our basic interests, satisfied rather than frustrated—it follows, if we are to be consistent, that all sentient animals have a degree of dignity, using the Latin word *dignitas,* meaning "worth" or "worthiness." Evolution proceeds in lineages usually from the less to the more complex, rather than the other direction, if there is a change in complexity in a lineage at all. What this means is that sentience would increase with greater cognitive faculties, such that animals that are not merely sentient but that have minds, with hopes and fears and personalities, will have higher degrees of sentience, and hence higher degrees of dignity. But no matter the degree, the baseline, Bentham's "insuperable line," would always be sentience itself.[13]

---

13. One might argue, as Goodpaster (1978) does, that from an evolutionary point of view sentience is an adaptation and hence a means, not an end, the end being the preservation of the life of the organism with the adaptation, so that the real criterion for "moral considerability" should be *being alive.* But this line of argument needs to be followed through. As Dawkins (1976) has shown, the logic of evolution is such that being alive is itself not an end but a means to something else, namely, the spread of the genes carried by the living organism. Unless one is willing to take the metaphor *selfish* in *selfish genes* literally, then, one would do better to confine "moral considerability" to *having interests,* which following Singer (1975, 7) and common sense is properly confined to sentient beings.

A full and complete method of naturalized normative ethics, of course, one that involves rationally extending sympathy, empathy, and fairness beyond our own species along with a strong desire to reduce pain and suffering as much as possible, would not accord dignity and moral concern to nonsentient beings, no matter how great our awe and reverence in the face of the diversity of life. But it would not view the acceptance of nonhuman animals into the circle of moral concern as lowering the dignity of man either. Instead, it would view having sentience as raising the dignity of those animals as fellow moral objects, as moral ends-in-themselves by virtue of their sentience.

We turn now to two matters of ethics and justice that are not only of national but of international concern, matters that are routinely debated in terms of universal human rights and that involve the United Nations and other international organizations. The first concerns waterboarding, a controversial interrogation technique. While the technique involves variations in methods and motives, we shall focus our discussion on a particular case that has gained wide international concern. On February 5, 2008, the director of the CIA, Michael Hayden, told Congress that his agency used waterboarding during 2002–2003 on three senior Al Qaeda leaders captured shortly after 9/11, one of whom was Khalid Sheikh Mohammed, the mastermind behind the 9/11 attacks. This was for the purpose of gaining information on Al Qaeda and preventing further attacks. According to Hayden, roughly one-quarter of the intelligence reports on Al Qaeda came from these interrogations and much of it was reliable. President George W. Bush subsequently admitted that he had authorized the waterboarding, and both he and especially Vice President Dick Cheney continue to defend it to this day.

The technique, as used by the CIA, involves strapping the subject supine to a long board and tilting it so that the head is a little lower than the feet. A cloth is then put over the subject's mouth and nose and water is poured on the face. Because of the tilt, very little if any water goes into the lungs, but the water cannot be expelled because of the cloth, which causes the gag reflex and the sensation of drowning. According to a CIA memo, Khalid Sheikh Mohammed was waterboarded a total of 183 times.

Shortly after Hayden's testimony, Louise Arbour, the UN's High Commissioner for Human Rights, told a news conference that "I would have no problem describing this practice as falling under the prohibition of torture," and she added that the violators should be prosecuted under the principle of "universal jurisdiction" as war criminals (Reuters February 8, 2008). This is no small matter. Article 17 of the Geneva Convention (III) (1949) bans the torture of prisoners of war for the purpose of gaining information. Article 5 of the Universal Declaration of Human Rights states that "No human shall be subjected to torture or to cruel, inhuman or degrading treatment or punishment." And the United Nations Convention Against Torture, which came into force in 1987, states in Article 12 that "Each State Party shall ensure that its competent authorities proceed to a prompt and impartial investigation, wherever there is reasonable ground to believe that an act of torture has been committed in any territory under its jurisdiction." The United States signed this document of international law in 1988 and ratified it in 1994.

Accordingly Ralph Nader, for example, wrote a letter to President Barack Obama to investigate Bush, Cheney, and their subordinates for violating international law (nader.org January 21, 2009), while in an open letter to Canadian Prime Minister Stephen Harper, in anticipation of President Bush's trip to British Columbia, Human Rights Watch (hrw.org October 11, 2011) wrote that the Canadian government, which ratified the Convention Against Torture in 1987, "is obligated to prosecute individuals suspected of committing torture found in its territory if other countries have failed to do so. The Obama administration has failed to investigate allegations of involvement in torture by Bush or other senior administration officials, and none are expected." A day later Amnesty International (amnesty.org October 12, 2011) called for the Canadian government to detain Bush and try him for "war crimes," given that "The former President specifically admitted to authorizing the 'water-boarding' of identified individuals, whose subjection to this torture technique has been confirmed," and that "even if one were to rely only upon information released by United States authorities, and by former US President George W. Bush himself—the available evidence gives rise to an obligation for Canada, should Mr Bush proceed with his visit on or around 20 October 2011, to investigate his alleged involvement in and responsibility for crimes under international law, including torture, and to secure his presence in Canada during that investigation."

One thing to notice is that the prosecution of Bush and Cheney for war crimes under international law is highly unlikely, whether the focus is on waterboarding or anything larger. In his book, in which he argues that Bush should be tried for murder, the famous prosecutor Vincent Bugliosi (2008, 269–271) notes that "war crimes," as defined by the International Criminal Court (ICC) in The Hague, is confined to large-scale human rights abuses, mainly genocide but also mass murder and mass rape, none of which were authorized by Bush or Cheney. Moreover, the ICC has jurisdiction only over signees of the ICC treaty, and that does not include the United States. The United Nations Security Council can indeed refer a case outside the ICC's jurisdiction for criminal prosecution of war crimes, but any one of the five permanent members of that Council, which includes the United States and Britain, has veto power. However, as Bugliosi further points out, Bush could be prosecuted for torture under the War Crimes Act, which was passed by a large majority of Congress in 1996 and signed into law by President Bill Clinton.

And on and on it goes. In an article published in *Vanity Fair* (August 1, 2008), titled "Believe Me, It's Torture," the controversial journalist and atheist Christopher Hitchens discusses his experience of being voluntarily waterboarded by a group of anonymous Special Forces veterans who had been trained in the technique. Hitchens writes: "You may have read by now the official lie about this treatment, which is that it 'simulates' the feeling of drowning. This is not the case. You feel that you are drowning because you *are* drowning—or, rather, being drowned, albeit slowly and under controlled conditions and at the mercy (or otherwise) of those who are applying the pressure."

Reignited by the killing of Osama bin Laden by U.S. Navy Seals on May 2, 2011, under order of President Obama (which itself is another topic for consideration), the debate centers around the word "torture," which is understandable given the role of the word in human rights documents and in international law. Those who believe that waterboarding is a violation of human rights and international law insist on calling waterboarding "torture," while those who defend waterboarding refuse to call it "torture" but instead an "enhanced interrogation technique." The topic continues to divide Americans and many others and to be a matter of international censure.

In all of this we need to go beyond the word "torture" and look at the big picture with the whole of our moral being, which includes our rationality, rather than with myopia, runaway emotions, or a robot-minded ideology.

Certainly, on the one hand, to watch someone being waterboarded is deeply disturbing. (You can watch Hitchens being waterboarded on YouTube.) Our feelings of sympathy and empathy are fired up, and there certainly seems no virtue in subjecting someone to such suffering. Our sense of altruistic fairness is also activated, as there is nothing reciprocal about the process.

And then there are the dangers to the recipients. Reported effects include broken fingers or limbs from trying to break the restraints, lung damage from water intake, increased cortisol levels from the stress (which can cause various health problems), long-term psychological trauma, and even death caused by a heart attack. In all of this it is difficult to get any statistical facts, since opponents emphasize the harm and proponents minimize it.

But there is more that needs to be considered, much more. For a start, thousands of elite American soldiers, such as Navy Seals, have received waterboarding as part of the SERE training program (Survival, Evasion, Resistance, Escape). Waterboarding is included in the highest level of the program, known as Level C, as preparation for possible capture and torture. There is no statistical study, or at least no published statistical study, on the physical and psychological long-term effects on these personnel. Nevertheless, since 2007 waterboarding has been discontinued in a number of SERE programs, but the reason typically given is that it failed to accomplish its purpose, which was to produce "psychological hardiness." In January 2009 Obama banned waterboarding as an interrogation technique, but the Department of Defense is silent on whether it still uses waterboarding as part of SERE training. Clearly politics plays a big role in all of this.

The biggest part of the picture is still missing, however. In addition to the handful of terrorists waterboarded under the Bush administration, one must add to the picture the death and trauma caused by terrorism, such as the almost 3,000 innocent people killed on 9/11, along with images of people jumping off the burning World Trade Center towers, thousands of people running for their lives through the streets while covered in soot, and the bravery of the many firefighters, paramedics, and police officers who risked their lives trying to save others (403 of them lost their lives in the process). Sympathy and empathy have to be applied here, too, to the victims, to their families and friends, and to the countless millions of others who were in some way negatively affected. And it is certainly no moral virtue to ignore all of this.

In addition, there is the issue of fairness. The terrorists involved with Al Qaeda do not have an agenda simply of spreading terror; their agenda is to kill innocent people, ultimately many millions of them, whom they call "infidels," in the name of their religion. The waterboarding of a small number of these terrorists, even if waterboarding itself produces the physical and psychological harm emphasized by its harshest critics, is hardly equal to, let alone greater than, the pain, suffering, and killing that is central to the agenda of these terrorists and that they have already accomplished, which itself is only a small fraction of their intentions.

In sum, the application of our whole moral being is required here, one that takes into account both sides of the matter, and it should be obvious to an impartial spectator which side should gain the majority of consideration. From the perspective of the method of naturalized normative ethics developed in this chapter, then, waterboarding, when conducted in circumstances such as the war on terrorism, is not immoral or unjust and should not be banned. It should not be taken lightly, of course, and should be used only under controlled and relatively rare circumstances, probably at the sole discretion of the duly elected head of state, when there is a reasonable expectation of gaining information that could save lives. An ounce of prevention is worth a pound of cure, after all, as per the old saying made famous by Benjamin Franklin (it did not originate with him but can be traced back to at least the thirteenth century).

The only question remaining is whether waterboarding is an ounce of prevention, whether it is effective in gaining information that has the reasonable potential of saving innocent lives. Many "experts" continue to claim that no reliable and useful information for the war on terrorism was gained from the waterboarding of Al Qaeda captives, and CSIS, for example, Canada's version of the CIA, has rejected information gained by the CIA from waterboarding (though it is unclear whether the reasons were epistemological or political). On the other hand, many others, including the CIA and the former Bush administration, continue to maintain that lifesaving information was in fact gained, including the location of bin Laden. It is a topic that divides Americans and many worldwide, mainly along party or ideological lines, which in turn makes it very difficult to ascertain the necessary facts. In this it is much like the cause of global warming, which is a further example of the fact that *politics does not determine good scholarship.*

The bottom line is that whether waterboarding can provide useful information for the war on terrorism is a factual matter, to be determined empirically, not politically, which requires an objective mind-set, and we will leave it at that. If there is a reasonable expectation that waterboarding can provide lifesaving information, then it should be employed, with the necessary precautions, but otherwise not.

Our final topic concerns political regime change, specifically the change from dictatorial to democratic governments, especially in the context of protest movements expressing the will of the people. Recent protests in Iran, Tunisia, Egypt, Libya, and Syria—the so-called Arab Spring—readily come to mind. Supposing that these protest movements not only are expressions of genuinely democratic beliefs and values but also represent the will of the majority of their peoples for a regime change to a democratic system (this is obviously a controversial supposition), what should democratic nations do in the case of such protests, especially when the dictatorial regimes are using guns on the protestors?

International response, of course, can and does range from public condemnation, including calls to respect the "universal human rights" of their people (e.g., Secretary of State Hillary Clinton), to economic sanctions, to public moral support for the protest movements, to financial support for these movements, to aiding these movements by giving them weapons, to military intervention such as bombing military bases, and finally to an all-out boots-on-the-ground attack against the home regime and its military, with the ultimate goal of taking out the dictator and his regime (I can't think of a single case where the dictator was female).

Aside from the issue of the violation of human rights by a government in terms of murder and torture, for example, which are clearly listed as negative human rights in the key human rights documents, what is the UN, and democratic nations in particular, to do when it has reason to believe that a nation wants to abolish a dictatorial regime and replace it with a democratic one? Is democratic participation a human right according to modern doctrine? And what should these bodies do when a nation really doesn't want a democracy? As the political scientist Shlomo Avineri puts it (quoted in Bugliosi 2008), "Democracy doesn't simply mean holding elections. First, you need a democratic culture—a tradition of voluntary associations, a tolerance for nonconformism and pluralism, a shared belief in the dignity of the individual, separation of political power from religious authority and a belief in the legitimacy of dissent" (265).[14] Should democracy be forced on a country without such an underlying culture for its own good, the way one might force nutrients into someone who refuses to eat and drink? What does the international human rights doctrine entail here?

According to Charles Beitz (2009), "Although it is not a consensus belief, the idea that there is a human right to democratic institutions is now a commonplace in international doctrine and practice" (174). The Universal Declaration of Human Rights (1948), however, the most important human rights document of them all, seems to make a stronger statement. Article 21 states clearly that "Everyone has the right to take part in the government of his country, directly or through freely chosen representatives" and that "The will of the people shall be the basis of the authority of government," with "periodic and genuine elections which shall be by universal and equal suffrage," while Article 29 specifically refers to "the general welfare in a democratic society."

It would seem, then, that democracy, according to modern human rights doctrine, is a positive right, such that if a political regime is denying its people this right against their will, then the international community must do something about it. But herein lurks a profound danger. As Jason Barry put it in a recent communication to me, "Is NE [the method of naturalized normative ethics developed in this chapter] less likely to be *abused* as justification for military conflict than human rights, and therefore a more robust ground for organizing international relations?"

A case in point is the recent war in Iraq. The original justification for the war by the Bush administration was the "clear and present danger" posed to the United States and other countries by Saddam Hussein and his weapons of mass

---

14. According to Mosab Hassan Yousef (2010), for example, an apostate to Christianity and the oldest son of one of the seven founders of Hamas, Islam contains an essential hierarchical contradiction in values, with "love and mercy" and "education and welfare" at higher rungs on a ladder (9), while the "highest rung" (12) "calls all Muslims to jihad, to struggle and contend with the world until they establish a global caliphate, led by one holy man who rules and speaks for Allah" (10). If he is right, then Muslim countries, inasmuch as they are Muslim, should be viewed, it would seem, as fundamentally antidemocratic. On the other hand, Judaism and Christianity undoubtedly also contain in their scriptures their own visions of theocratic world domination, and yet Jewish and Christian cultures have come to embrace genuinely democratic beliefs and values, which should give hope in the case of the Middle East.

destruction (a sentiment seconded by the U.S. Congress, by the way, at the time). As the evidence for the weapons of mass destruction failed to materialize during the war, the justification for the war shifted to human rights, both for Americans and Iraqis. In his Second Inaugural Address, for example, given on January 20, 2005, in which he specifically refers to the "Declaration of Independence" and to "human rights," Bush states that

> America's vital interests and our deepest beliefs are now one. From the day of our Founding, we have proclaimed that every man and woman on this earth has rights, and dignity, and matchless value, because they bear the image of the Maker of Heaven and earth. Across the generations we have proclaimed the imperative of self-government.... Advancing these ideals is the mission that created our Nation.... Now it is the urgent requirement of our nation's security, and the calling of our time. So it is the policy of the United States to seek and support the growth of democratic movements and institutions in every nation and culture, with the ultimate goal of ending tyranny in our world.

While it is true that the speech is qualified by not necessarily appealing to "the task of arms" and that "Freedom, by its nature, must be chosen, and defended by its citizens," it is also asserted that "we will defend ourselves and our friends" and that "The best hope for peace in our world is the expansion of freedom in all the world."

Whatever one thinks about the war in Iraq, specifically about the real reasons for it, is really beside the point here, which is that the universal human rights doctrine, involving the right to democracy, can indeed, by its very nature, be used to fight what in the end might be an unjust war.

If we go beyond human rights, however, and apply the whole of our moral being to the matter, what does the method developed in this chapter come up with? This is terribly complicated, but let me make a few points before closing.

On the one hand, we are shocked and horrified by the images of people peacefully protesting one minute and then lying in a pool of blood the next minute, and also being battered and rounded up for arrest. Our senses of sympathy and empathy are ignited, as well as our sense of altruism.

On the other hand, war is hell, and the images of lost lives and lost limbs of our own soldiers come to mind, as well as the tears of their loved ones here at home. And then there are the lives and limbs of a far greater number of people, more distant but just as real, the noncombatants who suffer in a war-torn country, and the horror that the entire country must endure.

But then there is the horror and hardship that these people endured for many decades before the war, under an undeniably brutal dictatorship. We value democracy, something they lack. We intuitively connect democracy with economic prosperity, and might feel guilty for it, privileged by the dumb luck of the time and place of our birth. We might even realize, as Steven Pinker (2011) puts it, that democracies "contain the seeds of expansion to groups that originally had been overlooked," and we might imagine ourselves as one of the many "overlooked" in nondemocratic countries. We might even know, what surely must seem obvious, backed by a statistical study Pinker cites, that democracies "go to war *less often* than nondemocracies, all else being equal" (281).

And then there is the observation, supported by a study cited by David Forsythe (2006), that "democracy does not last very long in the face of economic adversity," such that citizens can express "considerable sympathy for a return to authoritarian government," as in the case of Russia (270–271). Shall we have to support the economy of the newly made democracy, too? And if so, for how long?

In all of this, after applying the whole of our moral being to the topic, we might feel pulled simultaneously in different directions, with no one direction receiving even a mild consensus about what our governments and the UN should and should not do. That is the stuff of genuine moral dilemmas, and it is not to be unexpected, but thought through and felt through as best one can, with the result that there will be varying and conflicting opinions on the matter, with no one clear answer, even with the full benefit of hindsight.

Conclusion

The human rights memes that have come to control so many people's minds are not smart, they are not intelligent; they are mindless pieces of information and programming, subject to the blind forces of mutation, natural selection, drift, and symbiosis. And therein lies the good news. In the words of Richard Dawkins (1976), "We are built as gene machines and cultured as meme machines, but we have the power to turn against our creators. We, alone on earth, can rebel against the tyranny of the selfish replicators" (201).

To rebel, however, one first has to wake up, in the present case from the dogmatic slumber that is the myth of universal human rights. One has to awaken, rub one's eyes, and see that the Emperor has no clothes. One has to see that the original universal human rights meme complex, following its origin and spread a little over 360 years ago, has evolved into a babble of conflicting human rights claims and theories, its own *reductio ad absurdum,* and that it is mindless to believe that any of these particular memes are referentially true or justified given the basic facts of biological evolution.

Only then can one rebel. But what would rebellion here mean? It could mean many things, but let me suggest what I think it should mean. When one sees children suffering in poverty-stricken countries, or the faces of unfortunate prisoners in a death camp, or cows being herded carelessly and cruelly by a forklift truck, one has to be either extremely callous or an "unnatural monster" (a psychopath) to not be moved. What moves us, and what should move us strongly, is not their cries that their rights are being violated (most humans do not claim them when they are suffering, and animals could not claim them even if they knew how). Instead it is something palpably and indisputably real that moves us, on the one hand of course the sights and sounds of their suffering, and on the other hand, like vibrating strings or mirror reflections, our natural instincts for sympathy and empathy. It is primarily these instincts, along with instincts for altruism, fairness, and reason, and not beliefs like God or immortal souls or human rights, that fundamentally make us the moral creatures that we are, and accordingly the hope for the future of this world.

In short, rebellion should mean finding the Naturalia that is within you.

References

Ake, Claude. (1987). "The African Context of Human Rights." *Africa Today* 34 (142), 5–13. Reprinted in Larry May et al., eds. (2006). *Applied Ethics: A Multicultural Approach.* 4th ed. Upper Saddle River, NJ: Prentice Hall, 111–116.

Ali, Ahmed. (2001). *Al-Qur'ān: A Contemporary Translation.* Princeton, NJ: Princeton University Press.

Ames, Roger T., and Rosemont, Henry, Jr., trans. (1998). *The Analects of Confucius: A Philosophical Translation.* New York: Ballantine Books.

Armitage, David. (2004). "John Locke, Carolina, and the *Two Treatises of Government.*" *Political Theory* 32 (5), 602–627.

Asch, Solomon E. (1955). "Opinion and Social Pressure." *Scientific American* 193 (5), 31–35.

Ashcraft, Richard. (1986). *Revolutionary Politics & Locke's* Two Treatises of Government. Princeton, NJ: Princeton University Press.

———. (1992). "The Radical Dimensions of Locke's Political Thought: A Dialogic Essay on Some Problems of Interpretation." *History of Political Thought* 13 (4), 703–772.

———. (1994). "Locke's Political Philosophy." In Chappell (1994), 226–251.

Aunger, Robert, ed. (2000). *Darwinizing Culture: The Status of Memetics as a Science.* Oxford: Oxford University Press.

———. (2002). *The Electric Meme: A New Theory of How We Think.* New York: Free Press.

———. (2007). "Memes." In Dunbar and Barrett (2007), 599–604.

Babiak, Paul, and Hare, Robert D. (2006). *Snakes in Suits: When Psychopaths Go to Work.* New York: HarperCollins.

Baier, Annette C. (1987). "The Need for More than Justice." *Canadian Journal of Philosophy* 13, 41–56.

Barkow, Jerome H., Cosmides, Leda, and Tooby, John, eds. (1992). *The Adapted Mind: Evolutionary Psychology and the Generation of Culture.* Oxford: Oxford University Press.

Barnes, Jonathan, ed. (1984). *The Collected Works of Aristotle.* 2 vols. Princeton, NJ: Princeton University Press.

Baron-Cohen, Simon. (2007). "The Evolution of Empathizing and Systemizing: Assortative Mating of Two Strong Systemizers and the Cause of Autism." In Dunbar and Barrett (2007), 213–226.

Bauman, Richard A. (2000). *Human Rights in Ancient Rome*. New York: Routledge.

Bedau, Hugo Adam. (2000). "'Anarchical Fallacies': Bentham's Attack on Human Rights." *Human Rights Quarterly* 22, 261–279.

Beitz, Charles R. (2009). *The Idea of Human Rights*. Oxford: Oxford University Press.

Bell, Paul. (2002). "Would You Believe It?" *Mensa Magazine* (Feb.), 12–13.

Bentham, Jeremy. (1789). *An Introduction to the Principles of Morals and Legislation*. Henry Frowde, ed. (1907). *Jeremy Bentham: An Introduction to the Principles of Morals and Legislation*. Oxford: Oxford University Press.

Berman, David. (1988). *A History of Atheism in Britain: From Hobbes to Russell*. London: Croom Helm.

Biro, Val. (2005). *Hans Christian Andersen's Fairy Tales*. Worksop, UK: Award Publications.

Blackmore, Susan. (1999). *The Meme Machine*. Oxford: Oxford University Press.

Bobbio, Norberto. (1993). *Thomas Hobbes and the Natural Law Tradition*. Daniela Gobetti, trans. Chicago: University of Chicago Press.

Bogdanoff, M. D., et al. (1961). "The Modifying Effect of Conforming Behavior Upon Lipid Responses Accompanying CNS Arousal." *Clinical Review* 9, 35.

Bogin, Barry. (1990). "The Evolution of Human Childhood." *BioScience* 40 (1), 16–25.

Boone, Rebecca. (1997). "Review of *Early Modern Democracy in the Grisons*." *Journal of Interdisciplinary History* 28 (1), 131–132.

Brailsford, H. N. (1961). *The Levellers and the English Revolution*. London: Cresset Press. Christopher Hill, ed. (1983). Nottingham, UK: Spokesman.

Broom, Donald M. (2003). *The Evolution of Morality and Religion*. Cambridge: Cambridge University Press.

Bugliosi, Vincent. (2007). *Reclaiming History: The Assassination of President John F. Kennedy*. New York: W. W. Norton.

———. (2008). *The Prosecution of George W. Bush for Murder*. New York: Vanguard Press.

Bull, Hedley. (1990). "The Importance of Grotius in the Study of International Relations." In Bull et al. (1990), 65–93.

Bull, Hedley, Kingsbury, Benedict, and Roberts, Adam, eds. (1990). *Hugo Grotius and International Relations*. Oxford: Oxford University Press.

Bultmann, Rudolf. (1958). *Jesus Christ and Mythology*. New York: Charles Scribner's Sons.

Bunch, Charlotte. (1990). "Women's Rights as Human Rights: Toward a Re-Vision of Human Rights." *Human Rights Quarterly* 12 (4), 486–498.

Burns, J. H., ed. (1991). *The Cambridge History of Political Thought, 1450–1700*. Cambridge: Cambridge University Press.

Buss, David M. (2003). *The Evolution of Desire: Strategies of Human Mating*. Rev. ed. New York: Basic Books.

———. (2005a). *The Murderer Next Door: Why the Mind Is Designed to Kill*. New York: Penguin.

————, ed. (2005b). *The Handbook of Evolutionary Psychology.* Hoboken, NJ: John Wiley & Sons.

Campbell, A. C., trans. (1901). *Hugo Grotius: The Rights of War and Peace.* New York: M. W. Dunne.

Carcopino, Jérôme. (1941). *Daily Life in Ancient Rome.* E. O. Lorimer, trans. Harmondsworth, UK: Penguin Books.

Cavalieri, Paola, and Singer, Peter, eds. (1993). *The Great Ape Project: Equality Beyond Humanity.* New York: St. Martin's Press.

Chappell, Vere, ed. (1994). *The Cambridge Companion to Locke.* Cambridge: Cambridge University Press.

Christensen, Katherine. (1993). *Gratian: The Treatise on Laws with the Ordinary Gloss.* Augustine Thompson and James Gordley, trans. Washington, DC: Catholic University of America Press.

Clapham, Andrew (2007). *Human Rights: A Very Short Introduction.* Oxford: Oxford University Press.

Cohen, Elliot D. (1985). "Pure Legal Advocates and Moral Agents: Two Concepts of a Lawyer in an Adversary System." *Criminal Justice Studies* 4, 38–48.

Corbey, Raymond. (2005). *The Metaphysics of Apes: Negotiating the Animal–Human Boundary.* Cambridge: Cambridge University Press.

Courtois, Stéphane, et al.. (1999). *The Black Book of Communism: Crimes, Terror, Repression.* Cambridge, MA: Harvard University Press.

Coyne, Jerry A. (2009). *Why Evolution Is True.* London: Penguin Books.

Cranston, Maurice. (1967). "Human Rights, Real and Supposed." In D. D. Raphael, ed. *Political Theory and the Rights of Man.* London: Macmillan, 43–52. Reprinted in Hayden (2001), 163–173.

Crawford, Charles, and Krebs, Dennis L., eds. (1998). *Handbook of Evolutionary Psychology: Ideas, Issues, and Applications.* Mahwah, NJ: Lawrence Erlbaum Associates.

Curley, Edwin, ed. (1994). *Thomas Hobbes: Leviathan.* Indianapolis: Hackett.

Damer, T. Edward. (2005). *Attacking Faulty Reasoning.* Belmont, CA: Wadsworth.

Darwin, Charles. (1859). *On the Origin of Species by Means of Natural Selection.* London: John Murray.

————. (1871). *The Descent of Man, and Selection in Relation to Sex.* Part I. London: John Murray.

Davis, J. C. (1968). "The Levellers and Democracy." *Past and Present* 40, 174–180.

Dawkins, Richard. (1976). *The Selfish Gene.* Oxford: Oxford University Press.

————. (1986). *The Blind Watchmaker.* London: Longman Scientific & Technical.

————. (1993). "Gaps in the Mind." In Cavalieri and Singer (1993), 80–87.

————. (1998). *Unweaving the Rainbow: Science, Delusion and the Appetite for Wonder.* New York: Houghton Mifflin.

————. (2006). *The God Delusion.* New York: Houghton Mifflin.

————. (2009). *The Greatest Show on Earth: The Evidence for Evolution.* New York: Free Press.

Dennett, Daniel C. (1995). *Darwin's Dangerous Idea: Evolution and the Meanings of Life.* New York: Simon & Schuster.

Devall, Bill, and Sessions, George. (1985). *Deep Ecology: Living as if Nature Mattered.* Salt Lake City: Peregrine Smith Books.

de Waal, Frans. (1996). *Good Natured: The Origins of Right and Wrong in Humans and Other Animals.* Cambridge, MA: Harvard University Press.

———. (2006a). "Morally Evolved: Primate Social Instincts, Human Morality, and the Rise and Fall of the 'Veneer Theory.'" In Macedo and Ober (2006), 1–80.

———. (2006b). "The Tower of Morality." In Macedo and Ober (2006), 161–181.

———. (2009). *The Age of Empathy: Nature's Lessons for a Kinder Society.* Toronto: McClelland & Stewart.

Distin, Kate. (2005). *The Selfish Meme: A Critical Reassessment.* Cambridge: Cambridge University Press.

Donnelly, Jack. (2003). *Universal Human Rights in Theory and Practice.* 2nd ed. Ithaca, NY: Cornell University Press.

Dunbar, R. I. M., and Barrett, Louise, eds. (2007). *The Oxford Handbook of Evolutionary Psychology.* Oxford: Oxford University Press.

Dunn, John. (2006). *Democracy: A History.* London: Penguin Books.

Dworkin, Ronald. (1978). *Taking Rights Seriously.* Cambridge, MA: Harvard University Press.

Eldredge, Niles. (1985). *Time Frames: The Evolution of Punctuated Equilibria.* Princeton. NJ: Princeton University Press.

Eliot, T. S., trans. (1958). *Blaise Pascal: Pensées.* W. F. Trotter, trans. New York: Dutton.

English, John. (2009). *Just Watch Me: The Life of Pierre Elliott Trudeau, 1968–2000.* Toronto: Knopf Canada.

Evans, Tony. (2005). *The Politics of Human Rights: A Global Perspective.* 2nd ed. London: Pluto Press.

Fagan, Edward. (2009). *Human Rights: Confronting Myths and Misunderstandings.* Cheltenham, UK: Edward Elgar.

Fehrenbacher, Don E., ed. (1989). *Abraham Lincoln: Speeches and Writings 1859–1865.* New York: Library of America.

Figgis, John Neville. (1896). *The Theory of the Divine Right of Kings.* Cambridge: Cambridge University Press.

Forsythe, David P. (2006). *Human Rights in International Relations.* 2nd ed. Cambridge: Cambridge University Press.

Fortin, Ernest L. (1996). "On the Presumed Medieval Origin of Individual Rights." In J. Brian Benestad, ed. *Classical Christianity and the Political Order: Reflections on the Theologico-Political Problem.* Lanham, MD: Rowman & Littlefield, 243–264.

Foster, Serrin M. (2005). "Refuse to Choose: Women Deserve Better than Abortion." Feminists for Life.

Foucault, Michel. (1977). "Truth and Power." In Colin Gordon, ed. (1980). *Power/Knowledge: Selected Interviews & Other Writings 1972–1977.* New York: Pantheon.

Francese, Christopher. (2007). *Ancient Rome in So Many Words*. New York: Hippocrene Books.

Frankfurt, Harry G. (2006). *On Truth*. New York: Knopf.

Franklin, Julian H. (1978). *John Locke and the Theory of Sovereignty: Mixed Monarchy & the Right of Resistance in the Political Thought of the English Revolution*. Cambridge: Cambridge University Press.

Gazzaniga, Michael S. (2008). *Human: The Science Behind What Makes Us Unique*. New York: HarperCollins.

Gewirth, Alan. (1978). *Reason and Morality*. Chicago: University of Chicago Press.

———. (1996). *The Community of Rights*. Chicago: University of Chicago Press.

Ghiglieri, Michael P. (2000). *The Dark Side of Man: Tracing the Origins of Male Violence*. Cambridge, MA: Perseus Books.

Glendon, Mary Ann. (2001). *A World Made New: Eleanor Roosevelt and the Universal Declaration of Human Rights*. New York: Random House.

Goldie, Mark, ed. (1997). *Locke: Political Essays*. Cambridge: Cambridge University Press.

Goodpaster, Kenneth E. (1978). "On Being Morally Considerable." *Journal of Philosophy* 75 (6), 308–325.

Gould, Stephen Jay. (1981). *The Mismeasure of Man*. New York: W. W. Norton.

Gregor, Mary J., and Wood, Allen, eds. (1996). *Immanuel Kant: Practical Philosophy*. Cambridge: Cambridge University Press.

Grene, David, ed. (1989). *The Peloponnesian War, Thucydides: The Complete Hobbes Translation*. Chicago: University of Chicago Press.

Griffin, James. (2008). *On Human Rights*. Oxford: Oxford University Press.

Griffin, M. T., and Atkins, E. M., eds. and trans. (1991). *Cicero: On Duties*. Cambridge: Cambridge University Press.

Griswold, Charles L. Jr. (1991). "Rights and Wrongs: Jefferson, Slavery, and Philosophical Quandaries." In Lacey and Haakonssen (1991), 144–214.

Gutmann, Amy. (1993). "Can Virtue Be Taught to Lawyers?" *Stanford Law Review* 45, 1759–1771.

Haakonssen, Knud. (1985). "Hugo Grotius and the History of Political Thought." *Political Theory* 13 (2), 239–265.

———. (1991). "From Natural Law to the Rights of Man: A European Perspective on American Debates." In Lacey and Haakonssen (1991), 19–61.

Hale, William Harlan. (2001). *Ancient Greece*. New York: Simon & Schuster.

Hamer, Dean. (2004). *The God Gene: How Faith Is Hardwired into Our Genes*. New York: Doubleday.

Hare, Robert D. (1995). *Without Conscience: The Disturbing World of the Psychopaths Among Us*. New York: Pocket Books.

Harris, Marvin. (1989). *Our Kind: Who We Are, Where We Came From, Where We Are Going*. New York: Harper & Row.

Hassan, Riffat. (1996). "Rights of Women Within Islamic Communities." In Witte and van der Vyver (1996), 361–386.

Hayden, Patrick, ed. (2001). *The Philosophy of Human Rights*. St. Paul, MN: Paragon House.

Head, Randolph C. (1995). "William Tell and His Comrades: Association and Fraternity in the Propaganda of Fifteenth- and Sixteenth-Century Switzerland." *Journal of Modern History* 67 (3), 527–557.

Hegel, G. W. F. (1821). *Outlines of the Philosophy of Right*. T. M. Knox, trans., Stephen Houlgate, ed. (2008). *G. W. F. Hegel: Outlines of the Philosophy of Right*. Oxford: Oxford University Press.

Held, Virginia. (1998). "Feminist Reconceptualizations of Ethics." In Janet Kourney, ed. (1998). *Philosophy in a Feminist Voice*. Princeton, NJ: Princeton University Press, 92–115.

Henkin, Louis. (1990). *The Age of Rights*. New York: Columbia University Press.

Herbert, Gary B. (2002). *A Philosophical History of Rights*. New Brunswick, NJ: Transaction Publishers.

Hick, John. (1985). *The Problems of Religious Pluralism*. New York: St. Martin's Press.

Hill, Christopher, ed. (1983). *Winstanley: "The Law of Freedom" and Other Writings*. Cambridge: Cambridge University Press.

Hirschmann, Nancy J., and McClure, Kirstie M., eds. (2007). *Feminist Interpretations of John Locke*. University Park: Pennsylvania State University Press.

Hoekstra, Kinch. (2007). "Hobbes on the Natural Condition of Mankind." In Patricia Springborg, ed. (2007). *The Cambridge Companion to Hobbes's* Leviathan. Cambridge: Cambridge University Press, 109–127.

Honoré, Tony. (2002). *Ulpian: Pioneer of Human Rights*. 2nd ed. Oxford: Oxford University Press.

Houston, Alan Craig. (1993). "'A Way of Settlement': The Levellers, Monopolies and the Public Interest." *History of Political Thought* 14 (3), 381–420.

Hume, David. (1739). *A Treatise of Human Nature*. Volumes 1 and 2. David Fate Norton and Mary J. Norton, eds. (2007). Oxford: Oxford University Press.

———. (1740). *A Treatise of Human Nature*. Volume 3. David Fate Norton and Mary J. Norton, eds. (2007). Oxford: Oxford University Press.

———. (1748). *An Enquiry Concerning Human Understanding*. Tom L. Beauchamp, ed. (2000). Oxford: Oxford University Press.

———. (1751). *An Enquiry Concerning the Principles of Morals*. Tom L. Beauchamp, ed. (1998). Oxford: Oxford University Press.

Hunt, Lynn. (2007). *Inventing Human Rights: A History*. New York: W. W. Norton.

Hursthouse, Rosalind. (1991). "Virtue Theory and Abortion." *Philosophy & Public Affairs* 20, 223–246.

Hutcheson, Francis. (1725). *An Inquiry into the Original of Our Ideas of Beauty and Virtue*. Wolfgang Leidhold, ed. (2008). Rev. ed. Indianapolis: Liberty Fund.

———. (1728). *An Essay on the Nature and Conduct of the Passions and Affections, with Illustrations on the Moral Sense*. Aaron Garrett, ed. (2002). Indianapolis: Liberty Fund.

Hutson, James H. (1991). "The Bill of Rights and the American Revolutionary Experience." In Lacey and Haakonssen (1991), 62–97.

Ignatieff, Michael. (2007). *The Rights Revolution.* Toronto: Anansi.

Ishay, Micheline R., ed. (2007). *The Human Rights Reader.* 2nd ed. New York: Routledge.

———. (2008). *The History of Human Rights: From Ancient Times to the Globalization Era.* 2nd ed. Berkeley: University of California Press.

James, William. (1897). *The Will to Believe and Other Essays in Popular Philosophy.* New York: Longman's, Green & Co.

Jensen, Erik M. (1990). "The Imaginary Connection Between the Great Law of Peace and the United States Constitution: A Reply to Professor Schaaf." *American Indian Law Review* 15 (2), 295–308.

Jones, Owen D. (2005). "Evolutionary Psychology and the Law." In Buss (2005). *The Handbook of Evolutionary Psychology.* Hoboken, NJ: Wiley, 953–974.

Joyce, Richard. (2006). *The Evolution of Morality.* Cambridge, MA: MIT Press.

Kant, Immanuel. (1785). *Groundwork of the Metaphysics of Morals.* In Gregor and Wood (1996), 37–108.

———. (1797). *The Metaphysics of Morals.* In Gregor and Wood (1996), 353–603.

Kaufmann, Walter. (1958). *Critique of Religion and Philosophy.* New York: Harper & Row.

Kitcher, Philip. (2006). "Ethics and Evolution: How to Get Here from There." In Macedo and Ober (2006), 120–139.

Klucharev, Vasily, et al. (2009). "Reinforcement Learning Signal Predicts Social Conformity." *Neuron* 61, 140–151.

Kornblith, Hilary, ed. (1994). *Naturalizing Epistemology.* 2nd ed. Cambridge, MA: MIT Press.

Kramer, Matthew H. (1997). *John Locke and the Origins of Private Property: Philosophical Explorations of Individualism, Community, and Equality.* Cambridge: Cambridge University Press.

Lacey, Michael J., and Haakonssen, Knud, eds. (1991). *A Culture of Rights: The Bill of Rights in Philosophy, Politics, and Law—1791 and 1991.* Cambridge: Cambridge University Press.

Laland, Kevin N., and Brown, Gillian R. (2002). *Sense and Nonsense: Evolutionary Perspectives on Human Behavior.* Oxford: Oxford University Press.

Larson, Edward J., and Witham, Larry. (1999). "Scientists and Religion in America." *Scientific American* 281, 88–93.

Laslett, Peter, ed. (1988). *John Locke: Two Treatises of Government.* Cambridge: Cambridge University Press.

Leopold, Aldo. (1949). *A Sand County Almanac and Sketches Here and There.* Oxford: Oxford University Press.

Lipton, Peter. (1990). "Contrastive Explanation." In Dudley Knowles, ed. (1990). *Explanation and Its Limits.* Cambridge: Cambridge University Press, 247–266.

Low, Bobbi S. (2007). "Ecological and Socio-Cultural Impacts on Mating and Marriage Systems." In Dunbar and Barrett (2007), 449–462.

Lukes, Steven. (1993). "Five Fables About Human Rights." In Shute and Hurley (1993), 19–40.

Lutz, Donald S., ed. (1998). *Colonial Origins of the American Constitution: A Documentary History*. Indianapolis: Liberty Fund.

Lynch, Aaron. (1996). *Thought Contagion: How Belief Spreads Through Society*. New York: Basic Books.

Macedo, Stephen, and Ober, Josiah, eds. (2006). *Primates and Philosophers: How Morality Evolved*. Princeton, NJ: Princeton University Press.

MacIntyre, Alasdair. (1981). *After Virtue: A Study in Moral Theory*. 3rd ed. (2007). Notre Dame, IN: University of Notre Dame Press.

Mackie, J. L. (1977). *Ethics: Inventing Right and Wrong*. Harmondsworth, UK: Pelican Books.

Mahoney, Jack. (2007). *The Challenge of Human Rights: Origin, Development, and Significance*. Malden, MA: Blackwell.

Maienschein, Jane, and Ruse, Michael, eds. (1999). *Biology and the Foundations of Ethics*. Cambridge: Cambridge University Press.

Maier, Pauline. (1997). *American Scripture: Making the Declaration of Independence*. New York: Vintage Books.

Manning, J. G. (1995). "Demotic Egyptian Instruments of Transfer as Evidence for Private Ownership of Real Property." *Chicago-Kent Law Review* 71, 237–268.

Marquis, Don. (1989). "Why Abortion Is Immoral." *Journal of Philosophy* 86 (4), 183–202.

Marshall, John. (1994). *John Locke: Resistance, Religion and Responsibility*. Cambridge: Cambridge University Press.

Maslow, Abraham H. (1943). "A Theory of Human Motivation." *Psychological Review* 50 (4), 370–396.

Mayr, Ernst. (1988). *Toward a New Philosophy of Biology: Observations of an Evolutionist*. Cambridge, MA: Harvard University Press.

McInerney, Peter K. (1990). "Does a Fetus Already Have a Future-Like-Ours?" *Journal of Philosophy* 87 (5), 264–268.

McLuhan, Marshall. (1964). *Understanding Media: The Extensions of Man*. New York: McGraw-Hill.

Mencken, H. L. (1949). *A Mencken Chrestomathy*. New York: Knopf.

Milgram, Stanley. (1974). *Obedience to Authority: An Experimental View*. New York: Harper & Row.

Mill, John Stuart. (1859). *On Liberty*. In Warnock (2003), 88–180.

———. (1861). *Utilitarianism*. In Warnock (2003), 181–235.

Miller, Fred D. (1991). "Aristotle on Natural Law and Justice." In David Keyt and Fred D. Miller, eds. (1991). *A Companion to Aristotle's Politics*. Oxford: Blackwell, 279–306.

Miller, Kenneth R. (2008). *Only a Theory: Evolution and the Battle for America's Soul*. New York: Viking.

Milton, J. R. (1994). "Locke's Life and Times." In Chappell (1994), 5–25.

Moore, G. E. (1903). *Principia Ethica.* Cambridge: Cambridge University Press.

Morgentaler, Henry. (1996). "The Moral Case for Abortion." *Free Inquiry* 16 (3), 17+.

Morsink, Johannes. (1999). *The Universal Declaration of Human Rights: Origins, Drafting, & Intent.* Philadelphia: University of Pennsylvania Press.

Nagel, Thomas. (1986). *The View from Nowhere.* Oxford: Oxford University Press.

Noonan, John T. (1970). "An Almost Absolute Value in History." In John T. Noonan, ed. (1970). *Morality of Abortion: Legal and Historical Perspectives.* Cambridge, MA: Harvard University Press, 51–59.

Normand, Roger, and Zaidi, Sarah. (2008). *Human Rights at the UN: The Political History of Universal Justice.* Bloomington: Indiana University Press.

Nussbaum, Martha C. (1997). "Human Rights Theory: Capabilities and Human Rights." *Fordham Law Review* 66, 273–300. Reprinted in Hayden (2001), 212–240.

———. (1999). *Sex and Social Justice.* Oxford: Oxford University Press.

———. (2003). "Capabilities as Fundamental Entitlements: Sen and Social Justice." *Feminist Economics* 9 (2–3), 33–59.

———. (2006). *Frontiers of Justice: Disability, Nationality, Species Membership.* Cambridge, MA: Harvard University Press.

Oakley, Francis. (2005). *Natural Law, Laws of Nature, Natural Rights: Continuity and Discontinuity in the History of Ideas.* New York: Continuum.

O'Donovan, Oliver. (2009). "The Language of Rights and Conceptual History." *Journal of Religious Ethics* 37 (2), 193–207.

Orend, Brian. (2002). *Human Rights: Concept and Context.* Peterborough, ON: Broadview Press.

Paine, Thomas. (1791). *Rights of Man.* In Eric Foner, ed. (1995). *Thomas Paine: Collected Writings.* New York: Library of America, 433–661.

Peterson, Merrill D., ed. (1984). *Thomas Jefferson: Writings.* New York: Library of America.

Pinker, Steven. (1994). *The Language Instinct.* New York: William Morrow.

———. (2002). *The Blank Slate: The Modern Denial of Human Nature.* New York: Viking.

———. (2011). *The Better Angels of Our Nature: Why Violence Has Declined.* New York: Viking.

Pojman, Louis P., ed. (2003). *Philosophy of Religion: An Anthology.* Belmont, CA: Wadsworth.

Popham, Peter. (2007). "William Tell: Celebrating a Republican Icon." *The Independent* (Nov. 17).

Popper, Karl R. (1945). *The Open Society and Its Enemies, Volume I: The Spell of Plato.* London: Routledge & Kegan Paul.

Price, Peter W. (1991). "The Web of Life: Development over 3.8 Billion Years of Trophic Relationships." In Lynn Margulis and René Fester, eds. (1991). *Symbiosis as a Source of Evolutionary Innovation: Speciation and Morphogenesis.* Cambridge, MA: MIT Press, 262–272.

Primus, Richard A. (1999). *The American Language of Rights.* Cambridge: Cambridge University Press.

Quirk, Joe. (2006). *Sperm Are from Men, Eggs Are from Women: The Real Reason Men and Women Are Different.* Philadelphia: Running Press.

Rachels, James. (1990). *Created from Animals: The Moral Implications of Darwinism.* Oxford: Oxford University Press.

———. (2003). *The Elements of Moral Philosophy.* 4th ed. New York: McGraw-Hill.

Rakove, Jack N., ed. (1999). *James Madison: Writings.* New York: Library of America.

Railton, Peter. (1986). "Moral Realism." *Philosophical Review* 95, 163–207.

Rawls, John. (1971). *A Theory of Justice.* Cambridge, MA: Harvard University Press.

———. (1993). "The Law of Peoples." In Shute and Hurley (1993), 41–82.

Regan, Tom. (1983). *The Case for Animal Rights.* Berkeley: University of California Press.

Richerson, Peter J., and Boyd, Robert. (2005). *Not by Genes Alone: How Culture Transformed Human Evolution.* Chicago: University of Chicago Press.

Rizzolatti, Giacomo, and Fogassi, Leonardo. (2007). "Mirror Neurons and Social Cognition." In Dunbar and Barrett (2007), 179–195.

Robertson, Geoffrey. (2007). *The Levellers: The Putney Debates.* London: Verso.

Rorty, Richard. (1993). "Human Rights, Rationality, and Sentimentality." In Shute and Hurley (1993), 111–134.

Ruse, Michael. (1986). *Taking Darwin Seriously: A Naturalistic Approach to Philosophy.* Oxford: Basil Blackwell.

———. (2002). "Evolution and Ethics: The Sociobiological Approach." In Louis P. Pojman, ed. (2002). *Ethical Theory: Classical and Contemporary Approaches.* 4th ed. Belmont, CA: Wadsworth, 647–662.

Russell, Bertrand. (1940). *An Inquiry into Meaning and Truth.* London: George Allen & Unwin.

———. (1957). *Why I Am Not a Christian and Other Essays on Religion and Related Subjects.* Paul Edwards, ed. London: George Allen & Unwin.

Ryle, Gilbert. (1949). *The Concept of Mind.* London: Hutchinson.

Sablonier, Roger. (2008). *Gründungszeit ohne Eidgenossen: Politik und Gesellschaft in der Innerschwriz um 1300.* Baden, Germany: Hier und Jetzt Verlag.

Salmon, E. T. (1968). *A History of the Roman World From 30 B.C. to A.D. 138.* 6th ed. New York: Methuen.

Salmon, J. H. M. (1991). "Catholic Resistance Theory, Ultramontanism, and the Royalist Response, 1580–1620." In Burns (1991), 219–253.

Schellens, Max Solomon. (1959). "Aristotle on Natural Law." *Natural Law Forum* 4, 72–100.

Schmitt, David P. (2005). "Fundamentals of Human Mating Strategies." In Buss (2005), 258–291.

Schweitzer, Albert. (1933). *Out of My Life and Thought: An Autobiography.* A. B. Lemke, trans. New York: Holt, Rinehart, and Winston.

———. (1949). *The Philosophy of Civilization.* C. T. Campion, trans. New York: Macmillan.

Scott, Tom. (1995). "Liberty and Community in Medieval Switzerland." *German History* 13 (1), 98–113.

————. (2009). "Review of *Gründungszeit ohne Eidgenossen.*" *German History* 27 (4), 600–601.

Shapiro, Ian. (1986). *The Evolution of Rights in Liberal Theory.* Chicago: University of Chicago Press.

Sharp, Andrew, ed. (1998). *The English Levellers.* Cambridge: Cambridge University Press.

Shue, Henry. (1980). *Basic Rights: Subsistence, Affluence, and U.S. Foreign Policy.* 2nd ed. (1996). Princeton, NJ: Princeton University Press.

Shute, Stephen, and Hurley, Susan, eds. (1993). *On Human Rights: The Oxford Amnesty Lectures 1993.* New York: Basic Books.

Silk, Joan B. (2007). "Empathy, Sympathy, and Prosocial Preferences in Primates." In Dunbar and Barrett (2007), 115–126.

Simpson, D. P. (1968). *Cassell's Latin Dictionary.* New York: Wiley.

Simpson, George Gaylord. (1961). *Principles of Animal Taxonomy.* New York: Columbia University Press.

Singer, Peter. (1975). *Animal Liberation.* 2nd ed. (1990). New York: Avon Books.

————. (1993). *Practical Ethics.* 2nd ed. Cambridge: Cambridge University Press.

————. (2003). "Animal Liberation at 30." *New York Review of Books* 50 (8), 23–30. Reprinted in Robert J. Mulvaney, ed. (2009). *Classic Philosophical Questions.* 13th ed. Upper Saddle River, NJ: Prentice Hall, 207–219.

————. (2006). "Morality, Reason, and the Rights of Animals." In Macedo and Ober (2006), 140–158.

Slote, Michael. (2007). *The Ethics of Care and Empathy.* New York: Routledge.

Smith, Adam. (1759). *The Theory of Moral Sentiments.* Knud Haakonssen, ed. (2002). Cambridge: Cambridge University Press.

Smith, David Livingstone. (2007). *The Most Dangerous Animal: Human Nature and the Origins of War.* New York: St. Martin's Press.

————. (2011). *Less Than Human: Why We Demean, Enslave, and Exterminate Others.* New York: St. Martin's Press.

Sommerville, J. P. (1991). "Absolutism and Royalism." In Burns (1991), 347–373.

Spade, Paul Vincent. (1999). "Ockham's Nominalist Metaphysics: Some Main Themes." In Paul Vincent Spade, ed. (1999). *The Cambridge Companion to Ockham.* Cambridge: Cambridge University Press, 100–117.

Spelman, Elizabeth V. (1994). "Hairy Cobblers and Philosopher-Queens." In Nancy Tuana, ed. (1994). *Feminist Interpretations of Plato.* University Park: Pennsylvania State University Press, 87–107.

Stamos, David N. (2002). "Species, Languages, and the Horizontal/Vertical Distinction." *Biology & Philosophy* 17 (2), 171–198.

————. (2003). *The Species Problem: Biological Species, Ontology, and the Metaphysics of Biology.* Lanham, MD: Lexington Books.

————. (2007). *Darwin and the Nature of Species.* Albany: State University of New York Press.

————. (2008). *Evolution and the Big Questions: Sex, Race, Religion, and Other Matters.* Malden, MA: Blackwell.

————. (2010). "Quantum Indeterminism, Mutation, Natural Selection, and the Meaning of Life." In Chérif F. Matta, ed. (2010). *Quantum Biochemistry: Electronic Structure and Biological Activity.* Volume 2. Weinheim, Germany: Wiley-VCH, 837–872.

————. (2011). "The Philosophical Significance of Psychopaths: Postmodernism, Morality, and God." *Free Inquiry* 31 (5), 46–49.

Stassan, Glen H. (1992). *Just Peacemaking: Transforming Initiatives for Justice and Peace.* Louisville, KY: Westminster/John Knox Press, 137–163.

Stephens, William O., ed. (2006). *The Person: Readings in Human Nature.* Upper Saddle River, NJ: Pearson Prentice Hall.

Stevens, Jacqueline. (1996). "The Reasonableness of John Locke's Majority: Property Rights, Consent, and Resistance in the *Second Treatise.*" *Political Theory* 24 (3), 423–463.

Straumann, Benjamin. (2009). "Is Modern Liberty Ancient? Roman Remedies and Natural Rights in Hugo Grotius's Early Works on Natural Law." *Law and History Review* 27 (1), 55–85.

Strauss, Leo. (1953). *Natural Right and History.* Chicago: University of Chicago Press.

Sulloway, Frank J. (1996). *Born to Rebel: Birth Order, Family Dynamics, and Creative Lives.* New York: Pantheon Books.

Summers, Kirk. (1995). "Lucretius and the Epicurean Tradition of Piety." *Classical Philology* 90 (1), 32–57.

Svensson, Marina. (1999). "Book Review of *Confucianism and Human Rights.*" *Journal of Asian Studies* 58, 483–484.

Szasz, Thomas S. (1974). *The Myth of Mental Illness: Foundations of a Theory of Personal Conduct.* 2nd ed. New York: HarperCollins. Reprinted. (2010). New York: Harper Perennial.

Tattersall, Ian. (2000). "Once We Were Not Alone." *Scientific American* 282 (1), 56–67.

Taylor, Allen. (1971). "The Adversary System of Justice: An Ethical Jungle." *Journal of Critical Analysis* 3, 23–38.

Taylor, Paul W. (1981). "The Ethics of Respect for Nature." *Environmental Ethics* 3, 197–218. Reprinted in Jeffrey Olen and Vincent Barry, eds. (2002). *Applying Ethics: A Text with Readings.* 7th ed. Belmont, CA: Wadsworth, 517–528.

Thompson, Augustine, and Gordley, James, trans. (1993). *Gratian: The Treatise on Laws. (Decretum DD. 1–20) with the Ordinary Gloss.* Washington, DC: Catholic University Press.

Thompson, C. Bradley, ed. (2000). *The Revolutionary Writings of John Adams.* Indianapolis: Liberty Fund.

Thompson, Paul, ed. (1995). *Issues in Evolutionary Ethics.* Albany: State University of New York Press.

Thomson, Judith Jarvis. (1971). "A Defense of Abortion." *Philosophy & Public Affairs* 1, 47–66.

Tierney, Brian. (1997). *The Idea of Natural Rights: Studies on Natural Rights, Natural Law, and Church Law 1150–1625*. Grand Rapids, MI: William B. Eerdmans.

Tocqueville, Alexis de. (1835). *Democracy in America*. Arthur Goldhammer and Olivier Zunz, trans. and eds. (2004). *Alexis de Tocqueville: Democracy in America*. New York: Library of America.

Trivers, Robert. (2002). *Natural Selection and Social Theory: Selected Papers of Robert Trivers*. Oxford: Oxford University Press.

Trudeau, Pierre Elliott. (1993). *Memoirs*. Toronto: McClelland & Stewart.

Tuck, Richard. (1979). *Natural Rights Theories: Their Origin and Development*. Cambridge: Cambridge University Press.

———, ed. (2005). *Hugo Grotius: The Rights of War and Peace*. 3 vols. Indianapolis: Liberty Fund.

Tuck, Richard, and Silverthorne, Michael, eds. (1998). *Hobbes: On the Citizen*. Cambridge: Cambridge University Press.

Tucker, Robert C., ed. (1978). *The Marx-Engels Reader*. 2nd ed. New York: W. W. Norton.

Tully, James, ed. (1991). *Samuel Pufendorf: On the Duty of Man and Citizen According to Natural Law*. Michael Silverthorne, trans. Cambridge: Cambridge University Press.

Turco, Luigi. (2003). "Moral Sense and the Foundations of Morals." In Alexander Broadie, ed. (2003). *The Cambridge Companion to the Scottish Enlightenment*. Cambridge: Cambridge University Press, 136–156.

Tutu, Desmond. (1996). "Preface." In Witte and van der Vyver (1996), ix–xvi.

Vincent, R. J. (1990). "Grotius, Human Rights, and Intervention." In Bull et al. (1990), 241–256.

Vlastos, Gregory. (1962). "Justice and Equality." In Richard B. Brandt, ed. (1962). *Social Justice*. Englewood Cliffs, NJ: Prentice-Hall, 31–72. Reprinted in Jeremy Waldron, ed. (1984). *Theories of Rights*. Oxford: Oxford University Press, 41–76.

———. (1981). *Platonic Studies*. 2nd ed. Princeton, NJ: Princeton University Press.

Von Friedeburg, Robert. (2001). "Review of *Kommunalismus*." *English Historical Review* 116 (Feb.), 141–143.

Wade, Nicholas. (2009). *The Faith Instinct: How Religion Evolved and Why It Endures*. London: Penguin Books.

Warnock, Mary, ed. (2003). *John Stuart Mill: Utilitarianism and On Liberty*. 2nd ed. Malden, MA: Blackwell.

Warren, Mary Anne. (1989). "The Moral Significance of Birth." *Hypatia* 4 (3), 46–65.

Williams, Bernard. (1973). "Against Utilitarianism." In Bernard Williams and J. J. C. Smart, eds. (1973). *Utilitarianism: For and Against*. Cambridge: Cambridge University Press, 97–116.

Williams, George C. (1992). *Natural Selection: Domains, Levels, and Challenges*. Oxford: Oxford University Press.

Wills, Garry. (1978). *Inventing America: Jefferson's Declaration of Independence*. 2nd ed. (2002). New York: Houghton Mifflin.

Wilson, Edward O. (1975). *Sociobiology.* Abridged ed. (1980). Cambridge, MA: Harvard University Press.

———. (1978). *On Human Nature.* Cambridge, MA: Harvard University Press.

Witte, John Jr., and van der Vyver, Johan D., eds. (1996). *Religious Human Rights in Global Perspective: Religious Perspectives.* The Hague, Netherlands: Kluwer Law International.

Wittgenstein, Ludwig. (1922). *Tractatus Logico-Philosophicus.* D. F. Pears and B. F. McGuinness, trans. London: Routledge & Kegan Paul. Reprinted. (1961).

———. (1953). *Philosophical Investigations.* G. E. M. Anscombe, trans. Oxford: Basil Blackwell. 3rd ed. (1958).

Wollstonecraft, Mary. (1792). *A Vindication of the Rights of Woman.* Sylvana Tomaselli, ed. (1995). *A Vindication of the Rights of Men with A Vindication of the Rights of Woman and Hints.* Cambridge: Cambridge University Press.

Wolterstorff, Nicholas. (2008). *Justice: Rights and Wrongs.* Princeton, NJ: Princeton University Press.

Woolcock, Peter G. (1999). "The Case Against Evolutionary Ethics Today." In Jane Maienschein and Michael Ruse, eds. (1999). *Biology and the Foundation of Ethics.* Cambridge: Cambridge University Press, 276–306.

Woolhouse, Roger. (2007). *Locke: A Biography.* Cambridge: Cambridge University Press.

Wootton, David, ed. (1986). *Divine Right and Democracy: An Anthology of Political Writing in Stuart England.* New York: Penguin Books.

———. (1991). "Leveller Democracy and the Puritan Revolution." In Burns (1991), 412–442.

———. (1992). "John Locke and Richard Ashcraft's *Revolutionary Politics.*" *Political Studies* 40, 79–98.

———, ed. (1993). *John Locke: Political Writings.* New York: Penguin Books.

Yolton, John W. (1993). *A Locke Dictionary.* Cambridge, MA: Blackwell.

Yousef, Mosab Hassan. (2010). *Son of Hamas.* Carol Stream, IL: Tyndale House Publishers.

Zetzel, James E. G., ed. and trans. (1999). *Cicero: On the Commonwealth and On the Laws.* Cambridge: Cambridge University Press.

Zimbardo, Philip. (2007). *The Lucifer Effect: How Good People Turn Evil.* New York: Random House.

Zuckerman, Phil. (2007). "Atheism: Contemporary Numbers and Patterns." In Michael Martin, ed. (2007). *The Cambridge Companion to Atheism.* Cambridge: Cambridge University Press, 47–65.

Index

ontology, 4–5, 6, 20, 54, 61
Orend, Brian, 20–21, 44
ought implies can, 97
ought-is fallacy, 24, 57
Oxford University, 160
Overton, Richard, 13, 42, 154–156, 163, 168, 191, 192, 207, 208, 213
ownership, 146, 201. *See also* property

pain, 227, 231, 236, 238, 240–241, 257, 265
Paine, Thomas, 27, 29, 41, 42, 107, 168
Parfit, Derek, 49
Pascal, Blaise, 47, 48, 48n, 73
passive rights. *See* negative rights
Paul, 109–110
Pavlov, Alexei, 215
Pentateuch, 106
Pericles's Funeral Oration, 115–116
personhood, 50–54, 74, 81–82, 91–92, 96, 216, 247
pets, ix, 244
philanthropia, 115
philosophy, 54, 55
philosophy of religion, 28, 48n, 64
Pinker, Steven, 264
Plantinga, Alvin, 64
plate tectonics, 45
Plato, 4, 8, 12, 18, 116–118, 183, 231, 240
pleasure. *See* pain
policy and principle, 167, 191
political correctness, xi, 21, 24, 30, 31, 33
politics, and good scholarship, 4, 261
polygamous marriage, 252–253
Pope John XXII, 128
Popper, Karl, 117
positive rights, 143, 179, 262
postmodernism, 21–22, 22n, 42, 73, 86, 227, 231
potestas, 128
power, discourse of, 14, 196–200
predestination, 110
presentism, 23–24, 107, 111–112, 113, 114–115, 129–130, 131, 134
Price, Peter, 207
prima facie justification, 20
prima facie reason, 23, 64, 227, 236, 245
Primus, Richard, 167–168, 219

Prince, 52
Prince, Thomas, 154
principle and practice, 20, 168, 172
printing press, 206
properly basic beliefs, 64–65
property, 1, 128, 131, 136, 148, 154–157, 160–161, 162, 163, 164, 166, 174, 199, 201–202, 216
in ancient Egypt, 201
proof beyond a reasonable doubt, xi–xii, 4, 7, 15, 29, 42, 190, 247
psychopaths, 22n, 31, 76, 237, 238, 239, 240–241, 242, 243, 247, 249, 265
public good, 136
Pufendorf, Samuel, 13, 119, 142n, 145–149, 151, 187
punctuated equilibria, 38n, 83
punishment, 161, 162, 165, 166, 189
Putney Debates, 156–157, 158, 191, 198, 201
Pym, John, 157

question-begging definition, 74
Quirk, Joe, 30

races, human, 24, 30, 163, 171–172
Rachels, James, 231, 255–256
racism, 17, 24, 35, 71, 112, 119, 168, 254
Railton, Peter, 94
Rainborough, Thomas, 154, 156, 157, 201
Rawls, John, 10, 49, 52, 63, 65, 87–88, 96n, 216–217, 227–228, 236
reason/rationality, 31–32, 33–34, 73, 75, 116, 118, 161, 265
rebellion, 264–265
right of, 164, 170, 194
reciprocal altruism, 220, 231
reductio ad absurdum, 10, 18, 60, 157, 218, 264
Regan, Tom, 58–59
regime change, 261–264
religion, 178
Religulous, 178
Report to the Board of Trade on Poor Relief, 204
Richerson, Peter J., 183–184
right(s), logical geography of, 23, 50–51, 53, 77
Roosevelt, Eleanor, 195, 222
Rorty, Richard, 22, 73

About the Author

David N. Stamos teaches philosophy at York University in Toronto, Canada, and is the author of *Evolution and the Big Questions* (2008), *Darwin and the Nature of Species* (2007), and *The Species Problem* (2003). He has also published in a variety of journals, including *Philosophy of Science, Journal of the History of Biology, Biology & Philosophy,* and *The Evolutionary Review.*